CROSSMAN

by the same author

THE MAKING OF THE PRIME MINISTER (with Richard West)
THE CROSSMAN DIARIES: SELECTIONS (ed.)
RAB: THE LIFE OF R. A. BUTLER

CROSSMAN

The Pursuit of Power

Anthony Howard

JONATHAN CAPE
LONDON

First published 1990
© Anthony Howard 1990
Jonathan Cape Ltd, 20 Vauxhall Bridge Road, London SW1V 2SA

Anthony Howard has asserted his right to be identified as the author of this work

A CIP catalogue record for this book is available from the British Library

ISBN 0-224-02592-9

Printed in Great Britain by
Butler & Tanner Ltd, Frome and London

Contents

Illustrations

Preface

This is an authorised biography only in the sense that I was asked to undertake it by the executors of the Crossman literary estate, Anne Crossman, Michael Foot and Graham C. Greene. Although, in the course of writing it, I have probably wearied all three of them by the persistence of my inquiries, at no stage have they sought to influence my judgments or exercise any control over what I wrote. The responsibility for the book is mine alone.

To write a life of Crossman was something I had long wanted to do. This may well have been because he was the first politician to make any impact upon me. I can recall the occasion vividly and exactly. I first set eyes on my subject on 12 December 1949, when he came to address the Political and Literary Society of Westminster School, where I was a pupil. He was nearly forty-two, and I was fifteen. But in my mind's eye I can see him now – talking in that magnetic way that was entirely his own, using his hands as effectively as his voice (no one ever employed hands more expressively while speaking). That day he held twenty-three rather conservative schoolboys in thrall. We had been warned by our very conservative Head Master, J. T. Christie, a fellow Wykehamist, not to allow ourselves to be beguiled by his socialist arts of persuasion. But, in my own case, the warning was quite in vain. I was not only beguiled, but bewitched.

For the young, that was not an unusual experience with Crossman. No other politician of his generation was able to break through the age barrier with quite such effortless ease. For something approaching forty years he was the darling of every student debating hall – the automatic number one choice for any university union president or Labour club secretary when it came to drawing up a term's programme. This was one of the many things that made him suspect to his stuffier colleagues. Sometimes he was even referred to as 'the Peter Pan of

Politics' – but that particular gibe he always took as a compliment.

My own initial, wide-eyed admiration was inevitably tempered by later experience. There were aspects of his conduct – particularly during Labour's protracted civil war during the late 1950s and the early 1960s – that made me wonder, even as a political corre-spondent, whether Peter Pan had not grown up into a poor man's Machiavelli. (The nickname 'Double Crossman', however, was the irresistible sobriquet produced during his schooldays at Winchester and was not the subsequent invention of a Labour Party colleague.) In any event, through occasional bumpy episodes, we preserved a personal friendship that survived even the generally exhilarating but sometimes exasperating ordeal of working for him when he was editor of the *New Statesman* at the beginning of the 1970s. It was then that the notion was first mooted ('Like me, you've always really been a populariser') that I might edit a compact version of his *Diaries* after his death. Nothing was formally said that evening in the *New Statesman* boardroom about the longer-term project of a biography; but the idea that one day there would be one – and that I might even write it – loitered, I fancy, in both our minds.

In some ways, it is probably a disadvantage for a biographer to have known his subject – unless his aim is to be a first-hand chronicler, like Boswell. Since my own direct knowledge of Cross-man was confined to the last twenty-five years of his life – and during the earlier part of that period necessarily only at a distance – such an option was not open to me. When I started out on this book three years ago, I remember thinking nevertheless that a large part of my research would consist merely of checking my own memories and impressions of Crossman against the recollections of others who might well have known him better. But things did not work out like that at all. So much of his career was uncharted territory for me – and territory, moreover, from which the living witnesses had largely disappeared – that I found myself driven back to the normal basic tools of the biographer.

Contemporary documentary evidence has proved once again, as it did in my *Life of R. A. Butler*, far more of a precision instrument than oral interviews – grateful, as I am, to the many who granted them to me.* It would have been impossible to reconstruct Cross-

---

* I hope I shall be forgiven for not supplying a long list of names. It has always struck me as one of the more redundant rituals of modern biography, and not everyone I spoke to wished to be identified in any case. Where quotations from interviews appear in the text, they are normally attributed to their source in the Notes and References, pp. 319–54.

man's life at school, Oxford, with the Foreign Office in the war or after it in Parliament and on the Anglo-American Palestine Commission without the availability of written records (a lot of them, fortunately, survive in letters in his own hand). After 1951 the path in some respects became easier, for it was then that Crossman started keeping his own full, if somewhat intermittent, political diary (which he was to maintain, latterly in unpublished form, until the end of 1970).

That in itself, however, posed a different problem. Revealing and entertaining though it nearly always is, is it necessarily a reliable account of anything beyond his own often mercurial feelings and reactions? Harsh experience with his own versions of earlier events – notably, the circumstances attending his departure from New College, Oxford, in 1937 – persuaded me that it was safest to treat it with the same sceptical spirit I have always brought to bear on oral history. (It subsequently became exactly that, since in 1962 Crossman took to dictating straight into a tape recorder and no longer subjected himself even to the discipline of having his secretary take down or question what he said.) Both the *Backbench Diaries* and the *Diaries of a Cabinet Minister* were treasure chests in writing this book; but, if I appear to have made sparing use of direct quotation from them, it is because I consistently attempted to put the raw material of political history they contain to the test of other evidence. Only in those areas which convey Crossman's personal mood at various times did I abandon that attitude of scepticism and take his own entries at face value.

Apart from my overwhelming sense of gratitude to Anne Crossman, who freely made available to me all her husband's private papers, which had been kept since his death in 1974 at their home at Prescote, I must record a number of other debts. The prime one is owed to the Modern Records Centre at Warwick University, which already holds the largest collection of Crossman Papers and will now be given the rest. Its archivist, Richard Storey, was unfailingly supportive and helpful – indeed, towards the end, was all but acting as my (unpaid) researcher. The Middle East Centre at St Antony's College, Oxford, was also both forbearing and accommodating in allowing me to pay it a number of visits, as was the BBC Written Archives Centre at Caversham. The earliest expedition I made was to Winchester College, where the Headmaster, James Sabben-Clare, generously allowed me to see and quote from various College archives. His father, Ernest Sabben-Clare, offered equal encouragement at a crucial, initial stage by bolstering my confidence with written notes on Crossman both at school and Oxford – as did another Winchester and university contemporary, Michael Hope. Frank Longford provided the same self-denying service on Crossman's subsequent local political career in Oxford as don and city councillor.

Of the individuals directly concerned with the manuscript itself, the first mention must go, once more, to my former secretary, Isabel Boddy. She not only typed every word of it immaculately, but never once complained in face of my incurable habit of always dispatching amendments, additions and changes just at the moment that the final version of any chapter was supposedly completed. Another one-time *Observer* colleague, Blake Morrison (now literary editor of the *Independent on Sunday*), kindly volunteered critical guidance on the quality of Crossman's poetry and the relevance of his efforts to the poetic mood of the time. Simon Hoggart, the only person heroically to have read and annotated the whole manuscript, apart from Liz Cowen my meticulous and vigilant editor, rigorously applied even more astringent criticism to my own prose style – and deserves not only my thanks but the reader's gratitude for having done his best to break up the more interminable of my sentences. Any reverberations of a tin ear that remain are entirely the author's fault, as are all mistakes, misjudgments and misunderstandings of other people's roles as well as Crossman's.

ANTHONY HOWARD
March 1990

Acknowledgments

For permission to reprint copyright material the author and publishers would like to thank: John Murray for the extract from John Betjeman, 'The Wykehamist', p. 22, this poem is currently published in John Betjeman, *Collected Poems* (John Murray) and it is used by arrangement with John Murray (Publishers) Ltd; and Faber & Faber for the quotation from W. H. Auden, *The Orators*, p. 35, from *The English Auden: Poems, Essays and Dramatic Writings 1927–39*.

PICTURE CREDITS

The author and publishers are grateful to the following for permission to reproduce illustrations: Associated Newspapers plc/solo – 12, 13; Associated Press – 22, 26; Gabriel Carritt – 7; *Coventry Evening Telegraph* – 31; Anne Crossman – 4, 5, 9, 10, 11, 14, 15, 17, 19, 27, 28, 33; Hulton Picture Company – 18, 25, 32; Pictorial Press – 29; Popperfoto – 20, 23, 24; Syndication International – 21; Mary Woodhouse – 1, 2, 3, 6, 8.

1 The Claim to Fame

Few reputations fade more quickly than those of politicians. Often accorded too great a prominence during their lives, they tend to vanish into oblivion after their deaths. Richard Crossman remains a defiant exception. His posthumous fame exceeds any that he won in his lifetime.

While he lived, Crossman was never quite accepted as a politician of the first rank. In the high game of politics he was always the hare, and it is the tortoise that normally wins the race. Although from time to time he liked to flirt with the notion that he could become the leader of the Labour Party – and, once he had got into the Cabinet, Prime Minister as well – this was never a realistic prospect. During his six years as a Cabinet Minister he failed to realise his ambition even to be Foreign Secretary; and he never reached either of the other two great offices of State – the Home Office and the Treasury – which are regularly (if rashly) regarded as the stepping-stones to No. 10. Nor did he leave any lasting legislative memorial behind him. Labour's once-famous National Superannuation Plan, to which he devoted fifteen years of his life, lost its chance of getting on to the Statute Book when Harold Wilson called an election for June 1970. And that was not his only disappointment. A far-reaching scheme for House of Lords reform, with which he was almost as strongly identified, suffered the indignity of being withdrawn by the Government, the casualty of a backbench insurrection on both sides of the Commons.

How is it, then, that the fate that overtakes many more successful politicians should have spared Crossman? The answer is simple – and is to be found in four bulky volumes that contain his monument.* Opinions may still be divided about the reliability and accuracy of his *Diaries*; but over his aim and purpose in writing them there is no room for argument at all. Throughout his life, the charge most often brought against Crossman was that he was 'inconsistent'; but to one central belief he remained constant from his early days as a philosophy don in Oxford. He never wavered in his conviction that the basic flaw in the British political system was its allegiance to secrecy. He particularly resented the feelings of those in charge that the workings of Government were too sacred a mystery ever to be explained to the uninitiated. While he lived, Crossman consistently fought to break down that attitude; after his death, as he had planned all along, he smashed it wide open.

In some ways it was an improbable triumph, for Crossman was never an identikit iconoclast. With his educational background at Winchester and New College he always brought something of a patrician flavour to Labour politics. There were not many Labour MPs even of his generation who were members of both the Garrick and the Athenaeum, and he moved with equal ease in Tory as well as Labour circles. It helped that his interests ranged well beyond politics. He was a passionate lover of music and especially opera – on one occasion remarking that he would 'resign my Ministry and my seat in the Commons at any time if Harold [Wilson] will give me this one perk, a directorship of Covent Garden which gives me the right to see an opera two or three nights a week'.[1] All through his life, as well as writing regularly himself, he read omnivorously and voraciously – not just books on politics or public affairs but philosophy, theology (Reinhold Niebuhr was an early influence) and the whole range of English literature (when his children were young, he became a great reader aloud, particularly from Dickens). Unlike most politicians, he also liked the theatre, being a strong supporter of the Royal Court in its early adventurous days under George Devine. He would frequently sneak off there from the House of Commons, sometimes to his irritation having to miss the last act in order to return to vote at ten o'clock. All that, perhaps, provides the clue to a curious phrase he came increasingly to use about the last Labour leader whom he served. 'Wilson', he would declare, 'is just a little ball-bearing' – by which he meant that the leader of the

---

* Three successive volumes of Richard Crossman's *Diaries of a Cabinet Minister*, edited by Janet Morgan, were published in 1975, 1976 and 1977 respectively. A fourth volume of *Backbench Diaries* followed in 1981. A condensed version of the first three originally appeared in hardback in 1979, and has since been reprinted in paperback a number of times.

Labour Party was a man totally committed to the machinery of politics. Crossman – and it may be that this provides the secret of the contrast between their respective careers – was determined never to be just that.

But he was a singular figure for a left-wing politician in other respects. Despite his often-proclaimed pride in his 'bump of irreverence', he was not in any sense a natural nonconformist. He could display an oddly deferential attitude towards authority* – perhaps the product of his lifelong fascination with the concept of power. This could surface in unexpected ways. Someone who, as a schoolboy, was driven round Germany with him during a hot summer in the early 1950s still recalls how Crossman, sitting in the front passenger seat, would always scrupulously put his shirt back on before asking directions of any policeman.[2] It may not have been a conscious token of respect; but it certainly reflected an element in his character. Another long-term colleague on the *New Statesman* never forgot his experience of staying the night at Crossman's country home. They had both stayed up late talking – later perhaps than they had intended for his host suddenly announced that they had better go to bed as he needed to get up 'sharp' in the morning since he had agreed to be a godfather at the christening of a friend's baby. The guest was astonished: he had always looked on Crossman as a rationalist, if not an active atheist. He did not conceal his sense of surprise – only to have a long lecture delivered to him about the importance in a Christian country of subscribing to its prescribed forms. 'Otherwise', he recalls being briskly told, 'you simply went away and dug a hole for yourself.'[3] It was a revealing indication of Crossman's impatience with what he used disparagingly to call 'gesture politics' – meaning the kind of protests that brought no result except for an inner glow of self-satisfaction. This kind of robust attitude always cut him off from the sentimental Left, for whose more personal demonstrations he had very little sympathy. Unlike Aneurin Bevan and Michael Foot he never, for example, saw the point of refusing to wear a dinner jacket on formal occasions – although he did draw the line at a white tie (no doubt, for the practical reason that he did not possess an evening tail suit).

* When in 1972 the Northern Ireland Republican MP, Bernadette Devlin, assaulted the Conservative Home Secretary on the floor of the House of Commons, no one was more appalled than Crossman. Although away at the time through illness, he wrote to the then Leader of the House, Willie Whitelaw, to say he was thankful not to have been a witness to the scene.

To regard Crossman as a romantic rebel is, therefore, to misread his character. His interest invariably lay in what could be achieved rather than in what might idealistically be contemplated. It was because he saw stripping away the mumbo-jumbo that had been allowed to surround the workings of British Government as some-thing wholly realisable that he cheerfully dedicated his life to it. This meant, of course, that in his years in Cabinet he was *voyeur* and participant at one and the same time – and it may be that this limited his effectiveness as a Minister. But, if so, it was a price that he was more than willing to pay. What he wanted above all else was to push forward the frontiers of public knowledge about the way in which the country was governed – and to bring that off at all effectively he had always known that at some stage he would have to be a member of the Cabinet. Taking a reporter's notebook into the Forbidden City of Whitehall was bound to risk putting the Establishment on Red Alert. Crossman himself may never have realised how deter-mined the resistance would be.

The story of the great legal battle that preceded the publication of the first volume of the *Diaries of a Cabinet Minister* has already been told[4] and need not be repeated here. It would be remiss, however, not to notice the lessons to be drawn from it. The first, and most striking, is just how far those who wished to maintain the internal mechanisms of Cabinet Government as a secret garden of British politics (with no outsider allowed even a glimpse over the wall) had been lulled into a sense of false security. The controversy over the Crossman *Diaries* did not, after all, burst upon the world of White-hall unannounced in the mid-1970s. Twice in 1967 the matter of ministerial memoirs had been discussed by the Wilson Cabinet.[5] The question had been forced on to the agenda by what the Cabinet Secretary of the day, Sir Burke Trend, clearly took to be a highly alarming paragraph in the *Observer*[6] reporting the arrangements that various Ministers, including Crossman, were making with publishers. The one defence, therefore, not open to those who later professed themselves to be shocked and shaken by this breach of precedent and practice was that it had somehow stolen up on them unawares. That was so far from the case that the second discussion centred on a report from a Cabinet sub-committee headed by the Lord Chancellor, Lord Gardiner, which, being divided itself, failed to carry the Cabinet on any of its recommendations. This defeat was undoubtedly a blow to the Prime Minister, and it was wholly in character that he should there and then have decided to drop the issue. (Indeed, thereafter, Wilson simply rested content with personal entreaties that nothing should be published until Labour had put its fortunes to the test at a further general election.)

This meant, though, when the collision eventually came – after Wilson had returned to No. 10 Downing Street in March 1974 – that the Cabinet Office found itself completely unprepared. Looking back on the whole bizarre episode, which lasted from May 1974, when Dr Janet Morgan, the prospective editor of the *Diaries*, received the first 'fishing expedition' letter from the Cabinet Office to the Government's defeat in the High Court in October 1975, I was astonished to discover one conclusion staring me in the face. The unfortunate new Cabinet Secretary, Sir John Hunt, was trying to make the rules up as he went along. It was not his fault. He was acting – as the Prime Minister went to some pains to make clear – on his own, as an agent without a principal. No doubt he started off by believing that his case was stronger than it turned out to be: custom and usage, after all, were entirely on his side. But, from the moment in January 1975 that the *Sunday Times* successfully mounted its ambush – by starting to serialise extracts from the first volume of the *Diaries* without giving any of the advance undertakings that the Cabinet Office had vainly tried to procure – Sir John was fighting a rearguard action. His bluff had been called, and he was left in the position of the emperor without any clothes. This vision would have delighted Crossman, for whom such 'conventions' always existed to be challenged and, where possible, demolished. The *Sunday Times* may not have succeeded quite in doing that; after its first pre-emptive strike it entered into a comic arrangement whereby great chunks of text were sent week by week to the Cabinet Office, not for clearance but merely to provide the Cabinet Secretary with an opportunity (at not much notice) to make what representations he saw fit. Since, on Sir John's own admission, there was no question of a 'veto',[7] the newspaper enjoyed the upper hand: at the end of nine weeks, little was left of the Cabinet Secretary's famous 'parameters' – meaning the limits within which disclosure could be permitted – and still less of his blanket interdict against 'blow by blow' accounts of Cabinet meetings. It certainly looked like a substantial defeat for officialdom, secured posthumously by a marauder operating inside the citadel of Government.

Governments, however, do not like admitting defeats – and the story was by no means over. When embarrassed, it is generally the politician's inclination to kick for touch; and the Prime Minister's first move was probably predictable. On 11 April 1975 Harold

Wilson revealed the appointment of a blue riband Committee of six
Privy Councillors – headed by the eminent jurist, Lord Radcliffe –
'to consider the principles which should govern the publication by
former Ministers of memoirs and other works relating to their
experience as Ministers, and the arrangements which should be
made to give effect to those principles'.[8] Given the successful
serialisation of the *Diaries*, completed in the *Sunday Times* barely a
fortnight earlier, this necessarily smacked of locking the stable door
after the horse had bolted. But this was not a view accepted in
Whitehall; it remained determined to snatch a victory out of the
jaws of defeat. At issue, after all, was not just a newspaper serialisation but the publication of a book. And, over the latter, the
custodians of Government confidentiality plainly felt on surer
ground.

They had some reason for doing so. Not only was a combination
of two publishing houses – Crossman himself had finally agreed that
his diaries should be published jointly by Hamish Hamilton and
Jonathan Cape – rightly seen as a less formidable opponent than a
single powerful national newspaper. Worse, so far as the book was
concerned, the case for freedom of action had already been compromised. Under pressure from the Cabinet Office – and on the
advice of Lord Goodman – the three executors of the Crossman
literary estate had given the Cabinet Secretary the previous summer
the very undertaking that the *Sunday Times* had resolutely refused
to concede. In return for an expression of willingness on his part at
least to look at an edited (or bowdlerised) version of the *Diaries*,
they had promised to give fourteen days' notice of any ultimate
intention to publish. No doubt, at the time it had seemed a necessary concession – and at least it had had the merit of probing the
Cabinet Office's defences. But none the less it meant that the three
literary executors were caught in the trap that the *Sunday Times* had
avoided. They had acknowledged the obligation to seek official
permission before publishing.

Understandably, their initial reaction, after the conclusion of
the *Sunday Times* serialisation, was that all Sir John's original
'parameters' had ceased to have any application and that only matters on the perimeter, such as national security, would now need to
be negotiated. It did not take long for them to be disabused. A letter
from Lord Goodman to the Cabinet Secretary suggesting that the
successful publication of newspaper extracts had 'very radically
changed' the position brought a reply not from Sir John but from
the Treasury Solicitor, Sir Henry Ware, writing on behalf of the

Attorney-General, Sam Silkin. It was not accepted that the position had in any way changed: publication of the book would still not be in the public interest.

So eleven months after the first sign of trouble – the innocently inquisitive letter from Sir John Hunt to Dr Janet Morgan, the editor of the *Diaries* – the literary executors found themselves back at square one. For them it was probably the most dispiriting moment of the whole exercise, made worse by their knowledge that Crossman himself had been determined that the book should come out, coupled with an uncomfortable suspicion on their part that he might possibly have favoured a more robust approach than they had adopted. They realised, however, that they had exhausted the path of conciliation, and on 5 June 1975 at last served notice of their intention to publish. The response within a matter of days was a writ issued by the Attorney-General, applying for an injunction under the Common Law of confidentiality.

The form the writ took was in itself something of a surprise. It had been widely assumed that the Government would reach for the doomsday weapon of the Official Secrets Act. The original surmise was that the Attorney-General had been deflected from taking such a draconian step only by the fact that, in addition to the then managing director of Jonathan Cape, Graham C. Greene, the other executors were Crossman's widow, Anne, and a serving member of the then Labour Cabinet, Michael Foot. (Foot's own behaviour was exemplary throughout: as an old-fashioned traditionalist about Government as well as Parliament he by no means shared all Crossman's own campaigning enthusiasms,[9] but, having given his word to act on his behalf, he steadfastly refused to renege on his personal commitment.) The truth, however, was that the Attorney-General had been advised that he would be unlikely to succeed under any legal procedure linked to the Official Secrets Act. Crossman's death a year earlier had, as it were, cut the knot tying any information he had received as a Minister of the Crown to his own unauthorised disclosure of it. It was, therefore, not chivalry but lack of choice that compelled the Attorney-General to seek his remedy under the Common Law doctrine of confidentiality.

Confidentiality is an arcane area of the law and it cannot be said that this particular case did much to illuminate it. Heard before the Lord Chief Justice towards the end of July 1975, the trial, which went on for six days, was mainly notable for the appearance in the witness box of Sir John Hunt (the first, but not the last, Cabinet Secretary to take part in legal proceedings concerned with suppressing a book).* At the conclusion of the hearing, Lord Widgery announced that he would reserve judgment until the first day of the new law term, 1 October. If that was an anti-climax, it was more than made up for when the appointed day came.

On 1 October the Labour Party was assembled for its annual Conference at Blackpool – and for many of the rank-and-file delegates the news which arrived around lunchtime was the most exciting event of the day. The Lord Chief Justice ruled against the Attorney-General and upheld the right of Volume 1 of the *Diaries* to be published without even such trimming on the margin as the executors had volunteered to consider the previous April. In truth, it was not a very satisfactory judgment since it admitted the claim of confidentiality to cover such areas as Cabinet proceedings but simply asserted that, through the passage of time, it did not apply in this instance. For the executors (who had been joined as defendants by the *Sunday Times*, largely on its own initiative in publishing a further article)[10] it was, however, as complete a victory as it was a humiliation for the Government.

The epilogue, when it came in the shape of the *Report of the Committee of Privy Councillors on Ministerial Memoirs*[11] the following January, hardly seemed to matter. Again, though, it was not a wholly intellectually satisfying document. Alongside the still existing thirty-year rule covering official Government documents, it argued for a new fifteen-year time limit on Ministers so far as the obligations of confidentiality were concerned. The argument was not made with much conviction and the more important outcome of the Report was probably its forthright statement that 'legislation does not offer the right solution'.† Even so, there were those who feared that the fifteen-year time-span would be set in concrete and that there would be no further prospect of ex-Ministers writing with even relative candour about their recent experiences in Government. Fortunately, such apprehensions soon proved baseless in the light of the real contributions to modern political history made subsequently in their published *Diaries* by both Barbara Castle and Tony Benn.

If breaching what was always presented as a code of honour – but

---

* Sir Robert (later Lord) Armstrong gave similar evidence – with possibly more disastrous results, at least for his own reputation – in the case brought by the British Government against Peter Wright's *Spycatcher* in 1986.

† This apparently was prompted by a characteristic upper-class comment made to the Committee by the former Prime Minister, Harold Macmillan: 'Under any arrangement there will always be some cad who comes along to break the rules.'

was, in reality, no more than a mutual security pact – had represented an accidental achievement on Crossman's part, it would still be a more enduring monument than most politicians have to survive them. But 'accidental' was the one thing it was not. It was an integral part of his whole approach to politics. He may have lacked the moral fervour that some of his colleagues brought to the discussion of other issues – during his time in Cabinet perhaps most notably Rhodesia and Vietnam; but over his commitment to making democracy in Britain a reality, his own ardour was second to none. He displayed it passionately, perhaps even awkwardly, in some remarks he delivered at a dinner given on the day the 1945 Parliament opened. These are the notes he scribbled afterwards of what he had said:

> A Labour Government is a people's Government. It has got to have a new relation to the voters, to the people as a whole . . . Think about the people. Contact is not kept automatically in England, because the tradition here is aristocratic, i.e. leaving things to the people at the top and the people at the top regarding the people as rather a nuisance, a disturbing factor which must be 'squared'. That is the tradition our electors fought against . . . Strange how politicians develop a protective secretiveness. They love talking freely inside the 'closed circle', and making speeches outside it. And their speeches are very different from their talk. I want them to *talk* not only to their colleagues but to the people.[12]

At his best, that is what Crossman does in his *Diaries* – which is why they remain far more than a postscript to a life that, while seldom short of colour or controversy, started off by being thoroughly conventional.

2 *An Edwardian Childhood*

Richard Howard Stafford Crossman lived through five reigns. He was born on 15 December 1907, three years before Edward VII died; and it was in an essentially Edwardian household that he was brought up. Until just before his birth, his parents, like the lesser Forsytes, lived on the north (and unfashionable) side of the Park – in Porchester Terrace, Bayswater. But the potential addition of a third child to the family (they already had a daughter of four and a son of two) precipitated a move to what was then rural Essex. The only family home that Dick Crossman could recall in later life was a large, solid house at Buckhurst Hill on the edge of Epping Forest, near Woodford. Although by no means opulent or luxurious, its very name – Buckhurst Hill House – reflected its mahogany virtues.

These left an indelible impression on the second son of what was eventually to be a family of six. There was nothing unusual – in the pre-1914 world – about an upper-middle-class household gathering for family prayers at 7.55 every morning, or of the adults regularly dressing for dinner at eight o'clock each evening. What *was* striking was the rigid way this routine was adhered to right through the 1920s, when Dick Crossman was growing up, and on into the 1930s, when he had already fully earned his right to be considered the Prodigal Son.

The fact that such a regime should have endured for as long as it did bears its own witness to the distinctive character of each of the Crossman parents. They were, it is true, very different personalities – but at the same time wholly complementary. In age and background both were products of the Victorian era,* and their marriage

---

* Charles Stafford Crossman (knighted in 1934) was born in 1870 and died in 1941. Helen Elizabeth Crossman lived till 1960 and was born in 1876.

symbolised the then familiar union between trade and the pro-
fessions. Helen Elizabeth Crossman came from the family firm of
Howard of Ilford (pharmaceutical chemists whose brand of aspirin
survived on the market until the 1960s). Though, as a daughter born
into a Victorian manufacturing family, she was denied any proper
education, she was determined that her own children would not
suffer in the same way – and her three daughters, as well as the three
sons, all went away to boarding school. Throughout their youth, she
was the dominant presence in her children's lives – strong-minded,
energetic and eager to enter into every aspect of their activities.

Their father, one of eight children of a country doctor from Glou-
cestershire, could hardly have represented a sharper contrast. Of
yeoman rather than aristocratic stock – though there was a collateral
connection with the Danvers family,* which traced its lineage back
to the Plantagenets – Charles Stafford Crossman was a man of
exceptional intellectual ability and remarkable personal reserve. At
Winchester and New College, Oxford he had enjoyed a career of
unblemished academic distinction, just as his second son was to do
after him. That, however, was about all they shared in common.

Stafford Crossman, as he was generally known, believed above all
in the principle of order in human affairs.† Conventional by nature
and cautious by instinct, he was in many ways ideally cut out for the
profession he followed for more than thirty-five years, that of
Chancery barrister. (He eventually became a rather less successful
High Court judge – 'he had great difficulty in making up his mind'[1] –
but died within seven years of his appointment to the Bench,
thereby ensuring that his family received no pension.)

An essentially modest man, he was always conscious of his good
fortune in having had the opportunity to serve the love of his life,
the law. In fact, only a windfall inheritance from a childless uncle – a
farm estate near Bristol yielding the then lavish income of £500 a
year – had enabled him, after a year spent as a classics master at
Winchester, to be called to the Bar in the first place.[2] He was never,
though, in the least attracted by the more lurid, forensic side of the
profession: when, in later years, the question arose of his second,

---

* One of the odder aspects of Dick Crossman as a democrat was the enormous
pride he took in the fact that his ultimate home – Prescote Manor near Banbury –
should also have been for four centuries, starting in 1419, a house owned by the
Danvers family.

† His most enduring achievement was probably to draw up the rule book for the
Transport and General Workers' Union. It was a professional commission, but the
principles that Stafford Crossman laid down in 1921 survive intact to this day.

cleverest, son also becoming a barrister, he immediately abandoned all efforts to persuade him to do so in face of a brash declaration that the only thing that could conceivably make such a career worthwhile would be the prospect of becoming 'a famous criminal advocate'. Mr Justice Crossman (as he became in 1934) is said to have shuddered and encouraged him to become a don instead.[3]

In itself that was perhaps some indication of the gulf that was to develop between the reticent, reflective father and his equally able but fiercely ambitious second son. In the early years, however, it was naturally the influence of the father that prevailed, even if it was exercised far more gently than by many parents of the same era. According to his mother, 'as a little boy, Dick was the easiest of all my children'[4] – and there seems little doubt that his father also initially found him the most rewarding.

Every Saturday morning, starting at the age of seven, a small chair would be placed in Stafford Crossman's study and Dick would sit on it happily enough to be taught the rudiments of Latin. More than forty years later – when he was already a 54-year-old Labour MP – he was to look back on these as 'halcyon days';[5] and, whatever else he may later have said or written in criticism of his father, there would seem to be little basis here for a theory of an entire career being shaped by 'an Oedipus complex'.[6]

Indeed, Dick appears to have enjoyed an exceptionally harmonious childhood (if things changed later, that was hardly his parents' fault). It is not easy, of course, today to summon back the atmosphere of a pre-1914 middle-class home: the Crossman parents had been married in 1901 and all but one of their six children – Tom, their third son – were born before the outbreak of the First World War. By today's standards it was a fairly formal upbringing – with a day nursery, a night nursery, a nanny and an under-nurse, to say nothing of a parlour-maid, two other maids, a gardener and a gardener's boy. In the early 1900s that did not, however, rank as living in any great style. The children's maternal grandparents, who lived across the road, maintained the same full domestic staff with a coachman as well: in the Crossman family's eyes Devon House, which they would visit every Sunday, seemed a great deal grander than their own. Possibly to redress this balance – or to choke off any incipient materialism at an early stage – their mother always went out of her way to praise their father, even at the expense of her own parents and relatives; they, the children seem to have been given to understand, were merely 'in trade' whereas their father was both 'a scholar and a gentleman'.[7]

Through all his years at the Bar, Stafford Crossman remained, however, a fairly impecunious professional man. His eldest son estimated that his fees before he became a Junior Counsel to the Treasury in 1927, never came to more than £1,500 a year;[8] and, though family holidays were a regular part of the domestic rhythm, they were usually spent at the village of Ashmore in Dorset, which was virtually owned by another branch of the Howard family. Even in adult life, Dick was always ready to comment on the comfort of life at Ashmore[9] – and for all the children it clearly represented a refreshing change from the more austere regime at Buckhurst Hill.

The regime was dictated by their father's temperament: plain living, for Stafford Crossman, was in itself a mark of virtue – and certainly the necessary accompaniment to hard work. Every night, at ten o'clock, he would start preparing his briefs for the following day; and (in not merely the pre-television but the pre-radio age) the only evening recreation available to the children, once they were old enough to be allowed downstairs, came after dinner when their mother would read to them for an hour or so from a novel. At weekends there would be some relaxation of the routine – Buckhurst Hill House boasted a tennis court and inevitably it became the focal point for social activities. One couple who were regular Saturday afternoon visitors in the 1920s were a then rising young Labour MP and his wife, who lived just down the road some 200 yards from Woodford Green Station: conservative though he may have been by disposition, Stafford Crossman was ecumenical enough in outlook to number Clement and Violet Attlee among his and his wife's closest friends.* For Dick that may have been a mixed blessing; certainly afterwards he was inclined to blame the 'bolshie' impression he had made, as a schoolboy and an undergraduate, upon the future leader of his Party for his failure to achieve any form of preferment in the 1945–51 Attlee Governments.

For strangely, and rather against the odds, Buckhurst Hill was not an inhibited household. Plain living there may have been but – at least once the elder children became teenagers – there was less high thinking than boisterous argument. This was largely due to the children's mother, Helen Crossman, who was never quite able to adapt her own combative temperament to her husband's more docile nature. Perhaps reacting against her own Victorian upbringing, she was determined that her own children should not be repressed

---

* In 1960, as an ex-Prime Minister, Clement Attlee made a point of attending Dick Crossman's mother's funeral.

in any way. And if that meant awkward questions being asked about such matters as the Virgin Birth over the family dining-room table,[10] then that was a price she at least was prepared to pay. If a tension later developed in what was otherwise an ideal marriage, it was because her husband, who suffered badly from migraines, instinctively shrank from any form of domestic altercation.*

To begin with, though, few such problems presented themselves: from a Quaker background, Helen Crossman had developed into being a devout Anglo-Catholic. She, no doubt, felt that her policy of 'openness' on even the most delicate religious issues had been fully vindicated when her second son insisted that he should be confirmed at the same time as his elder brother, even though at that stage Dick was a mere eleven-year-old (his brother, Geoffrey, was already thirteen). The two boys were presented together for confirmation at their nearest Anglo-Catholic parish, St John's Loughton (to which the family would walk each Sunday two miles each way), in 1919.

That, however, proved to be the calm before the storm – something that Helen Crossman subsequently came ruefully to recognise. In old age she would sometimes remark: 'My great mistake lay in allowing Dick to come to religion so early, I should have known it would not stick.'[12] She was wrong, however, to reproach herself. What changed her second son's nature – and shaped his character – was not his home but his school.

---

* When a future daughter-in-law first visited the house as late as 1937 and found herself taken aback by the vigour of dinner-table discussions, she inquired of her host, Mr Justice Crossman, 'Is it always like this?' 'Yes,' he replied bleakly.[11]

3 The Wykehamist

One of Dick Crossman's favourite stories always centred on how, as a very small boy, one Saturday morning he was led by his father to an airing cupboard in an alcove off the kitchen at Buckhurst Hill House and shown two ancient black tin boxes. Their contents, he was proudly told, vindicated his claim to be 'Founder's Kin' – and, therefore, justified by descent from William of Wykeham to automatic admission to both Winchester and New College. In his more fanciful moments Dick would sometimes contrive to leave the impression that it was only his father's characteristic high-mindedness that had prevented this right from being exercised in his favour. In truth, the privilege attaching to 'Founder's Kin' – and the Crossman family's claim to it, through the female line of the Danvers family, was pretty tenuous – had been abolished as long ago as 1857:[1] there was never any question of Dick, or even of his father, being in any position to take advantage of it.

The only way, therefore, for Dick to get to Winchester was via the normal route of a scholastic forcing house. At the age of eight he was sent to Twyford School, a preparatory establishment conveniently sited in a village near Winchester, where his elder brother, Geoffrey, had preceded him. It was not an entirely happy choice. The school, at that time, was more games-minded than academic – with a headmaster, H. C. McDonnell, who was mainly interested in sport. Dick's arrival, given all the grounding he had gained in Latin from his father, also posed problems for his brother, whom he rapidly overtook both in term marks and exams. There was never any question, however, of Dick being held back – indeed, so far as his parents were concerned, rather the reverse. His brother, Geoffrey, was soon dispatched to Radley – and a new master promptly arrived who had been Stafford Crossman's own star pupil in the year he had spent as a classics 'don' at Winchester in the late 1890s. With the active encouragement of this particular classics teacher (H. V. Gillett), Dick, in June 1920, when he was only twelve years old, attained thirteenth place in what happened that year to be a particularly large and distinguished scholars' roll at Winchester.*

It was almost certainly what his father had always intended; but what he can hardly have foreseen was the appetite with which Dick would take to College life at Winchester. True to form, in later years Dick tended to romanticise his Winchester existence – 'For six years I fought first for survival and then for success, according to rules which barred very few holds,' he was to write in a book review in 1954.[2] But, in reality, there does not seem to have been much struggle at all. Like everyone else, Dick was placed in one of the five Chambers in College, each with between ten and twenty inmates selected, not on the basis of age or seniority, but as a cross-section of the scholars then working their way up through the school. Certainly, the life was hard – the scholars were expected to wash themselves under cold taps in a sort of bidet every morning (there were no baths of any kind) and the food, particularly on Fridays when there was fish, was, according to a contemporary, 'very bad indeed'.[3] But it provided exactly the competitive environment in which Dick was bound to thrive. He was later to suggest that College, when he entered it, was divided between 'athletes' and 'aesthetes';[4] if so, and even allowing for his good fortune in having the former Prime Minister's notably gentle son and future film director Anthony ('Puffin') Asquith as his first fag-master, Dick was hardly likely to be the victim of any such conflict. The one thing his contemporaries tend to remember about him was how 'big' and 'burly'[5] he was; he also very soon displayed a remarkable aptitude for the indigenous, somewhat arcane game of Winchester football – depending, as it does, far more on brute strength than any native ball-game sense (in which he was always notably lacking).

The truth was probably that Winchester offered the first proper forum in which Dick had had the opportunity to deploy the full force of his personality. Here a remarkable piece of contemporary testimony survives as to the impression he immediately created. It has always been the slightly precious Wykehamist custom for the senior member of any College Chamber to pass judgment on the

---

* Other members of it included Richard Wilberforce, later to become a Lord of Appeal in Ordinary, William Empson, the poet and critic, and John Willis, subsequently a Professor of Classics in Canada.

younger boys under his care. Possibly there was nothing especially surprising in the way in which Dick was loftily dismissed after his first year in College:

> R. Crossman was rather above himself but he has an amusing face. I hear that he is an amateur versifier of distinction. He was once transfixed with a long toasting fork by the analyst [meaning the writer of the annals] in a moment of exaltation.[6]

Typical enough *Tom Brown's Schooldays* stuff – though reflecting, perhaps, none too well on Britain's supposedly most academic public school. But it is interesting how often that same 'analyst' felt the need to invoke the influence of Crossman in composing his other character sketches. Thus one scholar's only claim to fame is found to consist in his having 'collaborated with Crossman to write an epic – nothing much else is known against him'; another is damned briefly as having 'modelled himself on Crossman'; while a third is characterised, even more brutally, as having 'displayed a dog-like devotion to Crossman, which is not reciprocated'.[7] Despite the tone of moral disapproval, such an evident impact on his fellows represented a considerable achievement for a thirteen-year-old.

And, to be fair, it was not long before the tone changed markedly. The next writer in the same Winchester archive had a different tale to tell:

> Crossman is a great personality. He came to Winchester very young and since then has had a triumphal progress. He was soon the acknowledged leader of his roll, and it was not long before he was appreciated to the full in yet higher circles.[8]

The latter, no doubt, was a veiled reference to Dick's undoubted success with Winchester's headmaster. Two views continue to exist about Monty Rendall (Headmaster of Winchester, 1911–24). One, embraced by some of his most distinguished pupils,* is that he was a charlatan; the other, championed by equally dutiful Wykehamists, is that – though undoubtedly an actor – he was also an inspired teacher. Dick, somewhat uncharacteristically, seems to have taken a middle way between the two viewpoints. He never sought to disguise that he found Rendall's classical scholarship 'rusted by years

---

* e.g. by Sir William Hayter, later British Ambassador to Moscow and Warden of New College, who claims never to have recovered from the shock of having been placed on Monty Rendall's knee and kissed by him.

of neglect' – a neglect certainly not helped by his 'delusion that the incantation of Pindar's Odes could be a substitute for seriously preparing the day's lesson';[9] but there was also an element of the showman in Rendall that found a response in his own nature.

Certainly, there can be no doubt that Dick owed his first Winchester headmaster a lot (he never seems to have enjoyed anything like the same rapport with the second master – and Rendall's successor as headmaster for his last two years at school – A. T. P. Williams, who went on to be Dean of Christ Church and Bishop of both Durham and Winchester). With his good looks, engaging personality and intellectual enthusiasm, Dick was, not surprisingly, just the type of schoolboy to appeal to Rendall (who never married). And he was clearly the beneficiary of the headmaster's direct personal patronage.

One of the stranger Winchester institutions used to be a society known as SROGUS – the initials standing for 'Shakespeare Reading Orpheus Glee United Society'. Defunct since 1960, in Crossman's day it met on Saturday evenings in the headmaster's house. Normally its membership was confined to some dozen senior boys, selected by the headmaster and drawn both from College and from the ranks of Commoners, who were all required to wear dinner jackets; presumably because, after the play-reading was over, they were allowed to stay up late for a buffet supper in the headmaster's own dining-room. Dick became a member of the society at the remarkably early age of fifteen, probably encountering there for the first time his future Party leader, the Commoner Hugh Gaitskell,* who was eighteen months older than he was and who left Winchester a full two years ahead of him. (Unkindly, on their first dramatic programme together, Gaitskell's reading was reported to be 'somewhat lifeless', while Dick's was characterised as having 'conviction and no small weight and force'.)[10] For the next three years – particularly during the two winter seasons remaining under Rendall – Dick became an established pillar of the society. He was not, of course, allowed the main parts – those, while he continued to reign as headmaster, were by tradition reserved for Rendall; but Dick did as well as anyone else in having his pick of the lesser roles. Between October 1923 and July 1924 – when Rendall retired and the society went into eclipse – he read Don John in *Much Ado About Nothing*, Roderigo in *Othello*, Cassius in *Julius Caesar* and

---

* Hugh Todd Naylor Gaitskell (1906–63). Labour MP, Leeds South, 1945–63. Chancellor of the Exchequer 1950–1. Leader of the Opposition 1955–63.

Falstaff in *Henry IV*, *Part One*; he also played the part of Hieronimo in a theatrical presentation of Thomas Kyd's *Spanish Tragedy*. Most memorably of all, however, in a full dramatic production of *Dr Faustus* in College Hall in Rendall's penultimate term as head-master he took the part of Mephistopheles – and was praised as having given 'a good picture of a soul tormented by remorse and driven, as by necessity, to do evil'.*[11]

Yet it was not merely as the headmaster's protégé that Dick flourished at Winchester. From the beginning he seems to have been recognised as a powerful personality. Partly, no doubt, it was a question of physique. The seventy scholars with their long black serge gowns and sleeved waistcoats tended to supply an aristocracy of brains rather than brawn: it was Dick's good fortune to embody both – and, therefore, to possess all the makings of a schoolboy hero. He was never the cleverest boy in the school: however hard he tried, Richard Wilberforce was always, at least, one place ahead of him (in their last competitive year together Wilberforce scooped up all four of Winchester's traditional classical prizes). But somehow that did not matter. To his contemporaries it was Dick who pro-vided the zest, the energy and the leadership – something that the school authorities tacitly acknowledged when they overlooked mere academic attainments and chose Dick first (in 1924–5) to be 'Prefect of School' and then (in 1925–6) elevated him to the top position of 'Prefect of Hall'.

It was a career of copybook public school success, all the more remarkable in that it had been achieved by a boy already of far from conventional cast of mind. In the 1924 mock election held by the debating society 'to elect a Member of Parliament for the Moberly Library Division of Hampshire' it was Dick, predictably, who was the Labour candidate – and though, like the first Ramsay Mac-Donald Government, he went down to defeat (gathering only twenty-one votes to 105 for the Conservative) he did so with all guns blazing:

The Conservative Party, in which Liberalism had apparently

* An irreverent view of these meetings of SROGUS was later to be offered by a somewhat older Winchester contemporary of Dick's. 'Rendall sat in the middle of a long table and read the principal male parts – Antony, Macbeth, King Lear and so forth; but there were often minor parts he could not resist, for example the fairies in *A Midsummer Night's Dream*, and these he would read in a diminished sing-song, wagging an enormous finger ... I may add that the soubrette parts were played by a little roly-poly boy named Richard Crossman.' Kenneth Clark, *Another Part of the Wood* (John Murray, 1974), pp. 64–5.

sought a refuge, stood now simply for stagnation: it was trying to
frighten people out of Socialism, which was nothing more terrible
than the co-ordination of effort along Socialist lines. Socialism
was the logical end of all the movements of today; to be afraid of
it was to be afraid of improvement, to stand against it was to stand
against change.[12]

If those were minority sentiments at Winchester, they were looked
upon as something far more alarming at Buckhurst Hill; and Dick
was probably right in tracing his alienation – at least from his father
– to the days when he would bring back to the family dining-table
the same robust debating techniques that he had learnt at school.
Nor were matters improved by his mother's consistent determination to enter into every aspect of her children's lives. Unlike her
husband, who tended to cleave to the quietist maxim, 'When you
don't agree, say nothing,' she insisted on entering every argument –
with results that nearly always ended in her humiliation. It cannot
have been a happy domestic scene – a fact that Dick recognised
when, of his father, he wrote years later: 'He could not forgive me
for cruelly and deliberately taking advantage of my mother's lack of
education. I could not forgive him for suffering in retracted silence,
instead of coming to her assistance, when his own values and
principles were under attack.'[13]

At Winchester no such problems arose. If Dick had already developed into an intellectual bully, then his role in that capacity was
simply seen as helping the education of his contemporaries.
Certainly, no one accused *him* of lacking chivalry: indeed, when
Monty Rendall, as a parting gift to the school, commissioned a
somewhat bizarre medieval triptych, designed to immortalise the
virtues of chivalry, Dick found himself selected as the artist's model
for one of the three panels devoted to the role of the scholar.

His father's apprehensions – which perhaps were provoked,
above anything else, by youthful arrogance – may not, however,
have been without foundation. It subsequently became one of his
son's more familiar boasts that never again – even as a Cabinet
Minister – did he enjoy the same power that he wielded as head boy
of Winchester.* And, slightly disturbingly, the contemporary
evidence suggests that he gloried in it. One of the duties of a Prefect
of Hall at Winchester is to preserve for posterity an account of his

---

* Stephen Spender recalls being told by Dick at Oxford in the late 1920s: 'Even
if I become Prime Minister, I'll never again be as great as I was at Winchester.'[14]

stewardship. Most of what Dick wrote in 1925–6 is, inevitably, fairly incestuous – barely intelligible to the non-Wykehamist; but there is one entry, in particular, that carries its own authentic authoritarian chill. Dated, simply, 'January 1926', it runs as follows:

> The Second Master [by then R. M. Wright] has had complaints from parents about beatings of which he knows nothing. He, therefore, asks the Prefect of Hall to inform him when any beating takes place. This is purely a matter of convenience for him. It has been agreed by him that he does not thereby gain the significant control of beating, nor is the Prefect of Hall 'raising leave' from him when he informs him of the fact. Indeed, it is better that he should be told after the event.[15]

It is unfair, of course, to judge anyone by something written at the age of eighteen – and full allowance should, no doubt, be made for the whole disciplinary ethos under which Dick had grown up at Winchester. Even so, it remains surprising that – far from being a rebel or even a reformer – Dick appears at the end of his schooldays to have emerged as the stout upholder of public school discipline. And the story is worse than that. A later, briefer entry, dated 'May 1926' (and again bearing the initials RHSC) reads simply: 'It should be placed on record here that the Ground Ash was abolished in February and a cane substituted as the official weapon.'[16]

That cryptic sentence conceals the background to what had caused this abrupt change in the instrument of punishment at Winchester. In his later journalistic incarnation all Dick's inquisitive instincts would certainly have been aroused by such a deadpan statement: so it is legitimate to reveal the story that lay behind it. Dick's own 'valet' – or fag – in College at Winchester was a boy called George Lowther Steer (who went on to become a distinguished journalist). In beating him for some offence Dick – employing the time-honoured Winchester weapon of chastisement – had cut him dangerously near the eye. The replacement of the ground ash – insisted on by the new headmaster, A. T. P. Williams – followed rapidly.[17]

None of this, however, subtracted from Dick's reputation. He had arrived at a school just emerging from the traumas of the First World War – and, largely owing to Rendall's obsession with the building of his 'War Cloister' as a memorial to the fallen, in some danger of still being dominated by them. What Winchester badly needed was a new folk hero, pointing the way forward rather than backward. Dick's exuberant gifts and articulate talents were ideally suited to fill that bill. It is always perilous to advance exaggerated claims after the event – but at least for a decade Dick does appear to have embodied the spirit of Winchester in a way that no one else could.

When, in 1931, John Betjeman published his poem 'The Wyke-hamist',[18] there seems to have been remarkably little question as to who had inspired it. Obviously, there was a certain licence involved, but its opening four lines reflected Dick's mental and muscular frame:

> Broad of Church and broad of mind
> Broad before and broad behind
> A keen ecclesiologist
> A rather dirty Wykehamist.

The rest of the poem may, if anything, have accentuated that initial derogatory tone – but at the age of twenty-four, and by then with some desire for celebrity developing, Dick was hardly going to mind about that.

4 Undergraduate and Don

The early years of Dick Crossman's university career have always been something of a mystery. He had arrived at Oxford – having effortlessly secured second place (to Richard Wilberforce) on New College's Winchester scholarship roll – easily the best known Wyke-hamist of his generation. And yet at Oxford his fame seemed, initially at least, to recede. Despite his claim, subsequently advanced in two BBC broadcasts,[1] to have been firmly 'politicised' by the General Strike (which had taken place in his final term at school), he took no part in the Oxford Union and never even joined the University Labour Club. Nor, unlike Hugh Gaitskell, was he one of those undergraduates who gathered at the feet of the reigning socialist guru, G. D. H. Cole – whose influence, though now largely forgotten, launched many young left-wing careers.

Perhaps the truth was contained in a startling confession Dick made many years later when addressing an Old Wykehamist dinner held in Bath after he had ceased to be a Cabinet Minister. He tried on this occasion to strike a balance as to what Winchester had, and had not, done for him. Even across the chasm of nearly half a century it is a sufficiently candid assessment of himself as a young man to be worth quoting:

What had the school done for me? Well, it had made me, intellec-tually, prematurely mature. Far too early maturity. Astonishing! Here I was reading Dostoevsky at 14 – and going to Oxford feeling everything was over. I had experienced everything – I had done everything in the world of intellect, culture and letters. I was over-developed intellectually when I went to Oxford but I was correspondingly under-developed in the problems of life – gauche, naive, boring, not used to handling myself with women.

That was the kind of person I was when I got to Oxford.[2]

If a harsh diagnosis, it was also probably an accurate one – and is borne out by the typically thorough exercise in personality development that Dick immediately embarked upon the moment he arrived in Oxford. With the sole exception of Douglas Jay,* (and since he had been a Commoner he hardly counted), he appears to have made a deliberate resolution to boycott all his former Winchester friends. In their place, he dedicated himself to cultivating friendships with people he regarded as 'creative writers'. In the climate of the time that necessarily meant poets (perhaps Dick's greatest disappointment in his last term at school had been his failure to win the Winchester poetry prize, which had gone instead to Douglas Jay). The circle he was determined to penetrate was assembled around the already legendary figure of W. H. Auden, then at Christ Church – and, thanks largely to an early friendship with Stephen Spender at University College – he soon established a place on the periphery. It was never, however, very secure (or even comfortable). Spender more than half a century later could still recall Dick blurting out: 'You know what I envy about you and your friends? You have *feelings* about other people. You see, I haven't got any.'[3]

No doubt, that was a typical remark designed to shock; but there was possibly an element of truth in it. The earliest diaries of Dick's to survive consist of a hard-bound notebook in which he wrote intermittently in 1928–9 – or half-way through his Oxford career. The entries in it are obsessed with sex, though hardly with love or even affection. One of them commemorates an Easter holiday spent in Cornwall with a young poet, and his evocation of it is explicit: 'He kept me in a little white-washed room for a fortnight because his mouth was against mine and we were completely together.'[4] Dick never sought to conceal the fact that in his early years at Oxford he had operated predominantly as a homosexual. Given the circle, dominated by W. H. Auden, which he had chosen to infiltrate, it was hardly likely that it would be otherwise.

Indeed, with Auden himself, he competed energetically for the allegiance of a particularly glamorous ex-Sedbergh schoolboy and noted rugby player at Christ Church named Gabriel Carritt (they were both disappointed – Carritt's own romantic interests at the time being focused on the Zuleika Dobson of her day, Elizabeth

* Labour MP, Battersea North, 1946–83. Financial Secretary to the Treasury 1950–1. President of the Board of Trade 1964–7. Created life peer 1987.

Harman, later the Countess of Longford). That did not, though, prevent either of them from making a number of trips to Sedbergh to watch the desired disport himself on the rugby field. But even at that stage of his life Dick was always ambivalent. He greatly admired, for example, Gabriel Carritt's mother, Winifred, the slightly unorthodox wife of a don at University College (Stephen Spender wrote a short story about both Dick and her – 'The Haymaking' – which appeared in *Oxford Outlook* in 1929). Nor did Dick himself ignore women in the diary entries he scribbled at the time, even recalling how on one occasion, a family Christmas party, a cousin (aged twelve) had clearly 'lured' him: 'she definitely wanted to be near me, sat on my knee and put her hands firmly on my arms so that my hands touched her cool skin'.[5] Not all experiences, however, were as rewarding: a casual pick-up of a girl in an Oxford cinema in January 1929 led to the gloomy reflection that 'the film was more real than our cuddling'.[6]

To his evident chagrin, everything suggests that Dick remained at least a heterosexual virgin while an undergraduate at Oxford. That may have been just as well: he was, after all, still a prize product of the classical scholarship battery farm of Winchester. And, despite his sexual and attempted emotional diversions, he was quite worldly enough to recognise that what mattered was getting a first in Classical Mods, just as his father had done before him. His initial comments on the coming ordeal were pretty fatalistic: 'Definitely now I am stale: still, it is too late now to do very much self-lashing into a visionary work-fervour.'[7] Nor did he sound much more cheerful once Mods had begun, though a more robust spirit soon asserted itself:

> It is an *awful* exam. But as it goes on you feel each day a great ton weight of stuff off. Each prepared book is a term's work, dismissed in three hours, so that you need never think of it again.
>
> As to doing well, you're too relieved at having the thing done to worry much. I only know that after 3 days all your papers are 20% to 30% below your level because your mind is fagged out: you just can't concentrate or arrange: you simply vomit stuff.
>
> But it is over now. I shall be very annoyed if I haven't got a first. There are 3 papers I know I made a mess of, 3 or 4 I am fairly confident about. The vast majority you just don't know if they are alpha or not.[8]

However, the examiners seem to have had little difficulty in recognising alpha quality when they saw it. Dick was duly placed in the First Class list. His reward was a holiday spent in Normandy with some Oxford friends and his eldest sister, Bridget (who herself had been an undergraduate at Lady Margaret Hall). It appears to have been a great success,[9] and was probably Dick's first trip abroad, although he went to Belgium later that same year with the family and a second cousin – almost old enough to be his mother – who had grown rather too fond of him. ('I suppose', Dick was to write some three months later, 'I did half fall in love with her in Belgium but since then have moved, leaving her stationary.')[10]

Dick's attractiveness to older women remained a factor throughout his youth. He had made a great hit while at Winchester with the mother of one of his schoolfriends, George Harwood: since she had married, for the second time, a classics don at Christ Church called John Murray, this friendship was fully maintained while he was still at Oxford – with Dick making frequent visits to their family home at Ewelme Down.[11] His relationships with older men tended to be rather more complicated – and, indeed, may have cost him his one chance of being an actor at Oxford, just as he had been at school. In the Trinity Term of 1928 the Oxford University Dramatic Society was due to produce a Greek play, which in those days it was required to do every three years. The choice was *The Clouds* by Aristophanes and initially Dick was cast in the main role of Socrates – on the strength of an audition he had given on his last day of taking Mods.[12] No sooner, however, did serious rehearsals start in the summer term than he found himself dropped from the cast. The official explanation given by the producer, a don called Cyril Bailey, was that he was not 'up to it'; a suspicion, however, lingered among his contemporaries that the real reason lay in a personality conflict – and in the desire of the producer to add a personal favourite of his to the cast.[13]

Dick does not, though, appear to have been much cast down by this disappointment. It was, no doubt, a help that his own interests continued to lie in writing his own verse rather than in speaking other people's. And there he soon enjoyed remarkable recognition, something that probably gave him as much satisfaction as anything else (apart from the academic results he achieved) that he did at Oxford. In the late 1920s *Oxford Poetry* was easily the most influential poetry anthology of its day. Auden's poetry had first appeared in it in 1926, and the following year he and Cecil Day Lewis wrote a Preface that was to serve as the first real manifesto on behalf of the generation that was to dominate poetry in the 1930s. Dick's appearance in it with three separate poems in 1929, therefore, fully vindicated his aspiration to be counted among the 'creative' figures of his own Oxford era. His contributions were not especially distinguished – as may be judged from the shortest of them entitled 'March Snow':

> Out on the field under a quiet sky
> The snow still lies in the furrows
> White body leaning upon dark strength
> But uncommingled –
>
> Let not my clay contaminate your snow
> Slipped from the upper firmament to discover
> The secrets of your country lover,
> But both lie easy till you know
> The fastnesses of this wide frame you cover –
> For then should winter soon be over
> And corn stand high
> Under a quiet sky.

Apart from its evident sexuality, there is not much to commend this poem. It displays an almost complete lack of rhythm – and tries to make up for it with exaggerated rhetorical devices and supposed poetic diction. Dick's two other poems in the same number of *Oxford Poetry* did reveal a more marked Audenesque influence – even if one of them ran (even in abbreviated form) to some eighty lines. The harsh truth probably was that Dick was never cut out to be a poet – though Auden's feigned lack of memory that he had ever tried to be one was something that wounded him deeply when they met over forty years later.[14] His subsequent television conversation with Auden in 1973 did little to suggest that any great rapport had survived between them from their Oxford years[15] – although Dick himself remained curiously proud of it.[16]

Yet at Oxford, as at school, Dick was not merely an aesthete. He regularly played rugby for his college and, in the view of one of his contemporaries, might even have gained a University Blue if Winchester had been a rugger rather than a soccer school.[17] He was an outdoor figure, regularly taking enormous walks in the countryside (on one occasion he hiked fifty-two miles in one day, from Oxford to Winchester, in the company of Douglas Jay).[18] No doubt this *corpore sano* aspect of his life had something to do with the decision of the New College authorities (with whom appointment to the post then lay) to invite him to become Steward, or President, of the

Junior Common Room during his final year. The approach, which was made early in the summer term of 1929, appears to have genuinely taken him by surprise. It certainly did much for his morale: he referred to it in his private diary of the time as being largely responsible for 'a sudden access of confidence in my powers'. He even mentioned the other interests he had been pursuing (including poetry) as being merely 'limbs of one wide tree'.[19]

His acceptance of this hallmark of official approval was also revealing in another way; for Dick had already entered into one of those elaborate student arrangements by which friends combine together to occupy 'digs' in their final year. His selection as Steward of the JCR meant that he had to live in College – and his delay in letting his friends know of this change in his circumstances (with all the dislocation it necessarily caused to long-agreed compacts) caused lasting offence to at least one of them.* Of course, Dick may have been bound by an oath of secrecy; but there was perhaps something ominously cavalier in the way other people's sensitivities never seem even to have entered his mind.

Presumably that was also part of the explanation for the marked lack of success Dick enjoyed with the leading university social figures of his time. Unlike John Betjeman, Hugh Gaitskell or (from a distance) Elizabeth Longford, he was never a frequenter of the two leading *salons* then run in Oxford by Maurice Bowra of Wadham and 'Sligger' Urquhart of Balliol:† he was, once, invited to lunch by Bowra but blotted his copybook by sending a note afterwards saying that, although he had enjoyed talking to *him*, he hadn't much cared for the other guests[20] – scarcely the type of remark calculated to please a man who prided himself above all on his gifts as a host.

Yet within the more austere walls of New College, Dick's lack of tact never seems to have counted against him – and he was always something of a protégé of the senior 'Greats' tutor (and leading Platonist of his day), H. W. B. Joseph. Almost certainly it was

---

* Douglas Jay, *Change and Fortune* (Hutchinson, 1980), p. 33: 'Crossman had forgotten to tell the rest of us. When he casually did, it was a stunning shock. We did not speak again for some years.'

† Dick did, however, stay as a member of a reading party at the then Urquhart-owned Chalet des Melèzes in the French Alps in the summer of 1928. He appears to have enjoyed it – describing it to his mother as 'a good place': undated letter written in pencil from the Chalet des Melèzes at St Gervais les Bains. Significantly or not, his father was also a member of the party.

Joseph's influence that lay behind an extraordinary offer made to
Dick in his penultimate term.

The background is provided in a series of letters he wrote to his
mother in February–March 1930. They begin by revealing that Sedbergh School (where he had become known through his visits to
watch Gabriel Carritt play rugby) had written to him offering him
'£350 p.a. and the top form'[21] if he would join the staff the following
September. The invitation was sufficiently attractive for Dick to
take it seriously – indeed, he discussed it with his parents, his
Oxford tutors and his former schoolmasters at Winchester. Their
advice, however, was uniformly against acceptance – with his Winchester counsellors, in particular, recommending instead that he
should 'spend a year or two abroad' once Greats was safely behind
him. Since this inevitably involved further parental subsidy it was
not especially welcome news at Buckhurst Hill – though, as a draft
letter from his mother shows, his father was still a dutiful enough
parent to shoulder the necessary burden, if on some fairly explicit
understandings:

> Daddy would be prepared to find £100-a-year for not more than
> two years provided that you are undertaking some definite work,
> not just wandering about. He feels there would be a very real
> danger of unsettling yourself for the routine work which has to be
> undertaken sooner or later if you were to spend two years in
> dilettante dabbling in many things. Daddy wants to add that if he
> got ill or anything the £100-a-year couldn't be forthcoming.
>
> Don't discuss your plans in detail with the family at present.
> This information is only to enable you to deal with the Sedbergh
> offer.[22]

As, no doubt, Stafford Crossman had gloomily foreseen, even the
guarded nature of his promise of help was sufficient for Dick to turn
Sedbergh down. However, his letter in reply intimating he had done
so was rather more significant for another piece of information it
contained:

> *In strictest confidence* I know there have been approaches made by
> Queen's to see if I should be a suitable Roman history don, as
> they want somebody who would have some influence with under-
> graduates and not be a mere student, and that there are *very
> vague* discussions at New College about the possibility of my
> being a philosophy tutor here.[23]

In the same letter Dick had gone on to emphasise that both possible

openings were 'the *merest suggestions*'[24] – but it did not take long for
the latter one at least to crystallise. Indeed, only one week later,
Dick was writing in understandable triumph:

> New College (money permitting) are forced by the Queen's offer
> to offer at once a fellowship in philosophy and history, after which
> I am to decide myself which to specialise in, with a chance of
> succeeding Joseph . . . I should not be wanted till next summer
> term so I should still have some time to work abroad myself.
> What do you think of that? It is rather exciting isn't it?[25]

It was not just 'exciting': even for the Oxford of 1930 it was quite
exceptional – for, as Dick's letter went on ruefully to note ('I shudder to think of Schools after all this'),[26] he had not yet even had his
encounter with the Greats examiners. Of course, the New College
dons, led by his own philosophy tutor, Joseph, were in a better
position than anyone else to form a view of his abilities – but a
decision taken so early was still a striking testament of faith in his
intellectual capacity. (There could, admittedly, have been another
motive operating: with typical bluntness, Dick himself commented
at the time, 'I think they realise how much might be done here to
better the relations between the two Common Rooms.')[27]

In any event Dick safely attained an unviva'd First in Greats –
though he held to his interpretation of what had prompted New
College to offer him a fellowship almost to the end of his days. In an
interview he gave three years before his death, he was still keen to
insist that his attraction for New College lay in the fact that he was 'a
terribly protected young man' who, with reasonable luck, could be
turned into 'a hard-working, rugger-playing don'.[28] If that was the
reason for the invitation to join the Senior Common Room, then
New College certainly blundered in the initial condition it imposed
upon his appointment. Because he was so young – not yet twenty-
three – it was apparently considered prudent that he should spend a
year abroad (with his fellowship and lectureship stipend of £500
halved) before making the transition from the Junior Common Room
to the Senior. It turned out to be a year – as Dick himself never tired
of repeating – that 'absolutely transformed me as a person'.[29]

The year was not marked by any dramatic developments at its
start. Dick did not leave England to go abroad until 20 October 1930
– or rather later than he would have had to go up to Oxford if he had
already been in full-time employment as a teaching don. And when
he did go, it was initially only to stay with some German Jewish

second cousins on his mother's side who, conveniently, lived in Frankfurt. The plan was that, as well as pursuing his studies in philosophy (there was a famous Aristotelian Professor at Frankfurt University at whose feet he sat), he should learn German; and, at least at first, the routine seems to have been placid enough. He reported to his mother within ten days of arriving:

> The household is exceedingly nice. The food very simple but well-cooked and nicely sufficient, the drinks tea and water. There is no sign of well-to-do-ness, no car, 2 servants (but they are cheap and plentiful here) and very little entertainment. I suppose I have spoken to no one save Jews since I arrived; if so Jews are very lovable people . . .
>
> Life is quiet but a good deal seems to happen in a quiet way. We breakfast at 9, and I go off to my German lesson at 10. We lunch at 2 when I am nearly fainting, and tea at 5. *Supper* not dinner is any time between 8 and 9, the later the faintier. My bedroom echoes with trams and motor-horns (Germans toot full blast for every 'peekingest' crossing) and my bed-covering is only a sheet and eiderdown (plus a duvet I can't keep on, or sweat if it does keep on – mostly they both fall off).[30]

Little, perhaps, there to cause any alarm at Buckhurst Hill – where there may even have been reassurance at the discovery that their son was plainly having difficulty in shaking off the habits and outlook of an English upbringing.

The first seeds of disquiet appear to have been sown three months later when Dick reached Berlin – which, possibly because of Auden's influence, was always the Mecca of his pilgrimage. There is a slightly nettled tone in a letter Dick wrote to his mother at the end of January 1931:

> As for money, I wonder if you are not making the mistake of thinking of concert-going or theatre-going as 'having a bust'. This is probably the only time for the next 6 years at least I shall have the chance (you can't in the Long Vacs because they aren't on). If there happen to be 4 good things in 4 days, and I feel strong enough to appreciate them, I go; perhaps next week there will be none . . .
>
> I consider I have had my money's-worth and, as I am going to have £500 a year in future, I think it would be folly to miss this chance of seeing German opera and theatre. It won't be 'going a

bust' either to go to Greece: it will be part of my training.[31]

Greece, with Italy and Sicily taken in on the way, was where Dick spent the spring of 1931. It was the first time he had been there, and it evoked all the predictable enthusiasm of a recent 'Greats' graduate: 'Greece is absolutely unbeatable, it is like Scotland or Ireland set in a Southern air and with a touch of the Orient in it, which gives it an added thrill . . . You live in a state of constantly holding your breath, and never the least knowing what glory is going to come.'[32] Until April, therefore, when Dick came home for a fortnight, nothing apart from his parents' worries that he was acquiring extravagant habits had occurred to suggest that his year abroad was going to alter the pattern of his life in any way. He was virtually the same classical enthusiast that his father had been before him (as he was not above hinting in his letters – 'It may have been fresher when Daddy was here and the excavations newer, but its message, I think in its life and countryside, remain pretty well the same').[33] The next three months, however, were to change all that.

In later years, it suited Dick to pretend that his year abroad had been all of one piece. The contemporary evidence suggests, however, quite otherwise. Even his letters home change quite distinctly in tone once he returns to Germany in May 1931. For the first time there is a sense of political awareness – and one of a remarkably intuitive kind. What, for example, can his father and mother have made of this oddly uninhibited declaration blurted out within a week of his leaving Buckhurst Hill in May 1931?

> The more I talk to people like Hans and Ernest [his Frankfurt cousins], the more one sees that what one complains of in England has bitten far deeper into Germany. Their 20 times greater sufferings have turned the young people into either terrific fanatics, rabid idealists, or into completely resigned cynics, and cynicism in Germany means in certain spheres brutality. It is the background of sheer suffering in Germany from 1918 to 1925 which haunts you as you talk. You can't *sympathise* because you have no idea what it was like.[34]

The implication must clearly be that someone had influenced Dick – and, interestingly, it was at about this time that he met the woman who was eventually to be his first wife. Erika Gluck (her maiden name was Lansdorf – though she had already been married twice, first to a wealthy Berlin art patron called Theo Simon, by the time Dick first encountered her) was a young woman who, even after she came to England, tended to expatiate on the sufferings of the German people.[35] She herself, though, even in the age of the collapse of the German currency, had enjoyed a distinctly sheltered upbringing, being brought up in some comfort as the daughter of a respected doctor of chemistry (her natural father was, however, a famous Berlin actor). At what stage – and how precisely – she bewitched Dick remains a mystery. But there can be little doubt that during his last three months in Germany – from May to August 1931 – she was the dominant presence in his life.

Erika was never, perhaps understandably, mentioned directly in any of Dick's own letters home – though, back in Berlin in the summer of 1931, he found himself more in the social swim than he had ever been before. Writing to his mother in June he described Berlin as a city composed of 'sets – and if you aren't in one, you are alone'; there was no element here, however, of self-pity, since he went on to mention having met 'a really very remarkable married woman of 32 or 33 [Erika would not have been flattered – she claimed to be twenty-six, even when Dick married her a year later] who holds the modern equivalent of a *salon*'. Whether this was really intended as even a veiled reference to Erika must remain doubtful – as Dick proceeded to characterise this particular hostess as 'not *at all* beautiful but with a superb sense of humour'.[36] It is more probable, indeed, that by then Erika rated in Dick's eyes as merely another star in the same firmament: his boast ever afterwards remained that he and Erika throughout that summer shared 'a couple of rooms which was next door to and top of Magnus Hirschfeld's Sexual Institute, where they were changing sexes!'[37]

It would probably be too much to claim that there was any deliberate allegory here – although Dick was always generous in boldly proclaiming that his first wife 'had solved my sexual hang-ups'.[38] Whatever the truth of that, Erika was indirectly responsible, perhaps even more importantly, for a second aspect of Dick's education. When he first met her, she was the courier for – and may also have been the mistress of* – Willi Münzenberg, a leading Berlin

* When this allegation appeared in a *Sunday Times* profile on 25 May 1969, almost forty years later, Erika – by now married for the seventh time – wrote indignantly from Switzerland to Dick to deny it. In his reply he claimed to have asked the editor to publish a correction – but there can be little doubt that he was the source of the original information. The correspondence – their first contact in more than three decades – must have intrigued the Civil Servants in Dick's private office, one of whom attached a note to Erika's initial letter inquiring, 'What is your first wife's full name, please?' only to be rewarded with the response 'I don't know!'[39]

Communist who was one of the most effective propaganda agents
ever to serve the Comintern (he was later to write *The Brown Book
of the Hitler Terror*). The chance throwing together of the young
Oxford don with this dedicated Communist publicist – Erika and
Dick even lived for a time in Münzenberg's Berlin flat – was perhaps
the principal reason why 1930–1 always afterwards ranked for Dick
as 'a seminal year in my life'.[40]

What appears to have happened is that Münzenberg took Dick
under his wing, possibly even hoping to recruit him to the Communist cause. In later years that became the centrepiece of Dick's
memory of his year in Germany – complete with chapter and verse
as to how and when the approach was made:

> Münzenberg took me out one day to dinner – he had this enor-
> mous Lincoln car. We had champagne, and he said: 'Now Dick
> the time has come for you to join the March of the Future. I'm
> going to Moscow today to fix things up with our friends over there
> – why not come with me and join us? I'll give you a job in the
> organisation. Be on the side of the Future.'[41]

As an account of an attempted Communist seduction it sounds a
little too glib to be wholly convincing – but what Münzenberg
certainly *did* do for Dick was to give him some insight into the
Communist mind. In particular, the discovery that the Communists
were more than ready to see the Weimar Republic destroyed by the
Nazis – provided that meant the end of the Social Democrats, too –
profoundly shocked him: it was eventually to make him a good deal
more resistant to the blandishments of Communism than most of his
left-wing contemporaries in Oxford.

However, when Dick returned from Germany in 1931, few people
thought of him as a left-wing figure at all – indeed, if anything, he
gave the impression of being so pro-German as to be in some danger
of being mistaken for a Nazi sympathiser.* He was, of course,
nothing of the kind – though the fact that he took Hitler and the
National Socialists seriously (refusing to regard them, as the Left
tended at that time to do, as 'mere tools of monopoly capitalism')

---

* According to an Oxford contemporary, there used to be long arguments at All
Souls, among at least the younger fellows, as to whether Dick was a Nazi or not.
They were eventually ended by the economic historian, Richard Pares,
magisterially declaring: 'The truth about Dick is that he is not a *Nazi* but a
German.'[42]

1 Helen Elizabeth Crossman

2 Charles Stafford Crossman

3 The six Crossman children with their father (*right*) in the garden of Buckhurst Hill House. Dick is standing back left

4 Dick (*seated centre*) as Captain of College VI, Winchester, in 1924

5 Dick (*standing left*) as Prefect of School in 1925, with William Hayter
(*seated centre*) and Richard Wilberforce (*seated right*)

6 Mr Justice Stafford Crossman. He was appointed to the Bench in 1934

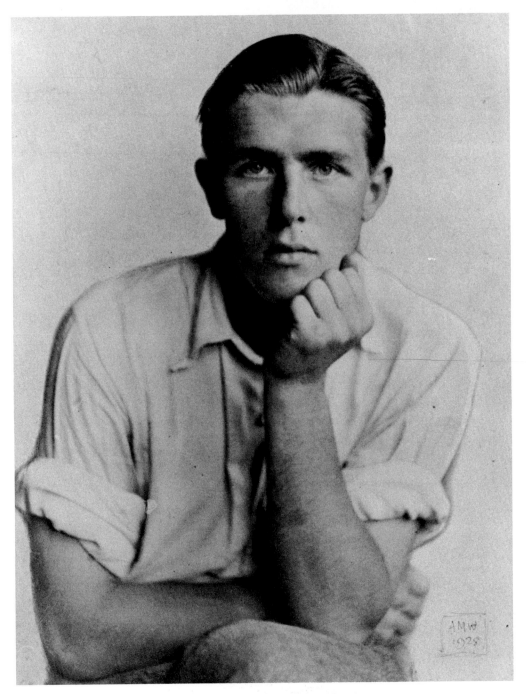

7 Dick as an Oxford undergraduate, photographed by his cousin
Amie Walters in 1928

did give rise to misunderstanding. In the early 1930s Dick found himself in the classic position of the messenger who brings the bad news: by insisting that National Socialism was a formidable, even revolutionary, movement with a broad base of popular support, he was telling Oxford in general, and the Left in particular, just what it did not want to hear.

His own friends, however, were naturally more interested in his personal circumstances than his political apprehensions. And here Dick seems to have made singularly little effort to keep his liaison with Erika any form of secret – indeed news got out about her almost the moment he returned.* That much can be deduced from W. H. Auden's poem *The Orators*, where his visit to the Carritt farmhouse in Pembrokeshire in August 1931 is commemorated by the two lines:

> The week the Labour Cabinet resigned
> Dick had returned from being in love.[43]

Since the Labour Cabinet resigned on 24 August 1931 and Dick returned only a week or so earlier, that implies a remarkable openness about his emotions.

Whether Dick was equally forthright with his parents remains doubtful. For not only was Erika a twice-divorced woman; she also had from her first marriage a daughter, Angelica, who was already four or five years old. Nevertheless, that Christmas of 1931 (without the daughter) she was formally introduced to the family at Buckhurst Hill. At first all went well, with Dick's mother in particular being bowled over by her[44] (that was not really surprising – Erika was, by general consent, fiercely attractive, possessing some of the looks and all of the poise of a celebrated German actress of the day, Elizabeth Bergner). No doubt, Dick's parents were also anxious to see at least one of their children married – his older brother and sister being at that stage still single. There was not much time, however, for the building of any such romantic dreams; for no sooner was Christmas over than Erika fell ill and the family GP was summoned to her bedside. The rest of the story has gone down into Crossman family folklore: the grave expression, the request for a private audience, the intimation of scandal, the eventual whispered

---

* To one *confidant* it had, in fact, surfaced even before that. Dick's correspondence with Christopher Cox, preserved at New College, reveals that he had kept nothing from his own young tutor.

word '*morphiniste*'.

As upright citizens, Stafford Crossman and his wife felt they had no option: as soon as Erika was fit to get up, she was ordered to leave the house. It was the one decision – though, innocently, they may not have realised it – that was guaranteed to seal their son's fate: if his parents, as Christians, were so deficient in charity, then he at least would show their values up by acting with chivalry. From the moment Erika was told to depart from Buckhurst Hill House, few – if any – of his friends doubted that he would end up marrying her (in fact, what doubts there were seem to have belonged to Dick – he was later to refer to his mistake in 'heroising' himself[45] and to admit that he knew the marriage was doomed even before he embarked on it).*

The one question that remains is how much Dick himself was taken aback by the discovery of Erika's drug addiction. It seems almost inconceivable that he could have lived with her for three months in Berlin and not recognised the tell-tale signs for what they were; yet there was always an element of naivety in Dick's make-up, and there may be some force behind the sisterly comment that Erika's undoubted sexual hold over Dick blinded him to absolutely everything else.[47] Certainly, what seems to be most vividly recalled about Erika is her physical attractiveness – even if sometimes expressed in fairly irreverent terms. Indeed, one contemporary Oxford anecdote ran as follows:

RHSC: I'm going to get married.
Stafford Crossman: Whom to?
RHSC: Erika Gluck.
Stafford Crossman: What does she do?
RHSC: She's a prostitute.
Stafford Crossman: In that case, why are you marrying her?
RHSC: But that's what people of your generation can *never* understand – it's precisely because she's a prostitute that I'm going to marry her.[48]

In any case, marry her Dick did – at Oxford Registry Office on 15 July 1932, though in the absence of both his parents. However, he found respectable enough witnesses in the shape of the wife of the Warden of New College (Lettice Fisher) and in his own old tutor,

---

* 'One day I told Erika I did not want to marry her but, if she held me to it, of course I would. She solemnly said that she would take the whole responsibility. That was cowardice on my part and folly on hers.'[46]

H. W. B. Joseph. There is even said to have been a service of blessing afterwards in New College Chapel – though, not being at that time a recognised service of the Church of England, no record of it survives.[49]

In a way, the conditions for Dick's start on marriage could hardly have been more auspicious. He was living in perhaps the most desirable of all New College's accommodation – The Barn in New College Lane, conveniently sited outside the college gates and thereby in no way inhibited by any provision about fellows having to be single if they wished to reside within college. He had successfully completed his first year as a philosophy tutor – and, indeed, had just secured as an assistant (though not as a fully fledged fellow) the young philosopher, Isaiah Berlin. He also enjoyed the patronage and good will – evidenced by his wife's readiness to be a witness at his wedding – of the college's Warden, the former Lloyd George Cabinet Minister and celebrated historian, H. A. L. Fisher.

Initially, there was no question either that Erika added a certain glamour – even a *frisson* of excitement – to Oxford's normally somewhat staid academic life. Sir Isaiah Berlin, for instance, recalls one day finding himself without the necessary cash to make a train journey to London. So he went to The Barn to borrow the money. A knock on the door was greeted with the shout 'Come on up, we're in bed.' On obeying the instruction, he was greeted with the vision – in the middle of the day – of Dick and Erika both in a large double bed in which they had clearly spent some time. Totally unembarrassed, Erika reached into her corsage and produced a £1 note – more than enough in those days to purchase a ticket to Paddington.

Inevitably, not everyone was charmed. Maurice Bowra's nickname for Dick's wife was reputed to be 'Erica – or tittle by tattle',[50] while others found themselves shocked by her readiness to leap on a dinner table, complete with candlesticks, and announce, by way of an entrance, 'Little Erika is here!'[51] It was not, of course, quite what Oxford was accustomed to – but that, for Dick himself, was only a benefit.

There can be no doubt that when Erika left him after a mere six months, it represented the gravest blow that Dick had yet suffered. The circumstances of her departure remain obscure – there is a family legend that she left for a skiing holiday at Christmas 1932 and, having fallen for a ski instructor, never returned. A more substantial explanation, certainly believed by Dick, was that, even while she was living in Oxford, she had formed an attachment with

another Oxford don, the agricultural economist, Dunstan Skilbeck*
(who went on to be the Principal of Wye College). Whatever the
cause, or the provocation, the fact remained that Erika, after the
end of 1932, never came back to Oxford.

For Dick, this was undoubtedly an intense humiliation. It was not
simply that, by marrying her, he had deliberately decided to defy his
parents and all the values they stood for. It was also that, by now
very much conscious that his capacities and abilities might one day
take him well beyond Oxford, he had involuntarily tied a quite
unnecessary ball and chain to his ankle.

---

* Many years later Dick used to like telling a story of how, when travelling in a
car with both Erika and Dunstan Skilbeck, he suddenly noticed from the back seat
that the latter, who was driving, was wearing a large hat. 'If I'd suddenly leant
forward and pushed it down over his eyes, all our problems could have been solved
in one jolly good smash up.'[52]

5 Broadcaster and Celebrity

It was wholly characteristic of Dick that he subsequently came to believe that the parting with Erika was the best thing that ever happened to him. And, in a strictly limited sense, that may have been true. The untidy nature of her disappearance – she even left behind at The Barn her Bavarian maid, Resi, who soon became Dick's mistress – meant that he had to go back to Germany frequently, if only to try and track down his errant wife. He would probably have maintained his interest in German politics in any case – Germany in the early 1930s was, after all, where all the political action was taking place; but the need to negotiate with Erika (and, at least initially, to try to persuade her to return) was what primarily motivated Dick to spend successive vacations there.

His first attempt at seeking a reconciliation with Erika degenerated rapidly into farce. In the summer of 1933 he persuaded a young graduate of New College, Ernest Sabben-Clare, at that time teaching at Winchester, to come out and stay (as he was led to believe) with both Dick and Erika in the Black Forest. When Sabben-Clare arrived, there was no sign of Dick and only the briefest sighting of Erika (accompanied on this occasion by her daughter, Angelica,* who had never been seen in England); there was just time for Erika to announce 'The marriage is finished', and to intimate that she was leaving immediately for Berlin. Sabben-Clare – and a fellow guest, a young woman from Yorkshire – were left to fend for themselves as best they could. It was, again, entirely typical of Dick that there was never any word of apology or explanation for this episode afterwards.[1]

---

* Angelica was the daughter of Erika's first marriage to Theo Simon. After the war she fell in love with, and married, one of her mother's ex-husbands.

Dick's own time in Germany, however, was not wasted; 1933 was the year Hitler took over, and he could claim to have had a ringside seat at the making of history. Later in his career he was to assert that his view was clear from the start – 'I was convinced that the Nazis couldn't be defeated without a war . . . I saw the war as essential . . . the Nazis were preparing to conquer the world.'[2] This was not quite the impression he left on his contemporaries at the time – nor, as we shall see, is it precisely the recollection that the public record bears out.

The great advantage to Dick of his early German experience was that it provided him with an expertise over and above that normally to be found in a philosophy don. He was not slow to use it. He soon took to drawing striking parallels between Plato and Hitler in the lectures he delivered – striding up and down in front of High Table – in New College Hall.[3] He was, in fact, as he soon discovered, a born lecturer – with all the self-confidence and power of the man who delights in argument for argument's sake. (There was a school of thought which maintained that this made him rather less successful as a tutor, and certainly only the ablest of his pupils found it easy to withstand his technique of listening to an essay and then brutally proceeding to prove to the writer the exact opposite of what he had written).[4] It was clearly, however, only a matter of time before his reputation as a lecturer – and particularly as an expositor of ideas – reached out beyond the university. And it was perhaps inevitable – in what Asa Briggs has called 'the golden age of wireless' – that the airwaves would provide the means by which it did so.

Dick started as a regular broadcaster in the spring of 1934 – when he was only just twenty-six years old. He appears to have made the acquaintance socially of the BBC's Director of Talks, Charles Siepmann; certainly the first letter he received from Siepmann implies the existence of a previous conversation between them:

20 April 1934

Dear Crossman,
    If you will prepare a ten-minute broadcast (not more than 1,100 words) on Labour Camps in Germany, we can include it at 9.10 p.m. in our programme of Tuesday next week. Unless I hear from you by Monday, first post, I shall assume that you can give this broadcast and be up in London that evening. There is no necessity to be here before 9 o'clock, and I shall be glad if you can let me have your script on Monday so that we can discuss any flagrant indiscretions on your part.

A date for a second talk is still uncertain, but we can talk about this when I see you, as I hope I shall do on Tuesday. Unfortunately I've got to dine out but if you can drop in during the day, I'd be delighted to see you and hear a lot more about what you have seen and heard.

Yours sincerely,
CHARLES SIEPMANN[5]

With full allowance made for the gentler manners and more relaxed approach of an earlier BBC age, it was an exceptionally friendly, if casual, letter – and it was plainly with distinct disappointment that Dick, the very next day, had to reply to it:

Saturday

Dear Siepmann,

I'm awfully sorry: I just can't on Tuesday as I have a 2 months' standing promise to speak at Charlbury (of all places!) on Tuesday, and the bills are out. I can't let down a newly-formed Labour party even for cash. I wonder if you can possibly arrange it later . . .[6]

The talk was rearranged for Wednesday 2 May – though, as a result of the delay, Dick found himself in the hands of another BBC producer, J. R. Ackerley (later to be literary editor of the *Listener*) who plainly took a more conscientious view of his responsibilities towards a new and inexperienced broadcaster:

About writing your manuscript, I assume that Siepmann has given you all the necessary instructions about this, since as far as I can see from our records you have never broadcast for us before. The matter is really quite simple and boils down to this – that the nearer you can get to sounding as if you were talking to somebody in an ordinary conversational way, the greater will be your success. This means, of course, that your script should be written in such a style as will enable you to read it in this way, and the style is therefore different from that one uses either for writing articles or for making the rather more formal public speech. I hope, also, that Siepmann told you that we cannot let you have more than ten minutes, which is approximately 1200 words.[7]

If there was a slightly pedagogic tone to that advice, Dick did not take offence – indeed, he was a model of modesty ('If I could come in at 5 p.m. for a rehearsal on Wednesday it might slightly warm my cold feet');[8] and the broadcast duly went out after the nine o'clock news on 2 May 1934. The principal interest it retains today is for the light it throws on Dick's views on Nazi Germany – and particularly its Youth Movement – a year after Hitler had come to power as Chancellor.

For the most part, the broadcast consisted of a simple description of a youth labour camp in Schleswig-Holstein that Dick had visited the previous month. He was not uncritical ('My first impressions were by no means reassuring . . . for English taste it all savours too much of the barracks'), but he was certainly much taken with the spirit and dedication of the young men whom he had met – so much so that he allowed himself to offer at least one hefty hostage to fortune:

> The spirit of the youth movement still inspires many of the young officers in the labour camps and fills many students with the belief that they are digging the foundation of a new German Socialism, not of the town and the machine but of the fields and the spade. For such workers the labour camps are indeed the centre of the Nazi endeavour. But one astounding contradiction remains. The revolt of youth has been drilled and disciplined into a conscript army, the rebels against law and militarism now march only too often under the command of old officers and click their heels like any hardened veteran ('Theirs not to reason why, theirs but to do and die'). And yet they are lovers of peace. I have not met a single young German who did not assure one – and it was sincere – that Germany has had enough of war – and civil war as well – and wants only order, peace and a decent livelihood.[9]

It was the kind of thing, of course, at the time that the British public was very anxious to hear – and it was not surprising that the talk was judged by Ackerley to be 'excellent from every point of view'.[10] Equally gratifyingly for Dick, he was promptly offered another opportunity to address the nation – indeed, Ackerley appears to have wanted him to return to the microphone the very next week, although Siepmann deemed this 'inadvisable' and suggested instead the 'fuller scope' offered by 'our late evening series on foreign affairs'.[11] Dick accepted the second proposal with alacrity and on 7 June 1934 was back delivering this time a twenty-minute talk entitled 'Germany: the Inner Conflict'. This turned out to be a far more academic and historical broadcast – there was a long, and slightly laboured, analogy between Nazi Germany and the ancient city state of Sparta – but, revealingly, once again Dick's admiration for 'the idealism' of the Hitler Youth Movement shone through.[12] It is hard to resist the suspicion that it was the ethos and spirit of the Hitler Youth which clouded Dick's vision: it was not so much that he endorsed their views – it was simply that he could not stop himself envying the zeal and certainty with which they were held.

At least Dick's first two broadcasts caused no sort of political flurry. That was not to prove true of the third – in which for the first time he displayed a true journalistic instinct. The Long Vacation of 1934 found Dick once again in southern Germany – and engaged in much the same business as before (this was the summer in which he finally steeled himself to inform Erika that he wanted a divorce). On Saturday 30 June, when he heard the news of the Night of the Long Knives – and the murder of Roehm – he was in the quiet university town of Heidelberg; but he immediately took himself off to the scene of the crime, Munich, where at least he could feel part of the story. From the point of view of *telling* it, however, he might just as well have remained in Heidelberg – for the only German city linked to London at that time by a radio circuit was Berlin. Nothing daunted, on the Monday – 2 July – Dick took himself off there, having failed to raise anyone at the BBC earlier on the telephone. It was a bold gamble – requiring, as he pointed out at the time, 'an investment of £20'[13] – but it paid off; by noon in Berlin he had heard that the BBC would, indeed, like him to broadcast and had cleared the relevant slot after that night's nine o'clock news. The result – written, he claimed, 'in an hour'[14] – was a ten-minute talk entitled simply 'Today in Germany' and broadcast that evening 'live' from the Nazi radio headquarters in Berlin.

Given the background, which included a three-hour session with the German censor in the Propaganda Ministry, it was a creditable and highly resourceful journalistic achievement – something that Dick himself clearly sensed:

> I've had a *gorgeous* time, feel very important, worked 36 hours without sleep and then slept on the train from Munich to Berlin, interviewed and looked and taxied round 2 cities, went on the spree last night with Erika's sister, went on the spree in Munich on Sunday alone. Smoked and drank like a journalist with the journalists . . . this is the life, provided it is not your main job.[15]

Nor was there anything professionally wrong with the talk Dick

actually gave. It was a good, crisp, vivid piece of on-the-spot reporting – but unfortunately lacked any hint of moral outrage at what had
occurred. It sounded almost as if Dick was overcome with admiration at the violent strike that Hitler had pulled off – and perhaps to
an extent he was (few things excited Dick more than the ruthless
exercise of naked power). Even when he tried an analogy with
Britain, the predominant impact he created was still one of awe:

> Imagine that it had happened in England. The Prime Minister
> arrives in an aeroplane at Edinburgh, arrests eight party leaders
> at 4 o'clock in the morning and by the afternoon the court martial
> is over and they are all dead, except the Prime Minister's personal
> friend who is shot the next day. Think of the sensation! But here
> everything goes on just as usual. A man said to me in a Munich
> café yesterday, 'The best thing about it is that he wasted no time.
> The scoundrels are dead now, and out of the way.' Not a single
> one of the many people I referred to this weekend would have
> disagreed. In fact it has been a personal triumph for Hitler, and
> has proved how completely dependent upon him the whole Nazi
> movement is. What Hitler says is law – and law in a very practical
> sense – as these events have proved.[16]

The message could hardly have been more direct or blunt – but it
was not perhaps one for the squeamish. Not surprisingly, there was
something of an outcry over the broadcast – provoking even the
Foreign Secretary of the day, Sir John Simon, to compose an internal Foreign Office minute: 'I have heard from several quarters complaints of the broadcast by the BBC from Berlin after the weekend
events in Germany. It seems to have been couched in a vein of
exultant approval of everything Hitler had done . . .'[17] That was, of
course, trying to have it both ways. Dick had been employed as a
reporter, not as a leader writer – and what he had done was to give
an honest account of the mood of a country he knew well. If that
proved unpalatable to a politician such as Sir John Simon, it was
presumably because he had cocooned himself for too long in
cotton-wool.

In any event, the broadcast – though it was later to do him some
damage politically* – does not seem to have harmed Dick at all in

---

* It was sometimes used against him by his fellow-travelling opponents in the
Oxford City Labour Party in the 1930s and, more remarkably, Auberon Waugh
was still to be found banging away about it in the columns of *Private Eye* in the
early 1970s.

the view of the BBC. Three weeks later, on 24 July, he was asked to give another talk (again from Berlin) and the circumstances surrounding this broadcast could hardly have been more helpful in removing any pro-Hitler taint that the previous one had left. The bizarre story of what occurred is perhaps most fairly summarised in the *Evening Standard* the following day:

> A technical hitch prevented listeners from hearing R. H. S. Crossman broadcasting on 'The German Scene' last night. The manuscript of the speech (which had been announced) had been submitted to Dr Goebbels, Director of Nazi Propaganda.
>
> Listeners heard the announcer say that the technical hitch would prevent Mr Crossman talking from Berlin. But the hitch was caused by the removal of the switch which connects the Berlin microphone to the landlines that travel to Rugby and Broadcasting House. The Hitler propaganda dept had evidently not approved of the impressions of an independent observer.
>
> The BBC, however, had secured in advance a copy of the speech and this was read to British listeners by Mr Stuart Hibberd, the chief announcer. It was definitely anti-Nazi in tone.[18]

It may not have been a deliberate early instance of 'jamming' – after all, as Dick himself observed, the Germans 'must have known the manuscript was in London'[19] – but the whole background certainly appeared suspicious. (The eventual finding of the BBC was characteristically ambivalent – 'There is no evidence to show it was a political act, but it may well have been'.)[20] As for the silenced broadcaster himself, he appears to have been more amused than irritated, writing to his original BBC mentor, Charles Siepmann, from Nuremberg station thirty-six hours later:

> Dear Charles,
>
> I am sorry England missed my lovely voice last night. I hope the announcer read the manuscript nicely and made all the points. I should much like to hear if the failure was purely technical and only in Germany. An SS man came in just as I was to start. I had a very richly humorous time with the Propaganda Ministry for an hour and a half explaining myself away; he couldn't understand English very well, so I had to translate myself into German . . .
>
> Finally, I told him that the BBC was his only friend in England and that I was so pro-Nazi that no Englishman would speak to

me.* So he cancelled his refusal, warning me that if the speech were delivered in Germany, it would be High Treason but he supposed the English mentality different.[21]

No doubt, what counted with Dick was the knowledge that he had come through his initial foreign correspondent's test with flying colours – having shown initiative on the first occasion and resource-fulness on the second.

Indeed, there is some evidence that at about this time Dick thought seriously about joining the BBC. An early letter survives in which he writes to Siepmann, 'If I come to you, you will have to give me occasional flights to fever spots to report – there is nothing I enjoy better than feeling myself in the minds of hallucinated but kindred people';[22] and certainly, as he grew older, Dick – forgetful possibly of his matrimonial entanglements in the Puritan age of Reith† – always liked to recall that as a young man he had 'intended to join the BBC'.[23] It is doubtful, however, if this aspiration can have lasted for long. Dick successfully cleared the hurdles of two more foreign broadcasts in 1934 – one on the German Church and one on the industrial and unemployment situation in Germany[24] – but an invitation to address a domestic theme soon revealed that he was not perhaps cast by nature to be a BBC 'type'.

At first, admittedly, there appeared to be few problems. The invitation from yet another BBC producer called G. N. Pocock was to join a series planned for early 1935 and entitled 'Youth Looks Ahead'. The idea, as Pocock initially described it, was 'to give young people still in their twenties a chance of explaining their point of view and philosophy of life, and I am choosing as far as possible young people with constructive ideas and an optimistic outlook'.[25] Probably that was when the alarm bells should have rung: for Dick, in contrast to some of the other potential contributors like the rising young headmaster of Uppingham, J. F. Wolfenden or the youth-ful Conservative barrister John Boyd-Carpenter, hardly seemed

* The perils of flippancy are illustrated by the fact that this plainly ironical statement was many years later to be taken seriously by a historian of the BBC and solemnly incorporated in a hostile biographical footnote about Crossman: W. J. West, *Truth Betrayed* (Duckworth, 1987), p. 27.

† Dick, in fact, on one occasion was wheeled in to see Reith, then Director-General of the BBC, and seems rather to have impressed him. An entry in the original MS of Reith's diaries for 2 March 1934 includes the passage: 'Saw one Crossman, whom Siepmann is putting up for a fairly important job – a Socialist but I liked him.' (This, of course, was before Dick had even attained his divorce from Erika.) BBC WAC, Caversham. Reith Diaries, vol. 4, 1934–6, p. 24.

likely to qualify as either 'constructive' or 'optimistic'.

The project nevertheless steamed ahead, with Dick submitting his script just before Christmas 1934. The first reaction, even from his old friend Charles Siepmann, was ominously guarded – 'I am not quite clear whether it is a mere *ballon d'essai* or whether you would like to submit it as your final script for consideration.'[26] That, however, was as nothing compared to what was to come. By the beginning of January 1935, the script had reached the desk of the Assistant Controller of Programmes, Major Gladstone Murray, and he lost no time in speaking out in no uncertain terms:

> I have read Crossman's typescript several times but I am unable to agree that it can stand as it is. There is not very much 'looking ahead' about it. Some disillusion, even bitter disillusion, is in keeping with that point of view but I think it balks too much. It may be that he would prefer to do the thing again rather than consider suggestions for a change. If, however, the present type-script is to stand, I have indicated what would have to come out. I wish he had given more space to the forward view.[27]

It was Dick's first collision with the BBC Establishment – and, on the whole, he did not emerge from it too badly. Siepmann was promptly called in to pour oil on troubled waters – and obviously did so to some effect ('It is not the point of view which you put forward that is in question but rather the method you have adopted for expressing it').[28] Dick himself was prudent enough to take a suitably contrite line, writing back one day later, enclosing an amended script, direct to Major Gladstone Murray: 'I really am not annoyed, nor do I think any of your people has done me down – for heaven's sake don't blame anyone in the BBC for my pig-headedness.'[29] That got the response that Dick must have hoped for, since within a week, after what appears to have been a summit lunch, Gladstone Murray was replying personally to Dick: 'As promised, I enclose a retyped copy of your script, which I think is excellent.'[30] (That was not strictly true: in an internal memo to the Director of Talks, Murray merely commented of Dick's amended script, 'I think it will do – anyway it is a vast improvement.')[31]

The fascinating aspect of this episode – which ended with the talk eventually going out on 4 February 1935 – was the uncharacteristic degree of diplomacy which Dick used in negotiating its passage through the shoals of the BBC bureaucracy. He obviously attached great importance to it, and was probably right to do so. As a forthright attack on Britain's class system, with particular reference to education, it certainly put him on the map politically – not least because the *Daily Herald* (then about to become Britain's largest selling newspaper) immediately commissioned him to write a follow-up article for its leader page: this appeared a week later, complete with photograph, which was captioned (no doubt to Major Gladstone Murray's irritation) 'R. H. S. Crossman Lecturer at Oxford University, whose broadcast "Youth Looks Ahead" caused widespread interest'.[32] Even more significant in the long term, the eventual success of the broadcast (Dick personally received over 150 letters) opened the door for what was to be, until his two BBC TV series entitled 'Crosstalk' in the early 1970s, his major piece of broadcasting exposure – his ten separate talks on the wireless early in 1936 under the collective rubric 'If Plato Lived Again'.

All in all, Dick could be forgiven if he felt at the beginning of 1935 that the world was at his feet. There remained, of course, the messy business of detaching himself from Erika – but even here, having settled the matter of divorce in the summer, he was starting to feel more self-confident. A striking letter he wrote (for once, to *both* his parents) on his twenty-seventh birthday, tells perhaps more about his new conquering mood than anything else:

> *The Barn,*
> *New College,*
> *Oxford*

Dear Duday and Mother,

Thank you both very much indeed for your letters and presents. I had a lovely birthday staying with Randall [Swingler]* and his wife in the Cotswolds – 4 perfect days of *doing nothing*, playing cards, walking, talking and getting wet in the rain. It has done me a power of good!

It is awfully good of you to arrange the £200. I do not think I need spend any of it as I have already paid £50 towards the expenses and am taking the allowance of £250 a year for Erika, which I am making (without *any* obligation) towards her training as a professional photographer, out of current income which happens to be good. If it goes on as good, I can carry on for 6 or 7 months and finish my first year of payments without touching the £200. I hope that may be so. It is most awfully nice of you to think

---

* Oxford contemporary and friend. Brother of Stephen Swingler, MP (1915–69), subsequently a Labour colleague of Dick's in the House of Commons.

of helping me in that way and I appreciate it enormously . . .

Life is alive, exciting and always expanding and every year one can scarcely believe the fool at the other end of the line of months was the same person. So far there is nothing I regret in all I have experienced and I have learnt, and learnt to see, that the personal (tho' the one thing worth having) is apt to slip out of crude and active hands like my own, or to be moulded by them into a crude and dead form.

Fortunately, I can do other things and at least marriage taught me how bad by nature *man* is, and how possessive and legalist by nature I am. I had no notion before how love of a person could vanish before possessive wrath at the violation of my *marriage rights*. I never learnt really to love Erika enough to lose her and still love her in the loss. Indeed, I feel I could just start doing so now, if she wanted and needed my love, which she does not in any way.

Still, I have learnt from my marriage something of the value of love against passion and possessiveness (both of us lived from those qualities) and I could not have learnt that in any other way. One has to be smashed if one is to be built as I am, full of gigantic vigour and dominant power. And I am lucky to know at 27 something few people know at 40. It gives a real basis to my educational and political activities . . .

I seem to have thought aloud. It is because of my talk in the 'Youth Looks Ahead' series where I want to talk of this, which I believe to be the real and only basis of Socialist activity. It is a society where persons can need each other and be to each other persons, not tools, that we have to build.

Enough! and so very many loving thanks,

DICK[33]

What the reception of this remarkably unbuttoned letter was at Buckhurst Hill can only be guessed at – but, almost certainly, it was a delighted one, with both his parents feeling at last that they were back into some kind of relationship with their prodigally gifted, if wayward, son. There was one fact, however, which Dick had omitted from it – a fact that had been cryptically revealed to a virtual stranger, a BBC producer called Lionel Fielden, in the summer of 1934.

Dick's second domestic broadcast for the BBC, delivered in London on 7 June 1934, had been preceded by a strange request: 'Could I possibly bring someone with me on 7 June as audience? I hate talking to a cubicle. Tell me, of course, if it would be against the rules.'[34]

Lionel Fielden, no doubt, believed he had coped very professionally. He replied amiably on 4 June:

Dear Crossman,
   Many thanks for your letter. By all means bring someone with
you on the 7th, but you must let me know the name. I can, of
course, call him Brown or Robinson if necessary. But it is one of
the laws of the Medes and the Persians that anyone who is to
enter the holy precincts of the studios shall be named.[35]

Alas, he had missed the point – and Dick was reduced to sending a
note saying simply, if slightly embarrassedly: 'Name, Mrs Baker is
the person I wish to bring.'[36] At least Fielden had stumbled on a
secret that was to take more than three years to come out either in
Oxford or at Buckhurst Hill.

6 An Oxford Scandal

There is no exact record of how and when Zita Baker – the wife of an Oxford zoologist with dining rights in the New College Senior Common Room* – first met Dick. It appears, however, to have been in the spring of 1934, although he may well have been aware of her existence before that. Zita (for 'Inezita') Baker ranked within the narrow confines of Oxford as something of a *femme fatale*. Born in the Canary Islands, the daughter of the cable manager in Tenerife, she had already been the mistress of Evan Durbin, Hugh Gaitskell's close friend who died in an untimely drowning accident three years after being elected as a Labour MP in 1945; she was also a girlfriend of Arthur Koestler† and known to have been more than a companion to Tom Harrisson (the founder of 'Mass Observation'), whom she accompanied, along with her husband, on the Oxford University Expedition to the New Hebrides in 1933. But, by the time Dick first encountered her, she was – superficially at least – a respectably married woman with two children, a girl and a boy, living in apparent domestic harmony at 94 Woodstock Road in north Oxford.

It was this vision of family security – all that he had failed to achieve with Erika – that appears, in the first instance, to have attracted Dick. Certainly by Christmas 1934, when their love affair had already been going for some six months, he thought nothing of announcing to her: 'It is an enormous great wad of comfort to think

---

* John Baker (1900–84) had a slightly disappointing career – not becoming a full fellow of New College until 1964. He was, however, elected an FRS in 1958; the Royal Society's biographical memoir of him recalls that he once summed up his own character as 'Sincerity 100%; tact nil.'

† Arthur Koestler (1905–83), author and polemicist, whose sexual appetite was legendary.

of 94 Woodstock Road – at least if you haven't a home yourself, it is
nice to think that the person you love is part of one.'[1] It may not
have been the most romantic of declarations – but, at least at the
start, both Dick and Zita appear to have been united by a common
resolution that they must, at all costs, behave sensibly. Zita had
joined Dick on holiday in the Swabian Alps that previous summer –
but she had been careful to take along with her as 'cover' not only
her eight-year-old daughter, Venice, but also a former boyfriend to
act as additional chaperon security.

It was useful, too, that Zita was known in Oxford as a reliable
typist; it meant, now that his journalistic practice was beginning to
grow (Dick started writing for both the *Spectator* and *The Economist* in the second half of 1934),* that there could be necessary
comings and goings between The Barn and 94 Woodstock Road
without any unwanted suspicions being raised. Still, even here there
was caution: their affair was largely conducted away from Oxford
and Zita herself does not appear to have paid a purely social call at
The Barn until the last day of 1934. The visit (unannounced on New
Year's Eve) was not a success – possibly because Zita had not until
then fully realised the role that Resi, Erika's former maid, played in
Dick's life. Certainly, the next day produced a flurry of letters with
Dick neatly evading the central issue by accusing his visitor of having 'gone home in a sensitive huff'[2] and Zita rather more robustly
replying, 'Hell, you are a swine.'[3]

Probably one of Zita's attractions for Dick was that, as very much
the modern woman, she sturdily refused to allow herself to be
walked over. She was in no sense Dick's intellectual equal – indeed,
she was not an intellectual at all. But, as well as being a firm Labour
Party supporter, she was a strong believer in feminine independence
and certainly in the early days held the whiphand in their relationship. It was Dick, for example, who pleaded with her to give up *her*
lovers:

> I've been wondering why it is I mind all your affairs. It is not open
> jealousy: god knows people need you and you help them. But I
> can't helping wanting speciality (is that the same at bottom as

* Dick was proud of his connection with the *Spectator* – sometimes claiming that
he 'wrote weekly for it', or even that he had 'a column in it'. If so, no trace
survives, though he did contribute three or four freelance articles between 1934 and
1936. His relationship with *The Economist* was owed entirely to the presence on its
staff of Douglas Jay and was restricted exclusively to reports on Germany, which
failed ultimately to meet the paper's requirements.

monogamy? I fear so!) and experiences with Erika bite deep.[4]

In other moods, however, it was precisely their lack of mutual possessiveness that commended their relationship to him:

> To get to non-possessiveness, as we two have got to it, is to remain interesting specimens in the sociological class-zoo. We have got to it within our own class as Zita and Dick, two modern Oxford unconventionals and we have, within the present social structure, attained the relationship which is aesthetically the most satisfying.[5]

Even in Dick's eyes it was not, of course, to stay that way for long. A poem he wrote for Zita, only a month later, demonstrated that at heart he remained a sexual romantic:

> Where gray winds blow
> Rain on bare skin
> Sways to and fro
> Out and in,
>
> Sways to and fro
> My lovely tree:
> Her leaves swing low
> Touching me
>
> Her leaves swing low –
> Oh sap flow free
> That she may grow
> Deep roots, deep roots in me.[6]

The difficulty, however, was that – initially at least – that was precisely what Zita did not want to do. She was perfectly content to have Dick as an admirer and lover but became apprehensive when he grew 'heavy'. It seems fair to conclude that her friends – of whom she had some remarkably loyal ones, particularly among women – shared her view. A letter from the novelist Naomi Mitchison at the beginning of 1935, suddenly inviting her to spend ten weeks in her company on a tour of the United States, hardly sounds as if it could have come right out of the blue. Zita immediately broached her problem with Dick – then supervising an undergraduate reading party at a farmhouse near Bridgwater – but her letter breaking the news indicated pretty firmly that her mind was already made up (the letter was plainly written in the immediate aftermath of their row over her New Year's Eve visit to The Barn):

> I have persisted in my resolution and have had an engaging grin on my face and a breeziness in my demeanour which my heart belies . . . And now Naomi writes and suggests the thing I have looked forward to enormously for years. But can I bear the Atlantic to separate us? I can, because by braving that kind of separation, the powers that assail the 'usness' weaken.[7]

That was almost certainly not the motive that Naomi Mitchison, already married and with five children of her own, had in mind: indeed, Zita's letter went on explicitly to state, 'It's no good not telling Naomi about you and I – I've had a letter from her and she *does* know.'[8] Dick appears to have put up little resistance; he may, of course, have been influenced by the fact that he had already been booked as a lecturer on a Greek cruise beginning as soon as the Oxford Hilary Term was over – and conceivably may even have seen Naomi Mitchison's proposal as relieving him of a twinge of guilt. In any event, Naomi and Zita pressed ahead with the plan and arrangements were soon in place for them both to leave for the United States on a cargo boat departing from Tilbury on 24 January 1935.

Before they left, however, Zita had already transacted one important piece of business on Dick's behalf:

> I went to the Oxford City Labour Party meeting last night and had some good fun over you. When the question of a Parliamentary Candidate came up, they read out three that had been recommended by HQ – all very dull. Then I got up and proposed you, putting forward all your assets in very glowing terms. I didn't give them to understand that you would certainly accept but that, if approached, you might consider it very seriously. Immediately I sat down, up shot two young chaps from Cowley saying that they strongly objected to your candidature as you were known as definitely to be pro-Nazi – had you not written a pro-Nazi article in a Nazi paper and also broadcast from Berlin? I pointed out (probably untruthfully) that the newspaper had only published those parts of your MSS which suited it. And, as to your broadcast, that was purely a news item and you were telling a straightforward tale of the 30 June shootings and their effect.

Then someone got up and proposed Gordon Walker.* They knew him pretty well because he helped a lot during the municipals – also I have a suspicion that it probably occurred to him that Oxford would have advantages as a constituency. I think he has been making himself pleasant to people. I spoke again and said that they ought to give you an opportunity of refuting the charges made – etc. etc. Eventually it was decided to ask both you and Gordon Walker to meet the party and then a choice would be made . . .

By the way. I don't believe you are a member of the party so I made you one and paid 10/– membership fee.⁹

The last paragraph was a clear indication of just how distant Dick's formal relationship was with the Labour Party, even as late as 1935.† Indeed, it was not the least of Zita's contributions to his career that she, above anyone else, was responsible for turning him from the outsider, 'bolshie' don into the loyal – though hardly ever orthodox – Party member. At first, however, Dick appears to have been mildly nettled, if also flattered, by her intervention:

Your letter was very exciting but rather awkward. I can't possibly stand in rivalry against Patrick! I wish to god, though, he would choose a more suitable place than Oxford for his Left-left wing propaganda. It is a hopeless place for that sort of appeal . . . Also Patrick is violently anti-WEA [Workers' Educational Association] and I want the Oxford Labour Party to see to it that the WEA gets to work to educate Oxford.

Still, I should love to meet the Party and tell them what I think – though I shan't give in one inch. They can take me as I really am or not at all. I should like to have heard you doing your stuff – thank you for 'membershipping' me.¹⁰

Politics apart, it was an exchange highly revealing of the parity that existed between them before Zita took off for the United States. If Dick was the rising celebrity, then she was his most powerful local supporter – it is conceivable, indeed, that it was the Oxford Labour

---

* Patrick Gordon Walker (1907–80) later to be a colleague of Dick's in Harold Wilson's 1964–70 Cabinet, was a don at Christ Church and at that stage a left-wing figure in local Oxford Labour politics. Labour MP, Smethwick 1945–64 and Leyton 1966–74. Created life peer 1974.

† Dick was, however, even by 1935 already playing a part in left-wing university politics as co-chairman with G. D. H. Cole of the Cole Group of progressive dons and undergraduates.

Party (with Dick on the fringe of it and she at the centre)* that had first brought them together. The next two and a half months, however, were to change the whole balance between them – not at all in the way that Naomi Mitchison had intended.

At first, admittedly, Dick reacted to the separation much as Naomi must have hoped. The imposed companionship of a still unsuspecting John Baker proved embarrassing to him – and it was not long before he was insisting:

> I think we have just *got* to realise the hard facts of my Oxford, my work etc and your John, your family etc – and that thinking in terms of disregarding those is just going to make us drift into a position where we shall be left alone bearing grudges . . .
> I do feel you've *got* to make me somehow fit in with John and 94 or else I've got to go away: otherwise I shall *have* you without respecting you. That sounds horrid but it is true.[11]

A week later Dick returned to the charge, mentioning that, when he had last met him, John had been so 'nice and so terribly "family" that finally I felt sick and guilty . . . we've just got to be above board or go to pieces. You've simply got to look after and *protect* John.'[12]

Unfortunately, however, Zita displayed no appetite for this type of advice at all. In fact, the more Dick urged caution, the more she embraced recklessness. Even before she had received Dick's admonitory letters, she was already writing:

> The funny thing about this separation is that it is making you more than ever my life and my background. I find myself thinking of coming back – not to Oxford or 94 but to you. I can't now think of 'us' in any other way. And I can't believe that you're thinking in different terms.[13]

In fact, the only sense in which they *were* thinking in the same terms lay in the need to stop deceiving Zita's husband – and even here they were approaching the problem from different angles. For Zita it meant telling him so that the die was cast; for Dick it meant simply seeing if a *ménage à trois* was possible – and, if it proved not to be, looking forward to 'lots of self-commiseration at my heroic self-sacrifice'.[14]

It is hard to avoid wondering why, if they were at such cross-

---

* Zita eventually became secretary of the constituency Labour Party, holding the post until she was driven to leave Oxford in late 1936.

purposes, Naomi Mitchison's hope[15] that the trip would end the affair went so badly wrong. The answer here probably lies in a factor that neither she, nor anyone else, could have anticipated. It was pure ill luck for John Baker that his wife's ten-week absence abroad should have coincided precisely with the period in his adult life when Dick began to feel total confidence in his own powers. If he had started off worrying about the implications of their affair for the future of his career, by the time Zita left the United States he was prepared to run virtually any risk.

The immediate cause of Dick's sudden readiness to throw caution to the winds lay as much in his public activities as in his personal feelings. By the time Zita returned he had just completed a series of ten evening lectures, given for both town and gown and delivered under the auspices of the WEA. Entitled, 'How Hitler Came to Power', they proved to be a triumph – playing to packed houses of 700 or more in the Examination Schools week after week. To Zita, who though 3,000 miles away, remained his one genuine *confidante*, he was quite honest about his reactions:

> The fact is that I've been rather carried away by this sudden apparent bout of success and it has made me lose half my point when I speak. It's made me a 'professional successful speaker'.
> Funny how suddenly it all came. On Thursday my chairman at Headington* said: 'Nine months ago none of us had heard of Mr Crossman'; nine months ago I had not met you either – and now you are not here to keep me in order when I've started doing the things you want me to do, so I'm not doing them so well! And you are not here to enjoy the success which would be a real one, I think, if you were here.[16]

There could scarcely have been a plainer indication of how Dick's public career had become intermingled in his mind with his private life – and, in many ways, justly so. Indeed, in a rather high-minded, Webbish way both Zita and he had often discussed the notion of their working together in a pure socialist partnership (although that was never really a runner, if only because of the marked imbalance in their abilities). What Zita had certainly earned, however, was her right to hear Dick's own characteristic confession: 'I can be a really

---

* Dick, having passed up the parliamentary candidature, was now keen to become a Labour representative on the Oxford City Council and this fringe area Oxford ward (not then part of the parliamentary constituency) promised his best chance.

great man but I haven't *started* yet. I've got the vitality and the brains but not the stuff – so it's all a bit hollow really.'[17]

If he was fishing for compliments, he certainly got none from Zita, who – knowing her partner – promptly replied:

> I'm damn glad that you're not content with being 'a professional public speaker'. You could do that so easily and well and make pots of money and be so respectable. I'm glad you feel the 'hollowness' inside you. That'll get filled up a good deal with me and what I give you, but I think it's also going to get filled up with some extra power and knowledge which you're going to get from a big struggle right outside yourself.[18]

One of the secrets of Zita's hold over Dick lay in her capacity for being tough – in the same letter she roundly rebuked him for not pursuing the Oxford parliamentary candidature and ridiculed his notion (soon abandoned) of going to stand in Canterbury* instead: 'I wouldn't be able to help you in Canterbury because Oxford is my town. They're my people and I like them. But that doesn't really matter – I expect you will be able to get lots of helpers . . .'[19]

In fact, Dick stood nowhere at the general election of November 1935 contenting himself in the same month with contesting the Oxford City Council ward of Headington where, unlike Gordon Walker, who went down to a substantial defeat, he gained a Council seat from an Independent with a thumping majority.† Labour with two gains made at Cowley from the Conservatives and one from the Liberals in the City's South ward, increased its representation on the City Council from two to six. Without any evident difficulty Dick assumed the leadership of the small group of Labour members on the City Council.

Headington was where Zita worked, too, during the election, but there was no sign of any whispering campaign directed against either of them. Nor for that matter – and despite all their good resolutions – is there any direct evidence that even at this stage John Baker knew their secret. He may, of course, have consented to be the complaisant husband – but that seems unlikely, since within New

---

* Dick had given his first external WEA lecture at Canterbury. The WEA secretary there was George Wigg (1900–83), later – as MP for Dudley – to be his colleague as Paymaster-General in the 1964 Wilson Goverment. Created a life peer in 1967.

† The *Oxford Times* headlined Dick's victory – 'Mr R. H. S. Crossman heads poll at Headington.' 'His majority of 499 over his nearest opponent', it reported, 'must have surprised many people'. *Oxford Times* (8 November 1935).

College (to which Baker was, after all, also attached) early in 1936 Dick was the beneficiary of a dramatic piece of preferment: with H. A. L. Fisher suddenly declared by his doctors to be in need of 'a rest', he was made the College's Sub-Warden just three months after he joined the City Council.

This appointment – which came to Dick on a complicated principle of rotation – occasioned a good many heavy academic jokes within the BBC. All through that autumn, quite apart from his new political role, Dick had been busy preparing his series of talks 'If Plato Lived Again', which were due for transmission the following year. He had already invoked Fisher's name when there seemed some possibility of his choice as speaker being blocked by the BBC's Board of Governors – writing to his new producer, Roger Wilson: 'It occurred to me if the "powers that be" don't recognise me as a philosopher ask them to inquire of my boss (H. A. L. Fisher). He will give them a judicial account of my activities here as a Platonist ... I don't want to be counted out because they think I'm a radical propagandist only.'[20]

Although the apprehensions were at a lower level than the Board of Governors – and were probably traceable to Dick's former critic over 'Youth Looks Ahead', Major Gladstone Murray* – Dick's new academic eminence can certainly have done him no harm. There was a flavour of the Senior Common Room about the BBC itself in those days – witness the letter that Roger Wilson wrote to him towards the end of January 1936:

> My dear Sub-Warden,
>   I felt in a fairly strong position when dealing with a Don junior in academic standing to myself and was proposing to ask you to come up on Tuesday 4 February early in the afternoon so that Charles Siepmann, you and I would have a real go at the question of broadcasting style ... But when the Corporation deals with a Sub-Warden, I am not certain that we can be quite so dictatorial. Perhaps you will give me your advice as R. H. S. Crossman – broadcaster.[22]

Beneath all the elaborate irony there remained, however, a problem.

---

* A hint of this is contained in Roger Wilson's reply to Dick: 'I was not worried about the line which would be taken by the Board, as I had no doubt your Warden's opinion [Fisher was a Governor of the BBC] would be decisive in your favour. I was much more worried by the fact that it might not get as far as the Board at all!'[21]

Dick had launched his major Plato series on 14 January 1936 and, although it was to be interrupted for two weeks by George V's death and funeral, the first reactions to it had been mixed – with even Zita commenting: 'By the way, Plato on Tuesday was fine, but you mustn't ever say "Some of you" again. You must talk to each person individually at his fireside.'[23] It was a well-taken point, with the professionals within the BBC appearing to feel much the same. On the same day Dick's producer, Roger Wilson, wrote to warn him that he had 'sounded a little patronising' and to advise for the future: 'If you go slower, you will be able to be more conversational and less "I'm telling you".'[24]

Dick's delivery, though – obviously by now custom-built for the lecture hall rather than the studio – was by no means Wilson's only difficulty. He had barely negotiated the production of the third talk before the following magisterial minute descended upon him in Broadcasting House. It emanated from the new Director of Talks, one J. M. Rose-Troop:

> Will you please tell Mr Crossman that he must not ask the Announcer to alter the announcement that has been agreed upon unless there is some serious mistake of fact? On 11 February he insisted that there should be substituted for one section of the announcement the statement that 'he [Socrates] was the first conscientious objector'. Apart from the impropriety of Mr Crossman asking for a change, I should not have been prepared in any circumstances to agree to this change being included in the announcement.[25]

Although Roger Wilson most chivalrously took full responsibility for the title alteration – the original one had been the rather flat-sounding 'The Search for Knowledge'[26] – Dick's habit of barging in and trampling on institutional customs and practices was plainly beginning to get up the BBC's nose. There was, for instance, later a long argument about his talk on 'Plato and Fascism' – or 'Plato Looks at Power States' (as the BBC finally neutrally put it) – with Zita urging him to stand firm in what was already almost a wifely manner:

> I think you're right to be strong about Fascism. If they were paying you a fabulous sum, then you might bother to change it. But the money you get in comparison with the sweat is mingy and

for that reason I don't see why you should put yourself out the least bit.[27]

In fact, Dick was not all that ill-rewarded: he was paid twelve guineas a talk, which in those days was quite a substantial sum. No doubt, the consciousness that they were paying him that kind of money – and, above all, that they were providing him with a superb platform – did something to explain the mounting irritation that gradually built up within at least some sections of the BBC hierarchy.

It finally exploded in an internal memo written by Dick's old enemy, Major Gladstone Murray. Dated 25 March 1936, it is worth quoting almost in full, if only because it is a genuine period piece:

> The study yesterday by D.R. [Director of Religion – at the time the Rev. F. A. Iremonger] and myself of Script No. 9 in the series 'If Plato Lived Again' confirms our misgivings about the eligibility of Mr Crossman for microphone work. The script examined contained several important errors of fact in quotations from the Bible. These, however, were not so serious as the general tone and trend of the talk. Although he was skilful enough to keep within his terms of reference for the most part, the talk was clearly using the series and the BBC as a medium for his own views and doctrines. He is, in essence, a 'disintegrator'. The remaining talks in the series will be examined with special vigilance.[28]

Alas, it was a little late for that. Showing a refreshing sense of priorities, Dick had deliberately withdrawn from talks ten and eleven in the series (leaving them in the charge of the philosophy don at Balliol, Charles Morris) so that he could go on holiday in the Channel Islands with Zita. Again, propriety was, to some extent, preserved by their going in the company of two married friends, Max and Mary Nicholson; the avowed intention was one of bird-watching on Sark, where Max Nicholson was conducting an ornithological survey. Suspicions, however, either at 94 Woodstock Road or at New College (where Dick was already under some pressure to leave The Barn on the ground that it was unsuitable for the Sub-Warden to be living there alone with a German maid),* might well

---

* Resi eventually left at the end of the Trinity Term 1936 and soon married a former boyfriend in her native Bavaria.

have been aroused in the light of one piece of evidence. Spurning the normal resort to such anonymous names as 'Smith' or 'Brown' Dick filled in the register in the various hotels in which they stayed with the *nom d'amour* of 'Mr and Mrs Cardigan-Barger'.[29]

Dick did, however, return in time to do the last talk in the series entitled 'Why Plato Failed' (which, unlike the one to which Major Gladstone Murray had taken exception, was, along with most of the earlier ones in the series, reprinted in the *Listener*). It is possible, however, that Gladstone Murray's writ was even more powerful than that. The fact that, once he had finished with Plato, Dick did not broadcast for the BBC again – apart from a couple of afternoon schools programmes – until 1939 would certainly seem to suggest that some sort of 'black spot' had been applied against him.*

For Dick, the closing off of the BBC as a source of income was clearly a blow – in 1936 he had earned nearly £200 from it (or the equivalent of two-fifths of his New College Fellow's stipend). And he was starting to have to reckon with the need for additional expenditure. During the summer of 1936, a state of armed truce still pertained at 94 Woodstock Road – but it was not to last for long. By the autumn, after John Baker had returned from a Long Vacation spent on a scientific expedition to Ceylon, Zita finally confirmed that she was 'in love with someone else' and in effect left home.[31]

It was not, however, to fly into the arms of Dick: they were both far too conscious of the dangers for that. The previous autumn of 1935 Zita had undergone an illegal abortion for fear of compromising Dick's career – though whether Dick ever knew about it remains uncertain (since it was clumsily handled, it may, however, have been the reason why she never subsequently had any children with him).[32]

It was hardly surprising that by the autumn of the following year not only Zita but her loyal female friends were beginning to get distinctly restive with Dick's detached attitude. He was even expressly accused by Naomi Mitchison of 'not having lifted a finger' to help Zita leave 94 Woodstock Road;[33] and Mary Nicholson, to whose Westminster flat Zita initially fled once she had left Oxford, also believed that Dick was tending to evade his responsibility for all that had occurred.[34] It was not, however, easy for Dick. In the first

---

* When Roger Wilson tried to infiltrate Dick back on to the air-waves in a series called 'This Planning Business' at the end of 1936, the message came from on high: 'Personally, I should prefer that we should give Mr Crossman a rest.' Charles Graves to J. M. Rose-Troop 18 December 1936.[30]

place, Zita does not appear to have been entirely sure what she wanted: in some moods she would suggest that the height of her aspiration was to live permanently with Dick, in others that her 'conscience' dictated that she must go back to her husband and her family.* The timing of the break-up could also hardly have been more unfortunate from Dick's point of view. Not only was he about to become Dean of New College – having ceased to be Sub-Warden on Fisher's return in October 1936 – and, therefore, directly responsible for the discipline and morals of all the undergraduates; he was also heavily involved that autumn in the municipal elections in Oxford and was well aware that any breath of scandal could easily thwart Labour's progress on the City Council.† There was a third complicating factor on the scene in the re-emergence in Zita's life of her former lover, Tom Harrisson, who began to press his own suit with alarming fervour. When Zita finally agreed to go to Bolton – the 'Worktown' of the Mass Observation Survey – to be a member of his polling investigation team, Dick found it hard to contain his jealousy.[36]

By the end of 1936 the only tidy element in an otherwise thoroughly messy picture was the firm indication that the unfortunate John Baker had himself formed an attachment to a woman of Russian upbringing called Liena. Unfortunately, she was also married, to Douglas Savage (of a newsagent's business of that name in Carfax). Eventually Douglas Savage was to be responsible for the dénouement to the whole complicated affair now involving not just one marriage but two; but, for the time being, at least it meant that John Baker was no longer wholly resistant to the idea of a divorce from Zita (though he still insisted on his prerogative of divorcing her rather than following the normal gentlemanly custom of those days of the wife divorcing the husband).

That immediately posed a real complication for Dick, though hardly for Zita. If he was to be cited as co-respondent, then what had been the point of all the subterfuge over the past three years? Catastrophically, Dick went for the soft option, if only to buy time

---

* There was a particularly bad wobble just before Zita's divorce case came up – with Dick hitting back with the slightly dangerous argument: 'You say it is "conscience" but conscience never pricks unless you still have a lot of wish left to do the things conscience tells.'[35]

† In fact Labour made limited, if slightly disappointing progress – gaining only two seats in November 1936. With the defection of Independents to its cause, it had now, however, risen to a group of 12 on the City Council of 68 (12 of them were still representatives appointed by the university).

(his seven-year fellowship at New College was up for renewal in October). One of Zita's early lovers had been a shop steward and prominent left-winger at the Pressed Steel works in Cowley called Frank Griffiths: how it was done remains a mystery, but somehow John Baker was prevailed upon to name him, rather than Dick, as the guilty party. The decree *nisi* went through on 16 February 1937 at Devon Assizes with barely an academic eyebrow being raised – though Dick, perhaps pushing his luck, confessed in a letter to Zita to being vastly irritated that the *Oxford Times* had failed in its report to give the name of the cited co-respondent.*

Dick could justifiably claim to have been the victim of the then archaic divorce laws with their emphasis on adultery as *the* 'matrimonial offence'; and at least it could be said on his behalf that he had behaved no worse than King Edward VIII with Wallis Simpson, whose own decree absolute was going through at much the same time.† Zita's fate, however, was hardly less enviable than Wallis's. True, she was not banished abroad – but banished she had to be. In the days of the King's Proctor – whose duty it was to sniff out any whiff of collusion on a divorce and then report the matter to the court, thereby blocking the decree absolute – she could not risk even being seen in Oxford. She was forced into the position (before she eventually went off to Bolton to work with Tom Harrisson) of being a wandering minstrel around the houses of her friends. Here Dick did betray some sympathy: 'Poor thing, carrying your home about. It's pretty trying having an empty, fixed home but I agree it's worse to have no home at all.'[39]

The heaviest blow for Zita, however, was an uncovenanted one that neither of them could have foreseen. In April 1937, at very short notice, Dick was selected as the Labour candidate in West Birmingham to fight the by-election there caused by the death of Sir Austen Chamberlain. It was just the side of Dick's activities in which Zita felt most at home – and which she had been largely responsible for developing; but on the advice of the agent, to whom Dick made a clean breast of things,[40] she was banned from making any appearance in the campaign at all (there was a proposal that she might be allowed to come on the afternoon of polling day itself but, understandably, it does not seem to have commended itself to

---

   * 'Blast the local Press. Why (when we've gone to all this trouble) should it fail to mention Frank Griffiths' name?'[37]
   † The parallels with the royal romance were in both their minds – with Dick at one stage confiding to Zita, 'I'm not going to make Edward's mistake of asking for advice before the absolute.'[38]

her). Here again, though, Dick did show some imaginative insight into what her feelings must have been, writing to her as the campaign opened: 'It is *horrible* your being left out of this but there will be lots of other elections in our lives, I rather think, and we may have enough of them before we are through.'[41] A few days later, apparently considering that his initial effort at comfort might not have worked, he risked a brisker variant on the same theme – 'I feel almost rather glad that I am going to learn to be a really good candidate by myself so I can show off to you next time.'[42]

In fact, Dick proved an excellent candidate, if a slightly euphoric one: at one stage being sufficiently carried away to confide in Zita, 'There is now just a chance that we shall pull it off.'[43] He had failed, of course, to reckon with the strength of the Chamberlain Birmingham machine – Neville Chamberlain, due to become Prime Minister the next month, sat for the neighbouring city constituency of Ladywood – and on 29 April Dick was defeated by 2,920 votes (significantly the constituency had on its register 6,000 business voters who did not even reside within its boundaries). It had been, though, a highly creditable achievement – Dick had reduced the Conservative majority of eighteen months earlier by some 4,500 and had put up the Labour vote by nearly 500 on a much lower poll. It may be, however, given the family background, that the thing which tickled him most was the 'awfully nice message'[44] he received from the leader of his Party, Clement Attlee: in it he was described as 'not only a distinguished scholar, but a recognised authority on the great problems which confront civilisation today'[45] – a far cry from the impact he had made as the *enfant terrible* of Buckhurst Hill only a few years earlier (see p. 13 above).

One place, however, where Dick's first parliamentary adventure had not won him golden opinions was back at New College, Oxford. With perhaps typical impetuosity he had gone off to fight the by-election without taking the precaution of clearing the matter with the college authorities – and they were far from being amused. The first sign Dick got of how seriously the matter was taken – as Dean, he had deserted his post for the first full week of term – came in the shape of 'a stinking letter all about disloyalty and dishonesty' from his former greatest ally, the Warden's wife, Lettice Fisher: that got short shrift from Dick ('I have answered it for once in straight words – the Bitch').[46] That may, however, have been a mistake – for Lettice Fisher was doing no more than reflect a very real anger within the Senior Common Room (Dick being no longer protected by his position as Sub-Warden) and he was soon to need all the friends he could get.

Theoretically, with the by-election behind him and Zita's final divorce decree due in August, the summer of 1937 should have been relatively untroubled. If it turned out not to be, it was largely because both Dick and Zita had chosen to ignore the warning contained in Sir Walter Scott's familiar lines:

> Oh, what a tangled web we weave
> When first we practise to deceive.

Admittedly, the way the web was finally untangled was sheer bad luck. Poor Douglas Savage, as the only individual counted out in the game of matrimonial musical chairs, finally got tired of writing anonymous menacing letters to John and Zita Baker: at some stage late that summer he resolved to take his story (and his complaint) direct to the Warden of New College. That might not have mattered – at least so far as Dick, the ultimate ricochet victim, was concerned – if he had only been sensible enough to take his friend and protector, H. A. L. Fisher, into his confidence. But that – perhaps because Fisher had the reputation of being 'a terrific prude'[47] – was something he had never done; in fact, he had done the opposite, allowing the Warden to slap down what he characteristically termed 'vile rumours' and even when Zita urged that he should own up, she was brusquely repulsed with the statement, 'If I'm going to leave Oxford, I don't want to be *forced out*.'[48] Nor did Dick in the end stick to his resolution, 'I shall tell the Fishers as soon as you are divorced fully.'[49] It was an expensive mistake, as the eventual showdown in October was to demonstrate.

Dick returned to Oxford after the Long Vacation of 1937 (some of it spent in Wales with Zita) aparently fully expecting to have his fellowship renewed for at least another year – which was all he wanted since the taste he had already acquired for politics (to say nothing of journalism) was already impelling him towards the wider world. Instead, however, he soon established that the Warden – by now fully apprised of Douglas Savage's story – had been making inquiries about him and Zita among his SCR colleagues and that one of them, the senior philosophy don, A. L. Smith (later himself to become Warden) 'had admitted my "guilt"'.[50] The rest of the tale, since the style is so characteristic, is probably best told by Dick himself:

I took the bull by the horns, interviewed the Warden and told him straight I wanted a non-teaching lectureship which would enable me to continue *lecturing* without corrupting the boys by my tutorials. Just after I came back up, Smith rang to say that he had spent a sleepless, conscience-troubled night and was enormously relieved to find he could back my new suggestion without scruples – so there is a good chance of my getting a £100 lectureship or at least £50 one. The Warden also seemed pleased. Anyway the meeting is over and I suppose my resignation has been accepted with acclamation.[51]*

There remained, of course, the loose ends to be tied up. Although no evidence survives to suggest that Dick got his £100, or even £50, lectureship, he was allowed to stay on the college strength for three months – and also to remain in The Barn. The ancestral memory in New College, however, is that it was almost as if he was 'under house arrest': certainly all individual teaching contact with pupils appears to have been cut off from the moment of his confession, though the duties of the Deanship were not immediately stripped from him. Even more significantly, when he eventually inquired whether he might bring Zita back to The Barn after their honeymoon, he was told that he might do so – but only on the strict condition that they had both vacated the premises by the time the undergraduates returned for the Hilary term.

Dick and Zita's marriage finally took place at Caxton Hall on 18 December 1937. This time there was no Mrs Fisher but at least some kind of seal of moral approval was conferred by the presence of Dick's mother.† (She even served as one of the two witnesses, just as the Warden's wife had done over five years earlier.)

There was another interesting connection between the two

---

* It has to be admitted that this contemporary chronicle is entirely at variance with a version of the same events that Dick gave in the course of a book review first published in the *New Statesman* (18 September 1954) and reprinted on pp. 3–9 of *The Charm of Politics*. There Dick has Fisher sending for him 'to tell him that he would recommend that his fellowship be renewed for seven years' but then urging that he should take the plunge into politics instead. The most charitable comment must be that even middle-aged men forget.

† Helen Crossman, though only warned of the impending marriage a week earlier, had already written a welcoming letter to Zita on joining the Crossman family. A measure of her perceptiveness and tact – not always acknowledged by Dick – can perhaps be judged by this passage from it: 'I have long realised that, after poor Dick's miserable experience, a quite ordinary marriage was not possible for him. I gather you, too, have had a disaster. I do hope you will both be able to heal these earlier wounds. Dick, as no doubt you know, has a wealth of affection to bestow.'[52]

ceremonies – in each case the age of his wife, as given on the marriage certificate, was noticeably older than that of the husband. When Dick was twenty-four, Erika gave her age as twenty-six, which may or may not have been the truth; with Dick just three days past his thirtieth birthday, Zita gave hers as thirty-four, which was undoubtedly a lie. She was, in fact, over seven years older than he was – something, in his innocent way, that he did not discover until after their marriage was ended by her death nearly fifteen years later.[53]

7   Prodigy Politician

The penalty of Athenian-style banishment New College imposed upon Dick was not as crippling as it might have appeared. In the first place, he was already a public figure in his own right – with a fame (thanks to broadcasting and his first, and best, book, *Plato To-day*)* reaching well beyond the confines of Oxford. And, second, whatever the constitutional powers of a 'Stated General Meeting'† at New College, his SCR colleagues' sentence could hardly be expected to thwart, or even take priority over, the democratic process. Once he had been evicted from The Barn, Dick defiantly resolved to stay within the city boundaries, setting up home with Zita at 64 Sandfield Road in Headington, the ward he unabashedly continued to represent as leader of the Labour Group on Oxford City Council.

Initially, though, the pressures – not least economic ones – tended to crowd in. Having lived in a 'tied cottage' all his professional life, for the first time Dick found himself thrust into the housing market. His original instinct was to rent – and he was prepared to pay up to the expensive limit (for those days) of £100 a year; no sooner, however, had he set eyes on 64 Sandfield Road – a large white house standing on the corner of a private road and with a balcony looking over the garden from its principal bedroom – than he decided that

---

* *Plato To-day* was first published in June 1937 by Allen & Unwin. It has remained in print ever since.

† At New College a 'Stated General Meeting' is the final decision-making body. Its minutes are about as illuminating as those of a British Cabinet. Thus, while the decision to extend 'Mr Crossman's fellowship on the same terms and conditions as before till 1 October 1939' is solemnly recorded in the minutes for 6 October 1937, not a word surfaces about the circumstances of his abrupt departure some three months later.

this was the home he wanted.[1] Unfortunately it proved to be for sale only, and Dick – having originally put in an offer of £1,000 – had eventually to pay £1,490 for it, which he still calculated was a good bargain. It meant, however, as he carefully spelt out to Zita, that they were going to be pretty hard up, especially as they would also need to buy a car* – if only to enable Zita to accompany Dick at least occasionally on his forays across the length and breadth of England lecturing for the Workers' Educational Association.[2]

His lecturing schedule was punishing. Monday to Wednesday were spent on alternate weeks in Staffordshire, every Thursday evening at Ashford in Kent, each Friday at Slough, with Swindon filling in for the Potteries in the weeks he did not go up north.[3] It was not perhaps the ideal basis on which to found a marriage, though Dick's first letter to his new wife – scribbled from Burton upon Trent – did at least include the tactful postscript: 'This is my first letter to the only Mrs Crossman my family now possesses.'[4] The initial tensions arose, perhaps predictably, over Zita's two children – Venice, who was already eleven and Gilbert, who was seven. Dick appears to have been anxious to provide a home for both of them; indeed, one of the attractions of 64 Sandfield Road was that it had five bedrooms and therefore posed no problems over accommodation. But what he was not prepared to do was to shoulder the entire financial burden for them; and very soon hostilities had opened up over the question of at least Gilbert's 'maintenance'. Before long this had developed into a running battle – with Zita, perhaps understandably, tending to take her ex-husband's side, thereby provoking Dick into displaying the unattractive, aggressive side of his nature:

> There are limits to what I will put up with from John. I have twice offered to help pay for Gilbert, and have received no word of thanks for my trouble. I do not dream of making the offer again. If John wishes to ask me for a favour, he can do so. But, until he does, I shall have nothing to do with it.
>
> I cannot see why it is tough that John should continue to pay for Gilbert when my salary has been cut. Nor can I see why you should fix this up without asking me about it. The normal thing would be for John, if he wants me to do it, to suggest a meeting or to write to me. As far as I know, Gilbert's education has been insured.

* Dick himself never drove a car. He had ridden a motor-bike as a young don at Oxford but gave up even that after having a bad smash riding from Wales to Cornwall in 1932.

So I think you had better tell John that I am quite ready to listen to any requests from him which he may care to make, and that he had better be civil about it. If he wishes to take the line that I have wronged him, I think he is perfectly entitled to do so. Nor should you continue to be friendly and nice to him while he behaves in this way. I should not be friendly to *anybody* who treated you as John thinks he can treat me.[5]

No doubt that is most charitably considered as an example – to use one of Dick's favourite phrases – of 'getting something off your chest'.* But it was not perhaps wholly surprising that, when Gilbert and Venice – who was sheltered to some extent from the battle because she was away at school at Dartington Hall – were asked to choose which parent they wished to live with, they should have opted for life with their father. (They were told to vote out of ten and tactfully brought in their verdict by six to four.)[6]

Thereafter Venice stuck by the decision, although Gilbert later went back to his mother: the presence of a seven-year-old in Sandfield Road can only have accentuated both Dick's and Zita's disappointment at failing to produce any children of their own.†

Not that in 1938 there was much time to repine over that or anything else. The year of Munich soon became, in effect, Dick's own *annus mirabilis*. In January, after toying with a number of other possible Labour parliamentary nominations, he made his official début as prospective Labour candidate for Coventry – then a single-Member seat narrowly held by a Conservative in 1935 but won by Labour in 1929.‡ In May he was sent by the *Daily Herald* to Prague to report on Hitler's challenge over the Sudetenland.[7] He produced four vivid reports from Czechoslovakia for the newspaper and some ecstatic private letters to Zita once Czech mobilisation appeared, if only transiently, to have stopped the threat of German invasion in its tracks ('We waited here for war and then knew guts had beaten Hitler').[8] Once safely home, Dick found himself fêted as the man

---

* The phrase appears later in the same letter: 'I have been wanting to get this off my chest for a good many months, and feel better now it is off my chest.'

† Slightly rashly, Dick – two months before they were married – had advised Zita to warn her ex-husband that they proposed to have 'one or two children'.

‡ Dick owed his selection, made at the end of 1937, to George Hodgkinson, secretary-agent of the Coventry Labour Party, who had served as one of the sub-agents in the West Birmingham by-election of April 1937. Hodgkinson's own account of the favourable impression Dick then made on him is given in his book, *Sent to Coventry* (Robert Maxwell, 1970), pp. 121–2.

who had seen history made; he was granted audiences both by Clement Attlee and Hugh Dalton and lost no time in organising a joint Labour Party/League of Nations Union rally in Coventry so that he could report back on how, for once, aggression had been repelled.[9]

Arguably, however, his most important encounter in that summer of 1938 was not with any politician but with an editor. Dick had written off and on for the *New Statesman and Nation* – though mainly in its literary back half – since November 1935. He had started off by reviewing books on philosophy but gradually had widened his scope and extended his range – writing, for example, for the first time in the paper's political front half, on the German Olympic Games of 1936[10] and a year later contributing a particularly trenchant article criticising the state of Labour Party organisation, following his own defeat in the West Birmingham by-election of April 1937.[11] He had never, however, considered himself primarily as a journalist* and was remarkably innocent of the metropolitan Press scene, even if his political allegiance had led him to contribute from time to time to Labour Party papers such as the *Daily Herald* and *Reynolds News*. It was, therefore, his good fortune that the editor of the *New Statesman* of the day – the illustrious Kingsley Martin, who went on to edit the paper for nearly thirty years – always liked to look upon himself as an academic almost as much as a journalist: few editors would have spotted the journalistic potential of a thirty-year-old 'unfrocked' philosophy don, but Kingsley Martin (touchingly proud of his own starred first at Cambridge) was one who did. They did not know each other well – indeed, they had probably not met till 1936 – but some time after Dick's fall from grace at New College, Kingsley Martin seems to have decided that he was just the sort of intellectual asset that the *New Statesman* needed.

Of course, in small weekly magazines nothing can be done suddenly. The *New Statesman* in the late 1930s (with a circulation only just breasting 30,000) already had its young man/dogsbody on the staff in the shape of Michael Foot† – and the paper's budget did not run to hiring someone else at whim. Providentially, however, in the summer of 1938 Foot was lured away to become a leader writer on Lord Beaverbrook's *Evening Standard*. This meant Kingsley Martin

---

* See above, p. 43: 'This is the life, provided it is not your main job.'
† Foot was to be a colleague and friend in the House of Commons almost throughout RHSC's parliamentary career, becoming leader of the Labour Party (1980–3) only, however, after Dick's death.

could follow what had probably been his inclination ever since he realised that Dick might become available. The offer seems to have been made with some rapidity[12] and, with Dick's appointment as assistant editor of the *New Statesman and Nation* in July 1938, one of the more incongruous alliances of modern British journalism was forged.

It was incongruous because Dick and Kingsley Martin – whatever their academic bonds – shared little in common in their political outlooks. The unkind judgment would be that Martin's success as an editor rested on his turning the *New Statesman* into a paper of emotional protest, even sometimes of political sentimentality: he certainly believed in agonising – no journalist ever wore his heart more publicly on his sleeve. Dick, on the other hand, prided himself above all on being tough-minded – and was rather keener on shocking other people's consciences than on appealing to them. He was also, though this has tended since to be overlooked, every inch a 'rogue' right-wing figure in the context of the Labour Party of the 1930s. The first political speech that he delivered – of which any record survives – is sufficient evidence of that. It was made in the year that he first became a Labour Councillor for Headington and was unorthodox enough in tone to attract the attention of the local Press:

> Socialists are very fond of talking of the influence of such people as the brewers behind the Conservative Party. But their influence is nothing like the influence which is imposed upon the Labour Party by its financial backers at Transport House – the trade unions. If you want to find a party that is dictated to by the financial powers behind it, it is the Labour Party.
>
> If you say that the Labour Party is the workers' party and that it has no other interests, you will never get a majority in this city. You will find that the English worker won't vote for a party which thinks only of the interests of a certain section of the community. One of the troubles of the Labour Party is that it is too class-conscious . . .
>
> Then there is the Labour Party intellectual who, psychologically, likes being in opposition. The Labour Party is gathering to itself all the cranks there are and all the minorities – anti-vivisectionists, internationalists and those who live for the brotherhood of man. Every minority movement naturally votes Labour because Labour is the party of opposition which will never get into power.[13]

Dick's subsequent years as a Labour Councillor may have smoothed out some of the anti-union edges that were apparent in 1935 – but his disdain for the woolly-minded intellectual ('anti-vivisectionists, internationalists and all those who live for the brotherhood of man') remained as strong as ever. But it was, of course, precisely this group of readers who comprised the natural audience of the *New Statesman*. Dick was certainly not guilty of hyperbole when he commented nearly thirty-five years later: 'I still think it *staggering* that Kingsley should have had the faith to take me on.'[14]

No doubt, it may have been done partly out of ignorance. A busy weekly editor was hardly likely to be a close follower of the various internecine struggles and quarrels within the Oxford Labour Party, though Dick's position there had been remarkably consistent. He may have liked to characterise himself as 'neither left nor right, just a sensible chap in local politics'[15] but that was not quite the case;* in internal Party controversy he tended to be found in the strong-arm, right-wing camp. That was certainly true of his attitude to the Communists and the Popular Front – unlike Patrick Gordon Walker and Frank Pakenham he actually opposed the Oxford City Party's endorsement of the 'fringe' Left's 'Unity Manifesto' of January 1937;[16] and it was striking how little, in contrast to other members of his generation, he allowed the Spanish Civil War to affect his political attitudes† – on one occasion cynically remarking on a WEA platform at Chorley: 'In Spanish affairs I trust Communists and Catholics about the same' (only to discover that his chairman was himself a Catholic).[18]

What, of course, may have clouded the issue, and confused memories, was Dick's role in the famous Oxford City 'Munich' by-election of October 1938. Here, admittedly, he was a supporter of the candidature of A. D. Lindsay, the Master of Balliol and outgoing University Vice-Chancellor – whom he almost certainly played some part in persuading to stand. But Lindsay was more a joint Liberal/Labour candidate than a 'Popular Front' one, in the way

* Dick, however, had every reason to feel proud of his record in local government. He was a very active Councillor, serving on the Watch, the Finance, the Parliamentary and the Public Assistance Committees. He maintained his involvement with the Council almost up to the outbreak of war, attending his last meeting (of the Watch Committee) on 27 July 1939.

† In 1973 a Birmingham University research student wrote to Dick querying the lack of emphasis 'the Spanish issue' appeared to have been given in his Birmingham West by-election campaign of April 1937. He received the typically forthright reply: 'I had never seen such slums and such poverty in my life and as a result perhaps it never occurred to me to mention Spain.'[17]

that phrase later came to be understood. The main initiative for giving a joint 'Independent Progressive' candidate the chance of a clear run against Quintin Hogg,* the young Fellow of All Souls who was defending the seat for the Chamberlain Government, had come from the Liberals. In making common cause with them Dick was doing no more than the anti-Munichites were ready to do at Westminster. Nevertheless his sin, in the eyes of the Labour Establishment, was that he had been a party to forcing a selected Labour candidate (Patrick Gordon Walker) to stand down – and that he had done so in a particularly visible manner: Dick had spoken at Lindsay's adoption meeting – where, significantly, the other three speakers were all Liberals.[19] But, if that was a sin, it can hardly at the time have appeared a very heinous one, even in the eyes of the Labour Party. Had not Patrick Gordon Walker himself, after all, spoken at Lindsay's eve-of-poll rally in Oxford Town Hall?

Still, as very much in those days 'a right-winger', Dick may have had second thoughts about his role. Significantly when, after Lindsay's defeat by 3,434 votes, an inquest on the by-election opened up in the correspondence columns of the *New Statesman* he played no part in it – leaving it to G. D. H. Cole to belabour the unfortunate Gordon Walker,† whose somewhat inconsistent conduct was cruelly declared to be 'inexcusable except on the assumption of temporary insanity'.[20] No reprisals were taken by Labour Party headquarters against Dick – though, according to an independent historian of the episode, 'he fell from favour with the National Executive'.[21]

With the Coventry nomination under his belt and the world of political journalism at his feet, Dick did not, however, have to worry about that. His main anxiety seems, indeed, to have remained Zita – for, although his new job at the *New Statesman* meant he no longer had to live his life in railway trains, it did require him to be in London, if only for the middle part of the week. At least, however, he could now get home to Oxford on most evenings – and when he didn't, he spent the night in an attic in Kingsley Martin's flat at 14 Buckingham Street, off the Strand.

---

* Quintin Hogg, Lord Hailsham, MP for Oxford City 1938–50, St Marylebone 1963–70, Lord Chancellor 1970–4 and 1979–87.

† Despite his ultimate appearance on Lindsay's platform, Gordon Walker had published a letter in the *Daily Herald* on 19 October 1938 in which he declared: 'I did not withdraw from the contest. I was withdrawn by my Party against my strong protest.' The letter, understandably, was run as a 'page lead' under the headline, 'It Was a Betrayal to Withdraw Me.' It incensed large sections of the Oxford City Labour Party and led to Frank Pakenham – rather than Patrick Gordon Walker – being selected as the next Labour candidate for the seat in January 1939.

This invitation was, in its way, a tribute to his editor's ecumenical spirit. It had soon become clear that, by appointing him to the staff, Martin had introduced something of a cuckoo into the *New States-man* nest. It was not that Dick failed to give professional satisfaction; indeed, he very soon developed the knack of writing paragraphs for the editor's 'London Diary' (always signed 'Critic') in Martin's own style. This was something, he secretly believed, that assured him security of tenure, whatever arguments they might otherwise have. But the arguments were real ones – and they tended to stem from the fact that Dick, at least by the time of Munich, thought that war was not only inevitable but necessary; Martin, on the other hand, believed that virtually any step was justifiable in order to avoid it. Predictably, this led to some glaring inconsistencies in the paper's line – with perhaps the worst one being the famous editorial 'Note' of 27 August 1938 in which the *New Statesman* virtually acceded to Hitler's frontier demands over Czechoslovakia even in advance of their being formally put forward. For Martin the outcry this caused – not least among his own friends in Prague – was a chastening experience;* and it may have eased Dick's problems during the Munich crisis when the paper took a noticeably more robust line.

Where, however, Dick was allowed a quite remarkable latitude was in his handling of other writers' copy. Perhaps the most famous – certainly the most familiar – bylines in the pre-war *New Statesman* were those of two academics: G. D. H. Cole of University College, Oxford and Harold Laski of the London School of Economics. Dick's reaction to their contributions, as given to his editor, was trenchant: 'I would say: "Look here, you can't print any more of this boring stuff from Cole and Laski. They're killing the paper. Let's have some *interesting* articles" – and little did I know what heresy I was uttering!'[23]

Heresy or not, Dick was right – and, in a strange way, Kingsley Martin himself (who was always much more interested in foreign articles than domestic ones) may even have known it. Certainly, while he would always apologise for Dick when such writers angrily complained, he would very rarely overturn his subordinate's decisions over articles – and there may even have been something to Dick's own suspicion that he had been deliberately brought in as the one spirit brash enough not to be intimidated by these household gods of the Left.[24]

* According to his biographer, in later years Kingsley Martin described this in an unpublished chapter of his autobiography as 'my worst editorial mistake'.[22]

Although he worked most of the week at the *New Statesman*, Dick did not entirely abandon his WEA lecturing. For one thing, after seven years at Oxford, he would have felt deprived if he had lost all opportunity of teaching; and, for another, he and Zita needed the money. The paper was paying him a salary of £400 a year – but Dick was understandably proud of the fact that even in his first year he managed, by his own efforts, to raise his income to £750 per annum. That, in those days, meant that it was perfectly possible to run a car, to take holidays abroad and (as Dick himself characteristically put it) 'to have Wine Society claret'.[25] He also received modest royalties from his books; as well as *Plato To-day*, which came out in June 1937, he had written – jointly with Naomi Mitchison – a slim volume on the politics and life of ancient Greece called simply *Socrates*. Very much a child's guide to both history and philosophy, it had also been published – as part of a children's series by the Hogarth Press – during the summer of 1937. Although, as even the *New Statesman* reviewer complained, it had something of 'the bland voice of the governess',[26] it enjoyed a reasonable success, and Dick was not ashamed of it: indeed, in later years – in marked contrast to Naomi Mitchison who was meticulous in acknowledging her co-author – he took to claiming sole credit for it in his *Who's Who* entry.

Plato To-day was always, however, to remain his favourite book[27] – and with good cause. In effect, a frontal assault on Plato as a fascist, it possesses all the verve and élan that the scripts of his 1936 broadcasts on the same subject lack. Described by his successor at New College, Sir Isaiah Berlin, as 'an interesting, original book of a rather maverick kind',[28] it has some claims to be considered the precursor of Sir Karl Popper's more famous work, *The Open Society*. Although its publication came too late to do him much good, it established Dick's right to be treated seriously by the Oxford philosophic community – despite the fact that its members had never felt disposed 'to look upon him as a brother'.[29]

But by 1938 all that was behind him. His own description of himself – admittedly delivered many years later – was 'a prodigy politician'.[30] That may have been pitching matters a bit high; he was not yet a Member of the House of Commons (although he plainly expected to become one within the next year or so). Dick may have anticipated, even in a sense have wanted, the war; but it must have been clear – although he probably could not have foreseen the wartime 'party truce' – that any outbreak of hostilities was liable to disrupt his own political ambitions.

For the moment, however, those remained not only serious but entirely consistent with his past record. If Dick enjoyed one triumph on the pre-war *New Statesman*, it lay in the way he – as the one member of its staff who knew anything about political organisation – swung the paper against Sir Stafford Cripps and his 'Unity Campaign'* for the Left. The long saga of Cripps's advocacy of a 'Popular Front', his resulting expulsion (along with Aneurin Bevan and George Strauss) by the NEC, and his subsequent decision to organise a 'petition' by the constituency Parties for his reinstatement at the 1939 annual Conference at Southport is too complicated a tale to be told here. It is enough perhaps to observe that, if any single grassroots political movement seemed tailor-made to appeal to all that the *New Statesman* had traditionally stood for, this was it.

Initially, there was certainly a good deal of ambivalence (Dick himself signed the 'petition' against Cripps's expulsion). Furthermore all the comments on the affair in the editor's own 'London Diary' tended to be sympathetic towards Cripps and hostile to the naked disciplinary attitude of the Labour Party's own Establishment. It was precisely that, however, which made the *coup de grâce*, when it came, all the more crushing. Dick wrote many brutal articles in the *New Statesman* but never a more savage indictment of any individual than that contained in his report on the Southport Conference of May 1939.† Headed 'Labour Lays a Ghost' it was a no-holds-barred assault upon Cripps: he had, *New Statesman* readers were told, 'not only antagonized the movement but (far more deadly) he has bored it . . . It is the voluntary liquidation of the Left that has made this conference important'.[32]

It can hardly have been the kind of thing that most of the *New Statesman*'s audience expected to hear – though it clearly delighted the Labour leadership (with Dalton cheerfully chortling in his *Diary*: 'I recognise signs of my own inspiration'[33]). And to be fair, there was never any reluctance on Dick's part to give Kingsley

---

* The original 'Unity Manifesto' – the work of the Communist Party, the Socialist League and the Independent Labour Party – had been published on 17 January 1937. Cripps, who financed the Socialist League, was the most prominent member of the orthodox Labour Party to give it support. Later, after the League had been wound up, he issued his own 'Unity Memorandum', circulating it to constituency Parties on 13 January 1939.

† It was all the more remarkable as Dick attended the Conference not merely as a journalist but as an accredited delegate. He had actually been mandated by the Oxford Constituency Labour Party to vote against Cripps's expulsion!

Martin the credit for having published it – on one occasion actually blurting out, 'I'm quite sure I myself would never have done so'.[34] Alas, however, it proved to be an isolated act of political courage on the part of the *New Statesman*'s editor, who became more and more of a tormented – not to say terrified* – soul as war approached through the summer of 1939.

Dick's own complaints became increasingly vocal. In August 1939 he wrote to Zita reporting on 'the usual tussle with Kingsley, only worse';[35] the week war broke out he speculated hopefully on the prospect of the editor's resignation (hinting that he thought 'the managing staff' would welcome it);[36] and finally his indignation boiled over in a letter to his wife beginning:

> If there is anything I hate more than Chamberlain, it is gutless socialists. Kingsley is now glooming around London, saying that the situation is hopeless. Dorothy† finds that this is an imperialist war after all. How I hate all that sort of humbug! They just find ways out and are not even as honest as Mr Chamberlain.[37]

All in all, it was probably just as well that Dick soon found himself removed from the *New Statesman*'s orbit by being drafted into the new Ministry of Information. At first, the prospect of 'war work' excited him: 'Well, I am a Civil Servant, liaison officer between the "Dynamo Group" (brains trust) and "Production" of home staff, salary £750 so that's not too bad',[38] but it did not take long for excitement to be replaced by disillusion. The harsh truth was that at the beginning of the war the Ministry of Information was a completely aimless organisation – a random collection of writers, journalists and academics hurriedly assembled in the Senate House of London University with remarkably little idea of what their purpose or their function was supposed to be. To begin with, Dick undoubtedly did his conscientious best, even trying to summon up enthusiasm for a public service poster campaign encouraging people to smile. But it was not long before he was confessing:

> So far this Ministry is not really there and is spending nearly all its

---

* At one stage, according to his biographer, Kingsley Martin even contemplated plastic surgery in order to escape capture – and what he believed would be certain execution – if the Germans invaded Britain.[31]

† Dorothy Woodman ran the Union of Democratic Control. She had lived with Kingsley Martin for many years and had a formidable influence – usually exercised in a fellow-travelling direction – upon his thinking.

time distributing jobs. Apart from my salary, I am still doubtful
what I am meant to do![39]

He was not alone in his bewilderment; Lord Beaverbrook's *Daily
Express* (which had taken a hostile attitude towards the Ministry
from the beginning) was soon daily announcing defections from it.
Dick's own resignation surfaced on 7 December 1939 and was
accompanied, at least in the *Express*, by a slightly portentous statement from a young man who was not yet thirty-two:

> Although my colleagues in the editorial division are willing and
> able to do a really good job of work, they have not been given a
> chance yet. I did not feel the work I was doing was sufficient to
> justify my salary nor did I see how, in present conditions, it was
> likely to become so in the future.[40]

The reference to 'present conditions' must have been intended as a
veiled criticism of 'the phoney war', by which Dick, along with
others, was becoming increasingly frustrated. Surprisingly,
however, the thought of volunteering for the forces – as Malcolm
Muggeridge, with whom he had shared an office in the University
Senate House, promptly did – does not seem to have occurred to
him. Instead, Dick limped back to the *New Statesman*, even setting
himself up in a bedsitting-room on the top floor of its Lincoln's Inn
Fields offices.

With his return, which must have been something of a humiliation, the fight appears to have gone out of him. There are no
further reports of 'tussles' with Kingsley Martin; if anything,
indeed, the peace-minded editor seems to have begun to influence
his more warlike colleague. A couple of signed articles that Dick
wrote in the first two months of 1940 serve as uncomfortable
reminders of just how difficult it had become to maintain a belliger-
ent spirit in face of a war in which little, if anything, ever seemed to
happen.

The first – proudly described by Kingsley Martin in an editorial as
'a striking article' containing 'propositions which will seem truisms
to some readers and infuriate others'[41] – was basically concerned
with the theme of whether there was any real compatibility between
the objectives of Britain and France. Entitled 'British War Aims
and French Security', its highbrow content fully reflected its
academic headline; and it would scarcely be worth disinterring
today were it not for the inclusion within it of two sentences reveal-

ing just how far Dick's own morale had slipped since the brave, buoyant days of September 1939:

> The only basis on which French security and Germany's reasonable rights can be reconciled is that Great Britain should accept its full share of responsibility for the maintenance of law and order in Europe. This is equally true whether the issue of the war is complete victory or stalemate and whatever the area of Europe that can be freed from Nazi domination.[42]

However it is looked at, that last phrase is surely capable of only one meaning: by 1940 even Dick was prepared to embrace the notion of 'a negotiated peace' – and furthermore was ready for it to be negotiated on the basis of leaving at least some subject peoples under Hitler's control. It was certainly not what he had believed six months earlier, nor is it at all what he would be proclaiming some six months later; but in the ordinary and reasonable meaning of words it is hard to see that there was anything much to separate him from, say, Lord Halifax,* in the third week of January 1940.

Dick's second article, which followed within a month, was probably even more vulnerable, at least in terms of its presentation. Headed 'What Can We Offer Germany?'[43] it sounded as if it was a deployment of the classic appeasement case; but in reality Dick was doing no more than offer a commentary on an already published declaration from the Labour Party entitled 'War and Peace'. Once again, however, some hostages were offered to fortune. There was, for instance, the blunt statement, 'Victory by old-fashioned means or by old-fashioned blockade is almost impossible for either side' and (perhaps even worse) the resigned admission, 'It is foolish – and impossible – to attempt the re-creation of Poland, Czechoslovakia and Austria as they were in 1933' – to say nothing of the now familiar forecast, 'A stalemate is probable.'[44] The main core of the article represented, however, a somewhat desperate effort to harness the chariots of war to the forward march of socialism.

Did Dick suffer any twinges of guilt about those two articles? The question is a legitimate one – if only because by June 1940 (with France overrun, the Low Countries occupied and Norway lost) Dick appeared to be posing it himself. In the last signed article he was to write in the *New Statesman* before returning to 'war work' he had

---

* As Foreign Secretary in, first, Chamberlain's and then (briefly) Churchill's Cabinet, Halifax persisted in exploring every possibility of a negotiated peace long after war had been declared.

this to say (and the personal echoes can hardly have escaped his more perceptive readers):

> Can it be that the controversy about war and peace aims which filled the winter months was just an *Ersatz* for real war? Certainly when you are fighting for bare existence the questions 'Why should we fight?' and 'What are we fighting for?' become superfluous. On the other hand, if we survive this summer, the creation of a Fifth Column in the Reich should be our main winter preoccupation.[45]

Those were prophetic words – for over the next five years Dick was to be engaged in doing exactly that.

8 Psychological Warrior

The exact date Dick began what he would always afterwards refer to as his 'top secret work' during the war remains cloudy. The truth seems to be that he drifted into it. Even during his time at the Ministry of Information he had been regularly broadcasting in the overseas service of the BBC and continued to do so once he had returned to the *New Statesman* in December 1939. He was no longer simply a freelance; he was one of a team delivering a series of daily talks* – addressed primarily to German workers – that the BBC put out in its European news service during the period of the phoney war. As slightly forlorn endeavours intended to appeal to the remnants of the Social Democratic opposition within the Third Reich, they do not seem to have been particularly effective; but at least they represented an attempt to deploy propaganda-by-wireless as a weapon of war.

The beginnings, though, appear to have been distinctly amateur. Dick would go into Broadcasting House every Wednesday evening to record a talk in German that would be put out early the next morning. The first effort to put things on a more formal footing arose when the Director-General who had succeeded Reith, F. W. Ogilvie, expressed an interest in seeing Dick. The casualness of the arrangements then prevailing is reflected in the note Dick wrote to the D-G in response to his invitation:

---

* Dick operated under the supervision of a BBC producer called Edward Shackleton. Later, as Lord Shackleton, he was to be Dick's Cabinet colleague in Harold Wilson's second Labour Government. Shackleton's immediate superior – and in effect the editor of the Workers' Talks series – was another future Cabinet colleague, Patrick Gordon Walker.

I seem to be in and about Broadcasting House a lot these days. Next Monday I am broadcasting at 1 o'clock and I am there again Wednesday evening if you would have time to see me for a moment.[1]

On that letter Ogilvie simply scribbled in his own handwriting: 'Saw Crossman for an hour and discussed his German broadcasts and home and foreign propaganda'.[2]

It hardly sounded as if, in the normal course of events, much would have flowed from that meeting. But events, of course, with the Germans invading the Low Countries early in May 1940 and the Dunkirk evacuation taking place by the end of the month, were ceasing to seem normal. And it was not perhaps a surprise that the new Prime Minister, Winston Churchill, who came to power on 10 May 1940, should have decided that the country's propaganda effort needed a radical overhaul.

For Dick initially that meant his recruitment to a clandestine branch of the War Office known as MI(R), standing for Military Intelligence (Research).[3] Its headquarters had been in a building off the Embankment named Electra House, but at the outbreak of war part of it had moved to the relative safety of the indoor riding school at Woburn Abbey in Bedfordshire. It was there that Dick – who seems to have been recommended to the War Office by Quintin Hogg, the victor of the 1938 Oxford by-election[4] – first surfaced in June 1940.

Woburn – or 'the Country Headquarters' as it became known in Intelligence parlance – was at that stage in something of a twilight era. While Neville Chamberlain remained Prime Minister, it had been the personal fiefdom of a Canadian named Sir Campbell Stuart, who had run British propaganda in enemy countries at the end of the First World War. His links, however, with the *ancien régime* – as well as being Chamberlain's hand-picked nominee, he was a close friend of Geoffrey Dawson, the appeasement-minded editor of *The Times* – meant that there was little room for him under the new dispensation; and he soon, wisely, withdrew to Canada for the duration of the war. That left Woburn operating in something of a vacuum – a vacuum, however, that was aggressively and noisily filled once Hugh Dalton, already the Minister for Economic Warfare, wrested control of what was then known as the Special Operations Executive (embracing both sabotage and subversion) by the middle of July 1940.

Dalton's arrival on the propaganda scene was good news for Dick. They had been allies during the 1930s in fighting against the prevalent pacifism within the Labour Party; and, although Dalton had reservations about Dick's character, he never had any illusions about his abilities.* One of his first actions on taking over responsibility for Woburn was to decide 'after some highly strung discussion' (presumably with the Foreign Office) that Dick 'should take charge at Woburn of our German Section, including the preparation of leaflets and of secret broadcasts' as well as 'continuing overt broadcasts in German through the BBC'.[6]

That description of Dick's 'top secret' war work was published as long ago as 1957. But, despite its slightly guarded language, it probably provides as good a clue as any to the essentially Jekyll and Hyde role that Dick played at least during the years 1940–3. In one incarnation he was the above-board broadcaster – advising the BBC on the points the Government wanted to be put across to the enemy, delivering talks himself in the German service and even taking part in a regular weekly brains trust called *Was wollen Sie wissen?* (What Do You Want to Know?');† the claim in this programme was that questions had come in from all over Europe but most of them, in fact, were carefully scripted by Dick himself or the producer, Leonard Miall, in the studio. This, however, was still an example of what Dalton called 'overt broadcasting' or what later came to be known as 'white' propaganda.

'Black' propaganda was very different. Here the entire *raison d'être* was deceit – whether in the pretence that a radio station was what it was not (i.e. that it was coming from inside Germany when it was, in fact, being broadcast from within the shores of Britain) or that leaflets, or even miniature newspapers, were being produced by resistance groups in Occupied Europe when they were, in truth, the skilled work of a secret branch of the Special Operations Executive in London. It was Dalton's inspiration to give Dick day-to-day charge of both the 'overt' and 'covert' aspects of these activities so far as they affected Germany; and although it caused some problems – as Dick later vividly put it, while his left hand could always

* Dalton was to write in his wartime diary on 17 September 1941: 'Crossman to dine. I view this able and energetic man with some detachment. He is loyal to his own career but only incidentally to anything or anyone else.'[5]

† This programme had a distinguished panel. In addition to Dick himself, the usual participants were Hugh Carleton Greene (then head of the German service and later Director-General of the BBC), the former university professor, Lindley Fraser (post-war head of the German service) and the well-known actor, Marius Goring, who acted as chairman.

know what his right was doing there were moments when his right hand could not be permitted to know what his left was up to[7] – it was probably the only way of making sure that the two sides of the same coin did not contradict each other.

On the sinister side the origins, admittedly, were very modest. Dick moved full-time to Woburn in July 1940 and, with Zita, took possession of a house named Dawn Edge in a village called Aspley Guise, a few miles from the Abbey.[8] This house became the headquarters of the first of the British clandestine radio stations – or 'research units' as they were always tactfully referred to even in official Government memoranda and minutes. Dawn Edge was run rather like a boarding house at a public school with Dick as 'housemaster' and Zita as 'matron' – both trying to keep in order the sometimes recalcitrant German left-wing *émigrés* who had been recruited as the broadcasters. The station was aptly named *Sender der Europäischen Revolution* ('The European Revolutionary Station'). It first broadcast on 7 October 1940 and continued doing so daily until 22 June 1942, always giving a left-wing view of events; it had originally been envisaged as 'an International Communist station'[9] – and, for that reason, was constantly regarded with some suspicion by both politicians and the Foreign Office. But perhaps its main defect was that it lacked the courage of its fraudulent convictions. At best, it never transmitted anything more than 'pale black' or 'grey' propaganda – since the team behind it always stopped short of offering the illusion that they were broadcasting from inside Germany.[10]

How much time and energy Dick devoted to superintending the output of *Sender der Europäischen Revolution* is not altogether clear. He certainly could not give it his whole attention, since for at least two days a week he was in London supervising the output of the BBC's own German service, recently moved to Bush House in Aldwych. (There he would have regular battles with Hugh Carleton Greene, who, as head of the German service, rightly resisted all efforts to inject too much propaganda into the service's news bulletins.) Dick was also an occasional attender at a curious joint Foreign Office/BBC body known as the Planning and Broadcasting Committee, which met daily and appears to have functioned as a kind of forerunner to the BBC's own subsequent time-wasting Programme Review Boards.* According to the surviving records, he

---

* Dick was later to write, in reference to the Planning and Broadcasting Committee, of its 'atmosphere of club chat and unconscious incompetence'. RHSC, notes on his American visit, entry dated 30 September 1942.

attended it, as a Government representative, for the first time on Saturday 29 June 1940 – even if as late as March 1941 he was still plaintively asking for 'a formal desk' to be kept available for him at Bush House.[11] The proceedings of this body were not momentous – witness the following early extract from its minutes:

> Mr Murray stated that Mr Sefton Delmer had suggested that he would be better employed in putting over talks of a comic, racy nature rather than the ideological talks he had up to now been asked to broadcast. The committee agreed with his suggestion in principle and took note of the fact that he was able to speak Berlin slang, and was capable of introducing comic songs into his talks where suitable.[12]

Dick had presumably known of the existence of Sefton Delmer long before that – he had, after all, been a famous correspondent for the *Daily Express* in Berlin for much of the 1930s; but this appears to have been the first moment at which their lives had formally crossed. They were to remain closely mingled for the next two and a half years.

Delmer, who did not officially join the Woburn community until the spring of 1941, was hardly the figure of fun that the minute above suggests. In fact, once installed a stone's throw from the Crossmans' house at a villa called Larchfield in Aspley Guise, he rapidly proved himself a master of the 'black' arts at which Dick had displayed the talents of a somewhat nervous novice. Delmer's *Gustav Siegfried Eins* ('George Sugar One') station soon stole all the thunder from the essentially earnest, missionary efforts of *Sender der Europäischen Revolution*. On *Gustav Siegfried Eins*, which started broadcasting on 23 May 1941 (conveniently some two weeks after Rudolf Hess's flight to Britain), there was no drawing back from deceit. The voice that spoke – always referred to as *Der Chef* – masqueraded as a high-ranking Prussian militarist (while actually belonging to a German-born Corporal in the Pioneer Corps); the message that was delivered never wavered – it was that of a patriot fed up with those on the Home Front who were not supporting Hitler zealously enough. *Der Chef* always came over as someone eager to prosecute the war (particularly against 'the Bolsheviks', once Russia had been invaded) far more vigorously than the 'traitors' at home allowed. Perhaps the best indication of the licence that the station enjoyed was that in its first broadcast – beamed from a transmitter secure in the Home Counties – the British Prime

Minister was referred to as 'that flat-footed bastard of a drunken old Jew, Churchill'.[13]

To the staff at Woburn it must have seemed as if Dick had significantly extended the frontiers of his personal empire. That was not, however, exactly the case: a secret document headed 'Decisions taken – weekend 24–25 May 1941'[14] makes it clear that higher authority had decreed almost from the start that Delmer and Dick should be co-equals, with the division of responsibility between them being almost exactly that between 'white' and 'black' propaganda (although Dick retained charge of the 'pale black' or 'grey' station functioning in his own house, Dawn Edge). Of course, by now he was also much more used to the ways of Whitehall than was Delmer; and it, therefore, fell to him to defend the interests of this secret subversive department when they came under attack, as from time to time they were probably bound to do.

The first such attack, rather woundingly, came from within. One of the inevitable consequences of Dick's arrival – followed almost a year later by that of Delmer – had been to upset those who had been at Woburn since the day war broke out (and who had managed to survive the enforced departure of Sir Campbell Stuart in June 1940). One of these was the distinguished former *Manchester Guardian* correspondent in Berlin, F. A. Voigt. Ten years older than Dick, he had served as 'Adviser on Germany' first to Campbell Stuart, and then to his immediate successor, Reginald Leeper of the Political Intelligence Department of the Foreign Office. Voigt's own anti-Nazi credentials could hardly have been more impressive. He had reported on the March 1933 elections which brought Hitler to power with such clarity and vigour that it was impossible for him thereafter to return to Germany; he had become, instead, the *Manchester Guardian*'s diplomatic correspondent. As such, he had always tended to follow the line taken by Robert Vansittart, Permanent Under-Secretary at the Foreign Office 1930–8, and then shunted into being merely 'Chief Diplomatic Adviser to the Foreign Secretary'. For him, as for Vansittart, there was no such thing as an opposition to Hitler in Germany, and anyone was wasting his time who believed that there was. He was, therefore, fundamentally out of sympathy with Dick's 'workers' broadcasts' and even more enraged by the presence of German *émigrés* attempting to preach socialist revolution within the Woburn complex.

It is possible, of course, that there were other reasons for his clash with Dick. His own title as 'Adviser on Germany to the Director of the Department' had become a pretty empty one following Dick's appointment as 'Head of the German Section'; it ceased to have any meaning at all once Dalton had put his own imprint on the whole tortuous Woburn chain of command. In any event, by the spring of 1941, Voigt's rage poured out into a 52-page memorandum to the Foreign Office. This was, in effect, a blanket indictment of all that the German Section – of what was still then known as SO1 – was trying to achieve. Its central thrust was pithily summed up in a minute that Con O'Neill, a former member of the Diplomatic Service and now in Military Intelligence (who served as Dick's alternate both at Woburn and at Bush House), promptly wrote in reply:

> The principal contention of this memorandum is that our propaganda to Germany is, in a last analysis, pro-German. Such a defect would, of course, be fatal.
>
> By attacking National Socialism instead of our real enemy, the German nation, we endear Hitler and the National Socialists to that nation and, instead of 'driving a wedge between them', we achieve the exact opposite (insofar as we achieve anything at all).[15]

With his message summed up in those blunt terms (and elsewhere O'Neill did not fail to detect that the whole thrust of the memorandum was directed personally at Dick) it was hard to see how Voigt could expect to survive as a member of the team. And he had, in fact, taken the precaution of resigning before his memorandum surfaced at Woburn, though not before it had been read within the Foreign Office.[16]

That was not, however, the last that Dick was to hear of Voigt – for he had powerful friends and knew how to mount a campaign from outside. It seems probable, indeed, that the three episodes over the next twelve months in which Dick found himself warding off attacks on both Delmer and himself were all Voigt-inspired. The first involved criticism expressed at ministerial level of the German Section's output – about which Dick heard from Sir Robert Bruce Lockhart, who had become in effect his new boss, ranking above Reginald Leeper, in August 1940. To his credit, Dick soon demonstrated that he could fight his own corner. His minute to Lockhart began in suitably abrasive form:

> I cannot help at the outset expressing my surprise that a discussion of our German service on a ministerial level should come out

of criticism on which the German section has had no opportunity to comment.[17]

No doubt, Dick had a shrewd idea of where that 'criticism' must have come from; but, having got that complaint off his chest, he was prudent enough to adopt an uncharacteristically emollient tone: 'No one recognises better than I how often we fail to do what we wish, how often our information fails to be phrased in precisely the right way for interesting Germany, how often the skeleton of the plan sticks out through the flesh of information.'[18]

By such diplomatic tactics this particular attack appears to have been effortlessly repulsed – indeed, within two months Dick was having a 'very friendly' meeting with Brendan Bracken, Churchill's Minister of Information, who assured him that he would never 'let him down in reply to a Parliamentary Question by some Tory who picks a phrase out of its context and suggests that our broadcasts are pro-German'.[19]

A much more damaging assault – if only because it went to the heart of the 'covert' side of Woburn's work – surfaced at roughly the same time. The September 1941 issue of the *National Review*, edited by Lady Milner, carried an editorial note criticising the moral tone of Delmer's radio station, *Gustav Siegfried Eins*, and hinting heavily that it was not as remote from British influence as it might seem. The initial instinct seems to have been to ignore this highly compromising criticism, at least in terms of any public controversy – although Brendan Bracken later sent a particularly sharp private letter to Lady Milner asking for an undertaking that it should not be repeated.[20] When, however, the allegations surfaced again in two Rothermere newspapers early in 1942, Dick was sufficiently incensed to dispatch a 'Most Secret' memorandum to the new Political Warfare Executive.* Dated '9 February 1942', it began:

The recent article by Quentin Varley in the *Daily Mail* and front-page splash by the Diplomatic Correspondent of the *Daily Dispatch* bring to a head a matter which for some weeks has been causing me concern. It is common knowledge that the former was inspired by Mr Voigt and the latter by Mr Loeb, both of whom

---

* The Political Warfare Executive became the supervising arm for British propaganda. Formed to bring some unity to the scattered work of those in three Ministries – the Foreign Office, the Ministry of Economic Warfare and the Ministry of Information – it functioned with reasonable effectiveness. This was largely thanks to its Director-General, Sir Robert Bruce Lockhart.

claim to have the ear of Lord Vansittart. These two gentlemen have for some months been carrying on a campaign in the Press and, even more in the clubs and lobbies, against PWE, more particularly its German Section. Mr Voigt has not been averse from using knowledge gained during his tenure of office in a secret department.[21]

In the light of the attitude Dick was later to adopt towards Cabinet secrets, it was perhaps an odd posture for him to take up. But, in fairness, there must always be a distinction between national security in wartime and the requirements of mere political confidentiality in peacetime. In any event, the use to which the Germans put the information that had obligingly been made available to them soon made Dick's point for him. Three months later, he wrote an even more magisterial minute, this time direct to Lockhart:

URGENT   MOST SECRET

To: The Director-General   *Date: 3 May 1942*

In the German weekly paper *Das Reich* of 26 April there appeared the first open attack in German propaganda on a German RU as worked from England. The relevant sentences run: 'This station has long been located by *Der Sender* [The German state radio service]. It was in Scotland – quite a long way from the Postsdamer Platz. And it is not an efficient German policeman who silenced it, but a British peer, by the name of Robert Vansittart. This man described it as intolerable that German *émigrés* working for the British propaganda service should try to turn the German people not only against Hitler but also against England . . .

After careful consideration of this passage, Delmer and I are both forced to the conclusion that it was the reference to this RU in the *National Review* which tipped the Germans off about the situation here and so provided them with an admirable weapon for discrediting the RU . . .

Delmer and I both feel that this is a cardinal matter of principle affecting the very existence of the work in which we are engaged. I do not see how we can continue the work unless the security necessary to its success is rigidly enforced.[22]

That minute is perhaps interesting for two reasons – first, for marking the one moment in the war when *Gustav Siegfried Eins* all but had its cover blown and, second, for what it reveals about the close working relationship which at that time existed between Delmer and Dick. They were not easily compatible characters – Delmer was Rabelaisian by nature and Falstaffian in appearance – and in the post-war years something of a well-mannered duel was to develop between them as to who deserved the greater credit for the success of British wartime propaganda (with Dick championing the cause of its 'white' aspects and Delmer the 'black'). But while it mattered – and when the future of the organisation for which they both worked was under threat – Dick always seems to have been prepared to throw a protective cloak around his more unorthodox colleague. Even when Delmer started deliberately injecting pornography into *Der Chef*'s scripts on *Gustav Siegfried Eins* no open criticism came from Dick. (It may, though, well have been his own socialist *émigrés* on the rival European Revolution station at Dawn Edge who translated *Der Chef*'s most offensive script – describing a sexual orgy organised by a German Admiral – and arranged for it to be passed to Sir Stafford Cripps. According to Delmer, Cripps promptly announced: 'If this is the kind of thing we have to do to win the war, I would rather lose it!')[23] However, throughout the two and a half years they worked together, Delmer perhaps never quite appreciated how fortunate he was. He seldom seems to have taken any political flak,* whereas Dick was almost constantly under fire, particularly from right-wing Conservatives in the House of Commons.†

Sometimes, of course, he brought his troubles upon himself. What Bruce Lockhart was later to call 'my most unpleasant experience of the war'[25] was directly Dick's fault. In retrospect it cannot help all looking a bit of a storm in a tea-cup; but it was perhaps typical of Dick's insensitivity that he should have trampled over what is always one of the most delicate frontiers in politics – that between Service Chiefs and the Ministers to whom they are responsible. What happened, briefly, was this. In July 1942 Air Marshal Arthur ('Bomber') Harris had been asked if he would contribute an article to a new miniature magazine that PWE proposed to have dropped over Germany. When the article came in and landed on Dick's desk, he thought it was far too good to be wasted on some

* Remarkably, Delmer's name never appears in Hugh Dalton's *Second World War Diary*.

† On 25 March 1942 the Foreign Secretary, Anthony Eden, had to receive a deputation of MPs in his room in the House of Commons and assure them that Dick was neither a Bolshevist nor a Fascist.[24]

RAF random drop.* He immediately set to work to change it into a broadcast that could be put out not just to Germany but in various languages, to all of Occupied Europe on the BBC's European service. At first sight, this might have appeared an imaginative decision; but, alas, it left entirely out of account the fact that, under wartime regulations, leaflets dropped on enemy territory were not open to discussion in Parliament whereas normal BBC foreign broadcasts (though not, of course, the clandestine ones emanating from Woburn) were part of the public domain. 'Bomber' Harris's language had been predictably robust – and, to be fair to Dick, he had toned it down a bit before knocking it into shape as a broadcast script. He had, for example, removed two sentences in which the Air Marshal originally wrote: 'America has hardly entered the fight yet. She is like a boxer donning his gloves before the fight, and let me tell you a secret – she is putting a horse-shoe in those gloves, just for luck.'[26]

Unfortunately, Dick had not sufficiently bowdlerised Harris's *penchant* for the bullying phrase. He had, for instance, left untouched a particularly menacing paragraph reading:

> You have no chance. Soon we shall be coming every night and every day. Rain, blow or snow – we and the Americans. I have just spent 8 months in America so I know exactly what is coming. We are going to scourge the Third Reich from end to end if you make it necessary for us to do so. You cannot stop it and you know it.

Worse than that, Dick had obviously thought the broadcast would benefit from a political *coda* at the end. He had written this himself and it ran as follows:

> One final thing. It is up to you to end the war and the bombing. You can overthrow the Nazis and make peace. It is not true that we plan a peace of revenge. That is a German propaganda lie. But we shall certainly make it impossible for any German government

---

* Dick always took a low view of the effectiveness of leaflets as an arm of propaganda. In a lecture delivered to the Royal United Services Institution on 20 February 1952 he declared: 'In the last war we wasted a great deal of paper on strategic leaflets. We asked the RAF on their bombing raids to drop leaflets, although they did not like doing it. The leaflets were dropped from a great height and drifted down in the countryside over an area of 50 square miles. It was a very wasteful way of getting information to the enemy when the radio could do it so much better.'

to start a total war again. And is not that as necessary in your interests as in ours?[27]

Quite apart from the inbuilt contradiction with the Air Marshal's own words ('You cannot stop it and you know it'), Dick had committed a grave constitutional sin – he had put political sentiments into the mouth of a serving officer. Retribution was not slow in coming. The broadcast – apparently avoiding any fail-safe checks – had gone out on the evening of 28 July 1942. Three days later Dick received this stern memo from Bruce Lockhart as Director-General of the Political Warfare Executive:

PERSONAL AND SECRET

Mr Crossman

The Minister of Information has directed me to obtain from you at the earliest possible moment a report on your activities in connection with the message broadcast to the German people in the name of Air Marshal Harris on July 28.

Your report should bear particular reference to the following two points:

(1) What authority did you obtain for broadcasting a message that was prepared for a miniature magazine to be dropped by air?

(2) On whose authority did you insert a political paragraph into a message to be delivered in the name of a Commander-in-Chief? I should be grateful if you would let me have this report in duplicate for submission to the two Ministers.*

R.H.B.L.[28]

It does not require any great intimacy with the workings of Whitehall to gather from the tone of that memo that a search for a scapegoat was afoot. And for the next two weeks – since he had no real answer to either of Bruce Lockhart's questions – Dick's job seems to have been on the line. The Coalition Government even had to endure the embarrassment of a debate in the House of Lords. There the veteran leader of the Labour Opposition, Lord Addison, not only took the obvious point that 'statements about the peace should be made by responsible Ministers' but went on roundly to say that the broadcast had been 'so bombastic that anyone might have thought Mussolini had made it – it is not a British habit to brag

---

* Anthony Eden, the Foreign Secretary, and Brendan Bracken, the Minister of Information. The Ministry of Economic Warfare was no longer concerned with propaganda to the enemy once Hugh Dalton left it in February 1942.

in advance'.[29] More seriously for the Government, his protest was endorsed by one Liberal and two Conservative peers.[30]

However, Dick was not entirely without supporters (though his name, of course, never surfaced in public). Since the text of the broadcast had been made available to the newspapers – standard practice with 'white' propaganda – there was a predictable Press flurry; yet the *News Chronicle* was not alone in wondering whether a mountain was not being made out of a molehill:

> Why all the fuss about Air Marshal Harris's broadcast message on the present and future bombing of Germany?
>
> All Sir Arthur did was to set forth, with brusque force, for the edification of the enemy, the strategical intention which the Air Minister himself has been pronouncing for months past.[31]

From the politicians' point of view that, of course, was precisely the question at issue; but, luckily, the Prime Minister himself – to whom the matter had to be referred – was never a man obsessed by the delicacies of protocol. The message eventually percolated down that Churchill 'had read the Air Marshal's message and had found it good'.[32] After that, it only remained for the disciplinary ends to be tied up – and, on the whole, Dick got off lightly. He received an official reprimand, if one expressed in markedly generous terms:

17 August 1942

My dear Dick,

The Ministerial Inquest on the Harris broadcast is now ended, and I have been instructed to take the necessary disciplinary action.

Ministerial criticism was directed mainly against mistakes in procedure and both Ministers were perturbed by the irresponsible manner in which a British Commander-in-Chief was invited to send a message of any kind to the German people without the prior approval of the responsible Ministers and the officials of PWE. The failure to ensure that the Commander-in-Chief was informed of the decision to broadcast a message given solely on the understanding that it was to be used as a leaflet was particularly unfortunate. Commanders-in-Chief are in a very different position from that of Ministers of the Crown and are entitled to proper protection.

The Ministers decided that the major, but not the whole, blame for this incident attaches to yourself. I consider your work of the greatest value to PWE. Otherwise I would not have wasted weeks of precious time in order to defend it. But I am not disposed to disagree with the ministerial verdict, and I think it a pity that you should sometimes jeopardise your own good work and the prestige of the department by excess of zeal and by a tendency to disregard the irksome but necessary rules of procedure which govern all forms of administrative life. It is not a question of what you think is the best propaganda. You have to be sure that this fits into the general pattern of HMG policy for which Ministers have to assume responsibility. There is no need for me to labour the points, for I am sure you understand them perfectly.

As regards action, I have given a personal guarantee that the errors of procedure will not recur, and I have to inform you that we have now reached a stage of the war when mistakes, not only of procedure but still more of policy and discretion, will have more serious consequences than heretofore. I am sure you will take these remarks in the spirit in which they are meant, act upon the advice and forget about an incident which has already wasted too much time.

Yours ever,

R.H.B.L.[33]

To that letter an obviously chastened Dick replied in an appropriately contrite fashion within a day or two:

Centre Block,
Bush House,
Aldwych WC2

Dear Director-General,

Thank you for your letter of the 17th. It gives me a chance to write what I have wanted for some time to say to you. No one has the right to expect his boss to waste a week defending him from execution. But you did; and the least I can do in return is to take your advice, suborn zeal and prove to you that I was worth the wasted week.

Yours ever,

DICK[34]

That exchange of letters – reflecting well, it should be said, on both parties – appears to have closed the incident. But it is hard to believe that it did not leave some sediment. Certainly, it seems suspicious that, within five weeks, Dick should have been packed off to the United States – the first visit he had ever made there. Other reasons could, however, have partly accounted for this American trip. In the first place, there was obviously a need for British psychological war experts to liaise with their American counterparts now that the United States had been in the war for nine months; and Dick, with his knowledge of Germany, was the obvious man to do it (the Queen's brother, David Bowes-Lyon, was already there heading a British Political Warfare mission in Washington but he was more of an administrator than a German expert).

Second, though, there could well have been personal motives that prompted Dick to welcome at least a temporary change of scene. His own 'pale black' European Revolution station at Woburn had ceased broadcasting on 22 June 1942 – largely because its German refugee staff had never really managed to grapple with the implications of the entry of the Soviet Union into the war a year earlier. Dick's own prime political patron, Hugh Dalton, had also been removed from the propaganda scene on being kicked upstairs from the Ministry of Economic Warfare to the Presidency of the Board of Trade. Dalton's departure meant that Woburn had ceased to be the centre for psychological warfare, at least so far as 'overt' propaganda was concerned. Dick was more and more based in London which, though it caused him no personal hardship, meant that a new home (in place of Dawn Edge) had to be found for Zita. She eventually settled at Town End Farm at Radnage in Buckinghamshire, which Dick leased in 1942. For the first time since 1940, when they moved from Oxford to Aspley Guise, Dick and his wife were, therefore, leading relatively separate existences. This, no doubt, made it all the more important for him to cement family ties;* and it so happened that both Zita's children, Venice and Gilbert, had been evacuated to America just after the beginning of the war. The trip to the United States thus gave Dick the opportunity of visiting them, which was more than their mother or father – at a time of strictly 'reserved air passages' – could possibly hope to do. (Dick duly went to see them in New Haven on his first available Sunday – something that both of them still remember.)

Despite all that, however, it still seems likely that there was an element of bureaucratic convenience in the decision to send Dick to Washington and New York at this particular juncture. Certainly, there was a perceptible echo of the controversy over the Air Marshal Harris broadcast in the somewhat inhibiting instructions with

---

* Dick's own family feeling may never have been particularly pronounced. The loss of his youngest brother Tom in an RAF flying accident in 1940, followed by the death of his father (Mr Justice Crossman) a year later, could well, however, have made him more conscious of the significance of the family as an institution.

which he was issued before he left. These came from Brigadier
Dallas Brooks, the War Office liaison officer to the Political Warfare Executive, and they were not perhaps as gracefully expressed as
they would have been had they been composed by Bruce Lockhart
himself:

> In connection with your forthcoming visit to the United States,
> you will abide by the following instructions:
>
> (1) In no circumstances are you to give an interview to the
> Press. You should try to avoid all contact with the Press.
>
> (2) It should be clearly understood that you are not in a
> position to commit HM Government to any line of action.
> Your mission must be confined: –
>
> (a) To a presentation and discussion of a draft appreciation of
> the situation in Germany.
>
> (b) To the preparation and discussion of the line to be adopted
> in interpreting developments in Germany in propaganda.
>
> (c) To discussing how (a) and (b) should be embodied in any
> joint plan for political warfare against Germany.
>
> *18 September 1942*   DSB, *Brigadier*[35]

It was a fairly peremptory note – and its tone was also partly
explained by the fact that Dick and Brigadier Brooks had already
had one run-in some six months earlier. In March 1942 Dick had
taken it upon himself to put forward a proposal for a PWE-inspired
Press campaign to be launched at home in favour of the lifting of the
blackout. The Brigadier had either failed to grasp what was in
Dick's mind or, if he did understand it, had dismissed it as 'too
clever by half'. Certainly, Dick appears to have been slightly
aggrieved by the refusal even to consider what he plainly regarded
as one of his more ingenious propaganda ploys:

> I fear I am returning again to the charge because I think our little
> idea has been misunderstood. My paper does *not* suggest the
> abolition of the blackout but only a Press campaign, organised by
> us, in favour of its abolition. You will see from my original para
> (4) that the proposal does not consider the possibility of the
> Government yielding to the campaign. What we need for our
> purposes is merely a public opinion impatient of the blackout,
> expressing their impatience and thus being a useful instrument of
> propaganda to Germany.[36]

Predictably, the idea still does not appear to have prospered – and it

may have been just as well (at least for his relationship with Brigadier Brooks) that Dick held most such inspirations in check during
his American visit.* In fact, the main untoward incident that
occurred arose from Dick's discovery that the Americans had for
some months been relying on the broadcasts delivered by *Der Chef*
on the *Gustav Siegfried Eins* station for their information about
German morale. (This had presented David Bowes-Lyon with a
very delicate problem; eventually he had obtained permission to go
to the White House and own up.)[37] The knowledge that this had
happened must, however, have had some impact on Dick's own
private reservations about the usefulness of 'black' propaganda.
Certainly, shortly after he returned from America in mid-October
1942, he was far from reassured to learn that plans were already
under way for the British 'black' propaganda effort to be stepped
up: his view seems to have been that, with a new station designed
specifically to demoralise German U-Boat crews[38] about to be
added to *Gustav Siegfried Eins*, Delmer's monster was in danger of
getting out of control.

How far this feeling of unease led Dick to look elsewhere for a
fresh role can only be a matter for conjecture.[39] Afterwards Dick
tended to pin the blame for his departure on the feud between Bush
House and Woburn, but there was never much secret that he dif-
fered with Delmer over the need to inject pornography into both
broadcasts and leaflets.† Delmer's position, though, had grown very
strong: there was even a suspicion that he operated in some way
under royal protection. (George VI had visited Woburn in November 1941[40] and had apparently been very impressed by what he saw
of the 'black' propaganda side of the business.) Now, with quite
independent links with Naval Intelligence forged through his new
U-Boat station, Delmer was almost invulnerable.

It took some time, however, for Dick to gain his release and
achieve another sphere in which to deploy his undoubted talents.
What came to his rescue were the 'Torch' Anglo-American land-
ings in North Africa in November 1942 and Harold Macmillan's

---

* A contemporary account does, however, have him saying to Colonel Bill
Donovan of the American OSS: 'We know you want us out of India – why not give
us North Africa instead?'
 † One of Delmer's more famous leaflets was a two-page folding affair. The first
page showed a bleak, snow-covered soldier's grave somewhere on the Russian
front; inside there was a picture of a naked flaxen-haired girl about to mount the
erect phallus of a dark-skinned man, who was plainly intended to be a foreign
worker. Delmer later played the same trick with Aryan girls and Japanese soldiers.

subsequent arrival in Algiers as Minister Resident in the Middle East (and, in effect, political adviser to General Eisenhower) one month later. This first joint Anglo-American military venture was supposed to be 'joint' at all levels and this meant that Macmillan had need of his own psychological warfare experts to match those of the Americans. No records reveal how the lot fell to Dick: the first intimation of his new role surfaces in a personal memo dated 10 February 1943 reminding the Director-General of PWE of the need to announce the name of his successor as head of the German Section 'before the end of this week as I shall be taking up my new appointment'.[41] Even so, nothing appears to have happened for some months. Indeed, the first recorded meeting between Macmillan and Dick did not take place till June 1943* – although the fact that Dick wrote afterwards of his period in Algiers as 'the most exhilarating five months of my life'[43] suggests that he probably arrived in May (he was invalided home in October).

The success of Dick's relationship with Macmillan was perhaps foreseeable – they were, after all, both intellectuals interested in books and ideas. Even so, for someone never much given to hero worship, Dick's attitude to his new boss was remarkable. Indeed, when he was desperately ill back in England with phlebitis in November 1943, Zita wrote a personal letter to Macmillan containing a striking personal confession:

> The other day, when he was at a very low ebb, he made me smile by saying 'Nowadays I sometimes think what I would like my last words to be and, I'm awfully sorry, but they're not addressed to you, they are to Harold Macmillan. Tell him that I wanted to go on working with him.'[44]

And, if on a different level, the regard was reciprocated.† In his own contemporary diary Macmillan was unstinting in his praise – referring to Dick one month as 'intelligent, humane and loyal' and then the next as 'a very able chap [who is] working splendidly'.[45]

Perhaps less predictably, as Macmillan also noted, Dick was a great success with the Americans – particularly with his own

---

* Macmillan mentions the presence of 'Dick Crossman (Political Warfare)' at dinner in his villa on 17 June 1943 in his diary, adding the comment: 'Pleasant talk about books and Greek philosophy. A nice change!'[42]

† Dick got a letter from Macmillan in December in which the latter wrote: 'I hope that the friendship that we have formed may be taken up at a later date and that perhaps we may find ourselves doing some work together in those years which will be dignified by the name of peace.' In fact, Macmillan and Dick spoke together only once after 1945.

opposite number, C. D. Jackson, formerly an executive with *Time* magazine (and later to become the man who broke up the marriage of the British Foreign Secretary, Anthony Eden). After years of constriction in Whitehall Dick obviously found the spirit of the New World, with its lack of inhibitions, particularly liberating:

> We enjoyed in those months one American quality which I think enabled all of us to do a better job than we had done before. In Britain, even in wartime, the instinctive reaction of those at the top to a new idea coming up from below is to crab it. But the American military mind delights in innovation, like the American civilian mind. One only has to convince an American general that one has found a way to shorten the war and reduce its casualties, and at once he is working out the logistics of trying it out.[46]

Dick always liked to quote one instance of that instinct in action – the Italian armistice negotiations of August 1943. In truth, the protracted way these were handled represented a great lost opportunity for the Allied cause; but it was Dick's own view that things would have been even worse but for the resourcefulness of Allied Force Headquarters in Algiers. According to his version of events, after waiting in vain for five days for any policy directive from Washington or London, following Marshal Badoglio's intimation of Italy's readiness to surrender, Macmillan proposed – and Eisenhower accepted – that AFHQ should simply draft an Anglo-American directive of its own and send it for clearance to the Combined Chiefs of Staff, the White House and No. 10. This duly happened – 'and from that moment on we realised that Eisenhower's Anglo-American command could always in an emergency reckon on bicker between London and Washington, bicker which could only be ended by our proposing the solution'.[47]

That Dick, who held no military rank and seldom himself ever wore uniform, should have come to have the respect that he did for serving officers was an improbable development; but he came greatly to prefer them to 'the trained diplomats' or 'elected politicians' with whom he had been accustomed to deal in London.[48] It was, therefore, more than a physical misfortune when a fierce wasp's sting in Algiers in October 1943 led to an alarming swelling in his leg and a serious attack of phlebitis. Macmillan arranged for him to be flown home, even solicitiously going to see him off at the airport. He was installed in a nursing home in Bentinck Street, where the phlebitis developed into a thrombosis; for a period it was feared that he might not live.* When he did recover (and it was March 1944 before he was fit again), PWE did its best to claim him back for its own London-based staff. It required all Dick's ingenuity to resist their efforts – and he risked some unpopularity with his former colleagues, including Bruce Lockhart, by lending himself to what was regarded as an American 'intrigue' to secure his services.[50] Their fear, of course, was that if Eisenhower's newly created Psychological Warfare Division – set up in Norfolk House in preparation for D-Day – succeeded in recruiting the most talented people, it would not be long before the military arm became the dominant partner to the civilian one in the propaganda war.

And that, in effect, was what happened. Dick was shrewd in judging that the future lay with Eisenhower – for once D-Day had taken place in June 1944 the Supreme Headquarters of the Allied Expeditionary Force necessarily became the hub even for political warfare. There was no way it could be otherwise: it is the Generals in the field who know, after all, what the enemy's problems are – and that is precisely the information that a psychological warrior needs if his own weaponry is to prove effective. Dick understood this very well – in fact, he always insisted that 'it is only when it has become clear to the enemy that outright victory is impossible that psychological warfare can be used fully and effectively'; and he maintained equally strongly that this was the stage at which 'the strictest co-ordination between psychological warfare strategy and the strategy of the military Commander' becomes imperative.[51]

It did not, of course, always work out like that. One of Dick's favourite anecdotes, used in many lectures afterwards,† concerned the visit that a VIP – Churchill, though Dick never said so – paid to Eisenhower's headquarters just outside Rheims in March 1945. There, as ill-luck would have it, the Prime Minister picked up and read a copy of the US Army paper *Stars and Stripes*. In it was a report of the broadcast instruction being issued to German civilians to keep off the roads so as not to impede the advance of the Allied armies. This instruction appalled Churchill; with memories of the

---

* Dick himself appears to have believed that he was going to die, even asking Zita on one occasion whether he should not see an Anglican priest. A stronger atheist than he was, she urged him to open the Bible at random and read out whatever passage his finger lighted upon. 'I did. I stuck my finger in Colossians. What I read was a verse of sheer nonsense about blood sacrifice. "All right," I said, "I won't see the priest." '[49]

† In the 1950s Dick became a familiar lecturer on psychological warfare at staff colleges. Even as a left-wing Labour MP, he addressed the Nato Defence College in Paris on no fewer than seven occasions.

Luftwaffe dive-bombing French refugees in 1940, he was all in favour of German civilians being incited to evacuate their homes and to crowd the roads in order to block the retreat of the German armies. The rest of the story is best told in Dick's own words:

> That night we received the order to reverse our whole propaganda campaign. I shall never forget the blackness of our despair. We realised that, if we carried out this Very Important Person's 'stunt', we should be breaking the solemn pledge by the Supreme Commander to the German people that no harm would come to them if they obeyed our orders. We also realised, I think, that militarily such a step would be of doubtful value. Our soldiers, unlike the Germans in France, would not shoot down helpless civilians; the crowding of the roads would, therefore, obstruct our Armies more than those of the enemy. Finally, we could not help remembering the indignation expressed in the name of democracy when the Germans had used these techniques four years previously.
>
> Eisenhower's Chief of Staff, General Bedell Smith, was called in, as he always was in a real crisis. 'Do something', he said, 'to satisfy the Old Man – one single thing – and then use your brains to ensure that it doesn't contradict or undermine our main campaign.'[52]

The 'single thing' that PWD eventually decided to do must have brought Dick a feeling of wry satisfaction. Since November 1943 Delmer had been running – with the aid of a new powerful medium-wave transmitter called 'Aspidistra' – a further 'black' station (*Soldatensuder West*) designed specifically to demoralise the German Army. The new orders were put out on this station, while the BBC, Radio Luxemburg and the American Broadcasting Station in Europe continued to broadcast messages in Eisenhower's name urging the civil population to 'stay put' and, if necessary, seek safety in their own cellars. In the murky world of reverse mirrors the opposite instruction to civilians (on *Soldatensuder West*) – to abandon their homes and flee to the east – was issued, appropriately, in the pretended name of the German authorities.[53]

That was virtually the final incident of the propaganda war, and it does something to explain Dick's ultimate conviction that it had been unwise to try to run 'black' propaganda alongside 'white'. The purposes and aims of the two approaches were, he rightly spotted, not just generally different but often diametrically opposed. The objective of 'black' propaganda was, after all, to corrupt and confuse the enemy, while 'white' propaganda had a much more responsible task: to get the enemy to believe that your word was to be trusted so that he would not resist any orders that were given to him. Eventually Dick even came to doubt whether 'victory would have been delayed for a day if "black" had been forbidden and all our efforts had been concentrated on perfecting a "white" propaganda designed first to win the confidence of the enemy in our truthfulness and then to impose our will upon him'.[54] And he was certainly entitled to claim that one of the most striking propaganda triumphs of the war lay in the discovery of the number of German soldiers who, by its end, carried a 'white' Eisenhower surrender pass in their pockets.

That was all the more astonishing an achievement as, at least since the Casablanca 'Unconditional Surrender' declaration of 1943, all those engaged in PWE or PWD had, in a sense, been fighting with at least one hand tied firmly behind their backs. It was not merely a matter of never being able to offer any inducement to particular units to capitulate in the field. 'Unconditional Surrender' also meant that no hope or encouragement could ever be held out to any resistance elements within Germany itself (hence the failure to exploit the Hitler bomb plot of 20 July 1944).* Dick, though, showed himself strangely ambivalent about the limitations imposed by the policy of 'Unconditional Surrender' maintaining, 'Surprisingly enough, we found more room for manoeuvre than might have been expected.' Yet if he was sceptical of the notion that 'our appeal to the German people would have been greatly strengthened if we had been able to make use of precise promises about the treatment to be accorded to Germany if Nazism were overthrown', he was equally clear, on strategic grounds, that 'the refusal to permit the Supreme Commander to state the terms and methods of military surrender certainly decreased the readiness of German commanders in the field to surrender, and so quite needlessly prolonged the war'.[55]

---

* Dick himself may well have felt a qualm of guilt about this. He had always tended to dismiss the possibility of there being any Establishment effort to overthrow Hitler. In May 1942 he had even written a private memorandum for the Foreign Office designed to undermine the credibility of an old friend from Oxford days, Adam von Trott, who had become a clandestine advocate of a negotiated peace. After von Trott was executed for his part in the attempt to kill Hitler, it was Dick who first suggested that he deserved a public memorial in his own native Hesse-Kassel.

As the war finally moved to its end, Dick's thoughts necessarily turned back more and more to politics. VE Day found him in Dachau conducting a group of film cameramen around the concentration camp: when, later on, someone questioned his insistence on taking down the details of everyone in the party, and having them recorded on the resulting, horrific, film, Dick sternly told him: 'One day there will be people who will stand up and say that there were no such things as concentration camps and that the whole thing was a frame-up by Hitler's enemies. We can't be too careful.'[56]

For Dick himself there could be no forgetting, either what the Nazis had done or how it had been allowed to happen.* In that sense, the war was a formative influence on both his character and outlook – probably as important an experience as any since Winchester. In career terms he had, of course, flourished – and it may be that Dick was always most at home in what was virtually an all-male environment. If he had not made himself popular, he had shown his capacity to exert authority – though not yet exercise direct power – over national policy. Whatever he was by 1945, he was no longer merely the carping journalistic critic, still less the ivory tower academic. He had become, in effect, a man of the administrative world – if one of independent, and sometimes inconvenient, convictions. He demonstrated those publicly almost as soon as he was released from PWD in order to fight Coventry East (the old seat had been cut in half) in the July general election. His first public initiative had nothing to do with his future constituents but was related entirely to the responsibilities he had left behind. Before he was even an elected MP, he chose in an *Observer* article to launch a frontal assault on the policies then being pursued by the Allied Military Government in Germany:

> From Russian-occupied Germany come sparse but consistent reports of revived industrial activity and of improved food supplies. On our side of the demarcation line, voice after voice is raised to prophesy famine conditions this winter in Germany; and to record an almost complete paralysis of the industrial scene . . .
> The root of the problem lies in the fatal desire displayed by the

---

* Dick retained particular feelings of bitterness towards those in the British middle classes who thought in the 1930s that the world could co-exist with Hitler. At the outbreak of war he gave a letter addressed to his mother and father to Naomi Mitchison and told her she was to hand it over to them in the event of his death. After Mr Justice Crossman's own death in 1941 Naomi Mitchison opened it – only to discover that it was 'a horrid letter saying that the war was all their fault'.[57]

British and American governments not to lag behind the Russians in 'toughness'. Time after time it was argued that, since the Russians would be utterly ruthless in Eastern Germany, Allied unity demanded a toughness on our part, in glaring contradiction with every dictate of expediency or commonsense. And so we fell into the old trap of believing our own propaganda, which asserted every day that it was dangerous to encourage anti-Fascist forces in Germany, lest they should turn out to be Fascists, after all.[58]

It was not perhaps a bad dying kick from the former psychological warrior who all along had maintained that such people as 'good Germans' *did* exist outside the cemeteries and the ovens. But in Foreign Office eyes it must have vindicated, rather than confounded, the character assessment that had been drawn up on Dick some three weeks earlier on his leaving the Political Intelligence Department (which all through the war had operated as the 'cover' for those working in both PWE and, later PWD). Written by the Director of PWE himself, Robert Bruce Lockhart, it is worth quoting in full – if only as a Whitehall collector's item:

Secretary of State
As from today Mr R. H. S. Crossman has resigned officially from the Political Intelligence Department on his adoption as the Labour candidate for Coventry. In accordance with the Treasury circular, his resignation is final.

You will be interested to know that Mr Crossman has received a special letter of thanks from General Bedell Smith and has been recommended for a United States decoration, which I understand is certain to be conferred.*

I should add that in a personal letter to me Brigadier-General Maclure, head of the SHAEF Psychological Warfare Division, has paid a remarkable tribute to Mr Crossman's work, which he describes as the most notable achievement in the whole field of political warfare.

In British eyes Mr Crossman is somewhat lacking in team spirit, and on more than one occasion his restless ambition has led him not only to take unjustifiable risks but to defy regulations which other temporary Civil Servants may find irksome but have to obey. On the other hand, with his agile mind, his almost daemonic energy, his considerable skill in broadcasting and in

* It was not. Dick did, however, receive an OBE in the Foreign Office list in 1945.

leaflet-writing, he has made a remarkable contribution to the whole technique of political warfare, especially in connection with military operations; and in making a final estimate of his work I have no hesitation in stating that his virtues greatly outweigh his faults. In other words, if he does not win a prize for good conduct, he certainly deserves a commendation for distinguished service.

R. H. BRUCE LOCKHART
7 June 1945[59]

The dichotomy in that last sentence was a neat one – and, though Bruce Lockhart can hardly have foreseen it, there would be any number of Labour politicans ready to endorse it over the next twenty-five years. In a sense, indeed, he could claim to have put his finger on the awkward antithesis that was to lie at the heart of Dick's political career.

9 Zionist Convert

The war meant that Coventry – for which he had been chosen as Labour candidate as long ago as 1937 – saw remarkably little of Dick. He managed to visit the city in the wake of the first Coventry saturation bombing of 14 November 1940 – but, as he himself expressively put it, 'by the time I got there the main panic had eased off and people had stopped sleeping in the fields outside'.[1] (There was no reproach in that: Zita had gone the day after the blitz, and only Dick's duties at Woburn had prevented him from getting there earlier.) He had, however, necessarily become something of a stranger to the local Labour Party. Perhaps for that reason, he appears to have suffered a twinge of apprehension once the Boundary Commission's recommendation for dividing the city into two parliamentary seats – East and West – was put into effect. Certainly at his farewell interview with Sir Robert Bruce Lockhart he tried 'to question the ruling about the finality of his resignation'.[2] According to Bruce Lockhart, he maintained he was doing so only 'as a matter of principle':[3] but it would have been surprising if the requirement to face a second selection conference, nearly eight years after his first in 1937, had not provoked a certain nervousness.

As things turned out, Dick had absolutely no need to worry. The Coventry Labour Party had already decided that the East division was the more winnable of the two seats and promptly awarded it to Dick (putting him through a mere *pro forma* selection conference, at which he was not even opposed). The only upset occurred in the West division, where George Hodgkinson, the man who was to be Dick's agent, had originally hoped to be the candidate. He was, however, disqualified by the National Executive on the grounds that he was a paid servant of the Party,[4] and the way was left open for an outsider to come in. Although there was at least one other strong local candidate, the nomination eventually went to a glamorous young Captain, dressed in the uniform of the Army Press Corps, who 'delivered a socialist message which caught the mood of everyone present'.[5] His name was Maurice Edelman and he was to be Dick's Labour colleague in representing Coventry for the next twenty-nine years.

The general election had been called for 5 July 1945 (although its result, because of the complicating factor of the Forces' vote from overseas, was not announced until 26 July). Immediately after severing all connections with the Foreign Office – his attempt to make his resignation conditional on getting elected predictably ran into the ground – Dick travelled up to Coventry. In later years he would normally stay with George Hodgkinson and his wife, Carrie, but on this first occasion he and Zita booked into a hotel. There was obviously a good deal of lost time to be made up and here Zita's help must have been invaluable. She had kept in close touch with the constituency Party throughout the war – representing Dick, for example, at the Coventry May Day celebrations in 1945 where the guest speaker was Aneurin Bevan ('he spoke without a single note and held the whole audience').[6] Dick's own recollections of the election campaign survive in a *New Statesman* article published just a week before the poll. It is clear that he had little or no intimation of the scale of the Labour landslide to come* – even if he could claim to have spotted one significant trend among the voters:

My first impression – after nearly two years overseas and out of contact with ordinary working people – is of the thoughtfulness and seriousness of the electorate. We are in considerable difficulties here because, in our print orders from Transport House, we alarmingly underestimated the reading capacity of the electorate. Every 2d or 3d pamphlet on sale at open air meetings is immediately snapped up. What we sell is taken home and thrown back at us at the next open air meeting, always in the form of precise and thoughtful questions as to what we shall do when we get to power.[7]

---

* According to Bruce Lockhart, Dick had started out in a mood of cynicism rather than optimism. 'He said that the next government would be a short-lived one whoever won. Selfishly, he would not mind very much if Labour were beaten. He would have more practice in opposition.' Kenneth Young (ed.), *The Diaries of Sir Robert Bruce Lockhart*, vol. II, 1939–1965 (Macmillan, 1980), p. 437. The remarks appear in the account of their farewell interview on 22 May 1945.

On his own likely result, Dick, however, was a good deal more cautious:

> Under normal conditions this should be a fairly safe Labour seat. But today there are four candidates – Conservative, Labour, Liberal and Communist; and it is possible that the Tory may squeeze in on a split Progressive vote. The Communists have been very active here during the war and are keen to test their strength – in the name of working-class unity, of course – against the Labour Party. The result may be a surprise to both.[8]

That the result – when it was eventually declared on 26 July – was 'a surprise' to Dick there can be no doubt. (On the eve of poll he had written down an estimate of his vote as 23,000 with the Communist getting 9,000.)[9] The actual outcome must, therefore, have been as encouraging to him as it was disappointing to the Communist candidate. Despite a fine record first in the International Brigade and then as a Captain in the British Army, he attained only 3,986 votes or a deposit-losing 7 per cent of the total poll, compared with Dick's 34,739 or a commanding 60 per cent of all the votes cast. The Labour majority was a handsome 18,749 over the Conservative, with the Liberal candidate coming bottom of the poll, 1,000 votes behind even the Communist. And that, of course, was merely a symptom of the Left's sweep across the country, with Labour winning no fewer than 393 seats – still its high-water mark – in a House of Commons with 640 Members.

There were 259 Labour MPs elected for the first time in 1945 and, even if Dick was better known than most of them, he can hardly have expected immediate ministerial preferment. In any event, he did not get it – though, startlingly, Ernest Bevin gave serious consideration to appointing him as his Parliamentary Private Secretary (drawing back from doing so only on the ground that it would mean 'he would have to give up journalism and he needs the money').[10] Three of the new intake were rewarded straight away with ministerial office – and only perhaps the fact that two of them (Harold Wilson and Hilary Marquand)* were former university teachers can have caused Dick a pang of passing jealousy. Even so, he was in no mood to take offence – witness his remark, before

---

* Harold Wilson, a pre-war don at University College, Oxford, went on to be Prime Minister. Hilary Marquand (1901–72), a former professor of industrial relations at Cardiff who became Minister of Health in Attlee's second Government, left the House of Commons in 1961.

these appointments were announced, that he 'did not want a junior job in the government but would prefer to go in in about eighteen months' to two years' time when he would have had some experience'.[11]

At first the thrill of being a Labour MP – after what was, in effect, an eight-year wait – seems to have been sufficient to keep Dick happy. He was intrigued enough after attending the first full sitting of the new Parliament, the opening day of the Debate on the Address on 16 August 1945, to make some immediate jottings. (The previous day, VJ Day, the House had simply heard the King's Speech and then processed over to St Margaret's for a service of thanksgiving for the victory over Japan.) As a consequence, the Commons, Dick noted on 16 August, still had 'a strong ceremonial atmosphere' and both the new Prime Minister and the new Leader of the Opposition had 'each in his own way conformed to the mood of the occasion'. There was no doubt, however, as to which of the two commanded his admiration: 'Mr Churchill gave what sounded like the last of his PM's war reports from the Leader of the Opposition's dispatch box and, relieved of responsibility, dazzled the new Members with a display of virtuosity and charm.' By contrast, Attlee struck him as merely having given 'a careful, well thought out statement of policy'.[12] If that was representative of the rival impressions made on the new Labour Members, then it may be that the Government was prudent in arranging for a six-week recess to follow what had merely been a four-day Debate on the Address.

For Dick the enforced holiday was certainly useful. Just before war broke out in 1939 he had published his third book, *Government and the Governed*, and he was now busy trying to bring it up to date. More of an academic textbook than either *Plato To-day* or *Socrates*, it had already been reprinted twice during the war; in its publishers' eyes – and perhaps those of its author, too – it thus had the potential of being turned into a modest money-spinner.* For this to be achieved, however, it was necessary – since, like all Dick's work, it was full of contemporary references – to make it read like a post-war book rather than a pre-war one; and that, given all that had happened in the six years, 1939–45, required fairly substantial revision. It was to this that Dick devoted the summer recess, while also getting used to his new home, Town End Farm, Radnage (already

---

* It eventually became one, going through a total of five editions and six reprints. It was published by Chatto & Windus, who, for the first thirty years of its life, brought it out only in 'a student's edition'.

enlivened by the return from the United States of Zita's children, Gilbert in 1943 and Venice in 1944).

In London, towards the end of the war, Dick and Zita had found a flat in Draycott Avenue, Chelsea, but they had been bombed out of it by a V1-bomb in 1944. So it was convenient that he had immediately been taken back on to the staff of the *New Statesman*, where Kingsley Martin renewed the invitation to share his flat at 14 Buckingham Street. With £400 a year from the paper on top of his £600 salary as an MP, Dick was thus better off than most of his Labour MP contemporaries – although no more affluent than he had been in his Foreign Office days when his salary had been £1,000 p.a. Nevertheless he and Zita had few economic – or even political – worries: the future, after the separation and disruption of the war, beckoned them forward calmly enough, especially after Dick had successfully got over the hurdle of his maiden speech on 26 October 1945.*

All that changed a few days later when Dick found himself approached by the Government Chief Whip in the members' lobby of the House of Commons. He had been expecting to go to Austria that weekend on a parliamentary delegation, and the first part of the news was a disappointment. He would not, after all, be going to Vienna, he was told: 'Ernest Bevin has got another job for you, something about Palestine. You will be hearing more soon'.[13] In fact, Dick did not hear anything for two weeks or more, and when he did, it was from a formal statement that the Foreign Secretary made to the whole House of Commons. On 13 November 1945 Ernest Bevin announced that the US Government had agreed to co-operate with Britain in setting up a joint commission to inquire not just into the future of Palestine but also into the plight of the Jewish victims of Nazi persecution in Europe.[14]

At that stage, no names were made public – and, although Dick correctly guessed that he was to be one of them, he was by no means certain that it was something he wanted to do. He sensibly sought out Bevin's Under-Secretary at the Foreign Office, Hector McNeil, and attempted to explain why he felt not particularly qualified for the role being held out to him. McNeil gave him short shrift: it was, he was briskly told, his 'big chance', Bevin deliberately wanted to

---

* This speech on 'Conditions in Europe' was in many ways an echo of Dick's *Observer* article of the previous May. Once again he drew attention to the Russian insistence on 'toughness' and the West's inability to match it with any policy of its own. When he sat down after speaking for fifteen minutes, *The Times* reported that, unusually for a maiden speaker, he was accorded 'loud cheers'.

try him out on 'a tough job', and 'you know perfectly well that you are not going to refuse'.[15] It was typical of Dick's honesty that he should have immediately given up pretending otherwise:

> In my heart of hearts I knew that he was right . . . The idea of an assignment was exciting. Though I denied it to myself, that is what I had missed since I flew back from Paris to fight the election. The House of Commons was a way of life, a new experience as exciting as the first weeks at boarding school. But life on the backbenches was not a *job*. Though it involved being away for four months, this Anglo-American Committee would mean that I would have a chance, not merely of making a speech or voting, but of formulating policy. Once again I would be back in the atmosphere I liked best – Anglo-American teamwork. I was glad the job had been offered to me, and I had no intention of refusing it.[16]

The names of the members of the Commission – six American and six British – were finally announced on 10 December and, before the end of the year, Dick found himself crossing the Atlantic on the *Queen Mary** – the Americans had insisted that the Commission's first hearings should be held in Washington. It cannot be said that his first letters back to Zita in England were entirely tactful. In a sense she was the victim of Dick's voluntary four-month absence – and all she got by way of consolation were sybaritic descriptions of luxury-liner life:

> I eat a four-course breakfast and a four-course dinner, with huge slices of roast beef. For lunch we have platefuls of exquisite sandwiches and a couple of lightly boiled eggs served in our cabins. Then we have tea in our cabins, where we eat the Christmas cakes we all bought. Heavens, rationing makes one greedy![17]

Also, it might be thought, insensitive. Certainly, it can scarcely have done much for Zita's own morale to discover that the same letter went on: 'The British are so conditioned to rationing that they do not fully realise their hardships. They have almost forgotten what

---

* Dick shared a cabin with his opposite number from the Tory benches in the House of Commons, Reginald Manningham-Buller (1905–80), later, as Lord Dilhorne, to be Lord Chancellor, 1962–4. They appear to have got on reasonably well, though Dick was unkindly amused when a gale blew overboard his colleague's hat *and* his glasses.

they are missing, or rather they remember plenty but only as a paradise which has disappeared.'[18]

Even if the point was valid, there must have been a less clumsy context in which to make it. It was perhaps just as well that the main theme of Dick's correspondence with his wife was the work of the Commission – and, even more interestingly, his own early views on the issue of Zionism. The tone in which these were expressed at least acquits Bevin of having made the kind of elementary blunder, of which he is sometimes accused, by appointing Dick to the Commission in the first place. Whatever else he was, the young Labour MP for Coventry East was not at that stage even a Zionist sympathiser:

> I begin to feel that in this world of 1945 Zionist assertion of the Jews as *a nation*, as distinct from race and nationhood, is really a part of anti-semitism. Whereas the few survivors of European Jewry should be liberated from that awful *separateness* which Hitler imposed – and reconstituted European with full rights and duties (as Englishmen or Americans) – Zionism maintains the spiritual concentration camp. In a sense, it is only the other side of the Nazi shield, the Jewish reaction to the German disease. It is the anti-semites and racialists who want to clear the Jews out of Europe and pack them together in Palestine.[19]

There was certainly nothing there to which Bevin – or even the traditionally pro-Arab British Foreign Office – could conceivably have taken exception. And they would have been reassured, too, to learn of Dick's simultaneous assessment of the mood of the British members of the Commission:

> With the doubtful exception of myself, all of us start with a blankness towards the philosophy of Zionism, which is virtually anti-Zionist. We all feel the whole idea of a Jewish national home is a *deadend* out of which Britain must be extricated: that, whereas it is obvious that Arab independence in the end *must* be granted, we have not a similar obligation to permit the Jews in Palestine the fulfilment of Zionism.[20]

Of course, it was always predictable that the British side of the Commission would turn out to be less sensitive to Zionist aspirations than their American counterparts. And initially, at least, the British members seem to have been irritated by the harangues to which they were subjected, once they had arrived in Washington,

8 Erika and Dick outside The Barn in New College Lane, Oxford
9–10 Zita on her way to the United States and in Memphis, Tennessee

11 Dick visiting a German work camp in 1934

12 Kingsley Martin as seen by Low

13 Dick as seen by Vicky

The Editor at work

from the representatives of American Jewry. Dick himself put the point vividly: 'There were moments when I felt more like a prisoner in the dock than a member of a committee of inquiry';[21] and the hearings, in the old State Department building next door to the White House, offered a field day to all those who felt that Britain had not done enough to help the Jews of Europe both before and during the Second World War. Perhaps alone among the British representatives, Dick in some ways found this experience salutary – writing in his diary for 3 January 1946, 'Having started on the *Queen Mary* very pro-Arab, I am now swinging over to the Jewish side' (though he was careful to add, 'Actually this sort of see-saw is quite irresistible when raw recruits begin learning a subject like this one.')[22] In truth, there will always be a difficulty about following the exact details of Dick's conversion to the Zionist cause. When he published his own account of his experience on the Anglo-American Commission in both Britain and the United States in 1947,* he had already made up his mind as to where he stood on the issue: inevitably, this led to certain adjustments in the description of his own journey down the Damascus road (significantly or not, neither of the two extracts given above features in it anywhere). What emerges clearly from his own private correspondence, however, is that he had made no final decision – and there were many wobbles on the way before that – until the Commission arrived in Jerusalem in March 1946.

The Commission had sentenced itself to a punishing programme of receiving evidence and listening to witnesses. After two weeks in Washington (and having endured a somewhat arduous return voyage on the *Queen Elizabeth*, for which the Foreign Office had botched the arrangements),[23] it set up business in London at the Royal Empire Society in Northumberland Avenue, where it started hearings on 25 January; since the first United Nations Assembly was taking place at the same time in Central Hall, it heard in London at least an initial presentation of the Arab case.

The most significant event of the London visit was, though, in Dick's eyes, a lunch that the Foreign Secretary gave for all the Commission members at the Dorchester Hotel. He was always to maintain afterwards that it was on this occasion Ernest Bevin undertook that, provided their Report was unanimous, he would 'personally do everything in his power to put it into effect'.[24]

---

* *Palestine Mission* was published by Hamish Hamilton in London and by Harper & Bros in New York.

Since this alleged promise became later Dick's main source of grievance against Bevin,* it is unfortunate that there is no official corroboration of it. But at least Dick made a note of it at the time – writing in the diary he kept of the London visit and sent on to Zita at Radnage:

> I went down to the House once or twice, once to vote for the Coalmines bill. A quarter of an hour with Dalton convinced me that, though he had moved the Labour Party Conference motion, he knew practically nothing of the issues involved but wanted to see enough immigration to prevent a Party revolt ... Attlee listened attentively but only permitted himself to say that the Zionist pressure was very irritating. Ernest Bevin, in a three-minute conversation, confined himself to asking me whether I had been circumcised. I saw him later about the inefficiency of the arrangements but we did not discuss politics. By the way, he made an excellent speech at a Dorchester lunch in which he promised to carry out whatever we recommended. This cheered the Americans and will, when we come to drafting the Report, make unanimity seem worthwhile.[26]

Even allowing for the minor discrepancy over whether the unanimity provision was put in by Bevin – or introduced by Dick himself as something that could usefully be extrapolated from his words† – it seems reasonably clear that the British Foreign Secretary did make some form of commitment to the Commission. It would have been rather odd if he had not. He, and the US Secretary of State, were after all, asking twelve busy and distinguished men to give up four months of their time to wrestle with one of the world's most awkward international problems – and at the very minimum Bevin owed them something for removing its weight 'from his shoulders for at least 120 days'.[27] If he gave no binding pledge, then in all probability he fell back on that familiar politician's device of offering a lick and a promise – which, alas, Dick took all too seriously.

---

* 'It was Ernie who had double-crossed me. I was absolutely furious. He forgot his solemn promise to us.'[25]

† The only roughly contemporary account supports this latter contention. In Bartley C. Crum, *Behind the Silken Curtain* (Simon & Schuster, New York, 1947) nothing is said about Bevin's words being in any way conditional. Crum, a Californian lawyer, was one of the six American members of the Commission. When Crum first made his allegation before his book was published, the Foreign Office issued a statement saying it 'had no record of such a remark'.

Once the London hearings were over, the Commission – which had been provided with its own RAF Dakota – flew to Vienna. The object here was not so much to take formal evidence as to examine conditions on the ground – and the Commission members soon fanned out inspecting Displaced Persons' camps in Germany, Poland, Czechoslovakia, Italy and Greece.[28] They did so, however, without Dick. A threatened return of his old phlebitis kept him in bed for ten days at Radnage and he rejoined his colleagues only when they were on the point of leaving Vienna for Cairo.

His absence hardly mattered – his colleagues, after all, were merely being brought face to face with the horrors, now slightly ameliorated, that Dick had seen for himself some eight months earlier. Inevitably the experience was shocking and distressing – and it appears to have been with some relief that the Commission and its staff left Europe for the Middle East. Their next stop was the secluded luxury of the Mena House Hotel just outside Cairo and near the Pyramids. Here the Commission's hearings took place in the hotel ballroom. They had been organised almost exclusively for the benefit of the Arab League – and Dick was not perhaps alone in finding them slightly bizarre:

> We soon realised that no serious hearings were possible. As in London, the Arabs were determined not to submit to the detailed cross-questioning which we had used in dealing with the Zionist spokesmen. Their purpose was to deliver to the committee, as a ritual act, a statement of the Arab attitude and to make it clear to us that this statement could not be modified or amended by any questions which we might ask.[29]

Nor was the whole pro-consular atmosphere of Egypt much more congenial, at least to Dick. He found the British Embassy – which had just been vacated by Lord Killearn* – highly unsympathetic ('They are all exquisite professional diplomatists, strutting about in high society, and treating the Egyptians like niggers');[30] and he was delighted with the comment he got from a young Egyptian law student who complained that the English always behaved 'like suzerains and never like friends'.[31]

It was not until the Commission reached Jerusalem – where it spent three weeks staying at the King David Hotel – that Dick really came into his own. It was his first visit to Palestine and he seems to

---

* Lord Killearn (1880–1964) was a diplomat of the old school. He had been in Cairo, first as High Commissioner and then as Ambassador, since 1934.

have fallen in love with the country straight away. His sympathies, though, were not engaged by one side alone – witness this excited paragraph in one of his letters to Zita: 'Just back from a *fierce* and vigorous informal discussion with Arab trade unionists and social- ists, all terrific anti-imperialists and also anti-Zionist to the nth degree. God! This is a country.'[32]

But Dick was quite candid enough to recognise that there was an imbalance, freely admitting: 'One of the troubles here is that there is such a *vast amount* of Jewish talent and such a tiny group of Arab intelligentsia.'[33] Not unexpectedly, this had the effect of tipping his sympathies back in favour of the underdog. Two days spent in Nablus and Ramallah almost had him sounding like a convert to the Arab cause:

> For the moment I feel like a man of the hills. It is all right for the Jews scientifically exploiting the coastal plain. That is a country where modern capitalism or socialism is justified by the return yielded by the land. But up on these hills, looking down on the sweltering plain below, you feel that the plain men have always been your natural enemy. Once it was the Jews in the hills who feared the Philistines coming up from the plain to modernise their archaic tribal way of life. Now it is the Arabs who look down and see everywhere the agents of the Jewish Agency spying out the hillsides and finding tricks for buying them against the laws.[34]

Of course, by then Dick had made up his own mind as to what the solution was – and this, in a sense, made it easier for him to spread his sympathies. He appears to have embraced partition as the only answer to the Arab/Jewish problem within a few days of arriving in Jerusalem, writing to Zita, 'suddenly my mind got made up'. It certainly made him more cheerful: 'So now, thank heavens, it's good hard politics and argument and in-fighting and out-fighting and all the things I enjoy.'[35] He was also not shy either of advertising his own success in terms of fame: 'Your husband for the moment is a celebrity and a headline every day in the local papers because he is, and can't help being, the most vital person here and the person they are anxious to convince.'[36]

On that last point Dick was certainly right – at least so far as Zionists were concerned. It was typical of his strange streak of naivety that he should never apparently have suspected that the invitations showering in upon him in Jerusalem were anything but spontaneous. 'Every other moment is taken by *endless* political hospitality – I have never lived in such a spotlight before and honestly it is great fun.'[37] As we now know, since it was revealed after his death,[38] he had been 'targeted' by the Jewish lobbyists ever since the Commission first assembled in Washington. An American who had worked with Dick in PWD during the war had even gone to the trouble of giving Dr Chaim Weizmann (the head of the Jewish Agency and the first President of Israel) a full briefing upon him:

> There is no one on the British side of the delegation that you have to fear except Dick Crossman. He's the brainiest of the lot, the most sophisticated, the most intelligent – a real socialist and a leftist socialist at that. He is a man to be watched and feared. Moreover, he is Ernie Bevin's appointment.[39]

The invitations which flowed in – to be Chaim Weizmann's guest at Rehovot, to dine with Ben-Gurion in the manager's suite of a Tel Aviv hotel, to lunch with the chairman of the Jewish Confederation of Labour, Golda Meir – were thus by no means an accident. With characteristic shrewdness, the Jewish community had decided that Dick was likely to be the pivotal figure on the Commission – and they were not mistaken. Their campaign of persuasion was, however, unnecessary: Dick, as has been noted, had made up his own mind within a day or two of arriving in Jerusalem.

However, his was only one voice out of twelve, and his problem lay in how to convert his colleagues. Basically, Dick had two objectives: to persuade the Commission to agree to the policy (supported by President Truman) of issuing 100,000 immediate entry certificates to Palestine for the Jewish refugees of Europe – there were 98,000 in the Displaced Persons' camps alone – and then to get them to recognise that a partition of Palestine was the only eventual political solution. When the Commission moved to Lausanne in Switzerland at the end of March in order to consider its Report, Dick soon discovered that he had a fight on his hands on both issues.

The fundamental division on the Commission was simple and predictable – the six American representatives leant towards the Jewish side and the British ones (minus Dick) inclined towards the Arabs. It would have been possible, therefore, for Dick to have secured a majority Report – if by a bare margin of seven to five – fairly easily; but he was not interested in that. It was now, indeed, that he brought into play his recollection of Ernest Bevin's remarks at the Dorchester Hotel lunch back in January – urging on his colleagues the imperative need for unanimity if all their work was not to go for nothing. With that as a lever, he began to detach one or two of the British members, at least on the issue of the entry certificates.

He soon learned, however, that on partition he could command the support of only two Americans – and that, from his point of view, was not enough. At a strategic moment Dick, therefore, shrewdly withdrew this proposal – and this almost certainly played some part in breaking what was threatening to be a total impasse. In the end, the Commission did come in with a united Report – although the differing accounts Dick gave in later years do not make it easy to tell how exactly this was achieved. What became his favourite version was given originally in an interview to Susan Barnes for the *Sunday Times* in 1970:

> The Commission had reached a deadlock. The six Americans and I were of one view, the five other English of another. At this point Philip Noel-Baker* arrived in Geneva. He was the Minister of State at the Foreign Office and specially responsible for the UN. His secretary and my secretary were friends. We all four dined together.
>
> Philip asked what was happening. I described deadlock. Philip said: 'That's terrible. I'll ask Sir John Singleton† [the chairman of the British side] to lunch and I'll tell him the Foreign Secretary wants a unanimous report.' He did. They signed. It wasn't until they got back to London that they found they'd signed the wrong report. I laughed like hell.[40]

A marvellous tale. The difficulty with it, however, is that it bears no relation to a private document Dick wrote for his own friend, the Under-Secretary at the Foreign Office, Hector McNeil, within two days of the Report being signed. Composed in Lausanne on Easter Sunday 1946 – the Report itself, with deliberate religious symbolism, was signed on Good Friday – it provides a much more sober (if also probably more truthful) version of what actually occurred:

Background of Report

The Report was, of course, a compromise document. A week

---

* Philip Noel-Baker (1889–1982) was at the time Minister of State at the Foreign Office. First elected Labour MP for Coventry in 1929, he went on to represent Derby (1936–70). Created a life peer 1977.

† Sir John Singleton (1885–1957) had been a High Court judge since 1934. He was raised to the Appeal Court in 1948.

before it was finished it seemed certain that there would be two, and probable that there would be three, reports. It seemed almost impossible to achieve unanimity.

The division was roughly as follows. Four Americans, headed by their Chairman, took the line: No Jewish or Arab State but 100,000 certificates to be issued immediately and unconditionally; the long-term policy was to be a complete reaffirmation of the Mandate . . .

The British had no united view but three of them, headed by Sir John Singleton, took the following line. We agree there should be no Jewish or Arab State. On everything else we disagree. We should only let in the 100,000 slowly and provided certain conditions are fulfilled, including the disbandment of the Jewish illegal army and the removal of the control of awarding certificates from the Jewish Agency . . .

At this stage there was a third group consisting of one Englishman and two Americans, in favour of partition – unless unanimity could be achieved on a uniting scheme.[41]

In so self-effacing a way did Dick refer to his own role – but the explanation for that modesty may have been supplied by the next paragraph, where he went on to describe how he eventually won over two of the British representatives – a veteran Labour peer and a retired Civil Servant.

Morrison, Leggett* and I were convinced that it would be disastrous if conflicting reports were issued . . . In particular we regarded as a gross error in tactics Sir John Singleton's demand that the entry of 100,000 should be made conditional on the disbandment of the Jewish illegal army. We argued that the attempt to impose such conditions would strengthen the hand of the extremists in Palestine – in particular making Weizmann's position impossible – and might well produce immediate hostilities between the British Army and the Jews.

This was by far the most ticklish point in the whole argument. We finally got unanimity by including in the factual report a full and objective statement of the facts about the illegal army and by drafting Recommendation 10.[42]

---

* Lord Morrison of Tottenham (1881–1953) had been a Labour MP for nearly twenty years before being created a peer in 1945. Sir Frederick Leggett (1884–1983) had been Deputy Secretary at the Ministry of Labour and National Service during the war.

The Report contained a mere ten recommendations in all, but, in fact, there was only one that mattered and that was not No. 10 (a bromide appeal to the Jewish Agency 'to resume active co-operation in the suppression of terrorism') but No. 2. Headed 'Refugee Immigration into Palestine', it had the temerity to call for action – action that could come only from the British Government as 'the Mandatory Power':

> We recommend (A) that 100,000 certificates be authorised immediately for the admission into Palestine of Jews who have been the victims of Nazi and Fascist oppression; (B) that these certificates be awarded as far as possible in 1946 and that actual immigration be pushed forward as rapidly as conditions will permit.[43]

It was for this that Dick had fought in the five weeks since the Commission had arrived in Jerusalem. Not least by his strategic sacrifice of his partition proposal, he could claim as much credit as anyone for the final unanimous Report.

Dick stayed on in Lausanne for a fortnight once the Commission had finished its work. There was a sound family reason for that. Both Zita and Venice (now in the WAAF and just recovered from diphtheria) had flown out to join him – Venice being installed in Dick's grand single room in the Beau-Rivage Hotel and her mother and stepfather finding refuge in a nearby *pension* at half the price.[44] This holiday was perhaps the least that Dick could do for Zita – for whom the Commission had meant an additional four-month separation added on to the years they had been apart during the war. There is some evidence to suggest that this had put their marriage under strain. Certainly, one letter that Dick wrote to his wife from Jerusalem was nothing if not tough:

Friday

My darling,

Now I have heard nothing since your letter of March 2nd, and no answer to my cable, and I wonder why. You should have been having a whole lot of letters by now and I am sure you have. I have only received four letters from you in a month and only two of them were proper letters and even now, when Venice is ill, you haven't written to me properly.

Somehow I think it is because you are hurt inside. It is not because you do not love me but I have bruised you or something so that you just do not want to love me while I am away for fear of getting hurt. I can try to understand it and accept it. Anyway, I tell myself, I am having a lovely time and she is not having a nice time, so why *should* she write to me. Why shouldn't she just try to keep me vaguely worried and uneasy by not writing? Then, also you don't tell me things. In one letter you mentioned the parliamentary letters, but in only one. You have never mentioned the 'little operation' which you thought of having or your plans for it. In fact, you have obviously decided to shut yourself up like an oyster until I come back. And I can't possibly blame you for doing it when I am once again away on a lovely job. But I don't like it because I know what months it will take for you to 'unthaw' when I come back and how unhappy we shall make each other in the process. The great difficulty for us is that you can neither talk nor even write to me anything you really feel, for fear of my arguing or in some way hurting you. Of course you write nice letters but you can never get anything really difficult out because I might trample on it.

Equally, we can't discuss anything (looking at it from my point of view) because you absolutely refuse to go on with a discussion after 10 minutes for fear of getting hurt. So the result is, we just don't know what is going on in each other's minds. Or rather, I don't know what is going on in your mind. Because I *do* tell you, but you *don't* tell me.

That is enough complaint for one letter. But don't go on being so bottled up and *cagey*. I know that, though you love me, you are always afraid of me somehow bashing you if you open out. But I think it is a risk you must take, and if you take it, you won't get bashed so often, at least I think you won't.[45]

That was, no doubt, no more than an all-too-typical Dick bully-ragging outburst. And, to be fair, it was to be balanced in the same month by other much more conciliatory statements ('I feel more and more that I am no good for practical politics and that I am always going to be someone who is trusted by nobody but you').[46] It is difficult, however, to resist the feeling that the war – followed by Dick's absence on the Palestine Commission – in some way changed his and Zita's relationship. It had, after all, always been her aspiration to share Dick's life, and, if possible, to participate in his work. That had not been practicable now for nearly four years (since they left Woburn) – and it was not perhaps the most considerate thing, now that normal life was about to be resumed, for Dick to blurt out in almost his final letter from Jerusalem: 'I can't tell you how I dread

going back to the *backbenches* and the NS and N after all this globe-
trotting and responsibility. *However* ... anyway summer in Radnage is lovely.'[47]

Dick was not to see all that much of Radnage in the summer
of 1946. When he returned to the House of Commons on 6 May,
it was to discover that the Government had, in effect, already
rejected the proposals of the Joint Commission.* He demanded –
and, more remarkably, got – an immediate interview with the
Prime Minister in No. 10. A legend has firmly attached itself to
this encounter; whether initially put about by Dick or not, it has
come to be accepted that he spoke without pause for some
twenty-five minutes and that, once he had finished, Attlee simply
looked up and said: 'Saw your mother the other day at Lord's –
she looked well.' Once again, however, this version of events
finds no support in the contemporary records. In fact, so incensed
was Dick by the thoroughly negative – almost resentful – attitude
taken up by the Prime Minister at their interview that he sat
down and wrote him a 1,000-word letter the morning after seeing
him. Its opening paragraph adequately disposes of the fable that
Attlee had refused to enter into any substantive discussion with
Dick:

7 May 1946

Dear Prime Minister,
    I was much depressed by hearing last night that I and my
colleagues had let you down so badly, and had produced a
Report which was, in your view, 'grossly unfair to Great
Britain'. I cannot help feeling that you are a little unfair to
us.[49]

For the next five typed pages Dick went on to spell out why he felt
that was the case – bringing up once again the alleged promise that
Bevin had delivered to the Commission at the outset of its work in
London. In his reply, Attlee ran true to form – writing just seventy-
five crisp words in his own hand:

---

* Attlee had given the official Government reaction to the Report in the Commons on 1 May. It was, at best, a temporising statement – containing a plea to the
Americans not to leave Britain to carry out the recommended policy 'single-
handed'. More revealing to Dick was the reaction of his acquaintances on the
fringes of the Government. 'Four months earlier when my appointment was
announced, they had been my warmest friends. They were friendly still, but with
the slightly self-conscious sympathy of a football team towards a member who has
just been dropped but hasn't yet been told it.'[48]

Private   *9.5.46*
My dear Dick,
      I am sorry if I appeared to you to be unfair to the Commission.
I certainly did not intend to do so. I fully realise the difficult task
you had in dealing with a most intractable problem. My
annoyance is with the Americans who forever lay heavy burdens
on us without lifting a little finger to help. Let us hope that they
will depart from their usual practice here.

Yours ever,

CLEM[50]

Although friendly enough, that note clearly represented a political
brush off – and Dick was driven to the conclusion that, if he was to
bring about any change in the Foreign Office attitude, he would
have to fight the Government in order to get it. That summer he
launched what was to develop into a three-year campaign* – a
campaign which eventually vindicated his own initial instinct in
favour of partition as the only viable solution to the problem of
Palestine. For the moment, however, the big political battalions
were all on the other side – and Dick's path became an increasingly
lonely one, even within the Labour Party. (This was especially so
after the bombing of the King David Hotel on 22 July 1946 with its
death toll of ninety-one people.) Dick refused, however, to be discouraged, seldom missing any opportunity to back the Jewish cause
in Parliament (his second Commons speech was in a debate on the
Palestine situation),[51] carrying the banner forward into a lecture at
Chatham House under Lord Astor's chairmanship[52] and even joining with Michael Foot in publishing a pamphlet headed bluntly and
evocatively *A Palestine Munich?*† That summer recess of 1946 he
spent writing what was to be his fourth book – his account of his
experiences on the Joint Commission entitled *Palestine Mission*,
which was eventually to be published to some acclaim in both
Britain and the United States.
      His efforts did not go unrequited – anyway outside Britain. He
received friendly letters of encouragement from two of his colleagues

* Dick's first shot was an article in the *New Statesman* (11 May 1946) headed
'War in Palestine?' Here he tackled head-on the Government's attempt to make
the disbandment of 'the illegal armies maintained in Palestine' a precondition of
any increase in immigration. This, so far as it affected the Haganah, was the very
proposal that the Commission itself had turned down.
      † The pamphlet – published by Gollancz at 6d – was, in fact, more the work of
Arthur Koestler than either of its two named authors. Koestler received 25 per cent
of the royalties.

on the American side of the Commission,[53] as well as a striking note
of gratitude from Dr Weizmann, who compared Dick's role to that
of Emile Zola in the *affaire Dreyfus* ('You may remember that at
that time Anatole France said that, for that moment, Zola spoke for
the conscience of the world. I felt the same when I read what you
have said recently.')[54] Most gratifyingly of all, he received out of the
blue a letter from possibly the most distinguished Jew of his age,
Albert Einstein. The letter began by praising him for his book *Plato
To-day*, which Einstein claimed he had only just read 'with great
admiration and delight'; but its real purpose, as Einstein went on to
make clear, was to congratulate him on 'the clear and upright' stand
he had taken against the policy of the British Government – while
tactfully adding: 'The fact that such independent criticism is possible
in England without grave consequences for the writer shows a
feature in English political life which deserves appreciation.'[55]

In fact, of course, for Dick there were 'grave consequences' – if
only in so far as his hopes remained alive for political preferment.
Given the embarrassment he had caused his Party – his most damaging attacks always centred on the pledges Labour had consistently
made in Opposition in terms of supporting 'a National Home' for
the Jews – there could no longer be any question of his joining the
Government, at least for as long as Ernest Bevin remained Foreign
Secretary. He found himself in the unpopular role of a member of
the awkward squad, inconveniently reminding the leaders of his
Party – now embroiled with all the economic problems of Government – of what they were most anxious to forget.

About whether Dick was right or wrong on Palestine – and, in
particular, on the Jewish claim to occupy what had traditionally
been an Arab land – there can be plenty of room for argument (and
the perspective is bound to look more complex towards the end of
the twentieth century than in 1946, the immediate aftermath of the
Holocaust). But where there need be no debate is over the nature of
the essentially disinterested decision that he made. He had everything to gain from taking the position that Ernest Bevin clearly
expected of him; he had nothing to expect in terms of reward from
kicking over the traces. Yet that is what he consciously did – and in
no fleeting, love-of-argument fashion. Zionism was to remain one
cause to which Dick remained constant throughout his life.[56]

10   *Backbench Rebel*

Before his appointment to the Palestine Commission, Dick's behaviour as a backbench Labour MP had been dutiful enough. His maiden speech had been judged to be a 'telling' one by the pro-Labour *Daily Herald*,[1] and it had certainly done him no harm in the eyes of the Party leadership. Moreover, conscious perhaps of his forthcoming responsibilities on a joint Anglo-American body, he had not joined in the first revolt against the new Government – the debate on the Bretton Woods Agreement on 13 December 1945 in which twenty-two Labour MPs defied the Whips and trooped into the division lobby, along with a random assortment of seventy-four Conservatives, to vote against the American Loan. Even more remarkably, his mood of restraint and responsibility survived at least for a while after it had become clear that the Government did not propose to act on the Palestine Commission's Report.

In those days the Party Conference was held not in the autumn but at Whitsun. Dick had thus been back barely a month from Lausanne before he went to Bournemouth to attend his first Labour Conference as an elected MP. It was only natural, given his Palestine experience, that he should want to speak in the foreign affairs debate held on 12 June 1946. He was duly called – and the point of view he adopted, on a resolution that had been put forward by Poale Zion, clearly came as a gratifying surprise to the Party leadership:

I wish to speak for a moment about Palestine and add something to what the mover and seconder of the resolution said on that subject. I think that they were right in telling the party that the Anglo-American Commission in broad outline, after a completely impartial study of the situation there, did confirm the party line

which has been held for 30 years . . . But I must add one other
thing. The resolution asks for a Jewish State in Palestine . . . We,
the six British and the six Americans, may have been wrong but
after 120 days we came to a unanimous conclusion that, if either
the Arabs are given what they want, an Arab State, or the Jews
are given what they want, namely a Jewish State, there can be no
peace or no prosperity for either side in Palestine.[2]

For Dick it was a notably loyalist utterance, since it ignored entirely
the initial battle he had fought on the Commission in favour of
partition. Not surprisingly, when he came to wind up the debate,
Ernest Bevin went out of his way to pay a tribute to Dick's
approach. He was, he declared, 'thankful to Mr Crossman for putting the point about the Jewish State so forcibly this morning'.[3]

As a honeymoon between the two of them, it was, however, to
prove all too brief – even if not quite as brief as Dick's enemies tried
subsequently to make out. Eight years later he was to come in for
some criticism in the House of Commons for having put his
signature to the Joint Commission Report – and then reneged on
one of its principal commitments by coming out in favour of a
Jewish State 'inside a week'.[4] He did nothing of the sort, as his
speech at the Bournemouth Party Conference adequately proves;
and if he did later modify his Conference stance against a separate
Jewish State, the responsibility for that lay with the actions of the
British Government.

The parting of the ways came for Dick when the British forces in
Palestine were ordered to round up 2,000 members of the Haganah,
the Jewish Home Guard, on the last Saturday of June 1946. On 1
July there was, as a consequence, an emergency debate in the
House of Commons, in which Dick made one of the most effective
interventions of his entire parliamentary career. Arguing that this
sort of repression would simply strengthen the hand of the terrorists
in the Stern Gang and the Irgun Zwai Leumi against the 'moder-
ates' like Weizmann and Ben-Gurion, he took the Government's
case apart, and left what passed for its 'even-handed' policy in
shreds. It was all the more impressive an achievement as Dick had
started out speaking 'in the teeth of furious hostility';* and it was
force of argument and analysis – rather than emotion – that turned
his speech into 'one of the supreme House of Commons moments of

---

* A constituent of Dick's, a Palestine policeman, had only a week earlier
become the latest British serviceman to be murdered in Palestine.

post-1945 history'.[5] Even so, however, Dick did not at that stage
come out in favour of an independent Jewish State. He was not
publicly to espouse that cause until he published an article in the
New Statesman that autumn called bluntly 'The Case for Partition'.[6]

By then, of course, Dick must have realised that he had burnt his
boats. An account of a talk he had given to a Zionist organisation in
London had already surfaced in a Jewish paper[7] – and a good part of
his second, and less successful, speech on Palestine in the Commons
that summer was taken up with defending himself from the charge
of having expressed sympathy with Jewish passive resistance.[8] It is
possible, too, that he had ceased to think of the House of Commons
as the be-all and end-all of his existence. In July, at the invitation of
its editor, Hugh Cudlipp, but at the instigation of its deputy chairman, Cecil Harmsworth King,[9] he had started contributing monthly
columns on world affairs to the *Sunday Pictorial* – a striking extension of his journalistic practice from a highbrow political weekly to a
mass-circulation popular Sunday newspaper. He had also become
something of a figure in the United States – and it was there that
he was invited, just after the end of the summer recess, to take
part in an 'International Forum' organised by the *New York Herald
Tribune*.

Dick and Zita – he had successfully insisted that his wife should
accompany him – flew to New York on 24 October and after a
gruelling eighteen-hour flight (with stop-overs, as was standard
practice at the time, at both Shannon and Gander) found themselves installed in some luxury at the Waldorf-Astoria. According to
Zita, who kept a diary of the trip, Dick was immediately accorded
'deferential treatment'[10] (there seems no doubt that her husband's
transatlantic celebrity status came as an agreeable, if slightly unsettling, surprise to her). To some extent, of course, this must have
been the product both of his war service at SHAEF and the fame he
had won, at least with the New York Jewish community, through his
views on Palestine. But in the immediate post-war world there was
also a consuming interest on the part of liberal Americans generally
in British politics: in that context Dick already qualified as 'a man to
watch'.[11] It did not take long even for Zita to become relatively
blasé: she soon thought nothing of writing of one of her husband's
many public appearances, 'Then Dick was introduced and, as usual,
it was mentioned that many people regarded him as a future Prime
Minister.'[12]

They had a full three weeks in the United States – with Dick, as
well as appearing at the *New York Herald Tribune* International

Forum, making speeches at both Harvard and Yale (where Zita was
able to meet the two families who had looked after her children
during the war); they also had the opportunity of watching the 1946
mid-term elections, which robbed President Truman of the
Democratic Party's majorities in both the House and the Senate. It
may be that this reverse for the Democrats had too great an
influence on Dick's interpretation of the United States. Certainly,
he filed a notably gloomy report to the *Sunday Pictorial* on the
weekend after the mid-term elections:

> America may not be politically isolationist today, but she is
> economically isolationist. We in Britain should be foolish to count
> on any understanding or co-operation from this post-war America
> in facing our own difficulties. America believes in free-for-all
> internally and externally. That means that we must look after
> ourselves and forget for all time the era of Roosevelt and
> lend-lease.[13]

It is equally plausible, however, that the facts were simply being
made to fit a pre-ordained thesis – for Dick, who left Zita behind in
the States to stay for an extra week with her children's benefactors
at Yale, must have known when he flew back to England that he was
returning to face a foreign policy showdown with his own Party's
leaders. It had started, admittedly, quietly enough. Before departing for New York Dick had been one of the twenty-one signatories
to a private letter to the Prime Minister calling for a switch to a more
socialist foreign policy. Attlee, typically, does not appear to have
given any considered response to this missive;[14] but arrangements
were made for its signatories to enter into discussions with Hector
McNeil, recently promoted to be Minister of State at the Foreign
Office. Dick, who had not returned from New York until Sunday,
10 November, was not party to any of these informal talks; but he
immediately became an eager participant in the resolve – reached
on 11 November, the day before the second session of the 1945
Parliament opened – to mount a more formal, public attack on the
Labour Government. This was to be done by the somewhat unusual
method (for members of the governing Party) of putting down an
amendment to the King's Speech. The decision to take this course
was made on the afternoon of 12 November and the amendment,
complete with six formal signatures and fifty-one others, all endorsing a call for the Government 'to review and recast its conduct of
international affairs', duly appeared in the Commons Order Paper

the following morning. The fat, as even Dick perceived in unrepentantly reporting developments to Zita, was then well and truly in the fire:

14 November 1946

My own darling,

Yesterday was a terrifically exciting day as you have probably read in this morning's newspapers. At the Parliamentary [Party] meeting Attlee started off with a furious rebuke to us for a disloyal and unsporting indictment of the Government. Michael Foot, Benn Levy* and I all spoke quite briefly. The trouble is that, as usual in such revolts, we were very wrong on procedure. We had tabled our amendment without warning Attlee or Hector [McNeil], with whom we were discussing the original letter, and we had tabled it on Monday evening, sorry Tuesday, despite the fact that the Party meeting was on the next morning. We should, of course, have gone to the Party first.

Anyway, the boys on the platform had us on procedure which was a fortunate thing as the whole debate was on that and not on the foreign policy issue. Herbert [Morrison]† made an extremely placatory speech, merely asking that all amendments (there were two others besides ours) should be taken off the Order Paper and stressing that we were not mere Communists but well intentioned people. Finally we lost by 128 votes to 33 and Wigg and I both guessed that the group would disintegrate as we were formally threatened with disciplinary action.

I had a drink before lunch with Herbert Morrison who was extremely friendly and made all sorts of promises about giving us time to discuss the matter in the party if we withdrew. He also made it pretty clear that he had some personal sympathy with our criticisms and at one point seemed almost to be saying, 'If you want to change a Foreign Secretary, why not ask me to help you?'![15]

Dick's mood of excitement was understandable enough – it is not, after all, every day that a senior member of the Government makes

* Benn Levy (1900–73), a well-known British playwright, was Labour MP for Eton and Slough 1945–50.

† Herbert Morrison (1880–1965), Labour MP for East Lewisham, was Lord President of the Council and Leader of the House of Commons 1945–51. He subsequently became Ernest Bevin's successor as Foreign Secretary for six months before the defeat of the 1945–51 Government in the general election of October 1951. Created a life peer in 1959.

his feelings clear about an equally senior Cabinet colleague to a back-bencher of little more than a year's standing. The anti-Bevin forces, however, refused to be bought off. That same evening a meeting attended by some forty of them decided – despite Dick's and George Wigg's original forebodings – to press ahead with their parliamentary rebellion. Initially, Dick once again was exultant, carefully explaining to Zita: 'We're not just intellectuals. I have been thinking about this for so long with my head that I had forgotten that other people have hearts and feel passionately.'[16] But his most ominous message to his wife, who in some ways had a shrewder tactical sense than he did, was contained in almost a throw-away line:

> In this morning's papers the Labour revolt is the main headline news and my name heads the list merely because I came alphabetically first among the six members who originally tabled the amendment. However, it has been decided that, if the Speaker calls it, I should move.[17]

The Speaker, Colonel Harry Clifton Brown, much to the fury of the Government, *did* call the rebels' amendment; Dick, to a packed House on Monday 18 November 1946, thus found himself in his first full starring role in a set-piece Commons engagement.

It turned out to be something of a poisoned chalice – as Zita, had she been in England rather than the United States, might have been able to foresee. The main trouble was that the amendment had been drafted in such a way as to attract every possible avenue of support: the fellow travellers, the proponents of world government, even the legatees of the old League of Nations Union – each had obeisance made to them. Dick, therefore, made an elementary blunder, which Attlee, in replying to the debate, ruthlessly exploited, in not mentioning the United Nations once. Even in terms of dialectical technique, it was not Dick's finest hour, possibly because he did not himself fully believe in half the things the catch-all amendment said. He made it clear, for example, that he personally did not equate 'American capitalism' with 'Soviet Communism' – although the amendment he was moving appeared to do exactly that; and, as a relative newcomer to the Commons, he may not have helped his cause by brashly declaring, 'We get the impression that not only is there a complete Anglo-American tie-up but a tie-up between the two frontbenches.'[18] When Attlee came to reply, it soon became a case of the massacre of the innocents – with the Prime Minister tartly announcing, to Labour loyalist cheers, that the amendment was 'misconceived, mistimed and based on a misconception of fact'.[19]

Even then, however, Dick's humiliation was not complete. In the last moments of the debate he rose to his feet and stumblingly – initially he failed to find the correct parliamentary formula – tried to prevent the rebels' amendment from being put to the vote. He was thwarted in his effort to exploit this procedural device, when a pair of Independent Labour Party Members from Glasgow – supported by a number of Conservatives anxious to embarrass the Labour Government – loudly shouted 'No' when the Speaker formally asked the leave of the House for the amendment to be withdrawn.[20] The two ILP MPs duly provided the necessary Tellers for a vote to be taken, but that was all they could do. The much-vaunted Labour foreign policy rebellion was eventually crushed (with the help of the Conservative Opposition) by 353 to nil.

However, that meant that something like 100 Labour Members had refrained from going into the division lobby in support of Ernest Bevin's policies. And it was from this deliberate abstention – of which the Conservative newspapers made a good deal[21] – that the rebels had to derive what comfort they could. For Dick personally, however, there can be no question that the occasion had been a setback: he was left in the never very dignified parliamentary posture of apparently being willing to wound but afraid to strike. He did not make a speech in the Commons again for nearly three months.

Other motives, though, could have played a part in that decision. One of the more notable facts about Dick as a parliamentarian was that he never aspired to be any kind of backbench headline-hunter. The *Hansard* reports of the 1945–51 Parliaments suggest that he did not ask a single parliamentary question; and he tended to ration his speeches to those topics on which he felt he could address the House with some authority. In the early days that meant predominantly Germany and Palestine, gradually widening out into a frontal assault on British foreign policy generally. But by early 1947 he had also begun to take an interest in defence matters.

It was defence that provided the occasion for his second, and rather more effective, backbench insurrection. The New Year of 1947 had opened badly for the Labour Government – with 'the big freeze' of January and February leading to fuel cuts and industrial lay-offs. In a letter to his old PWD friend C. D. Jackson (now back with the Time-Life organisation in New York) Dick insisted on keeping up a brave front, sounding what might have been a defiant echo of 1940:

> We are still in the middle of the fuel crisis here which means that Britain is at its best and that people are more cheerful than they have been for weeks! I was in Coventry last weekend and found the engineers really quite glad to have a little enforced holiday since they have a guaranteed week, and they were all contrasting the atmosphere with the great lockout of 1922. Still, I wish this country did not wait until things were really bad before pulling its socks up.[22]

Dick went on to spell out one way in which he felt this would have to be done – though the measures he envisaged can hardly have been palatable to a loyal employee of the Henry Luce empire:

> We must cut down imports on cigarettes and films and we must cut our arms estimates and the size of our armed forces. All these things may not be desirable but they are inevitable since Anglo-American relations are no longer based on lend-lease ... The brutal fact is that our economic situation is such that we cannot afford the armaments to continue.[23]

That was the case that Dick proceeded to develop in the House of Commons against a necessarily groggy Government when the National Service Bill came up for its second reading on 1 April 1947. He did so, however, on this occasion with some finesse – not opposing peacetime conscription in principle but insisting that a national serviceman's time with the Colours should be kept to one year only (rather than the eighteen months that the Government proposed) and arguing strongly that conscripts should never be used for 'garrison work overseas'.[24] During the debate this meant that Dick attracted opprobium from both supporters of the Government Bill and from its outright critics – eighty-five of whom (pacifists and fellow travellers, together with the twelve-strong Parliamentary Liberal Party) marched into the division lobby to vote against the whole concept of peacetime conscription. Dick did not join them – indeed, he actually voted for the Government Bill, but only on the understanding that he was reserving the right to move an amendment on the Bill's Committee Stage incorporating the reservations that he held. Given the size of the revolt – and the threatened economic position of the Government – this was enough to do the trick. In one of the swiftest about turns of post-war politics, the

Government within two days tabled an official amendment of its own reducing the term of National Service from eighteen months to twelve.*[25]

It was a remarkable tribute – as the Press was not slow to point out[26] – to the influence of a 39-year-old back-bencher; and, had Dick been prepared to rest on it, it might even have restored his reputation with his elders and betters on the Labour Front Bench. Characteristically, though, he burst into a frenzy of fresh activity. The Easter weekend of 1947 found him – in the company of Michael Foot and Ian Mikardo† – at home at Radnage working on the draft of a 'Red Paper', later to gain renown as the pamphlet *Keep Left*.[27] The three MPs, supported by two secretaries and sustained by Zita, kept at the rush of writing from the morning of Good Friday to the afternoon of Easter Monday – 'it all went very smoothly and happily'.[28]

Politically, however, that was not to prove true of the results of their labours. Although *Keep Left* reads today like a singularly rational and perceptive document – correctly forecasting, for example, that making the pound convertible with the dollar (which Hugh Dalton, as Chancellor, rashly proceeded to do in July) would prove to be a disaster for Britain – there is no question that at the time it looked like the first formal flag of revolt run up from within the Party against both the domestic and foreign policies of the Attlee Government. This was partly a consequence of its presentation. Although written by just three MPs, it was offered to the political world as representing the considered views of fifteen backbench Labour MPs (one of whom, remarkably, given his future right-wing career, was Woodrow Wyatt‡). Three MPs might have been regarded as little more than a harmless cabal; fifteen came to resemble something much more like an active conspiracy – especially as the pamphlet casually revealed that they had been in the habit of meeting together regularly. Once again, it was either Dick's good fortune or ill luck that, in strict alphabetical order, his name

* No national serviceman, in fact, served for a mere twelve months. Before the Government's amendment could come into effect, the period had been changed again to eighteen months and was extended to two years in September 1950.

† Ian Mikardo was Labour MP for Reading 1945–59 and for Poplar 1964–87. He served for more than a quarter of a century on the Labour Party's National Executive, being first elected in 1950.

‡ Woodrow Wyatt, a colleague of Dick's on the staff of the *New Statesman* at the time, was Labour MP for Aston, Birmingham 1945–55 and for Bosworth 1959–70. He later became a journalistic flail of the Left and was created a life peer by Mrs Thatcher in 1987.

appeared on top of all the others on the pamphlet's cover. For that reason alone, his identification with the pamphlet – and the group – was to become as strong as anyone's in the minds of both the Party and the public.

So far as the wary view taken by the Government Whips was concerned, that by itself would have been bad enough. But no sooner had the pamphlet been sent to press than Dick embarked on another and even more unorthodox political activity. The origins of this remain a matter of some dispute – so all that can be done is to set out the public facts as they are known.

Henry Wallace, who had been for one term Roosevelt's Vice-President before being dropped in favour of Harry Truman, had resigned from the Democratic Administration as Secretary of Commerce the previous autumn: he had promptly been appointed to be editor of the American liberal magazine, the *New Republic* (at that stage owned by Michael Straight, who many years later admitted to having been recruited as a Communist agent by Anthony Blunt while an undergraduate at Cambridge).[29] Somehow the idea seems to have taken root that it would be a good promotional stunt for the *New Statesman* if an American liberal were invited over to Britain in order to establish a link between 'progressive forces' in both countries. The choice eventually fell on Henry Wallace – though other names (like that of Chester Bowles, later Governor of Connecticut and US Ambassador to India) were apparently considered. Who bore the responsibility for issuing the invitation is where the argument begins – with Kingsley Martin always afterwards maintaining that not just the invitation but the whole notion of such a visit had been entirely Dick's own.[30] Whatever the truth of that – and the contemporary evidence is not conclusive either way – Dick certainly seems to have borne the brunt of organising Wallace's meetings, including one at which he spoke to an all-Party gathering at the House of Commons.

In a limited sense, Wallace's tour – starting off at the Methodist Central Hall, Westminster, he went on to address large paying audiences up and down the land – was a remarkable success. It certainly brought the *New Statesman* a great deal of publicity, but it was not perhaps the kind of publicity that it needed; for even before he arrived, in the week after Easter, the Communist *Daily Worker* was ominously singing anthems in his praise.[31] The truth was that the *New Statesman* had blundered: no one on its staff seems to have known enough about American liberal politics to realise that, unwittingly, Wallace had become a wholly isolated figure manipulated by

Communists. Typically, Dick subsequently claimed that he knew all that perfectly well. Wallace had come to Britain, he revealed to the *Saturday Evening Post* nine months later, bearing a message 'signed by a lot of Communist stooges – but what were we to do? Cancel the invitation? It would hardly have been polite.'[32]

It is not the most convincing of explanations to account for an episode that was to cause Dick a good deal of embarrassment – and it is not, in fact, supported by what he wrote privately in the immediate aftermath of the Wallace visit to his old American friend, C. D. Jackson. There, his tone, if condescending, was distinctly indulgent:

> Henry Wallace caused much less commotion here than he apparently did over with you. We have a soft spot for politicians who resign on principle – that is why Eden still has such a high reputation.* Wallace is a lousy speaker even if you help him to compose his speech but he is a thoroughly nice, good man and, as you know, we divide people into good and bad. No one cared about internal squabbles between one section of American liberals or the other. They were merely welcoming a good American who seemed to feel himself thoroughly at home in our atmosphere and I think most people felt rather sorry for him, poor man, at having to go home where nobody seemed to agree with him.[33]

It is hard to resist the conclusion that at the time Dick was as misled as anyone – and that his subsequent outburst to the *Saturday Evening Post* (which was to do his hopes of succeeding Kingsley Martin no good at all) must in some measure have been a piece of self-compensation at finding himself 'conned'.

Yet all that, though it undoubtedly compromised Dick with his transatlantic friends,† was as nothing to the public bruise that was to be inflicted on his reputation one month later. It is conceivable that Dick's whole burst of political energy in the spring of 1947 had been deliberately calculated in order to help him to storm his way on to the National Executive Committee at the Party Conference held at Margate that Whitsun. Certainly, in 1947 he stood for the first time

---

* This reference to the former Conservative Foreign Secretary was – unless an accident – a typical piece of belligerence on Dick's part. See p. 101 above.

† Joseph Alsop wrote a particularly brutal column about Dick and Henry Wallace in the *New York Herald Tribune* (16 April 1946). C. D. Jackson sent a copy of it to Dick – with only the half-jovial comment attached: 'You nasty old man!'

for election to the constituency section; and the vote he got – 334,000 or runner up to the seven elected candidates – was extremely impressive for an initial outing. He was still, however, over 100,000 votes behind the Old Guard – people like Morrison, Dalton and Noel-Baker – who all kept their seats. Was Dick disappointed? With everything in the eyes of the Left going for him – the victory on the length of national service, the *Keep Left* pamphlet, even the packed Henry Wallace meetings – it seems likely that he was. Significantly, he did not risk standing again for another five years.

That was not, however, the main reverse he suffered at the Conference. At Margate on 29 May this came in a wholly different form, plainly premeditated but, so far as Dick was concerned, entirely unforeseen. From the day it opened he had a highly energetic Conference – rising on the first day to challenge the status of a Transport House pamphlet entitled *Cards on the Table* (designed as a reply to *Keep Left*) which all the delegates had found waiting for them on their seats. Dick asked all the right questions: who had authorised its publication, had it been approved by the Foreign Secretary or Foreign Office officials, was it written 'solely by Denis Healey'*?[34] Initially, he got an equivocal, temporising reply from Hugh Dalton on the platform – but, whether Dick realised it or not, he was playing with fire. Two days later he risked being burnt again by speaking in favour of a manpower resolution, which included a demand for drastic cuts in the armed forces: he made a fine knockabout speech, complete with a reference to there being altogether too many 'soldiers littered about the place'.[35] Everyone knew, however, that the major confrontation of the Conference would come in the foreign affairs debate on its last full day. Once more, Dick successfully caught the chairman's eye and made a critical, if slightly offbeat, intervention about the Government's policy towards the British zone in Germany: 'I hope the Foreign Secretary will say bluntly to the Americans that we cannot go on spending £80 million a year on importing food and raw materials for the British zone of Germany if we are going to have food cuts in this country at the same time.'[36] With that one sentence, he had prepared the faggots for his own Conference martyrdom; for, although in reply-

---

* It was. Denis Healey at the time was Secretary to the International Department of the Labour Party. He became a Labour MP, for Leeds East, in 1952 and subsequently, as Minister of Defence, served alongside Dick, with whom he never got on, in the 1964–70 Labour Cabinet. He was Chancellor of the Exchequer 1974–9, and deputy leader of the Labour Party 1980–3.

ing to the debate after lunch, Ernest Bevin spoke for over an hour and a half, there was only one remark in his mammoth *tour d'horizon* that later went into Labour Party legend. It came dramatically when the Foreign Secretary, having talked about how even Ministers were entitled to expect loyalty from the Labour movement, suddenly spat out in reference to the Commons rebellion of the previous November: 'On the very day I was trying to get the agreement with the Americans to prevent the bread ration from going down – on that very day I was stabbed in the back.'[37]

Inevitably, that phrase – 'stab in the back' – made all the headlines, and no one had much doubt at whom the charge was primarily aimed. With characteristic candour Dick acknowledged the extent of Bevin's triumph. He wrote in the *New Statesman* the following week:

> This year's Labour Party conference settled one thing at least. As long as he wants to do so, Ernest Bevin will control not merely the Cabinet but the whole Labour movement . . . No one should be under any delusion about the extent of Bevin's victory. He carried the delegates with him in his demand that his policy should be condemned or accepted as a whole and in the implication which ran through his whole speech that criticism of it was an act of disloyalty.[38]

It was fortunate for Dick that he had not then made any personal attack on Bevin. Indeed, in a speech at Deal – while the Conference was only half-way through – he had gone out of his way to declare, in reference to the Foreign Secretary, 'None of us wants his job.'[39] However, that never inhibited Bevin from referring to him as 'that wicked man';[40] and it may be that Dick later deceived himself into believing that 'Ernie was always ready to talk to me' – even if he was careful to advance as the reason: 'I think he quite liked a little opposition as long as he was certain he could smash it.'[41] There was, in fact, a side of Bevin that appealed to Dick, fascinated, as he was, by the ruthless use of power. No figure in the Labour movement was more aggressive in its exercise, and this aspect of Bevin's character commanded Dick's sneaking admiration. Hence his often related anecdote of how Bevin had deliberately softened him up before the Margate debate – by cordially buying him a drink in the bar at lunchtime – and his conviction that this hospitable gesture had been deliberately made in order that the personal shock of the 'stab in the back' charge would be all the greater. Revealingly, where most people would have borne resentment over being misled in that way, Dick – telling the story – would always add admiringly, 'That's how he smashed me.'[42] He may have grown to detest Bevin; he never despised him.

Still, if only because of their continuing running battle over Palestine, it was the Foreign Secretary who had become easily his most powerful enemy. How much Dick minded about being kept out of the Government, it is hard to tell;* but his own original timetable for being brought in was already beginning to run out† – and the experience of exclusion cannot have been made any easier to bear by the elevation to full ministerial status that autumn of such contemporaries of his as Hugh Gaitskell, Harold Wilson and Frank Pakenham.

Dick's own life, though, had its compensations. To begin with, there was his monthly column in the *Sunday Pictorial*, over which he took great pains and which must have made his salary at least equal to that of any junior Minister. There was also the question of his growing fame – both at home and abroad. This led not just to frequent BBC broadcasts but to a number of foreign trips (something largely denied at the time to most other British citizens through the stern requirements of foreign exchange control). By means of invitations to lecture, Dick was able to go abroad to Brussels in the summer of 1947 – which Zita, who accompanied him, found 'even more expensive than New York'[43] – and, again, to the States in the autumn. The latter trip, the result of an invitation to address a New York liberal dinner, was a fleeting visit, lasting just inside a week; but at least it provided Dick with the opportunity to catch up on the United Nations side of the Palestine dispute. He journeyed out twice from New York to Lake Success on Long Island (then the UN headquarters) to listen to the deliberations of an *ad hoc* committee of the General Assembly. This body had been charged with the task of considering the Report of the UN Special Committee on Palestine, which on a majority finding had just recommended the division of Palestine into separate Jewish and

---

* *Newsweek*, in what reads suspiciously like a story planted by Dick, reported on the eve of the Labour Party Conference that his 'stature as a rebel' is something 'he frankly enjoys'.

† See p. 111. Robert Bruce Lockhart's claim that Dick told him he would prefer to wait to join the Government for eighteen months or two years is not, however, wholly borne out by a note Dick made at the time, where he writes of having spent the first few days at Westminster in August 1945 'strenuously denying to oneself that there is any chance of being offered a job, but still subconsciously waiting . . .'

Arab States. The British Government fought a dogged, protracted, rearguard action against this recommendation; but, ever since the turning back of the refugee ship *Exodus* in the summer of 1947, with all its inevitable unfavourable publicity for Bevin's policy,* the will to maintain the Palestine Mandate had largely vanished in Britain. At the UN Dick at least had the consolation of seeing his own views vindicated: the surprise switch of the Soviet delegation from opposition to support of partition meant that the battle was effectively over. It may have taken until 1 December 1947 for the US to round up the necessary votes for a two-thirds General Assembly majority in favour of the partition plan; but even by the time Dick arrived in the second week of October, it was clear that that was the way things were going. He contributed an article to the *New Statesman* which, although simply entitled 'Politics at Lake Success' was, in fact, just as much about politics in the British Labour Party.[44] It says, though, something for Dick's developing political antennae that he should have resisted the temptation simply to gloat.[45] The victory over Bevin had ultimately been his, and for the moment that was enough.

For Dick, however, it had been bought at a rather high cost. He had consistently taken a gloomy view of Truman's America – and yet here was the White House, even more than the State Department, ramming through his own solution for the Palestine problem. Equally embarrassingly, Truman's Secretary of State, General George Marshall, had earlier that summer confounded all the warnings Dick had been in the habit of delivering about the United States' new economic isolationist tendencies. 'The Marshall Plan' of economic aid for Europe, first proposed by the Secretary of State at Harvard on 5 June 1947, contradicted virtually everything that Dick had been telling the readers of the *Sunday Pictorial* – to say nothing of undermining the central thesis of his two foreign affairs speeches delivered first in the Commons and then at the Party Conference. To his credit, however, Dick was never a man for half measures. If he had got something wrong, he was quite prepared to say so – witness the recantation that he delivered in the Commons in his first speech of 1948:

> I will be frank. My own views about America have changed a
> great deal in the last six months. Many Members have had a

* On 7 September 1947 Dick wrote a particularly vigorous column in the *Sunday Pictorial* headed 'The Jews: An Appalling Blunder', criticising the eventual decision to send some of the refugees back to Germany.

similar experience. I could not have believed six months ago that
a plan of this sort would have been worked out in this detail with
as few political conditions. It is an amazing tribute to Mr Marshall's personality that he has disciplined all the forces against him
in America itself and has at least got this policy presented to
Congress in a form as acceptable as it is to Western Europe.[46]

In later years Dick was to make no effort to conceal the somersault
he performed over his attitude to the United States. He had originally, he would explain, been a 'Third Force' man – wanting Britain
to take the lead in a United Europe designed to hold the balance
between the Soviet Union and the United States.[47] But round about
1947–8 something occurred to force him to change his view. Dick's
own subsequent claim that the sole factor influencing him was the
initiative of the Marshall Plan did not tell the whole story. An
equally decisive element in the shift of his position was a visit he
paid to Czechoslovakia (with Michael Foot and George Wigg) in the
immediate aftermath of the Communist take-over of February 1948.
Dick had always felt close to the Czech Social Democrats, through
his association with their great champion, Robert Bruce Lockhart,
during the war; and there can be little doubt that the Communist
coup – and the death of Jan Masaryk – awoke for him a number of
echoes from pre-war Germany. In fact, on his return from his five-
day visit to Prague in March 1948, he was quite explicit about it.
Reporting that what he had found was 'a very quiet, cold terror', he
went on to explain that it was not always necessary to have a revolution in order to seize power: 'You get power first in a coalition –
then you eliminate the coalition.'[48] (This, of course, was exactly
what the National Socialists had done in Germany, and the fact that
the parallel was in Dick's mind is suggestive of his new strong anti-
Communist mood – a mood that was soon, surprisingly, to turn him
into 'a firm Nato man'.)[49]

There was a literary by-product, too, of Dick's revulsion from
post-war Communism. Arguably, the book for which he is best
known – apart from his *Diaries* – is one that he merely edited.
Entitled *The God that Failed** it is a collection of six essays by former intellectual supporters of, or sympathisers with, the Communist

---

* The title was not Dick's own. It came, as he generously makes clear in a
footnote to his Introduction, from one of the contributors, the Oxford don, Enid
Starkie. The book was published in Britain by Hamish Hamilton and by Harper &
Bros in the United States in January 1950. The English edition went through five
impressions in a year.

Party who had since renounced the faith. It owed its inspiration to an argument Dick had had with Arthur Koestler while staying with him at his mountain-top cottage in North Wales. (Zita had remained friendly with Koestler since the days before her marriage and his remote Welsh retreat, near Blaenau Ffestiniog, had served as a holiday home for her and Gilbert while he was growing up.) What happened on this occasion – if Dick's account can be accepted at face value[50] – was that he and his host fell into a furious discussion after dinner as to what made people become Communists in the 1930s. No doubt, Dick – having avoided the temptation himself – was predictably superior. In any event, he records Koestler as having burst out in some exasperation:

> Either you can't or you won't understand. It's the same with all you comfortable, insular Anglo-Saxon anti-Communists. You hate our Cassandra cries and resent us as allies but, when all is said, we are the only people on your side who know what it's all about.[51]

Eventually calm seems to have prevailed sufficiently for Dick to come up with the idea that personal histories of what prompted individual intellectuals to join the Communist Party – and what later led them to withdraw from it – had all the potential in it for a book. And two years later – in a political climate that could hardly have been more propitious – the work materialised

For Dick there were, none the less, certain risks in the enterprise. Coventry had been remarkably supportive of him in his battles with Ernest Bevin* but it was very much a left-wing city; the last thing his local Party would expect of its MP was that he should wear the badge of any sort of professional anti-Communist. Fortunately for Dick, though, the tide even on the 'progressive Left' was beginning to turn – though, revealingly, he still found it necessary to insist in the City Labour Party's local paper: 'No one wants heresy hunting in Coventry . . . My views have remained unchanged ever since I was first elected.'[53] The latter part of that statement was not, of course, strictly true, although Dick was at least entitled to claim that the Communists themselves had altered the rules of the game. So

---

* On 28 May 1948, a fortnight after the formal foundation of the State of Israel, the Coventry East General Management Committee unanimously passed a resolution declaring that 'Comrade Crossman's pursuance of a just solution of the Palestine problem, as revealed by his work on the Anglo-American Commission of 1946 followed by his speeches from time to time in the Commons, should be rewarded by the sincere appreciation of all within the Party.'[52]

enraged, indeed, was the Communist Party's leadership by the Labour Government's acceptance of the Marshall Plan that it began to threaten war on the industrial front – warning that increased production in Britain could from now on only benefit American 'imperialism'. It was the kind of challenge that enabled Dick to appear, at least locally, in the unaccustomed role of the antagonist of 'moles' and 'subversives'.

Even at Westminster, Dick had begun to wear what was almost a mask of respectability. In 1948 he embarked on no major policy revolts, keeping his dissent from the official Government line to such forgivable issues, for an MP from a car manufacturing city, as urging the abolition of the basic petrol ration. There appears, in fact, to have been some hope in the higher reaches of the Labour Party that he had at last started to 'settle down' – and, in a personal sense at least, that was true. In the summer of 1948 Dick and Zita managed finally to move out from their attic rooms in Kingsley Martin's flat in Buckingham Street, finding a house of their own at 9 Vincent Square, Westminster (it was to remain Dick's London home, rented from the Church Commissioners, until his death in 1974). For Zita, in particular, this was a change for the better: she had never liked Buckingham Street – 'she found it intolerable because it was so filthy'[54] – and the move also meant that she could incorporate herself more fully in Dick's political life.* They did not, however, leave Town End Farm, Radnage – keeping it for weekends and maintaining, with the help of a housekeeper and a gardener, the smallholding of chickens, beehives and fruit growing that Zita had built up during the war.[55]

His move away from living, as well as working, under Kingsley Martin's shadow also had a liberating effect on Dick. The positions he took up in 1948 – a tough line in justification of the Berlin airlift, endorsement of the Marshall Plan, even forthright support for the foundation of NATO – were certainly not ones designed to appeal automatically to the editor of the *New Statesman*. According to Dick's subsequent version of their relationship, the summer of 1948 marked the beginning of their estrangement,† with Martin

---

* She may never, however, have been able to do this as closely as she would have liked. Dick's long-time secretary, Rose Cohen, who stayed with him till the 1960s, was a highly professional amanuensis in both his political and journalistic activities.

† Kingsley Martin himself dated it earlier, tracing his distrust of Dick back to his role over the Henry Wallace visit in the spring of 1947 and his repudiation of it later to the *Saturday Evening Post*. See p. 137 above.

particularly holding against him the 'political' way in which he had run the paper while he himself was away on holiday.[56] Dick remained, however, very much an integral member of the *New Statesman* staff, going to its Lincoln's Inn Fields offices every morning and playing an aggressive, if not always decisive, role in determining the paper's editorial line. He was still given a free hand in any signed articles that he wrote, but over leading articles and comments there began to build up a conflict similar to that which had characterised his association with the paper in the years before the war.

By early 1949 that association was subtly to change. Dick had been writing for the *Sunday Pictorial* on a monthly basis since halfway through 1946; towards the end of 1948 he was asked whether he would like to make this a weekly column. Financially, the offer was too attractive to refuse – though, politically, now that he seemed to be on the road to rehabilitation with the Party hierarchy,* Dick should have seen that there were bound to be dangers. (These were not only political either: all editors are jealous and it was probably inevitable that Kingsley Martin would come to look on his own prospective heir in a rather different light now that he was a regular columnist in another, if very different, paper.)

At first, admittedly, no problems seemed to arise. Dick's opening weekly column, published on 2 January 1949, read like a Labour Party handout. Headed 'The British People Can Be Proud', it reviewed the progress the nation – and the world – had made over the past year. There was certainly nothing in it to cause any distress on the Government Front Bench (or even, it might be added unkindly, any envy to the editor of the *New Statesman*). The second column carried a more ominous heading: written from the home of Dick's old admirer and now Israel's President, Chaim Weizmann, it was entitled 'My Report on the State of Israel'. However, it managed to stay broadly within the bounds of political propriety – even if there was a sting in the tail. Having recorded the remarkable achievements of the State of Israel, since it came into existence on 15 May 1948, Dick could not resist making his last paragraph a pungent quotation from a Major in the Israeli Army: 'If we were to put up a statue to the Englishman who did most to create the State of Israel, we should have to choose Ernest Bevin. By trying to destroy us he gave us no alternative to taking our destiny in our own hands.'[57]

It was hardly the kind of barb calculated to please the Foreign

---

* The Cross-Bencher column in the *Sunday Express* (12 December 1948) had even speculated on Dick's imminent prospects of joining the Government.

Secretary; but at least Dick could claim that he was doing no more than the traditional job of a foreign correspondent by reporting a view held in the country he was visiting. No such defence was open to him over the article, also sent from Weizmann's home in Rehovot, that appeared the following week. Placed by the editor, Hugh Cudlipp, on the front page of the *Sunday Pictorial*, it was given the headline 'I Accuse Bevin' and amounted to an all-out personal attack on the intransigence and obstinacy still being displayed by the Foreign Secretary in refusing to come to terms with the existence of Israel.[58] If it had been filed by an ordinary journalist, it would no doubt have caused offence; written by a Labour MP, it provoked a predictable uproar. In a personal sense, Dick was certainly courageous – only the previous week five British Spitfires, supporting the Egyptian forces in the Negev Desert, had been shot down by the Israeli Air Force; but politically his action was little short of suicidal. It certainly put paid to a whole year of political good behaviour.

Having sent such an explosive report from what was in effect a battle front abroad, Dick clearly had no option but to follow through in the House of Commons once he got home. His original dispatch had referred to the need for Bevin to do 'some explaining' when the House of Commons resumed after the Christmas recess;[59] and he welcomed the full-scale Palestine debate that the Government eventually conceded for the last week of January. This debate turned out to be a historic turning point; for the first time the Conservative Opposition, very much at Churchill's own insistence,[60] voted against the Labour Government's Palestine policy – and, with the bipartisan front broken, Bevin had little choice but to throw in the towel. Dick seems to have expected him to do so during the debate[61] – the immediate point at issue was the British Government's readiness to accord *de facto* recognition to the new State of Israel – and he was infuriated when in his opening speech the Foreign Secretary refused to make any such announcement.

The consequence was one of the great philippics of the 1945–50 Parliament, with Dick sparing his old antagonist nothing:

Because the Foreign Secretary was afraid of a Jewish State he has created one. Because he was afraid of terrorism, he has made terrorists. Because he was afraid of immigration he has achieved the immigration of 140,000 people in nine months. Because he wanted to build the Arab Legion it has gone in ruins. Everything

14–15 Dick in civvies and in uniform

16 Broadcasting *Was wollen Sie wissen?* from Bush House; Dick (*seated left*) with Hugh Greene next to him

17 The 1945 election in Coventry, Dick and Zita (*centre*)

18 Labour celebrates election victory. From left: Herbert Morrison,
Clement Attlee, his wife Violet (*seated*) and (*right*) Arthur Greenwood
and Ernest Bevin

he tried to do failed. Everything he tried to prevent has come about . . . Prejudice, to my mind, has blinded the Foreign Secretary, and compelled this country to accept a grave diplomatic defeat and humiliation.[62]

That was strong stuff even from a rebel back-bencher – and the political correspondent who judged that 'with this one speech Crossman deliberately threw away all chances of promotion'[63] was scarcely making any very rash forecast. Still, he could certainly claim to have made an impact: a Conservative newspaper called his contribution to the debate 'the best backbench speech of this Parliament'[64] and, to even the score, the left-wing *Tribune* considered that he had delivered 'the speech of a lifetime'.[65]

What mattered most for Dick, though, was the moral defeat he inflicted on Bevin. More than sixty Labour MPs joined him in refusing to vote for the Government motion and, with the Conservatives opposing it, the Labour majority fell to an (for that Parliament) alarming ninety. There was even speculation that the debate had made the Foreign Secretary's position vulnerable and that 'were he not so powerful a figure in the Government his resignation would be probable'.[66] Nothing, of course, like that could be allowed to occur within a year or so of a general election. But it must have been a bitter pill for Bevin when, three days after the debate, it was quietly announced that Britain had at last joined the United States in formally granting recognition to Israel.

For Dick, that represented the culmination of a three-year campaign – and one in which he could claim almost total consistency. It had not, however, been won without cost: at the moment of victory, Dick had to face trouble in his constituency. In the Coventry Labour Party the fact that Dick and Winston Churchill should have spoken with virtually one voice was not something that was easily understood. (Moreover, local paper headlines like 'MP Defends His Action in Supporting the Jews'[67] – before the debate even took place – reflected an unattractive undertow of anti-semitic Labour feeling.) Worse trouble soon followed. Perhaps rashly, Dick had decided to take cover after the Palestine debate by going on a five-week trip to the United States – with all expenses paid by the *Sunday Pictorial*. This does not appear to have been a decision that commended itself to his constituency; certainly before he left Dick found it necessary to declare defiantly at a public meeting, 'Don't write letters attacking your MP for not concerning himself with Coventry's affairs because he goes abroad. There are good, sound

Coventry business interests concerned.'[68] (Perhaps wisely, since he was basically on a journalistic assignment, Dick did not specify what these were.)

How assiduous a constituency MP was Dick? It is hard to answer that question without understanding something about Coventry. Very much a car workers' city, often at the time compared to Detroit, its political life was dominated by the trade unions.* The last thing men like Jack Jones and Cyril Taylor, local chieftains, respectively for the Transport Workers and the Engineers, would have welcomed was trespassing on what they regarded as their patch by the city's two MPs. The same went for members of the City Council, who took their civic responsibilities very seriously and saw it as their job to create a model socialist community. If Dick had begun to run into criticism locally over 'absenteeism', it was a sure sign of disquiet over his political outlook. The fact was that Coventry stood no less staunchly for the doctrine of working-class solidarity than did Ernie Bevin himself; and any threats to Dick only surfaced at such moments when his activities appeared to be damaging the wider unity of the Labour movement.

It was just as well, therefore, that Bevin's surrender over recognition virtually ended the internal Party controversy. The Israeli Army's victory over the Arabs enabled Dick to concentrate on what Coventry rightly regarded as more relevant bread-and-butter issues. And here Dick, partly as a result of his American trip, could claim to have displayed some foresight. The first thing that struck him on his return, he wrote in the *Sunday Pictorial*, was 'the mood of complacency which prevails among some Government supporters'.[69] He proceeded to explain why he did not share it – displaying, as things turned out, a remarkable economic shrewdness:

> The next 18 months are going to provide the first real test of the British recovery. We have expanded our exports to 170 per cent of pre-war figures. But this has been achieved in a sellers' market, and at a time when Germany and Japan were completely knocked out and the USA was not in full competition with us. This year, just at the moment when buyers are beginning to jib at our high prices, German competition will begin to make itself felt and the recession in the USA may well force American manufacturers to

---

* There was no doubt of the political muscle exercised by the trade unions in Coventry. Dick was, no doubt, exaggerating – but only marginally – when he told the *Harvard Crimson* in April 1970 that his own voters in Coventry East 'would elect the back-end of a jackass if it wore the Labour Party label'.

begin an export drive. Unless we can lower our prices our export figures are bound to decline.[70]

It was very much the message that Sir Stafford Cripps, who had succeeded Hugh Dalton as Chancellor in November 1947, delivered in his Budget that same week.[71] There is no evidence that Dick was ever particularly close to Cripps; but the fact that his old Oxford contemporary Douglas Jay was now Economic Secretary to the Treasury may serve to explain the stern economic line that Dick took throughout the summer of 1949. It even led him, on the eve of the Party Conference at Blackpool, to come out against the abolition of controls and to emerge as the champion of continued rationing – explaining that both should be regarded as 'the normal instruments of Socialist planning in a mixed economy'.[72] (This was perhaps the first example of what became an enduring habit of Dick's of always trying to make a left-wing virtue out of an economic necessity.)

It was, again, wholly in character that Dick should have displayed a sense of excitement at what he boldly termed 'the coming crisis'.[73] The young don who all those years before had been tempted by the notion of 'a jolly good smash-up' to solve the problems of his personal life (see p. 38) never quite rid himself of the feeling that 'a world crash' could have an equally salutary effect in political terms. From his weekly pulpit in the *Sunday Pictorial* he monitored the progress of the American economic recession with increasing zeal ('for the seventh month in succession American unemployment figures have risen');[74] and he thought nothing of advising the Prime Minister to waste no time and call a general election before the Four Horsemen of the Apocalypse arrived.[75] It was all too public advice that must have caused a shudder in Transport House – only perhaps equalled by the collective shiver that must have gone through the Treasury when Dick insisted on discussing the pros and cons of devaluation almost four months before Cripps was driven to reduce the dollar value of the pound from $4.03 to $2.80.* He seems, in fact, to have spent the latter part of 1949 in a mood of some political irresponsibility. Was it the consequence of personal disappointment, was it the result of political frustration – or was it simply his own way of reminding the Government that he could still be more of a nuisance outside than within?

---

* The decision in principle to devalue the pound was taken by the Cabinet on 24 July but no announcement was made until 18 September. The new rate seems to have been settled earlier that month in Washington.

Some plausibility is lent to that last interpretation by a couple of stories that surfaced in the Sunday newspapers[76] in the same week that Attlee announced the calling of a general election for 23 February 1950. Perhaps mischievously, they both suggested that Aneurin Bevan, the architect of the National Health Service, had proposed to the Prime Minister that after the election he should succeed to the Foreign Office if Ernest Bevin found himself forced to leave it through ill health. The most intriguing detail in each of the stories was, however, the suggestion that, if Bevan succeeded in his ambition, he would ask for Dick to be appointed as his Under-Secretary. It all sounded, as the *Manchester Guardian* promptly noted the next day, 'wholly improbable'[77] – but Dick's colleagues were probably not wrong in seeing it as evidence that his ministerial ambitions had not even yet been finally abandoned.

The release of a new pamphlet – *Keeping Left*[78] designed as a sequel to *Keep Left* of three years earlier – at the start of the campaign was also interpreted in some quarters as reflecting Dick's renewed aspirations for office. Significantly or not, it dealt only cursorily with foreign affairs and concentrated instead on taking stock of the record of the Government at home and trying to draw socialist lessons from it. Once again, it was the collective work of a number of authors – even if this time the cover bore a mere twelve signatures rather than the previous fifteen. Yet the pamphlet's emphasis on the importance of controls (described as 'essential and permanent bulwarks of a socialist full-employment and fair-shares policy') left little doubt as to the identity of at least one of the guiding hands behind it. For obvious reasons, its tone was rather different from that of its forerunner. Although the exact timing of its publication was a matter of luck rather than good management, its authors plainly realised that it was likely to be launched on the world in a pre-election atmosphere; they were, therefore, anxious not to lend any aid and comfort to the Opposition – the most significant hostage that they offered to fortune lay in their advocacy of a national wages policy (hardly something that the Conservatives of that era could exploit). Revealingly, the main attack upon *Keeping Left* came not from any Tory newspaper but from the Communist *Daily Worker* – where its authors found themselves collectively denounced as '12 right-wingers':[79] but for an Oxford veteran of Communist attacks that was hardly a matter of much concern.

Even in Coventry, the Communist Party had by 1950 become the least of Dick's worries. The Yangtse incident of April 1949 – in which Commander J. S. Kerans ran the gauntlet of Chinese artillery batteries on either side of the river and enabled his ship the *Amethyst* to escape into the open sea – had stirred deep patriotic sentiments not least on the part of the industrial working class.* The British Communist Party thus went into the February 1950 general election with no hope at all of repeating even its 1945 showing. In Coventry East the retribution exacted by the voters was particularly savage. The same Communist candidate who in 1945 had attained nearly 4,000 votes this time could scrape together only 487. That did not save Dick, however, from seeing his own vote go down both in percentage and absolute terms; compared with 1945 his majority was reduced from 18,749 to 13,453. This result, though, may well have been affected by boundary redistribution (a third city seat, Coventry South, came into being for the first time at this election) and in any case was rather better than that achieved by Labour nationally. The Party had never expected to hold on to its overall Commons majority of nearly 150 but to see it slashed to a bare six was undoubtedly a shock.

The initial reaction, in a political world unused to small majorities, was that the task of governing had been rendered impossible – a reaction which Dick fully endorsed. 'There are', he wrote on the Sunday after the election, 'only two possibilities: there can either be a national coalition or another election.'[80] He was, he explained, opposed to the first but could see no alternative to the second. Attlee, however, had other ideas. The defiant wartime slogan 'Business as Usual' was adopted by Downing Street and the Prime Minister moved swiftly to get the message across that, so far as his Government was concerned, very little, if anything, had changed. That, of course, ruled out – another disappointment for Dick – any wide-ranging reconstruction of the Government; all Attlee's principal colleagues stayed at their posts and the most significant change in the ministerial line up was the introduction of Hugh Gaitskell into the Treasury as Minister of Economic Affairs. (There was one other change that for Dick may have been more personally wounding – his old Oxford rival, Patrick Gordon Walker, was dramatically promoted from being Under-Secretary in the Department to Secretary of State for Commonwealth Relations with a seat in the Cabinet.)

---

* Dick himself, typically, took a minority view. 'British warships', he wrote in the *Sunday Pictorial*, 'are as out of place on the Yangtse as Chinese warships would be on the Thames.'

Dick's own view was that the Party had thrown the election away
– and he had no doubt where the responsibility for that lay:

> Herbert Morrison got his way, as he usually does, and persuaded
> the party to water down its Socialism in an effort to appease the
> middle-class vote . . . Enough confusion was created to prevent
> the nation from taking the decision which was required and which
> I am firmly convinced would have been taken if it had been
> presented with a clearcut choice.[81]

It says something for the primary allegiance which Dick continued
to yield to the Labour Party that he should have followed that
newspaper attack up with a surprisingly humble letter to Morrison:

> *Personal and Confidential*   *13 March 1950*
> Dear Herbert,
>   When, in the past, I have sent you a paper, you have always
> encouraged me by apparently liking to read it. I am sending you
> these rather lengthy notes because I publicly criticised you on the
> Sunday after the election, and I don't think I have any right to do
> that without letting you know in detail and in private why I did so.
>   As you will see, my own very strong feeling is that there is no
> reason for any acute policy differences between different wings of
> the Party, provided that we define our Socialism in terms not of the
> controversies of the 1930s but of the facts of the past four years.
>   Yours sincerely,
>   DICK[82]

The last sentence was almost an echo of the central message of
Keeping Left – and Morrison could perhaps have been forgiven if he
felt he was re-reading off a typescript what had already appeared in
a printed pamphlet. Nevertheless his reaction seems to have been
polite enough: certainly, within a fortnight Dick felt sufficiently
encouraged to send him a 'revised and somewhat expanded'[83] version of the original document. A substantial part of it was concerned
with criticisms of the Party organisation – and on that Morrison may
well have felt resentful, since he was effectively in charge of it. What
must, though, have delighted him, as one of the most stalwart right-
wing members of the Cabinet, was this blunt unilateral declaration
(going well beyond *Keeping Left*) on Dick's part:

> I doubt if anyone now denies that the proposals for new national-
> isation [these included sugar, cement and water] in our election

manifesto – whatever their individual merits – looked very silly in the election campaign. Frankly, they were irrelevant. If they were calculated to appease Left-wing Socialists, they certainly did not accomplish that purpose; and they certainly lost us floating votes because they seemed to imply a vague threat of unlimited nationalisation.[84]

It was a classic definition of what was later to be termed 'the revisionist' case;[85] and even if it was combined – as it was – with an attack on the whole concept of the centralised, Morrisonian public corporation, it would have been surprising if as astute a political operator as Labour's chief tactician had not spotted the value of such a left-wing conversion to pragmatism. It appears anyway that he did: Dick's covering letter accompanying the second draft of his 'Notes for the attention of the Lord President' included the slightly defensive comment: 'I have no objection to your showing these to anyone in their present form. I have, however, left the document in the form of a private note to you, since I do not wish to seem anxious to push my views onto the National Executive.'[86]

For Dick, it was an uncharacteristically bashful attitude but – perhaps because he was in the process of falling out with his old left-wing friends without finding any new ones – he kept a surprisingly low political profile throughout the twenty-month history of the 1950–1 Parliament. What drift there was, though, seems throughout to have been to the Cold War right.*

Dick became a surprisingly strong advocate of Britain joining in the negotiations that led to the formation of the Iron and Steel Community – warning prophetically in the Commons: 'My greatest fear is that for overriding reasons of French prestige and German national policy a treaty could very easily be signed between these two nations which might exclude us for ever.'[88] He got into a slightly undignified public quarrel with the Soviet writer, Ilya Ehrenburg – invited to Britain by the British Peace Committee – over what the latter had, or had not, said in the course of a private meeting with

---

* There were still limits, however, at which Dick drew the line. A dinner party in the House of Commons in September 1950 in honour of Arthur Koestler (author of the most praised essay in *The God that Failed*) ended in a violent altercation between Dick and his chief guest. Koestler accused the British Labour Party of not doing enough to counteract Communist influence in Europe and Dick retaliated by charging Koestler with telling 'anti-British lies'. So acrimonious did the atmosphere become that Koestler and his wife marched out of the dinner, collected their bags from 9 Vincent Square, where they were staying, and booked into a hotel.[87]

the *New Statesman* staff; the quarrel, which led to a protest from
Ehrenburg in the Letters column of *The Times*,[89] was largely Dick's
own fault (he had quoted an alleged remark of Ehrenburg's that
Britain was 'physically and morally incapable of waging war' in a
Commons defence debate).[90] And, most mystifying of all, he
initially gave his whole-hearted support to the rearmament programme announced by the British Government in the wake of the
outbreak of the Korean War of June 1950. On the issue that within a
year was to split the Labour Party the speech he made in the Commons was one of the strongest utterances in the whole debate:

> The prime object of this rearmament plan is to meet the situation
> presented by the precedent of Korea. Up to Korea the Commu-
> nists in the Kremlin have done everything short of war. In the
> case of Korea a secondhand war was started. What we have to do
> now is, by next summer, to have sufficient strength so that no
> further experiments of this sort can be undertaken.[91]

It was hardly the easiest of positions from which to have to extricate
oneself – but by the following April, when Aneurin Bevan, Harold
Wilson and John Freeman* all resigned from the Government, citing as their reason the crippling burden of the rearmament programme, Dick somehow managed it. Their resignations, he
informed a wondering political world, had been 'absolutely right':
Hugh Gaitskell's† Budget had been 'wrong because it gave rearmament an absolute priority'.[92]

To the charge of inconsistency Dick was entitled, admittedly, to
plead changed circumstances. The rearmament programme to
which he had given such positive support was one envisaging an
expenditure of £3.6 billion over three years; that total had since
been raised to £4.7 billion. Moreover, the Americans had not fulfilled their part of the bargain, failing to make any dollars available for
the purchase of vital raw materials. And, if that were not considered
justification enough, what about the conduct of General Douglas D.
MacArthur as Commander of the UN forces? Had he not, before

---

* John Freeman was Labour MP for Watford 1945–55. He had been a
Parliamentary Under-Secretary at the War Office 1946–7 and at the Ministry of
Supply 1947–51. After his resignation, he joined the staff of the *New Statesman*,
becoming its deputy editor in 1958 and then its editor in 1961. He was subsequently
High Commissioner in India and then Ambassador to the United States.

† Hugh Gaitskell had become Chancellor of the Exchequer when Sir Stafford
Cripps resigned on grounds of ill health in October 1950.

his dismissal,* threatened to transform a local conflict into a world war by his reckless desire for 'total victory'?

The fact that Dick never felt constrained, at least in public, to offer any such excuses was arguably the most revealing aspect of the whole episode. The plain truth was that – after his various chops and changes during the previous six years – this latest reversal of his position astonished no one; it was merely what was expected of him. No one in the House of Commons denied his brilliance. Few even in the Labour Party placed much faith in his judgment. Their reservations were not so much intellectual as moral, and were perhaps best summed up by the Prime Minister himself. When Hugh Gaitskell, shortly after ceasing to be Chancellor, boldly risked saying to Attlee that, on grounds of ability alone, Dick should have been given a place in his Government, he received the brisk reply: 'Certainly not. Known him since he was a boy. You can't trust him at all.'[93] It could hardly be considered an impartial comment – the running battle with Bevin had attended to that; but it must still have been a melancholy reflection for Dick that, in telling the story, Gaitskell could always count on getting an equally amused reaction – whether on the Left or the Right.

* Gratifyingly for Dick, three days after he had demanded MacArthur's dismissal on 8 April 1951 in the *Sunday Pictorial*, President Truman obliged and fired him.

11   *Independent Bevanite*

Aneurin Bevan's resignation from the Government in April 1951 transformed Dick's view of his own prospects within the Labour Party. For the first time he felt identified not just with a solid body of opinion within the movement but also with what he was convinced would be the wave of the future. He lost no time in characterising the Attlee administration as 'only a Caretaker Government'[1] and grew increasingly impatient with its infuriating capacity for clinging to office. (In July 1951, he declared: 'I believe the Labour Government finished its job somewhere in 1948 or 1949.')[2] When the Prime Minister eventually announced a fresh general election for 25 October 1951, Dick greeted the decision with ill-concealed relief. This was not because he expected Labour to win but because he could see no point in maintaining in office an exhausted Government, bereft of its major personalities. The resignations of both Aneurin Bevan and Harold Wilson from the Labour Cabinet had been preceded by the retirement on grounds of ill health of Stafford Cripps in October 1950, and by the death of Ernest Bevin in April 1951.* With Herbert Morrison an inadequate substitute at the Foreign Office and Hugh Gaitskell an already embattled Chancellor at the Treasury, the Government bore little resemblance to the confident team that had been elected only six years earlier on the slogan, 'Let us face the future'.

For Dick, going into Opposition was now the precondition for the Party coming to grips with the future. From his point of view, the result of the 1951 general election was probably just about as satisfactory as it could have been. Labour was defeated but by no

---

* Bevin died just six weeks after Attlee had removed him from the Foreign Office to the sinecure post of Lord Privy Seal.

means humiliated: it attained the highest aggregate national vote in the whole of its history (13,948,385 – or nearly 225,000 *more* than the Conservatives) only to see its representation in the House of Commons reduced by 20, from 315 to 295. This was enough to give the Conservatives an overall majority of 17 – again a margin that in the more leisurely days of the early 1950s seemed to the political pundits hardly sufficient to sustain a Government on any long-term basis.[3] Dick's own result in Coventry – a majority down from 13,453 to 12,671 – reflected that in the nation at large: for the first time he had a straight fight and, though the absence of a Liberal candidate enabled him to increase his own vote, his Conservative opponent obtained a rather larger share of the former Liberal poll than he did. That was the pattern throughout the country; and the key to the somewhat bizarre result may well have lain in the Liberal Party's decision to field a mere 109 candidates compared with the 475 it had put forward in 1950.

Dick, however, was in no mood to nurse any grievance about that. Within two days of the last results coming in, he was boldly declaring to the Labour students at Oxford that he was convinced that 'within 12 months Bevanism which, under the last Labour Government was a heresy, will have become the official party policy'.[4] Nor was that his only source of consolation. In the House of Commons he discovered an entirely new atmosphere, delightedly reporting on the day the new Parliament opened:

> What is really significant is the cheerfulness and morale of the Party, compared with its state of semi-disintegration just before the election. What a difference it makes not to be scared of losing your seat! They are even almost friendly to the Bevanites, out of general sense of well-being.[5]

As a forecast of the mood of the Parliamentary Labour Party over the next three and a half years, that was to prove a little rash. But it may well have been justified at the time it was delivered.

One indication of how slowly Labour's civil war developed is to be found in a book that Dick put together, and which was published within six months of the new Parliament assembling. Entitled *New Fabian Essays*, it was designed as a follow up to the famous *Fabian Essays* the Webbs and others had produced over sixty years earlier. The new volume, admittedly, had its origins back in the days of the first Attlee Government – it had first been discussed at a weekend Fabian conference held at Buscot Park in July 1949;[6] but all the essays in it had been finally written in the wake of the election defeat. The most striking aspect of them was the range of viewpoints that they managed to embrace. Dick may have been the editor but other contributors included Roy Jenkins,* Anthony Crosland† and even Denis Healey. The Preface to the original edition was written by Attlee himself. Whatever differing political views they put forward – and they were not, in fact, all that contrasting (Jenkins, for example, wrote an essay in praise of equality) – the sheer catholic nature of the enterprise hardly suggested that any indelible battle lines were already drawn up.

Dick, whose own essay 'Towards a Philosophy of Socialism' was one of the weightier contributions, was probably right, however, in reflecting afterwards that the book's impact had been blunted by the political climate in which it eventually appeared. Writing in 1970 he described the book's reception as 'cold but respectful' and put that down to the fact that by May 1952, when it first came out, 'Labour politics were dominated by the Bevanite split'.[7] What, therefore, had happened between November 1951 and May of the following year to bring about such a change of mood within the Party?

The answer, of course, lies in the first of the Bevanite rebellions, which took place at the end of the defence debate on 5 March 1952. On that date some fifty-seven Labour MPs withheld their support from the official Opposition amendment, on the ground that it condoned the rearmament programme, and then proceeded, while the rest of the Party abstained, to vote against the Conservative Government's Defence White Paper. As in November 1946 in the famous Debate on the Address, Dick was once again given the starring role as the spokesman for the rebels. If only because of his speech in September 1950 endorsing the rearmament programme, he was clearly in some difficulty – but his candour seems to have carried him through:

Times have completely changed – that, I should have thought, is

* Roy Jenkins, first elected a Labour MP in 1948, was to be a colleague – and, in some senses, a friend of Dick's – in the Wilson Cabinet, which he joined as Home Secretary in December 1965. He later became Chancellor of the Exchequer (1967–70) and after four years as President of the European Commission (1977–81) was briefly transmogrified into the first leader of the SDP (1982–3). Created a life peer in 1987, he was in the same year elected Chancellor of Oxford University.

† Anthony Crosland (1918–77), never a particular friend of Dick's, was first elected a Labour MP in 1950. Ideological opponents, they fought the battle over 'revisionism' against each other in the early 1960s. Crosland eventually became Foreign Secretary in the Callaghan Government before dying prematurely.

something we all have to recognise. None of us, or very few of us, on this side of the House can deny responsibility for acquiescing in last year's big defence programme. We cannot criticise each other for not discovering until too late its disastrous effects. But what I urge upon the House is that we should learn the lessons of the last 12 months and what it does to a relatively free economy to inject too much defence into it.[8]

In cold print that may not look particularly convincing – but Dick, often his own harshest critic, was certainly pleased by his performance. He described it excitedly in his diary as 'an occasion all right, because when my name went up there was a general move into the Chamber' – and went on to relate how much he had been helped by 'Churchill's coming back for the whole speech so that I could direct it against the Tories'. His real source of gratification was perhaps, though, concealed in the comment, 'Nye could not have been more generous.'[9]

The difficulty with understanding the internal politics of the Labour Party throughout this period lies in the degree to which they were dominated by one individual. Hugh Gaitskell may have had his own reasons for saying so, but when early in 1955, in a conversation with Dick, he defined Bevanism exasperatedly as 'only a conspiracy to seize the leadership for Aneurin Bevan'[10] he was not all that wide of the mark. Certainly, the Bevanites – as their name suggests – were always a group based on a personality rather than a policy; no other Opposition figure in modern British politics has ever enjoyed the same dominant position over his followers. For someone as conscious of his own powers as Dick was, that might have been expected to cause difficulties. In the early days at least it did not – although he was later to recall realistically (though not resentfully): 'Of course, before Nye resigned in 1951 I was much better known in my own right because I was then leading the Keep Left Group.'[11]

At what precise moment the Keep Left Group – from which Aneurin Bevan had always maintained his distance while in Cabinet – ceased to exist as a separate entity and merged into a loose confederation of Bevanites is by no means clear. It was probably significant that when a policy pamphlet entitled *One Way Only* was produced as early as July 1951, it should have carried only the bylines of Aneurin Bevan, Harold Wilson and John Freeman; it was also certainly no accident that it was published by *Tribune* rather than the *New Statesman* (Bevan's attitude towards the latter paper was generally suspicious, whereas his links with *Tribune*, having been a founder member of its editorial board, were extremely close). Even before the general election of October 1951, Wilson and Freeman – though rather less often Bevan – had taken to attending the weekly meetings of the Keep Left Group; but the sea change in its nature and composition – to say nothing of its title – appears to have occurred at or around the time of the defence rebellion of March 1952. That was natural enough. If some fifty-seven Labour MPs were prepared to risk all sorts of disciplinary sanctions – including withdrawal of the Whip – then it was clearly a tactical imperative not only that they stood together but that they should have the opportunity of taking counsel collectively. (The Keep Left Group, which recruited by invitation only, had never had more than twenty-two members – increased to twenty-five when Bevan, Wilson and Freeman formally joined it in June 1951.)[12]

In the event, no dire penalties followed the Bevanites' first open demonstration of strength at the end of the debate on the Defence White Paper. Attlee and the Shadow Cabinet had wanted, at the very least, a vote of censure carried against those who had flouted the official Party line (combined with signed undertakings from each of them of future good behaviour), but the leadership was thwarted by a feeling among 'middle of the road' Labour MPs that nothing was to be gained by invoking all the clanking machinery of disciplinary procedures. The most a Party meeting, summoned specifically to discuss the issue, would agree to was a reimposition of the Parliamentary Labour Party's own standing orders, which had been suspended since 1945. This meant that in future it would be an offence for any Labour MP – except on grounds of a narrowly defined 'conscience clause' – to do anything but vote in accordance with majority decisions; but it also, of course, implied a recognition that those who had deliberately chosen to kick over the traces in the defence debate had done nothing for which they could be brought to book.

Dick himself was understandably triumphant at the eventual outcome – and lost no time in spelling out the main lesson he had learnt from it to his constituency Party:

> If a fortnight ago, the leadership had done what they intended and delivered their ultimatum [meaning the demand for signed undertakings as to the rebels' future conduct], we should not have accepted it. We should have been bound to accept expulsion. It was an issue of absolute principle. It was because we had enough people to call their bluff, so to speak, that it did not happen.[13]

Never slow to spot the part raw power plays in politics, Dick had undoubtedly put his finger on the central dilemma that confronted the leadership. Whatever disciplinary action they might initially have contemplated, it was simply not feasible to start a process which – provided the rebels all stood together – could easily have ended with the expulsion of almost one-fifth of the parliamentary Party. However, the version of events that Dick gave to his constituency by no means told the whole story. It was he, in fact, who had had to pull back Aneurin Bevan from his initial inclination to embark on a campaign of open defiance – candidly warning him at a meeting at Bevan's house in Cliveden Place that there 'could be no future in the wilderness'.[14] It was an early indication of the tensions that would later arise between Bevan, a figure cast essentially in a Coriolanus mould, and Dick, who never aspired to be anything else but an exponent of *Realpolitik*.

The relationship between them was always bound to be delicate. In the early days it was eased by Bevan himself. Conscious probably that Dick possessed his own fame and reputation, he made no effort to muscle in on his position as spokesman for the left-wing group of Labour MPs: in both the first foreign affairs debate of the new Parliament held on 20 November 1951 and in the defence debate of 5 March Bevan merely skulked on the back-benches while the man the *Observer* was already calling his 'principal lieutenant'[15] held the stage. For Dick himself, however, that newspaper characterisation may have been hurtful. Certainly, once the defence rebellion was over – and the threat of disciplinary sanctions had been effectively foreclosed by the strength of the Bevanite revolt – he quickly proceeded to serve notice that he was still his own man. He did so at a meeting at Staveley near Chesterfield in terms which were hardly designed to commend themselves to the more hero-worshipping of his Bevanite colleagues:

> I don't think Aneurin Bevan would claim that he has the quality of an angel, but he is no fool. As long as Clem Attlee is prepared to lead our party, and is able to do so, no one is going to be fool enough or knave enough to challenge him.[16]

There was one Establishment quarter at least where that message must have been received with relief. When the *Daily Express* had first disclosed, back in May 1951, that the Cabinet resignations might well mean the development of 'a Party within a Party',[17] it had caused some agitation within the BBC (which had increasingly come to rely on Dick as an all-purpose performer in programmes like 'The Week in Westminster' and 'Any Questions'). A contemporary internal memo, written by the producer of 'The Week in Westminster' and addressed to the Head of Talks, marvellously reflects the anxieties of the period:

> I have had a talk with E.R. Thompson [then the BBC's parliamentary correspondent] and he agrees that the *Express* story is substantially correct, though its treatment is undoubtedly an exaggeration of the facts. A meeting *has* been held, Crossman is active apparently, to re-form a Keep Left Group excluding some of the original members in 1946 . . . Thompson and I agree that the only safe way of considering a speaker's acceptability in the role of banner-bearer for the Labour Party is to study his *public* utterances and his *authentic* private view on each occasion that he is proposed. The Labour Party is in a state of flux at the moment, and this seems likely to last for a while. I think the only way one can regard Crossman is as a highly individual propagandist, who may have reasons and motives of his own for allying himself with Bevan.[18]

It has, admittedly, a splendidly Establishment flavour to it – revealed by its all too apparent apprehension that someone, previously regarded as a reliable exponent of official Labour policy, might be in danger of letting the side down. But its diagnosis was not wholly wrong, as the events of the next few years were to prove.

The differences between the two men had less to do with any views Dick may have held about policy than with the reservations he came increasingly to feel about Bevan personally. These are indicated in the diary he kept at the time, but they are more eloquently expressed in a letter he wrote many years later. In 1968 the then editor of the *Dictionary of National Biography*, E. T. Williams, sent him a copy of his own essay that he was proposing to include in the 1970 edition of the *DNB*: it provoked an astonishing onslaught on Nye by way of response:

> You seem to detect 'the development of statesmanlike qualities' in his later days. In my experience, Nye remained his unpredictable, irascible, brilliant and occasionally cowardly self throughout. Indeed, his trouble was precisely that he did not grow up and remained a man of immense promise which rarely bore fruit . . . In the common cliché he did have an artistic temperament, though others would have called it a feminine temperament.

His real weaknesses were, first and foremost, his indolence. The only time when he really worked steadily was when he was a Departmental Minister. Then the Civil Service and the discipline of over-work put corsets round him and forced him to go into training. Even so, he rarely did his homework. . . .

His second defect was a streak of cowardice. To put it bluntly, at critical moments he was inclined not to be there – an attack of bronchitis, perhaps, or just a sheer disappearance to his house in the country in order to avoid an unpleasant meeting or postpone a decision. In a Prime Minister this defect may be turned to advantage, since half the job consists of avoiding rows and decisions; but in a leader of a faction or an opposition, it has the effect of demoralising those around you. I was not the only Bevanite who adored him as a boon companion but who secretly knew he should never be Leader of the Party.[19]

It is only fair to add that that was Dick's judgment delivered nearly a decade after Nye Bevan's death – and it may well not have represented his mood at the outset of his Bevanite journey. Indeed, the period when he was probably closest to Nye was in the early days of their political association. There was a personal reason for that – and one that had little to do with politics as such.

By the summer of 1952 Dick and Zita had been married for nearly fifteen years. What had started out as a passionate commitment on each side had become a more humdrum relationship – with Zita wryly describing herself as 'the girl with the tools, the plumber's mate'.[20] If it was not quite the role in a joint socialist partnership to which she had originally aspired,[21] it was certainly one that she had come to accept without rancour. After the war, too, she had begun to develop her own interests – becoming a voluntary worker at a Family Planning Clinic in North Kensington and taking a particular interest in the welfare of the children at a Lambeth school of which she was a governor. It was while making one of her regular visits to this school that, virtually without warning,* she keeled over and collapsed with a cerebral haemorrhage on 3 July 1952.

Zita was taken to Westminster Hospital, whither Dick was immediately summoned from near-by Vincent Square. In no very robust state of health himself – he had just had his appendix out at the trade union Manor House Hospital, although the cause of the

---

* Dick was later to recall that Zita, untypically, had complained earlier that morning of not having slept well and had seemed 'very out of sorts'.[22]

trouble seems to have been a long-standing stomach ulcer – he characteristically insisted that the doctors should tell him the truth. They did so: the best hope they could hold out was that Zita might survive for a time, but only as a human vegetable. She had been taken into the casualty ward and, in the light of the doctors' prognosis, Dick declined to have her moved (he was shocked afterwards to discover that Zita would probably not have been admitted to a famous teaching hospital like Westminster in the first place, had not the doctors assumed that he would wish to have her moved to a private room). Fortunately, the end was not long in coming. There was time for both Zita's children – Venice and Gilbert – to come and see their mother and, as is the way with relatives in such cases, even Dick seems to have persuaded himself briefly that what he took to be a flicker of recognition could yet confound the doctor's verdict. A second haemorrhage soon robbed Dick of any such hopes – and late in the evening of Saturday 5 July 1952 he did something of which Zita herself would certainly not have approved (see note, p. 102). He went to knock on the door of his local vicarage and, finding the vicar of the church at the other side of Vincent Square at home, humbly asked him to come and say some prayers at his wife's bedside. The vicar, George Reindorp, who went on to be Bishop of both Guildford and Salisbury, never forgot his opening words: 'Padre, I am not a member of your flock but my wife is dying in Westminster Hospital . . .'[23]

Zita died on the morning of Sunday 6 July, without ever regaining consciousness. The cruel shock of all that had happened so fast proved too much for Dick and by that same evening he himself was back in Manor House Hospital with a badly bleeding ulcer. Although he remained there for nearly a fortnight, he was allowed out on Thursday 10 July to attend his wife's funeral held at Radnage, where they had kept their country home. It was designed as a family occasion – even John Baker, Zita's first husband, came over from Oxford – but Dick was enormously touched by the number of their political friends who took the trouble to turn up. Prominent among them were Aneurin Bevan and his wife, Jennie Lee – and nearly forty years later George Reindorp, who took the service, could still recall how 'Nye with his wonderful Welsh voice led the singing'.[24] There is no doubt that Zita's death made Dick suddenly seem a strangely vulnerable figure – and the support of his friends, especially perhaps of Nye, came to matter a great deal to him. He meticulously recorded those who came to see him in hospital and the names of those who wrote, noting sharply that from Clem Attlee came 'no letter, nor a flower'.[25] That was an odd omission on the part of the leader of his own Party – made all the more wounding, so far as Dick was concerned, as one letter of condolence he *did* receive came from the Conservative Chancellor of the Exchequer, Rab Butler. Dick was much affected by this chivalrous gesture – as is evident from the warmth of the letter he wrote back in reply:

Manor House Hospital   *9 July 1952*

My dear Butler,
    I hope you will excuse me dictating this reply to your extremely nice letter. About the only thing which makes life tolerable at this sort of moment is the kind of thoughts which prompted you to write.
    I hope it will not embarrass you if I tell you something now. For quite a number of years, half-jokingly and half-seriously, my wife had maintained that you were her favourite politician. We were dining in the House last Wednesday night, a few hours before she was struck down, when she maintained this to a group of Labour MPs who were sitting round her. When one of them asked why she held this strange view, she replied: 'I'd like Dick one day to have the same sort of position within the Labour Party as Rab Butler has in the Tory Party, even though he's unpopular.'
    I think you will have an inkling of what she meant, and the fact that she meant it made me more pleased to get your letter than I can tell you.
                    Yours sincerely,
                        DICK CROSSMAN[26]

The letter is a touching one, not least because it reveals Dick's anxiety to have Zita regarded as someone with a distinctive personality of her own. She had certainly been that when they first met eighteen years earlier in Oxford, and it may be that Dick felt a degree of guilt that his own subsequent public career had tended to cast her into the shadows. There is some evidence for the existence of such a feeling in a comment Dick made in his diary, within two days of returning to the House of Commons, on 23 July 1952:

It was nice with what extraordinary unanimity people felt that it was somehow unheard of that it should be Zita who had died. A few, no doubt, had regarded her as my wife in the background, but I think that the vast majority of people that met her knew that

Zita was an odd character in her own right and had a vitality completely of her own.[27]

To the end, though, there were aspects of Zita that remained elusive even to Dick. Carrie Hodgkinson, the widow of his agent in Coventry, could still recall thirty-five years later the genuine shock that he experienced on discovering – because of the need to provide personal details on a death certificate – that his wife had been not, as he had believed, two years older than he was but seven[28] (Zita was fifty-one when she died while Dick was still only forty-four). It had been in many ways an unorthodox marriage and the question is still perhaps open as to how far, at least once the war was over, it had been a happy one.* There is no doubt, however, that for a time anyway the suddenness of Zita's death knocked Dick sideways.

In August 1952 it even led him to contemplate leaving politics. While Zita was still alive, he had heard rumours that he might be asked to become Principal of the University College of North Staffordshire, the first of the future post-war universities planted very much in his old WEA territory of the north-west. North Staffordshire, or the University of Keele as it later became, had already attracted A. D. Lindsay, the former Master of Balliol and candidate in the famous Oxford by-election of 1938, as its first Principal,† and it was his death in March 1952, within three years of his appointment, that had created the vacancy. At first the idea of succeeding Lindsay seems to have appealed to Dick – and on his own admission, he was slightly taken aback when Zita, having been told of the rumour, appeared unenthusiastic.[29]

The wheels of the selection process, however, continued to turn – and at the end of the summer parliamentary session Dick received a much more formal approach. It came in the shape of a letter addressed not to Dick himself but to his parliamentary colleague, George Wigg, who had been authorised to raise the matter with him. Since the letter originated from an influential quarter – A. H. Blake, the Director of Education for Burton upon Trent, and a member of the University College Council – Dick decided that it deserved to be

---

* Certainly Dick's predominant feeling in the immediate aftermath of Zita's death seems to have been one of guilt. An astonishingly candid letter he wrote thanking Tom Driberg for a note of sympathy includes the confession: 'I stubbornly refused to learn from her when she was alive the real meaning of love.' Francis Wheen, Driberg's biographer, generously showed me this letter.

† A. D. Lindsay had been raised to the peerage in 1945 as Lord Lindsay of Birker.

treated seriously. He obviously reflected very carefully before replying to it:

11 August 1952

Dear Mr Blake,
    George Wigg passed on to me last Thursday your letter to him
of 6 August, and I have left myself the week-end to think it over.
May I, first of all, tell you what a very great honour I feel it to be
that you should consider me as a possibility to succeed A. D.
Lindsay.
    I find it extremely difficult to answer your question. For one
thing, as you may possibly know, my wife died suddenly a month
ago, and I frankly do not yet quite know how I shall face the
world after I have got used to the shock. If she had been alive, I
should have found it much easier to make the big decision, which
an affirmative answer would imply, of resigning from Parliament
and devoting myself to the University College.
    There is another and more mundane reason for my difficulty. I
am standing for the National Executive of the Labour Party, the
ballot for which takes place at the beginning of the Party Conference at Morecambe at the end of September. If, by any
chance, I were elected to the National Executive, I should feel it
out of the question to refuse the responsibilities to which I had
been elected. . .

Yours sincerely,
DICK CROSSMAN[30]

As things worked out, Dick's 'more mundane' proviso solved his
dilemma for him. On 30 September at Morecambe he was, indeed,
to his considerable gratification, elected to the Labour Party's
National Executive – beginning a term of service on that body that
was to last, until he voluntarily ended it, for fifteen years. For Dick,
who was never to be elected by his parliamentary colleagues to the
Shadow Cabinet (although he was once, very briefly, co-opted to it
to fill a vacancy)* this conferment of approval by the mass Party
mattered a lot and was to have a considerable influence on shaping
his political attitudes over the next decade. He owed his success

---

* This happened in October 1960 when Anthony Greenwood resigned from the
Shadow Cabinet in order to oppose Hugh Gaitskell for the leadership (a move he
did not finally make because Harold Wilson stood in his place). Dick was a co-
opted member of the Shadow Cabinet, during late October and early November,
only for a matter of weeks.

originally almost entirely to his association with the Bevanites: Morecambe 1952 was the year in which the followers of Aneurin Bevan made virtually a clean sweep of the seven constituency section seats, dislodging both Herbert Morrison and Hugh Dalton in the process. Dick squeezed on in the last place (attaining 620,000 votes to Bevan's own 965,000). After all the years of non-recognition of his talents by the parliamentary Party, it was scarcely surprising if the sense of finally being accepted by Labour's rank and file tasted rather sweet.

Dick was not, however, to enjoy it for long; within twenty-four hours it had gone distinctly sour. For that he had only himself to blame, as he later came to recognise. Never armed with the most sensitive fingertips in politics, he always rated the psychological blunder he made at Morecambe on 1 October 1952 as among the worst of his whole career. It came about innocently enough. Having prepared a five-minute speech for the foreign affairs debate, Dick suddenly thought – apparently on the way to the rostrum[31] – that the Conference might expect him to make some allusion to the agreeable change in his status that the National Executive elections, announced the previous day, had brought about. He proceeded to do so in the clumsiest way possible – starting off with a real 'thudder' of a joke and then going on to make things a great deal worse by seeming to convict himself out of his own mouth of being the most shameless sort of opportunist:

> I think conference will appreciate what I mean when I say that I feel somewhat embarrassed, because I am mentally and physically suspended between the platform and the floor. I will tell conference quite frankly that for the very lively and fiery things I decided to say yesterday, I felt – and I think conference will know the reason why – it was wiser to substitute less controversial things today.[32]

Immediately, according to that same day's *Evening Standard*, 'a storm of booing broke out which lasted for some minutes growing louder'. Nor was the *Standard*'s reporter slow to indicate the reason – 'Mr Crossman seemed to have said that violent remarks were for those climbing to power and should be dropped when they had achieved their aim.'[33] It was, on any judgment, a classic 'clanger', as Dick himself was candid enough to concede when he described in the *Sunday Pictorial* the following weekend how 'the booing nearly blew me off the rostrum – I have never felt such a backfire'.[34]

The view among his critics was that Dick never quite understood why what he had said provoked such uproar.* That, however, was far from the case. Even on the day of his humiliation he wrote in his diary: 'What one learnt, of course, is the intense suspicion with which I am viewed by my own supporters . . . the one person who shouldn't try, even in a joke, to be fair is the politician suspected of trimming.'[35] The incident was certainly branded on Dick's memory – and he did not fully regain his confidence as a Party Conference speaker until five years later when he won a standing ovation for his remarkable *tour de force* in expounding Labour's pensions policy.[36]

Another more notable consequence of the Morecambe Conference led Dick straight into a collision with his old Winchester and Oxford contemporary, Hugh Gaitskell. Not content with delivering a speech at Stalybridge denouncing Communist infiltration of the movement on the Sunday after the Conference, Gaitskell went on immediately to contribute an article to the *Daily Herald* in which he wrote scathingly of 'the Bevanite press propaganda machine' and explicitly identified Dick's column in the *Sunday Pictorial* as an integral part of it.[37] Curiously, this seems to have got under Dick's skin, though Gaitskell may well have been less than tactful in introducing into his article a quote from the *Manchester Guardian* in which the Bevanite journalists were described as 'masters of invective and malignant vituperation'.[38] It was this that gave Dick his opening to write a hurt letter of protest to Gaitskell the week after the article came out (the delay was, no doubt, caused by Dick going through his cuttings and pulling out every single reference he had made to Gaitskell over the past two years). This at least enabled him to end his letter with a challenge:

> I expect you find it difficult to take columnising as seriously as I do, but I have felt it a minor triumph to maintain in the *Sunday Pictorial* a column on the intellectual level and with the fairness which I have tried to give mine. And, since I know that you genuinely believe in fairness, I am asking you to do this:
>
> (a) If you feel I have merely selected passages to prove my case, please come to my house for an hour and read through the file.

* Writing in the *Spectator* a full three years later ('Quest for Crossman', 7 October 1955), the journalist Henry Fairlie summoned up a vision of Dick 'pacing up and down the corridor behind the conference hall asking in genuine bewilderment, "What did I do wrong?"' Against the background of his own contemporary diary it sounds a bit of a fisherman's tale.

(b) If this convinces you that you have made a very unfair accusation against a colleague, will you put it right?[39]

Gaitskell, however, was far too old a dog to be caught by a trick like that – and promptly replied amiably but firmly to Dick, yielding not an inch of the case he had made in the *Herald*:

Many thanks for your letter and the enclosures. As I rather suspected, you and I take a completely different view of what is and what is not 'personal' and 'vituperation'. I would gladly come round and look through the file at your house sometime, but meanwhile there are several of the passages which you have typed out which pretty well illustrate my point of view. Let me add that I, of course, do not for one moment doubt that you sincerely thought that all this was perfectly fair and reasonable. The trouble is that I do not think you ever realised just how much we resented it from a colleague. You once said to me – some five years ago – that you found it very hard to combine journalism and politics. I think that is the real trouble.[40]

It may not have provided a wholly convincing response to Dick's dual challenge – but Gaitskell had probably taken the best course open to him by shifting the dispute on to territory where Dick always felt faintly uneasy. He liked to believe that he used his pen to forward the cause of the Labour Party; but he did nothing of the kind (if he had done, he would have produced copy as boring as that of the *Daily Herald* – a 'responsible' paper singled out for praise by Gaitskell).

The inconvenient truth was that Dick believed in the power of ideas in politics – and this was bound to put him frequently at loggerheads with a Party leadership (for whom ideas all too often seemed dangerous things, best kept under control). From its point of view, Dick was probably at his safest as a journalist when he operated abroad: at least his overseas trips kept him out of Machiavellian mischief at home. But Dick was also an admirable foreign reporter in his own right – something he demonstrated at the end of 1952 when he spent the Christmas recess touring the Middle East on behalf of the *Sunday Pictorial*. He went first to Israel, then crossed into Jordan – but spent most of his time in Egypt, the first time he had been there since the days of the Anglo-American Commission hearings at the Mena House Hotel of 1946. He found a country transformed following the Army coup of the summer of

1952 – and grasped very quickly the need for the British Government to reach an accommodation with the new regime over the Canal Zone and the 80,000 UK troops who were still stationed there. He filed reports first in the *Sunday Pictorial*[41] and then in the *New Statesman*[42] pressing the case for the evacuation of the Canal Zone as quickly as possible – advice that was probably more palatable to the Foreign Office than to the ranks of the 'Suez Group' Tory back-benchers in the Commons. Most remarkably of all, in a period of just a fortnight, he met and talked not only to General Neguib (the nominal head of the coup), but also to Colonel Nasser and Colonel Sadat – the three men who successively were to rule Egypt over the next thirty years (the last two even became correspondents of his – each writing him a letter applauding the stand he was taking in the House of Commons in the early months of 1953).[43]

It was possibly characteristic of Dick's priorities that his visit to Egypt prevented him from attending the first 1953 meeting of the National Executive – though he noted, with typical journalistic cheerfulness, that he was able to 'read every detail of it in the *Daily Express* the next day'.[44] The National Executive soon proved to be hardly the kind of spiritual home he had obviously looked forward to when he was first elected. The difficulty was that the Bevanites had only six votes. Time and again they were crushed by the combined forces of the twelve trade union members, the five-strong women's section and the leadership (represented by the leader, the treasurer and the docile nominee of the Co-ops). Dick, having believed he was about to enter paradise, found himself instead in purgatory – and a great deal of the frustration he experienced in 1953 centred on the monthly NEC meetings. These normally culminated in explosions of anger directed at its left-wing members – who also happened to be the Party's prime Press communicators.

Here Dick found himself in a slightly invidious position. The target the right wing always had in its sights was not the *Sunday Pictorial* or even the *New Statesman*: invariably, it was the Bevanite weekly, *Tribune*. This left Dick in trouble on two fronts – first, with Kingsley Martin, who resented the publicity *Tribune* was getting in preference to the *New Statesman* and, second, with the *Tribune* board, who insisted on running their own paper as an independent fiefdom beholden to no one, least of all their co-belligerents on the Left. One of Dick's main problems in the early months of 1953 lay in trying to make sure that *Tribune* was never left out on a lonely limb of its own, where it always ran the risk of being summarily chopped off by the axe of right-wing discipline.

In this respect, he was not helped by the erratic behaviour of Aneurin Bevan. The only Bevanite elected to the Shadow Cabinet (Dick himself had prudently not stood for it), Nye, although he had agreed to the formal (and enforced) disbandment of the Bevanite group in November 1953, continued to follow a personally wayward course. In an effort to concert a political strategy that all the leading Bevanites could support, Dick took in the New Year to holding weekly Tuesday lunches at 9 Vincent Square. These were supposed to be attended by the five other Bevanite members of the National Executive together with the three members of the editorial board of *Tribune* – but, predictably, the most consistent absentee was Bevan himself (to be fair, he was often away on foreign travels). The result was probably inevitable: by the time of the long parliamentary doldrums of the late summer, Dick went through a bad attack of disillusionment with politics. He reflected more than once upon how much he preferred the life of a journalist to that of an MP[45] – and at one stage even seems to have considered defecting from the *Sunday Pictorial* to the *Daily Express*. He was certainly summoned to Cherkley, Lord Beaverbrook's country house outside Leatherhead, and given the full seduction treatment.[46] In the end, however, nothing came of it – in Dick's own view because Beaverbrook was disappointed with his lack of application to politics.*

It may be, of course, that Dick was simply depressed. It was just a year, after all, since his wife had died. So it was a considerate gesture on the part of his literary agent, Helga Greene (the first wife of Hugh Greene), to suggest that he spend some part of the summer recess driving through Austria and Germany with her and her teenage son, James. It was the second such holiday Dick had had abroad with Helga and she had certainly done her best to cheer him up – indeed a long-standing friendship between them, going back to Dick's wartime days at the BBC, seems to have ripened, after Zita's death, into an affair. (Helga Greene never concealed that she would like to have married Dick.)[48] It was thus perhaps not the most tactful thing in the world for Dick to blurt out over a restaurant

---

* 'We sat on the south terrace in a lovely sunset, drinking, while he tried me out. After some desultory conversation he said, "Next week will be critical in Parliament. Reputations will be made or marred. There is Dalton and Bevan on Monday on the last day of the Budget ... Will you be taking part?" I said I only spoke really on defence and foreign affairs, and he was obviously deeply shocked. "It's no good specialising," he said. "One's got to put oneself forward whenever there is a chance." '[47] *Backbench Diaries*, p. 219.

lunch in Austria to Helga and her fifteen-year-old son James: 'Of course I should have committed suicide when Zita died – I realise that now.'[49] It seemed to James that the remark was not simply thrown off in a desire to shock, that he was genuinely upset; at the same lunch Dick went on to give a long disquisition on the character of the Grand Inquisitor in *The Brothers Karamazov*. None of this stopped him, however, from making a very good meal off a blue trout.[50] The holiday seems to have been quite a success, with Dick – always the born enthusiast and teacher – making a particular hit with James Greene.*

Early September found Dick back in London to discover, as he put it, 'a delicious quiet'.[51] It was temporarily disrupted by a request from the *Sunday Pictorial* that he should review Hugh Cudlipp's new book about the *Daily Mirror, Publish and Be Damned*. Since Cudlipp was, in effect, his patron at the *Pictorial*, it was an awkward task – but, after agitated consultations not only with Hugh Cudlipp but with Cecil Harmsworth King as well, Dick brought it off with some aplomb.[52]

Towards the end of the month Dick's mind became increasingly centred on the Labour Party Conference, due to be held that year at Margate. Perhaps conscious of his catastrophe of a speech the previous year, Dick grew uncharacteristically apprehensive over the fate of his seat on the National Executive. It was, therefore, a great relief when he learned that his vote had actually gone up by over 150,000 and that he was no longer the bottom of the seven constituency representatives elected (his 788,000 votes had enabled him to overhaul Ian Mikardo). Dick himself put this success down to the pulling power of the *Sunday Pictorial* with Labour delegates; certainly it had not been a year in which he had made much of a splash politically. In fact, with the exception of the perennial running rows over *Tribune*, 1953 proved to be very much a year of armed truce in Labour's civil war – with even Bevan himself reaping the benefit of the lull in hostilities by being elected ninth rather than twelfth in the annual November Shadow Cabinet ballot. For Dick, however, politics had, temporarily at least, lost all zest. He made one long speech in the Commons at the end of the year – concentrating

---

* 'I fell for him completely. He had a great spontaneity and naturalness. I liked him enormously.' Ironically, James Greene later learned from his mother that the reason Dick gave for not wishing to get married to her was that he could not face bringing up two stepchildren – James had an elder brother – 'for the second time round'.

on the negotiations with Egypt over the future of the Canal Zone[53] –
and was delighted (though slightly disbelieving) when Bevan
remarked 'it was the best speech I had ever made'.[54] For the rest,
his mood was probably summed up by the very last paragraph he
wrote in his diary at the end of the year:

> Nye and I agreed that there has never been a Government which
> by its incompetence has given an Opposition so many opportuni-
> ties and that there has never been an Opposition which by its
> incompetence and division has muffed so many opportunities.
> But I should add that the left-wing of the Labour Party (or should
> one still call it Bevanism?) is also collapsing as a force. With no
> one standing for anything anywhere, British politics drifts. One is
> left with the feeling that life will really start when one gets into an
> aeroplane as a journalist on the way to Africa.[55]

For once, perhaps Dick was not being quite his usual open, frank
self. Life, in a different sense, had already re-started for him that
autumn.

One of the few Oxfordshire country houses where he always had
been assured of a welcome as a young socialist don was Prescote
Manor, Banbury, the home of A. P. McDougall, a farmer and
auctioneer of anti-Conservative inclinations. Originally introduced
to Prescote and its owner, Patrick McDougall, by his first wife's
friend, Dunstan Skilbeck, Dick had become something of a regular
visitor in the mid-1930s – attracting the particular interest of the
McDougalls' sole child, Anne, then a fourteen-year-old schoolgirl.
At that stage Dick was clearly a much more fascinating figure to her
than she was to him – but the thirteen-year age difference between
them tended to matter less as the years went by. By a curious chance
after the war, they were thrown together in a quite different context. At Dick's suggestion, Anne McDougall had become secretary
to his fellow Coventry MP, Maurice Edelman, in 1948 – and
although she dealt mainly with constituency business, she could
hardly help being aware of her girlhood hero's presence (especially
at election times in Coventry). After Zita's death, Dick again
became a frequent visitor to Prescote, and also began to see something of Anne, who, having parted from Maurice Edelman, was now
working for a firm of design consultants in London. No one, least of
all Anne's father, seems, however, to have detected that there was a
romance blossoming – and it was Dick who first blew their cover by
sending an indiscreet cable from Cairo (the first stop of his African

trip) to Anne at Prescote. Since it was Christmastime, the cable was not delivered but read over the telephone – to, as ill luck would have it, Anne's father. Understandably, he demanded to know what was going on and so became the first person to learn of their impending engagement. That was formally announced at the end of January 1954.*

This was Dick's first visit to Africa – and although it produced two articles for the *New Statesman*[56] it did not leave him with any abiding interest in the affairs of that continent. His trip, however, aroused some controversy, arising at its starting point in Cairo. Criticising the meeting he had had with General Neguib, the *Daily Express* accused him of 'barging in on a head of Government' and rudely asked, 'What makes this conceited MP for Coventry think he has any influence on British foreign policy?'[57] But the truth was that, on the Middle East at least, Dick did have some influence because he had taken the trouble to make himself an expert on the region and, to some extent, was able to be a sounding board for the views of the Foreign Office as against those of the increasingly vociferous 'Suez Group' on the Tory back-benches. An indication of the antagonism he aroused in those quarters is to be found in an extraordinary attack upon him (combining snobbery with condescension) that appeared in the normally civilised columns of *Time and Tide* at the beginning of January 1954:

> Crossman is not a Communist or a fellow-traveller but he is that most pernicious of all characters in our national life, the persistent anti-patriot. And he has the talent of deploying *New Statesman* arguments at *Sunday Pictorial* level. *New Statesman* arguments were pernicious enough when they destroyed the morale of a whole generation of dons, schoolmasters, journalists and education officers; given the popular emotional twist that appeals to millions of typists, office-boys and conscripts, they can wreck what remains of our strength as a nation.[58]

Of course, not all Tories took that view. Dick always remained on extremely cordial terms with his House of Commons 'pair', the wealthy stockbroker, Sir Alexander Spearman† and he had a

---

* Dick did not learn of Anne's acceptance of his proposal until he returned to London on 15 January 1954.

† Sir Alexander Spearman (1917–77) was Conservative MP for Scarborough and Whitby 1941–66. It was in his London home that the Tory rebels against the Suez invasion of 1956 initially gathered.

long-standing friendly, joshing relationship (born of a succession of one-night stands in university debating halls) with that rising Tory star of the TV screen, Sir Robert Boothby.* He also, perhaps more than most Labour MPs, moved about in London society – never having any qualms about going to parties given by those with whom he politically disagreed.

What he was not so good at was keeping his social lines open within the armed encampment of the Labour Party. One of his fiancée's first parliamentary encounters taught her how soon a conversation with Dick could degenerate into a massive political quarrel. Dick's victim on this occasion was the inoffensive (and ineffective) Labour front-bencher, Sir Frank Soskice.† He had come up to the couple in the Central Lobby, mainly to make Anne's acquaintance. In no time he found himself being told that his support of Ernest Bevin's policy all those years ago had made him 'an accomplice to genocide' – although, Dick brutally added, that would, no doubt, not stop him the next morning from 'going to the Israeli Independence Day and drinking their good drink, having forgiven them for all the ill we have done them'.[59]

Unprovoked onslaughts of that kind may not have mattered to Dick so long as he knew that there was a kraal of Bevanites with whom he could always seek companionship and refuge. But in 1954 divisions broke out in the Bevanite camp causing wounds to Dick's own personal relationship with Bevan which never wholly healed. The original fault was not Dick's. On Tuesday 13 April 1954 there had been the normal lunch of the six Bevanite members of the National Executive and the editorial board of *Tribune* at 9 Vincent Square. Nye himself had been present for once, and the main item of discussion was to work out a concerted line on the Indo-China war, where the threat to the beleaguered French garrison at Dien Bien Phu had raised the risk of American intervention. According to Dick, the group had spent some time 'steaming Nye up to the need for a strong party line' – but with consequences they can hardly have foreseen. When the lunch broke up, Dick went off to a routine meeting of the Labour Party's International Sub-Committee, while Nye left for the floor of the House of Commons where, as a member

* Robert Boothby (1900–86) created a life peer in 1958, was Conservative MP for East Aberdeenshire 1924–58.

† Frank Soskice (1902–79), created a life peer as Lord Stow Hill in 1966, was first elected a Labour MP in 1945. Solicitor-General and then Attorney-General under Attlee, he briefly became Dick's Cabinet colleague as Home Secretary in the 1964–6 Wilson Government.

of the Shadow Cabinet, he was in charge for the Opposition of that day's business on the Government's Rent Bill. Before, however, that was reached, the Foreign Secretary, Anthony Eden, made a statement at the end of Question Time on the Indo-China crisis. This drew some fairly non-committal reactions from Attlee – although at one point he did seem to be prepared to go along with the notion of a new treaty alliance in south-east Asia, provided it embraced Asian nations as well as European ones.

For some reason, this had an incendiary impact on Bevan. In no time he was on his feet – pushing past his leader to get to the dispatch box – in order to denounce any such idea: it amounted, he declared, to a deliberate policy of 'surrender to American press-ure'.[60] Although the demarcation lines of Shadow Cabinet respon-sibilities were not in those days quite as rigid as they have since become, it was by any standards a bad breach of parliamentary manners. Bevan had seemed to be repudiating the line taken on behalf of the Opposition by his leader and, therefore, had discom-fited the benches behind him while delighting the Tories sitting opposite him. Nevertheless, the incident could probably have been smoothed over by an apology – but an apology was the one thing Bevan was in no mood to give. At two successive meetings of the Shadow Cabinet – on the evenings of 13 and 14 April 1954 – he refused to retract anything he had said, walking out of the second one when Attlee himself made it clear that he refused to qualify in any way the official stand he had taken on behalf of the Opposition. On making for the door, Bevan had intimated his intention of leaving the Front Bench 'after Easter' – and that same night he made it a fact by announcing to the weekly parliamentary meeting that he had already resigned from the Front Bench.[61]

While the scene in the House of Commons was taking place, Dick himself had been upstairs in a Commons Committee Room trying to negotiate through the NEC International Sub-Committee a relatively anodyne statement on the implications to world peace of the situation in Indo-China. Since Dick and Nye had been together at lunch only a few hours earlier, it is the lack of co-ordination on the part of the Bevanites that provides the most astonishing aspect of the whole affair. Certainly, that became the burden of Dick's grievance against Bevan's behaviour.*

---

* 'Certainly at lunch Nye hadn't indicated he was going to take this line and I am pretty sure he didn't even know Indo-China would be up for discussion.' *Back-bench Diaries*, p. 311.

That it was ill-considered – and certainly not thought through – is probably best indicated by the trail of recrimination and division Bevan's outburst left in its wake. When he first uttered his resignation threat to the Shadow Cabinet, he can hardly have taken into account the quandary in which it would place another leading member of the Bevanite group. The runner up in the previous November's Shadow Cabinet elections had been Harold Wilson – and, by the ordinary standing orders of the Parliamentary Labour Party, he would automatically succeed to a seat in the Shadow Cabinet if any vacancy among the twelve elected members occurred during the year. Should he refuse to do so? It appears to have been the almost unanimous view among the Bevanites that Wilson had no choice: it was unthinkable that any one of their number should weaken their leader's protest by even appearing to acquiesce in a collective responsibility that he had found intolerable. As the original co-resignee from the Labour Cabinet of 1951, along with Aneurin Bevan, Wilson was, of course, in a difficult position – but it soon became clear that he did not necessarily accept the counsel of his Bevanite comrades. 'No annihilation without representation'[62] he said grimly to Dick on the telephone the morning after Bevan's formal promulgation of his resignation at the party meeting – and there was sufficient cold anger in his voice[63] to convince Dick that he was about to make a bid for freedom. From then on he seems to have resolved to cast himself in the role of Wilson's adviser.

For Dick, the opportunity to play an influential part in reshaping the future of the Left within the Parliamentary Labour Party must have appeared irresistible – but he had placed himself in a very delicate situation. It was bad enough that, through the leader column of the *New Statesman*, he had to comment on Bevan's wholly unpredictable action; the criticism there was surprisingly tough ('By his impulsive gesture, Mr Bevan has postponed – possibly for ever – his chances of succeeding to the socialist leadership').[64] It was worse, in some ways, that in the *Sunday Pictorial* he had to put his name to a column headed 'After Bevan's Walk-Out', though the tone here was markedly more gentle ('Aneurin Bevan is not a man who worries about short-term tactics . . . he is a man who must speak his mind even if it costs him his political career').[65] Worst of all, however, was his rash acceptance of the role of go-between between a leader who in the last resort regarded all his followers as 'dispensable' and a follower who was no longer happy to go on being regarded as 'Nye's little dog'.[66]

A letter Dick wrote to Harold Wilson – marked 'Personal and

Confidential' – within ten days of the dramatic *démarche* provoked by Bevan's resignation offers its own testimony of how ill-suited Dick was for the part in which he had cast himself. In the first place, he entirely misread Harold Wilson's intentions: his assumption evidently was that there was no question of Wilson joining the Shadow Cabinet except as the result of a fresh ballot – yet within a fortnight Wilson tamely agreed to being co-opted. Second, far from reconciling the two principals, Dick seems to have done his unwitting worst to exacerbate their relationship. It is hard to conceive of anything more liable to fuel Bevan's resentment than Dick telling him that 'what he had done was to weaken his own position' and strengthen Wilson's.[67] All in all, it was something of a miracle that Bevan even agreed to appear at the next Bevanite lunch, held after the Easter recess, on 27 April at 9 Vincent Square.

The atmosphere there, though, was never to be quite the same again. However hard he tried, Bevan could not conceal his feeling that what Wilson proposed to do amounted to 'gross personal disloyalty'.[68] Nor did Dick help matters by first privately and then publicly championing Wilson's right to make his own decision: the final affront to Bevan came when Dick, in his column in the *Sunday Pictorial*, spiritedly defended Wilson's eventual action in taking his seat around the Shadow Cabinet table.[69] Whatever the reservations held by other members of the group over their leader's initial impetuosity, no other Bevanite joined Dick in the highly unpopular stand he took.

It says something, therefore, for old-time bonds of personal friendship – if no longer quite of political comradeship – that when Dick and Anne got married at Caxton Hall on Thursday 3 June, the two most illustrious guests who turned up were Nye Bevan and his wife, Jennie Lee. (Suspiciously or not, in a galaxy of other Bevanites, a notable absentee was Harold Wilson.) Almost unprecedentedly while Parliament was sitting, Dick was allowed a three-week break from his column by the *Sunday Pictorial* – and he and Anne spent their honeymoon in Italy and Yugoslavia. By the time they returned, the House of Commons was already in the dog days of July* – and, apart from a premonition (as events turned out, well

---

* These, however, were enlivened, so far as the Government benches were concerned, by a crushing rejoinder Churchill made to Dick when the latter sought to interrupt him during a foreign affairs debate. 'The Hon. Member', the Prime Minister declared, 'is never lucky in the coincidence of his facts with the truth.' *Hansard* (14 July 1954), vol. 430, col. 496.

founded) that Bevan had made a serious blunder in sacrificing his place on the National Executive in order to challenge Gaitskell for the Party treasurership, politics seems to have been the least of Dick's preoccupations.

There was a reason for that, if a rather surprising one for a left-winger. When Anne married Dick, it seems to have been tacitly assumed that her father would now have no alternative but to sell Prescote Manor and the farm attached to it on which she had been brought up. (The farm was in a run-down state and needed a great deal of money spending on it.) It had initially been accepted by both Anne and Dick as the only sensible decision, much as they regretted the need for it. But almost as soon as they returned from their honeymoon, Dick, at least, seems to have begun to have second thoughts – and simultaneously Anne's father appears to have listened to advice from his friends that it was quite the wrong moment to get out of land. The result was that during the first weekend of August everything was put into reverse. An accountant was summoned to Prescote and the decision was taken that, instead of the estate being put up for sale, it should pass to Dick and Anne as a post-nuptial gift (with all the tax advantages that followed from that). The accountant also patiently explained that the expense of investing even as much as £10,000 in the farm need not necessarily detract from Dick's income – as it could always be set off against his earnings elsewhere.

Both Dick and his father-in-law appear to have been slightly shocked at the ease with which such tax matters could be arranged, but the outcome was still very satisfying to both of them. It meant that Anne's father could go on living at Prescote – he did so for another five years until he died in 1959 – and the only difference was that the estate now legally belonged to his daughter and her husband rather than to himself. If Dick felt any compunction about becoming (as he put it characteristically) 'that wicked thing, an urban gentleman farmer', it was a feeling that, revealingly, seems to have surfaced mainly in relation to Aneurin Bevan. Nye had just sold his London house in Cliveden Place in order to buy a farm of fifty-four acres in the Chilterns; and yet here was Dick the sudden owner of an estate of 360 acres – or (again as he characteristically put it) the equivalent of a Russian 'Kulak'.[70]

Prescote did not, though, start off by occupying the dominant place in Dick's and Anne's lives. They set up their own home at 9 Vincent Square – which, since Zita's death, had served as bachelor quarters for Dick (shared from time to time with fellow Bevanite

MPs). The house, therefore, needed a certain amount doing to it – and it may not have been an unmixed blow to Anne when Dick took himself off to the United States on a *Sunday Pictorial* assignment for half of September. As if to remove any suspicions that he had lurched to the Right, Dick took a sternly anti-American line on this trip – so much so that when he returned his normal column did not appear. In its place there was a question-and-answer feature in which he was called to account for his own anti-American views[71] (considerably to the Left of those of the *Sunday Pictorial*). To be fair to Dick, he was visiting the United States at the tail end of the McCarthy era of Communist witch-hunting, and he was particularly disturbed by the case of the nuclear physicist, J. Robert Oppenheimer, who had recently had his security clearance withdrawn.[72]

Back in Britain, in plenty of time for that year's Labour Party Conference, Dick – along with every other delegate – realised from the outset that it was bound to be dominated by the subject of German rearmament. The dispute over this had trundled through the Commons ever since the spring – when the Labour leadership had mustered a majority of just two votes at a PLP meeting – and it was generally conceded that the final battle over the Labour Party's stand would have to be fought out on the Conference floor at Scarborough. Dick had always been an opponent of rearming Germany but it had never been an issue on which he was prepared to go to the wall. In fact, at Scarborough he formed the view that it would actually be better for the Party if the leadership's policy prevailed[73] – which it did, if only by a quarter-of-a-million votes. The truth was that Dick – perhaps because of the time he had spent in Germany as a young man – could never quite work up the same intensity of anti-German feeling that affected some other Labour supporters across the Party spectrum.*

German rearmament apart, Labour's 1954 Conference was pretty dull. For the first time Dick spoke from the platform – replying on behalf of the Executive to a relatively low-key debate on legal aid and suffering the indignity of being corrected by a lady magistrate on a technical point.[74] He also once again improved his position in the elections for the National Executive, coming fifth – ahead not only of Ian Mikardo but also of his rival MP-columnist on *Reynolds*

---

* One of the most passionate opponents of German rearmament was Dick's old patron at Woburn, Hugh Dalton. The strength of Dalton's feelings on the subject even caused a temporary estrangement between him and Hugh Gaitskell.

News, Tom Driberg.* In Dick's eyes none of this, however, compensated for the loss of Nye Bevan from the Executive. He went down to a resounding defeat (by more than two to one) in his contest for the treasurership against Hugh Gaitskell. In company with most of the other Bevanites, Dick appears to have left Scarborough in a thoroughly dispirited mood.

The main reason behind the general gloom was the realisation on the Left that their standard-bearer of the past three years had fallen on his own sword. Without a power base either in the Shadow Cabinet or on the National Executive, Nye Bevan was beginning to look an almost irrelevant figure – something that Harold Wilson had obviously taken on board when he quietly remarked to Dick that it would now be up to the two of them 'to carry the parliamentary burden'.[75] There was some justification, however, for taking such a view – since Bevan's own reaction to his defeat had been to declare that he would spend a year campaigning among rank-and-file trade unionists in order to introduce genuine democracy in place of the block vote.

From the beginning Dick felt this was a forlorn cause - and once again his view was to be vindicated. His immediate preoccupation, however, was to prevent Bevan, like some latter-day Cincinnatus, from simply retiring to his farm. Since the Left had made their whole investment in a personality, there was always a sense in which they needed Bevan more than he needed them. There could, in short, be no Bevanism without Bevan – and Dick, whatever their quarrels and differences, had always fully understood that. From his vantage point as the convenor of the Vincent Square Tuesday gatherings, he probably did more than anyone else in the closing months of 1954 to keep Bevan's interests even marginally focused on the House of Commons.

* Tom Driberg (1905–76), first elected an Independent MP for Maldon at a by-election in 1942, became Labour MP for the same constituency 1945–55. He subsequently was Labour MP for Barking 1959–74. Created a life peer as Lord Bradwell in 1975, he served on the NEC 1949–72.

12   *Temporary Gaitskellite*

If 1954 had not been a very good year for the Bevanites, 1955 was to prove a lot worse. It was a year marked by quarrels and recriminations, one of which was to lead to Dick's final separation from the Bevanite cause. Before that happened, however, British politics itself had gone through a major transformation: the replacement of Churchill by Eden as Prime Minister, a general election in which the Conservatives increased their majority from seventeen to sixty and Attlee's retirement after a record-breaking twenty years as leader of the Labour Party. There was even a significant change in Dick's own journalistic life – the wrench of leaving the *New Statesman*, which he had first joined in 1938, and becoming instead a twice-weekly columnist on the mass-circulation *Daily Mirror*.

It was a switch Dick did not make formally until the autumn of 1955 but it had cast its shadow before it. In December 1954 a disobliging paragraph had appeared in the *Observer* speculating on the eventual succession to Kingsley Martin's editorial chair. Although it did not favour his prospects – he was branded as 'too erratic'[1] – Dick responded to it with some insouciance: on the evidence of his own diary, he appears to have been genuinely bemused by the hysterical reactions it provoked in the *New Statesman*'s offices, particularly on the part of Kingsley Martin himself (whom Dick described as being 'inflamed and in a state of high tension').[2] In face of a threat of libel proceedings,[3] the *Observer* promptly apologised and the next week withdrew its suggestion that Kingsley Martin's mantle was about to fall on John Freeman,[4] Dick's Bevanite colleague who had joined the paper in 1951. The truth was, however, that a casual gossip paragraph had put its finger on a very sensitive spot. Ever since Freeman had announced his intention of retiring from the House of Commons at the end of the

1951 Parliament, Dick's position as heir apparent at Great Turnstile had been under serious threat. Kingsley Martin had never wanted him as his successor, and in John Freeman – less colourful but a good deal more dependable – he had found the ideal means with which to block him. It was typical of Dick's strange streak of innocence that it should have taken him so long to wake up to what was going on. When he finally did, he proceeded to behave with an almost elephantine clumsiness.

That particular drama was not to be played out until the summer, however; before that, Dick had had to battle through the most difficult episode of his whole Bevanite phase. The issue this time was a new one – the H-bomb, which the British Government had announced its decision to manufacture in the Defence White Paper of February 1955. That immediately posed a dilemma for the Bevanites. Collectively, they needed to resolve whether or not to oppose the production of a British thermo-nuclear weapon. In an effort to determine the terms of the debate, Dick had joined his old (non-Bevanite) friend George Wigg in contributing a three-and-a-half page defence supplement to the *New Statesman* within ten days of the Government's announcement.[5] It was a remarkably tough-minded piece – in effect pointing out that there were now only two courses open to Britain: following the kind of neutralist policy in world affairs adopted by Nehru's India or accepting a nuclear strategy and trying to ensure that it led to an entire reappraisal of the arms race. Backed by the military expertise of George Wigg, Dick eventually came down in favour of the second – not surprisingly provoking Kingsley Martin to add a prophylactic note at the top of their article, which was headed 'The H-bomb: a Fearful Choice',[6] carefully explaining that their views were not necessarily those of the paper.

Nor, it soon became clear, did they command the support of most Bevanites. Yet here Dick had a legitimate grievance. Before writing the article, he had gone to some trouble to establish what position Bevan proposed to take. He had been astounded to discover that his robust view was that 'the British people were not prepared to see themselves denied a modern weapon'.[7] It seems unlikely that Dick had misrepresented Bevan's initial reaction as he went on to explain with characteristic candour: 'If Nye hadn't talked as he did on Tuesday, I think I would probably have come down in favour of opposing the decision but I was extremely impressed by his argument that public opinion was not ripe for that.'[8] Neither the political insurance he had taken out, nor the personal influence Bevan had evidently exercised upon him, ultimately did Dick much good. Even before his own article was published, he discovered that Bevan had changed his mind – and was due that week to answer a reader's question in *Tribune* with a demand for the removal of all American bases from British soil.[9]

Understandably, thereafter Dick would always refer to this incident as the occasion Nye 'ratted' on him. It undoubtedly lent an edge to their relationship during what was to be the most threatening crisis of Bevan's career – the all-out attempt to expel him from the Party in March 1955. For, not content with putting his anti-H-bomb views forward in *Tribune*, Bevan had gone on to give virtually a repeat performance of his SEATO attack upon Attlee in the Commons debate on the Defence White Paper at the beginning of March. Intervening from the back-benches, he delivered a powerful speech that, at least in its peroration, appeared to be a calculated assault not on the policy of the Government but on the official attitude taken up by his own Front Bench.[10] Worse, however, soon followed. Attlee wound up the debate for the Opposition; just as he was sitting down, he was ambushed by a question from Bevan demanding an assurance that the official Labour amendment was not intended to endorse the Government's view that we 'should use thermo-nuclear weapons, in circumstances of hostilities, although they were not used against us'.[11] Attlee, plainly discomfited, gave an equivocal reply – only to be rewarded with an audible, 'That's no answer, that's no answer'[12] from a now obviously angry Bevan. Thirty minutes later he joined sixty-one other Labour MPs in ostentatiously abstaining on the Opposition's own amendment.

Just why this particular action of Bevan's should have been regarded as a hanging offence by his opponents within the Party has never been quite clear. The whole parliamentary Party, after all, had good reason to know that he had an excitable temperament and that his behaviour was often unpredictable (even as they entered the Chamber for the start of the second day of the debate, Nye had murmured to Dick, 'I'm still completely in two minds what I should do').[13] It may be, however, that the disciplinarians of the Right realised that they would never catch him again at such a disadvantage; for, although Bevan had carried the pacifist and moral protest wings of the Labour Party with him, he had been unable even to persuade all the Bevanites to support him. Three who did not join him in his public demonstration of protest – but who went dutifully into the lobby in support of the official Opposition amendment – were Harold Wilson, John Freeman and Dick.

Still, in theory at least, the number who had abstained should have protected Bevan's position. As in the original defence debate of March 1952, it simply was not practicable to invoke disciplinary procedures against as many as sixty-two Labour MPs. But by his action in challenging the Party's leadership on the floor of the House Bevan had delivered himself into the hands of his enemies. His gesture in putting his question – and thereby undermining Attlee's authority – meant that he could be placed in a quite different category from all the other Labour MPs who had abstained.

At first Bevan himself does not seem to have realised this – indeed, in the Smoking Room after the debate he was, as Dick noticed, in avuncular mood. 'Nothing has changed,' he told Dick, 'it will all be as before.'[14] It was a prediction Dick was prudent enough to question. By the weekend it was clear that the knives were out in earnest – and that Bevan was going to need all the friends he had got. It was over this need for solidarity that Dick committed his first blunder. Nettled by an outright attack on his own views in *Tribune*[15] – and infuriated by a front-page story in the *Daily Express*[16] suggesting that he and other Bevanites were ready to resign from the Party and fight the coming election as unofficial Labour candidates if Bevan was expelled – he made the mistake of issuing a statement to his own local paper in Coventry. No doubt, Dick intended it to be no more than a repudiation of the *Daily Express* report, but by describing that story as 'untrue and grotesque' he had given the opening for the *Coventry Evening Telegraph* to create further trouble. Not surprisingly, the paper headed its own story: 'Crossman: I will not resign'[17] – and Dick was left to pick up the pieces as best he could both with his fellow-Bevanites and with his own constituency Party, which took a stronger pro-Bevan line than he did.* The truth was that, if the original *Daily Express* story had been damaging, Dick's attempted correction of it had been even more compromising – encouraging the right-wing forces intent on Bevan's expulsion to believe that they could get away with it.

His relations were certainly soured with Bevan, who expected his

---

* Exceptionally, in the immediate aftermath of his support of the official Opposition amendment, Dick felt it necessary to write a letter to the secretary of his constituency Party justifying the stand he had taken. Explaining that he had written 'extremely frankly about the rift which has sundered Harold Wilson, John Freeman and myself from Nye', he instructed Ted Davies to '*destroy this letter after reading it to the Executive*'. Characteristically, however, he retained a copy of it in his own files.

own supporters to resign (at least from the National Executive) if the ultimate penalty of his own expulsion from the Party was successfully exacted. Dick discovered that for himself when he bravely went to visit him, along with two Bevanite colleagues, at Nye's farm in the Chilterns on Friday 10 March.[18] It was not a very cordial meeting – probably predictably so – since Dick had also used his column in the *Sunday Pictorial* the previous Sunday to criticise Bevan's 'confused, and confusing, behaviour'.[19] Dick, of course was in a slightly different position from the other Bevanites, as he still felt wounded by what he regarded as his own betrayal by Bevan on the issue of the H-bomb (which had left *him* exposed and out on a limb, after the publication of the *New Statesman* defence supplement). But, with his taste for *Realpolitik*, Dick was not blind to the compensations which might flow from that. Even before Bevan had pulled the rug out from underneath him, he had written in his diary: 'The ironical thing is that, purely from my own personal point of view in the Party, it would do me a power of good if Nye were to come out against making the H-bomb, disagreeing with me, since I have a very powerful case and would then be seen to be independent of him.'[20] It was as near as Dick ever came to facing up to the fact that, for an essentially free spirit, the previous four years had not been wholly easy.

In any event, they were now over. Dick did his idiosyncratic best to avert the threat of Bevan's expulsion – at one stage even inviting Hugh Gaitskell to Vincent Square for a drink to try to warn him of the perils of the course on which he had so enthusiastically set out. Yet again it proved to be a not very fruitful meeting – all Dick got for his pains was a ludicrous lecture on the 'extraordinary parallels between Nye and Adolf Hitler'.[21] In the end, though, Bevan was saved – and Gaitskell frustrated – by an external event as much as anything else. Before the crucial National Executive meeting at which Bevan's immediate expulsion was due to be voted upon, the *Daily Express* came up with a scoop predicting that Churchill would resign before Easter and that a general election would take place in June.[22] Inevitably, that gave pause even to the lynch mob within the Labour Party. Although some (including Gaitskell) took the view that the only thing to go for was a clean break, the idea of a major Party convulsion on the eve of an election caused others to stay their hands. At the National Executive meeting on 23 March Bevan was spared from expulsion by one vote – although he was still required to go through the indignity of providing assurances to a special sub-committee of the NEC as to his future conduct (assurances that the full NEC accepted, if in a distinctly grudging spirit, at a further meeting on 30 March).

It was a deliverance which Dick greeted with considerable relief. Yet that all could not possibly be 'as before' is perhaps best illustrated by a clearly carefully thought out letter that he wrote to Bevan on the day after Bevan's reprieve was formally ratified. After dealing with a fresh quarrel that had arisen between them over a sentence Dick had included in a *New Statesman* unsigned leader the previous week,* the letter went on to address the reasons for the deterioration in their relationship:

> What I think you sometimes forget is that, on the few critical occasions when we have discussed either strategy or tactics in the last 12 months, I have been in disagreement with you, and said so . . . I believe your strategic aim is fantastically over-ambitious: my own is limited to trying to restore a proper balance between Right and Left in the Party, by strengthening the Left.
>
> In so far as my 'piddling little aim', as you would no doubt call it, coincides with yours we work happily together. But when actions you take for your strategy militate against what I am trying to do, we disagree – and it's silly for either of us to charge the other with treachery and disloyalty. Inevitably, I regard some of your actions as wild and harmful to the cause. Inevitably, you regard my unenthusiastic comment on those actions as equivocal. Surely we can only work together if we both accept what you so often say – that we have a fundamental difference. I do accept that about you. But I sometimes get the feeling that you feel you cannot or should not work with anybody with whom you have such a fundamental difference.
>
> One of the main reasons why I like working with you is because I don't always agree with you and because your mind works in a totally different way from mine, which is immensely refreshing. But it would be disloyal of me to disguise from you (and, to be fair, I never have) that in my view your general line in the past 14 months has taken you further from effective power and nearer to the danger you mentioned of becoming a Jimmy Maxton. In the

* The sentence that caused offence was an unpredictable one. Dick had written: 'The vast majority of Labour supporters pin their faith on Mr Attlee as their leader, accept Mr Gaitskell as their financial expert and look up to Aneurin Bevan as the spokesman and inspirer of their Socialist faith.' For some reason Bevan chose to take this as an attempt to 'marginalise' him – to put him, as he expressed it, 'in the position of Jimmy Maxton' (the romantic but ineffective leader of the ILP who had died in 1946).

last three weeks this deterioration, as I regard it, has been miraculously stopped by the over-confidence and stupidity of your enemies, and another superb opportunity has been presented.[23]

Despite its tactful *coda*, the letter sounds like a declaration of independence – and after March 1955, though courtesies continued to be maintained, any close working relationship between Dick and Bevan was never fully restored. Significantly, in contrast to 1950 and 1951, Bevan did not come to Coventry to support Dick and the other two Labour candidates in the election campaign ('He explained at length how his diary is booked up').[24] The election, held on 26 May, seems also to have reinforced Dick's fears about the damage Bevan's conduct had inflicted on the Party. His feelings over this, however, could well have been exacerbated by a rash mood of optimism which seems to have overtaken him once the election was announced.

With rather less sagacity than he normally displayed on purely electoral matters, Dick appears initially to have persuaded himself that the Labour Party could win. Certainly, he was sufficiently carried away to reveal, if only in the confessional of his own diary: 'I would be prepared to bet that, if we win the Election, Attlee will be prepared to offer me and other left-wingers jobs in his Cabinet'.[25] Moreover, he went on to declare his conviction that 'a Labour triumph in the municipals [council elections were due to take place on 12 May, a fortnight before the general election] will bring us a long way towards victory'.[26] For once, Dick was totally deceived about the mood of the country and in particular about the anti-Labour backlash operating in Coventry.

When the municipal election results were declared there, they revealed – as Dick put it in a letter to his stepson, then working in Nigeria – 'a violent reaction against the Left'.[27] The general election results a fortnight later were little, if any, better – indeed, as Dick ruefully confessed in a letter to the psephologist, David Butler, 'Coventry showed the worst swing against Labour in the country'.[28] Dick's own majority plummeted from 12,671 to 6,104 and Maurice Edelman did worse, seeing his majority go down from 9,588 to 3,173 (to add insult to injury the city's remaining Labour MP, Elaine Burton,* who had voted against Bevan in the PLP and almost lost her candidature in the process, fared significantly better, containing the anti-Labour swing in her constituency to 4 per cent compared

---

* Elaine Burton, a former champion runner, was Labour MP for Coventry South 1950–9. Created a life peeress in 1962, she subsequently joined the SDP.

with 6 per cent in the other two divisions of the city). The lesson was certainly not lost on Dick, who candidly reported to his regional organiser, 'I would guess that Elaine Burton gained somewhat by the fact that they had tried to throw her out as a candidate'.[29]

Elsewhere, admittedly, Labour did less badly – indeed, its national share of the vote declined by only 1·9 per cent. This, however, was still enough to enable the Conservatives, under Eden's leadership, to increase their parliamentary representation from 320 to 345 (the total membership of the House of Commons had gone up from 625 to 630); equally significantly, they managed to turn the tables on the quixotic 1951 result by attaining almost a million votes more than the Labour Party. Once he had abandoned his initial sense of ill-founded optimism, Dick was oddly sanguine about the eventual outcome – actually admitting to his stepson, 'From the country's point of view this was palpably the right result'.[30]

In saying that, however, he was probably motivated by his feeling that it was bound to assist changes at the top of the Labour Party – indeed, in that same letter to Gilbert Baker, he frankly confessed: 'I am now looking forward with the keenest anticipation to the re-assembly of Parliament to see what the Labour Party will do'.[31] As it turned out, to Dick's obvious frustration and disappointment, it did very little. With the exception of Hugh Dalton's public initiative in writing to Attlee suggesting that the time had come for the veterans to depart from the Shadow Cabinet – a move that shamed three or four others into going with him – the post-election pattern proved to be very much 'business as usual'. Even Dick's own hopes of being elected for the first time to the Shadow Cabinet came to nothing. Although Harold Wilson was easily re-elected and Bevan secured seventh place (thirty votes behind Wilson), Dick could muster the support of only sixty-two of his parliamentary colleagues, placing him in a not very consequential twentieth place in the ballot.

It was at this moment, certainly of political despondency and possibly to some extent of personal despair over his ambitions, that Hugh Cudlipp of the *Mirror* chose to renew a proposition that had been broached before. He did it in the first instance rather cunningly by asking Dick's views as to whether a colleague of his in the Commons (the much younger Labour MP, Wilfred Fienburgh)*

---

* Wilfred Fienburgh (1919–58) was Labour MP for North Islington 1951–8, when he was killed in a car crash. An accomplished journalist, he also wrote a controversial political novel, *No Love for Johnnie* (Hutchinson, 1959) that was published only after his death.

could conceivably make a regular *Daily Mirror* columnist. No doubt according to Cudlipp's design, Dick took the bait; after an initial feint in favour of Denis Healey – summarily dismissed by Cudlipp on the ground that 'he can't write' – the discussion between them proceeded to Dick's own availability. Cudlipp said all the right things, even conjuring up the vision of a regular *Daily Mirror* columnist having the chance to become 'a British Walter Lippmann'.*[32] It was enough for Dick to get hooked and, although nothing was immediately resolved, Cudlipp must have had the satisfaction of realising that he already had Dick wriggling on the line.

However, before he consented to being landed on the bank Dick decided on one last attempt in the area where his ambitions really lay. Kingsley Martin had been away when Cudlipp made his offer and Dick was not able to talk to him until half-way through July. By then Martin had been apprised of what was afoot by John Freeman, who initially seems to have persuaded Dick that 'rather than lose me he would like to see Kingsley resign and me take his place, in which case he would serve under me'.[33] It may be, of course, that Dick misread the signals conveyed in any such conversation: certainly, the received account later in *New Statesman* circles was that Dick had tried to hold a pistol to Kingsley Martin's head and that he had been outwitted by John Freeman, who had the good sense to realise that what the paper would most need by way of replacement was the services of a fluent, polemical writer. For that role, there was an obvious candidate – the then very young Paul Johnson† employed at the time by the magazine, *Réalités* in Paris, but who also served as the *New Statesman*'s Paris correspondent. Some time in July 1955 Freeman went to Paris and over dinner suggested to Paul Johnson that there might be a prospect of joining the *New Statesman*'s London staff – an offer that greatly attracted him.[34]

All that, however, was unknown to Dick. He blundered into his negotiations with Kingsley Martin – designed in his own mind to secure his editor's enforced retirement, if not immediately, then at least in a specified time-span – with absolutely no understanding of the cards that had been stacked against him. At first things appeared to go rather promisingly. Dick invited Kingsley to lunch at 9 Vincent

---

* Walter Lippmann (1882–1974) was probably the most illustrious of all American columnists. He wrote his 'Today and Tomorrow' column twice a week for thirty-five years.

† Paul Johnson succeeded John Freeman as editor of the *New Statesman* in 1965. He was, in turn, succeeded by Dick Crossman in 1970.

Square on 14 July and laid out his terms for staying on the paper and turning down the *Mirror* offer. It seems probable that he said altogether too much – though, poignantly, he recorded at the time: 'Kingsley took it all quite well'.[35] The next morning, however, things turned out differently. At 8.30 a.m. Dick received a phone call from the editor he had worked for over the past eighteen years giving him, in effect, the sack. 'I've thought it over,' declared Martin on the telephone, 'and it's quite definite that there is no room for the three of us [meaning himself, Freeman and Dick] on the paper.'[36]

In honesty, he probably should have said 'the two of us'. For whatever the exact date of Kingsley Martin's private memorandum about Dick – and internal evidence tends to suggest that it *was* written in 1955 – it is reasonably clear that, quite apart from the *Saturday Evening Post*/Henry Wallace episode (see p. 136) – his editor's view about him had become intensely moralistic. It is perhaps best expressed in the simple statement, 'I have never worked on the paper with anyone so brilliant but so impurely motivated.' As if that were not enough, Martin concluded his memorandum with the comment: 'I think he lacks the qualities which will bind a staff in loyalty to him and the integrity, disinterestedness and judgment that will make him a good editor.'[37]

If those represented his editor's considered views – and there can be little doubt that they did – then Dick's attempted putsch must have been doomed before it started. There was, though, genuine regret at his departure. John Freeman, in particular, wrote him a chivalrous letter:

Personal and Confidential   *15 July 1955*

My dear Dick,

I think the loss of you to the *Statesman* is a terrible blow, and one which I had most sincerely hoped to avoid; but the blow is to us rather than to you. Were I in your position I think that, on the whole, I should welcome the prospect of doing the sort of work which you are now going to undertake; and I am sure you are right in saying that your chances of inheriting the editorial chair at Great Turnstile in the long run are made neither worse nor better by your going off now. . . .

I would just like to say that the last few days have been exceptionally unpleasant ones for me, since I cannot help being aware of the fact that, had I never arrived at Great Turnstile, it is almost certain that the present situation would not have arisen. Nevertheless, I think you probably do understand – and I would certainly wish you to – that I have tried my best to behave towards you as a good colleague; for many reasons, not the least of which is that I regard you as a very much better journalist than I am.[38]

The editor's own formal response was, admittedly, a good deal bleaker:

21 July 1955

Dear Dick,
    Very many thanks for your letter. I shall present it to tomorrow's *NS and N* Board and explain why you are leaving the paper. I know the directors will feel the same sense of loss as I do and, at the same time, fully understand your motives. . . .[39]

Dick himself appears to have been genuinely taken aback by the speed and decisiveness with which he was bundled out. It was, of course, entirely his own fault: after all, he had precipitated the crisis. But that he had never expected it to end in this way is shown by a letter he wrote to the managing director of the *New Statesman*, John Roberts (well known to be at odds with the editor), on the day of his departure:

Personal and Confidential   *17 August 1955*

Dear John,
    I am writing to you because, as the Duke of Windsor said, 'at long last' I am entitled to do so, since I finished my last week on the *New Statesman* today.
    As soon as Hugh Cudlipp put the proposal to me that I should join the *Mirror*, I had wanted to discuss it with you but, as you will recall, Kingsley was at that time in Moscow and it was John Freeman's view, with which I concurred, that Kingsley, as Editor, would strongly and legitimately resent it if I discussed it with you before I discussed it with him. All I did, therefore, was to make sure that the *Mirror* had no objection to there being a 3-week period after Kingsley came back in which I could finally make up my mind after discussing it with the *New Statesman*. To my great surprise, this 3-week period disappeared because, within 24 hours of returning from Moscow, Kingsley had made up his mind emphatically and rang me up very early in the morning to tell me that on no account could there possibly be a whole-time job for

me on the *Statesman* and that was his final decision. All I could do was to write him a letter accepting this decision but asking for an assurance, which he readily gave on his own behalf, that leaving the *Statesman* would not prejudice my chances if ever the editorship were open.

I want to repeat to you something I made clear to Kingsley both before and after the *Mirror* offer. For some 18 months now I have realised that any Ministerial ambitions I may have had – and they were less than some people imagine – are unlikely to be realised and that my future lies in the realm of ideas and public opinion . . . I want to tell you that the centre of my life remains the kind of writing that I can only do on the *New Statesman* . . . I shall continue to harbour the hope, or illusion, that my stint at the *Daily Mirror* will prove to be only an interruption of my activities at Great Turnstile.[40]

If any proof were needed that Dick had been driven into a corner of his own construction, it is contained in that letter. In face of it, there can be little doubt that his original intention had been – as is not unknown among journalists – to use an outside offer merely to improve his position and prospects within an organisation to which he was already attached. By overplaying his hand, however, he had delivered himself into the hands of his chief critic, who behaved with something less than magnanimity right to the end. The most eloquent postscript to Dick's departure from the *New Statesman* is reflected in a note he wrote to John Freeman, who had been away on holiday, two days after leaving:

19 August 1955

What might amuse you was my last day at the *Statesman*. I went in vaguely imagining that after 18 years' service, we might part over a (cheap, of course) bottle of red wine. But no. At 12.30 Kingsley looked into my room and said, 'I've got to go off to lunch early with Owen Lattimore.'* Then Lattimore came along the passage and said (I had my coat off), 'Are you putting your coat on?' Kingsley looked embarrassed and said, 'Would you like to come, too?' I said I preferred to have sandwiches.[41]

Fortunately for Dick, there was a gap between his humiliating last

---

* Owen Lattimore (1900–89) was an American Sinologist who had fallen victim to McCarthyism. He eventually found refuge in the Department of Chinese Studies at Leeds University.

days at the *New Statesman* and his striking up at the *Daily Mirror* –
most of which he spent on holiday with Anne in Italy, eventually
joining up with Hugh Gaitskell ('who couldn't have been more
polite')[42] at a Congress of Cultural Freedom meeting in Milan. Even
while he was away, however, his future welfare was being attended
to by a then relatively unknown lawyer called Arnold Goodman,*
whom his old friend George Wigg had put in his path. His contract
with the *Mirror* was notably generous: he was to get £3,000 a year
with £1,000 fixed expenses (he had latterly been paid thirty-five
guineas a week on the *Pictorial*) and the paper, quite exceptionally,
offered him a four-year security of tenure. That there were still
some lacunae left for the resourceful Arnold Goodman to exploit is
revealed by a good-humoured but still perhaps slightly irritated
letter that Dick received from Hugh Cudlipp – who was, after all,
staking quite a lot by introducing a serious political column into a
popular newspaper:

12 August 1955

My dear Dick,

It happens that I am just setting off for Germany and will not be
back until Thursday next so unfortunately I have not the time at
the moment to deal with your letter in detail. But in general you
may take it from me that:

i) The *Daily Mirror* likes its employees to enjoy their
holidays. It believes, with the Socialist Party, in paid
holidays as opposed to unpaid holiday. Your lawyer's fears
are unjustified.

ii) Nor are we renowned for deserting our employees and
contributors when they are ill. Your Mr Goodman is
unduly perturbed also about this point.

iii) You state that your desire is 'to ensure that the *Daily
Mirror* does not kill me or dry me up within a short time by
over-production'. Our present contributors are looking
remarkably well, and if your Mr Goodman is as rosy-
cheeked as they are he also has nothing to worry about.

iv) I have never altered an article signed by a writer without his
consent during the long period I have been associated with
this business, and I am not likely to change my principles
now.

* Senior partner of Goodman, Derrick & Co., he was also Harold Wilson's legal
adviser. Created a life peer in 1965, he was chairman of the Arts Council 1965–72
and Master of University College, Oxford 1976–86.

I will iron out all these points formally when I come back, but in the meantime I suggest that you and Mr Goodman relax. Frankly, I am not half so worried as you appear to be about the whole transaction.

Cheer up,
HUGH[43]

Dick's column did not appear in the *Mirror* until Tuesday 20 September. By good fortune, it happened to be a day with a major running news story – and Dick, having scrapped his original effort, was able to devote his main item to the Diplomatic Service spies, Guy Burgess and Donald Maclean, who, it had just been belatedly confirmed, were KGB agents.[44] Even so, it was in some ways an indication of Dick's natural solipsism that he should have been 'somewhat disconcerted to find that the whole front page had led it, too'.*[45]

Apart from launching his new column, the main focus of Dick's interest – once he had returned from holiday – was the Labour Party Conference. Exceptionally it met in 1955 after rather than before the Conservative one, enabling Dick (wearing his new *Mirror* hat) to get his first glimpse of how the Tories organised these gatherings[46] before making his way to Margate to join his own Party's annual Conference. As always, he was faintly apprehensive about his seat on the National Executive, wondering if his much-publicised recruitment by the *Daily Mirror*† would have done him any damage with the comrades. He need not have worried: the NEC results, announced on Tuesday 11 October, revealed that with 897,000 votes he had gone up to fourth place in the constituency section, the best performance in these particular popularity stakes he was ever to enjoy. Two days later he had possibly the greater satisfaction of making his first successful speech from the platform. Called upon to reply to a debate on pensions, he displayed a sufficient mastery of the subject to cause the *Manchester Guardian* to wonder whether his

---

* One of Dick's more engaging characteristics lay in his ability to pick up jargon and then get it slightly wrong. He presumably had heard someone use the phrase 'a page lead' and then compressed it in his mind to make his own use of it. Alas, he converted it into a proof more of amateurism than of professionalism.

† The first report of Dick's joining the *Mirror* had appeared in the journalists' trade paper, *World's Press News* dated 29 July. It was immediately followed up by the *Evening Standard*. The *Mirror* – reproducing a paragraph from the London Diary in the *New Statesman* – announced it only on 10 August, but subsequently trumpeted the news of Dick's arrival in advertisements.

talents 'need any longer be reserved for foreign affairs and defence'.[47]

Inevitably, however, the subject that dominated the Conference was the future of the leadership. Attlee's initial instinct had been to retire after the election defeat, but he was prevailed upon, not least by Dalton (who specifically excepted him from his call for the veterans to depart), to stay at his post. He was by no means an unwilling recipient of such advice, since his prompt departure would almost certainly have favoured the prospects of Herbert Morrison, whom Attlee had never given the slightest sign of wanting as his successor. Having lost two elections, however, it was clear that Attlee, who was already seventy-two, could not be expected to fight a third – and the only real question lay in the timing of his retirement. Here an interesting sub-plot developed at Margate. The crushing second defeat of Aneurin Bevan by Hugh Gaitskell for the Party treasurership (Gaitskell put up his 1954 margin of victory of over two to one to more than four to one) meant that the Left was not at all keen to see any immediate contest for the leadership. Indeed, at that year's annual Party demonstration – in those days always held on the Sunday evening before the Conference proper started – Barbara Castle, on behalf of the Bevanites, drew a touching picture of evil forces being prepared to hustle poor deserving Clem Attlee off the stage before he was ready to go.[48] Since, however, PLP elections were not due that autumn (the new Eden Government having decided to run the parliamentary session through to October 1956) no imminent threat existed to Attlee's position. The matter had, in effect, been left for him to decide – though one or two other people were beginning to give voice to their own views.

Among them, somewhat to Dick's embarrassment, was Hugh Cudlipp. The *Mirror*, with its attachment to youth, was quite clear that what the Labour Party needed was a new, and younger, leader – and it had already selected its candidate, Hugh Gaitskell. This put Dick in an awkward position with his Bevanite colleagues – all of whom were actively campaigning for Attlee to remain, if only to give Bevan time to improve his own prospects. Such was Dick's dislike of Attlee that he would probably never have found it easy to line up with them anyway (and not only that – he was also the only Bevanite who, through having known him for something like thirty-five years, maintained any sort of relationship with Gaitskell). The longer the hidden power struggle went on, therefore, the more delicate Dick's predicament was bound to become – torn between his old political colleagues on one side and his new journalistic associates (combined perhaps with his personal aspirations) on the other.

Luckily for Dick, the dénouement came with some abruptness. On 7 December Attlee tartly told the weekly Parliamentary Labour Party meeting that he was announcing his resignation – explaining that he found it 'regrettable' that, despite an original intimation on his part of a willingness to carry on, 'there has scarcely been a week pass without one prominent member of the Party or another talking about my impending retirement'.[49] That, however, solved only one half of Dick's dilemma. He could hardly write a political column – least of all in a popular newspaper – and not have a view as to who the next leader of the Labour Party should be. How was he going to square the romanticism of his Bevanite past with his increasing sense of realism about not merely the inevitability of but the need for a Gaitskell victory?

Fortunately for Dick, Bevan himself rode to his rescue this time. In a last despairing attempt to thwart a Gaitskell victory, Bevan acceded to a request by ten elderly Labour MPs to give Herbert Morrison a clear run. He was ready, he declared, to stand down from the contest provided Hugh Gaitskell would do the same – Gaitskell, not unnaturally, refused. But Bevan's action meant that Dick had been provided with his loop-hole. Describing it as 'a damaging manœuvre' in his *Mirror* column,[50] he as good as announced his own support of Gaitskell some four days before Labour MPs were due to vote. Fortunately, when they did, the result proved to be decisive and clearcut: Gaitskell received 157 votes, Bevan 70 and the wretched Morrison only 40. At least Dick had nimbly jumped on to the winning side – but the incident inevitably left a good deal of bitterness among his former Bevanite colleagues. He was roundly denounced in the columns of *Tribune* by Michael Foot (writing under the pseudonym of John Marullus)[51] and, when he sought to defend himself, became the object of an even more violent assault by his NEC colleague, Ian Mikardo. This attack appeared in the form of an open letter in *Tribune* – and as an indication of the venom with which Dick had come to be regarded by his Bevanite colleagues some of it is worth quoting:

Dear Dick,

I've had an opportunity of reading your letter which appears on p.3 of this paper. It demands an answer. I want to answer it, because I've been for so long your friend, your colleague in many enterprises and your defender.

It will not be news to you that since 1945 you've had (as I and others have had) many detractors in the Labour Party and especially in the PLP. In particular, many left-wingers in the party have always feared that in a crisis you would sacrifice your political philosophy to your 'realistic' interest in power politics. Some of them, including some of your close friends, have often warned me and others against you. Be careful of Dick, they've said: he'll let you down in the end.

It's against these attacks that I've always freely defended you. I've believed that some of your detractors were motivated by nothing more than jealousy of your superior intellect.

I don't claim any credit for this record; it's a poor specimen that won't stand up for his friend. But I do claim that it gives me the right to tell you openly and publicly why a lot of people in the constituency parties who voted you onto the National Executive Committee were horrified by your *Daily Mirror* column of 10 December. . . .

Yours fraternally,

IAN[52]

The only phrase Mikardo failed to use was that reflected in the familiar charge of 'Double Crossman' – although that represented the thrust of his whole argument. It was undoubtedly an unpleasant letter, but was it an unjustified one? Probably Dick had been a little too slick in exploiting the loop-hole that Bevan had opened up by his apparent endorsement of Morrison's claims to the leadership. For the truth was that Dick's own mind had been made up, at least since the Margate Conference, that there was no alternative to Gaitskell's succession. Nor had he reached that conclusion in any reluctant spirit – as a letter he wrote to Labour's new leader on the day after he was elected adequately demonstrates:

I am *unqualifiedly* glad that you are now the Leader. I am also even gladder that there is now no fence with each of us on his own side. Personally – and because I like Dora* very much – it is nice to feel we can be friends again.

But I want you also to know that I am not a bandwagon kind of person. My value to the Party, so far as I have one, is as an awkward, independent ideas man who can always be relied upon to chase an idea further than is convenient.

* Dora was Hugh Gaitskell's wife, whom he had married in 1937. She was created a life peeress on the nomination of Harold Wilson in 1963. She died, twenty-six years after her husband, in 1989.

Be that as it may, yesterday was a very good day for the Party.[53]

Gaitskell replied gracefully to Dick's letter on Boxing Day 1955, repudiating any suggestion that he had ever regarded him as 'a bandwagon sort of person' ('I could make out something of a case for you jumping *off* rather than *on* during the last 10 years!').[54]

Perhaps more significantly, he immediately took up Dick's characterisation of himself as 'an ideas man' and proceeded to harness his abilities to the service of the Party. There was nothing Gaitskell could do about adding Dick to his expanding Front Bench team – he was regarded at that time with too much suspicion in all sections of the Party for that. But he did the next best thing by making him a member of an informal foreign affairs steering group intended to guide the sometimes faltering footsteps of the Shadow Foreign Secretary, Alfred Robens.*[55] Even more to the point, the new leader soon made it clear to Dick that he looked to him, following his Conference speech of the previous autumn, to come up with a 'half-pay on retirement' pensions plan with which Labour could fight the next election.

So for the first few months of Hugh Gaitskell's leadership, Dick found himself in the unaccustomed role of backroom boy. Of course, he still had an outlet for his views in his regular *Mirror* column – but that had the effect of making his utterances of less interest to other political journalists than they had been before: no newspaper ever likes taking in another's washing. Certainly, 1956 turned into a relatively quiet year for Dick – marred only by an undignified spat he got into with the Lord Provost and Corporation of Glasgow over some criticisms he had made in the House about the conduct of the Highland Light Infantry in Cyprus.[56] Early in the year he also caused some alarm to Gaitskell[57] by proposing to publish a Fabian Tract entitled *Socialism and the New Despotism* – in itself merely an expansion of two articles he had published some sixteen months earlier in the *New Statesman*.[58] Initially Gaitskell wanted the pamphlet stopped but, on discovering it was too late to do that, Dick merely removed all the more incendiary passages, particularly those concerning the trade unions. It was an exercise that he carried out with some aplomb: when the Tract eventually appeared in February, it received the remarkable accolade, for a

---

* Alfred Robens was Labour MP for Wansbeck 1945–50 and for Blyth 1950–60. Minister of Labour and National Service in 1951, he was appointed chairman of the National Coal Board by the Macmillan Government in 1960. He held the post for ten years and was created a life peer in 1961.

former *New Statesman* staff member, of a highly favourable leading article in *The Economist*.[59]

The general impression – at least among his former left-wing colleagues – was that Dick had consented to be bound over to be of good behaviour. During its first year (in contrast to what was to happen later) even his column in the *Daily Mirror* caused no offence, and his removal from the critical, querulous ambience of the *New Statesman* was obviously regarded as a reassuring sign by the Party leadership. The phrase that tended to be used by Hugh Gaitskell and his friends was that he had 'settled down' – and there was probably some truth in that. Here Prescote, where he and Anne now spent most weekends, probably had an influence: a year or two earlier it would have been difficult to imagine Dick opening a British Legion fête[60] – but he had begun to take his role as, in effect, the village squire rather seriously. He took particular pride in the development of the farm. He had appointed a manager, Dennis Pritchett, at the beginning of the year (and Dick was soon proudly recording, 'He has put Prescote ahead of every other farm in Warwickshire this season.')[61]

It was not perhaps surprising that politics, or at least parliamentary politics, ceased to be his central preoccupation. He made a highly praised speech[62] in the debate arising from the embarrassing Commander Crabb affair,* which formed an awkward aftermath to the April visit of Bulganin and Khrushchev to Britain, and followed it up a month later with an equally well-received contribution to a debate on Parliament and the Executive.[63] (Dick, of course, still had no specific Front Bench responsibilities – hence the nature of the roving commission he was able to exercise from the back-benches.) One mystery, however, has always been the remarkably quiet role that Dick played during the Suez controversy, which dominated the House of Commons from the end of July to December 1956. Even four years later the *Observer* was to comment, 'There is nothing odder in recent times than his comparative silence at the time of Suez'[64] – and the implication plainly was that Dick, with his close

* The Admiralty announced the presumed death of Commander Crabb on 29 April explaining that he had failed to return from a test dive in the area of Portsmouth. Ten days later, in response to a Soviet note of protest, the Government in effect admitted that he was the frogman whom the Russians had detected swimming underneath the cruiser that had brought Bulganin and Khrushchev to Britain. Commander Crabb's body was never recovered, which led to some speculation that he had been taken prisoner by the Soviet Navy: the greater likelihood remains, though, that he was killed by one of the cruiser's propellers as it started up.

ties to both Egypt and Israel, found the issue personally difficult. As so often in politics, however, accident played a greater part than design. When the crisis broke, with Nasser's nationalisation of the Suez Canal Company on 26 July, Dick was about to leave for Canada – where he and Anne spent the month of August as guests of the Canadian Broadcasting Corporation and the Canadian Institute of Public Affairs. When they returned at the beginning of September, the Labour Party's line was already established and, apart from defending it in his *Mirror* column, Dick's sole intervention was to deliver a vigorous speech in the Commons denouncing the propaganda errors the Government had made[65] (which he followed up with a letter to *The Times* rebuking Professor Max Beloff for suggesting that there had been a shift on the part of Labour back-benchers to a pro-Nasser position).[66] Admittedly, one day later he did tell his constituency Party that the crisis had so far resulted in 'a resounding victory for Nasser'[67] – but that could be explained by the way in which the Eden Government had been let down by the American Secretary of State, John Foster Dulles, at the London conference of the Suez Canal Users' Association (an abortive US proposal that got nowhere in face of Nasser's refusal to accept it). In the face of its collapse Dick, never wholly sharing the Left's horror of military adventures, expressly charged Eden with 'having drawn the sword, only to put it back again'.[68]

After the joint British-French announcement on 23 September that the two countries were prepared to refer the question to the UN, Dick seems to have taken the view that the crisis was over (even complaining that he was 'sick to death of writing about it').[69] As usual, at this time of year, his central concern became the annual Labour Party Conference and, in particular, his own continued membership of the National Executive. He held on to his seat comfortably enough – going down only one place from fourth to fifth – and was much relieved at doing so after a year in which he had effectively parted company with the Bevanites. But the mood at Blackpool was, as Dick noted, one of 'unity'[70] – a mood reflected in the Conference's narrow decision finally to elect Aneurin Bevan to the Party treasurership in preference to the right-wing candidate, George Brown.* Far from welcoming the new atmosphere of amity,

---

* George Brown (1914–85) was Labour MP for Belper 1945–70 and was to be a colleague of Dick's in the first two Wilson Cabinets before resigning as Foreign Secretary in March 1968. He was created a life peer as Lord George-Brown in 1970 and, after having served as deputy leader of the Labour Party 1960–70, left the Party in 1976.

Dick found it distinctly dispiriting – even going so far as to admit: 'I do not think I have ever enjoyed a Labour Party Conference less than this one.'[71] But that may have been because he went to it by himself – having discouraged Anne from accompanying him because 'I disliked the idea of her being there if I was knocked off the Executive'.[72]

It could also, though, have been because Dick himself was not at the top of his form. Certainly, one week later at the Conservative Conference at Llandudno – which he visited for the second year running in his capacity as a *Mirror* columnist – he became ill with what was later diagnosed as pneumonia, although he did not realise it at the time. Within a week he was in hospital with what was officially described as 'pleurisy'[73] and he was out of action until the Anglo-French invasion of Egypt had already taken place. The mystery of Dick's 'silence' over Suez is, therefore, nothing like as curious as it can be made to seem: he was simply in no fit state to play his usual energetic part. He did, however, make a brief speech in the House of Commons on 13 November, in which he called the Prime Minister 'a weak, vain man who is going to bring this country to further disaster unless we get rid of him soon',[74] and he also fully backed the *Mirror*'s none too popular anti-Eden stand in his column.[75]

He took some time fully to recover from his first serious bout of illness since 1943 and at the beginning of December left with Anne for a fortnight's recuperative holiday in Israel. This, inevitably, aroused suspicions that he was engaged in a secret investigation of the role 'collusion' might have played in the Suez episode; but, although Dick subsequently became one of the strongest advocates of the need for an official parliamentary inquiry on this point, there is no reason to believe that his holiday provided him with much evidence for the case he would later develop. He spent most of his time lying in the sun by the Sea of Galilee and in his one talk with Ben-Gurion, at the end of his visit, he seems to have been more concerned with rebuilding bridges between the British Labour Party and the Israeli Government than opening up any new points of difference.[76]

Dick's return to Britain on 16 December more or less coincided with Eden's own arrival back from his ill-fated trip to Goldeneye in Jamaica.* Dick was a witness to the Prime Minister's first reappear-

---

* The Prime Minister, on the advice of his doctors, had left for three weeks of 'rest' at Ian Fleming's villa on 24 November. He returned to London on 14 December with his political position considerably eroded.

ance in the House of Commons after almost a month and, although
he seems initially to have felt the Press exaggerated the 'chilly
reception' the Prime Minister received, it did not take long for him
to form the view that Eden's days were numbered. In this he was,
no doubt, assisted by Aneurin Bevan, whom – to Dick's pleasure –
Gaitskell had just appointed 'Shadow' Foreign Secretary in succession to Alfred Robens. By the end of 1956 the two of them were
back on sufficiently good terms for Nye to confide to Dick in the
Commons Smoking Room that 'he thought the Tories needed a
scapegoat and that in due course Eden would be made that
scapegoat'.[77]

Bevan's prophecy was soon vindicated. Dick was out of the
country – lecturing at the NATO staff college in Paris – the day
Eden resigned, and when he returned the next morning, Thursday
10 January 1957, it was to a country that, though it had lost one
Prime Minister, still did not have a new one.* Curiously, for a
scholar of the constitution, Dick was highly impatient with the row
that the Labour Party, in the absence of Gaitskell (also away, lecturing at Harvard), tried to create over the way the Royal Prerogative
had been exercised to bring about Harold Macmillan's accession: 'If
the Tories choose to have their Leader selected by the Queen that's
their own affair.'[78] But he was probably correct in his conclusion
that all the Shadow Cabinet had achieved by seeking to stir up a
constitutional controversy was to close ranks within the Establishment. Equally strikingly, Dick does not appear to have been at all
excited by the notion of his own old boss from his wartime days in
Algiers becoming the Queen's First Minister: there is no evidence
that he wrote to Macmillan or, indeed, that he offered any gesture
of sympathy to the disappointed R. A. Butler who had, after all,
behaved very generously to him when Zita had died five years
earlier.

The truth was that by 1957 Dick had come to view politics almost
entirely in a Labour Party context. One reason for this was his
increasing preoccupation with his work on the Labour National
Superannuation Scheme – which he spent the early months of 1957
navigating through not just the policy machinery of the Party but
that of the TUC as well. It was, in many ways, an uncharacteristic

---

* Eden formally resigned at Buckingham Palace on the evening of Wednesday 9
January, having alerted the Queen to his intention the previous day at Sandringham. Macmillan did not kiss hands until just after lunch on Thursday 10
January, the Palace having in the meantime conducted soundings with various Tory
grandees.

achievement for Dick, requiring tact, diplomacy and a good deal of forbearance in face of minds less agile than his own. The detail of the document – eventually published on 15 May* – was largely the work of other hands; Dick had had the wisdom to recruit to his working party a number of experts in the field, including three academics from the London School of Economics, Richard Titmuss, Brian Abel-Smith and Peter Townsend. That, as he realised, was the secret of his success in overcoming the normal inertia of Transport House. In his own mind he had proved that it was, after all, 'possible to make the Labour Party adopt a new policy'.[79]

But Dick's own role – not least as a communicator selling the novel concept of 'half-pay on retirement' – was also crucial: he wrote the document himself and for the following months, culminating in his triumph at the Brighton Party Conference in the autumn, became easily its most energetic exponent. Of course, the premise of the plan was an ever-expanding economy – and, although that may have looked a rational enough forecast in 1957, it was already to seem a rash prediction by the time of the Wilson Government of the 1960s (which never succeeded in getting the scheme on to the Statute Book). Still, Gaitskell's skill in directing Dick's energies to a single piece of creative policy-making had certainly paid off; it was one of Gaitskell's closest friends, Douglas Jay (not always Dick's most fervent admirer), who many years later was to describe the part he played in converting the Labour Party to a whole new attitude towards pensions as 'the best job I ever saw done in Opposition'.[80]

For the leadership, of course, it also had the beneficial by-product of keeping Dick out of mischief. So absorbed had he been in the task of domestic policy-making that his old stamping grounds of defence and foreign policy attracted singularly little of Dick's attention through most of 1957. Even the famous Defence White Paper in April, announcing the abolition of conscription and Britain's future reliance on the nuclear deterrent, failed to provoke Dick into any indiscretion – though he did take advantage of it to comment in favour of Britain founding what was later to be known as 'the non-nuclear club'.[81] As for foreign policy, his only excursion in this area

* Soon after it was published, Dick's father-in-law wrote him a letter which obviously enormously gratified him. Patrick McDougall, who was to die in February 1959, wrote: 'Were I a young man, I should speak for it, I should work for it, I should fight for it; almost it would make me wish that I could roll back the years.' Dick preserved the letter, dated 27 May 1957, in his 'Autobiography' file.

was to visit, along with Aneurin Bevan and the Labour Party's general secretary, Morgan Phillips, the Congress of the Italian Socialist Party held in Venice in February – but this, thanks to a report in the *Spectator*, was to turn into a legal rather than a political *cause célèbre*.

Since Dick's role in the resulting libel action – heard in the High Court in November – was subsequently to become one of the more controversial episodes of his career, it is only fair to start with its origins. On 1 March 1957 the *Spectator* carried a piece written by one of its regular contributors, Jenny Nicholson, giving a somewhat knock-about account of what had taken place at the twenty-third Congress of the PSI. Its tone was mocking – Pietro Nenni's PSI had voted at the Congress in favour of reunification with Giuseppe Saragat's more right-wing PSDI – and, no doubt for that reason, the article was headed 'Death in Venice'. As a piece of lively, irreverent journalism, there was nothing particularly wrong with it, except for this passage concerning the three British observers:

> And then there was the occasional appearance of Messrs. Bevan, Morgan Phillips* and Richard Crossman who puzzled the Italians by their capacity to fill themselves like tanks with whisky and coffee, while they (because of their livers and also because they are abstemious by nature) were keeping going on mineral water and an occasional coffee. Although the Italians were never sure the British delegation was sober, they always attributed to them an immense political acumen.[82]

Although those two sentences did not contain a direct allegation of drunkenness, it was certainly implied – and it was wholly predictable that, within four days, the *Spectator* should have received a letter from Goodman, Derrick & Co (on behalf of Bevan, Phillips and Dick) complaining of 'a serious libel' and demanding 'to hear from you, by return please, as to your proposals for dealing with the matter'.[83]

At this stage, there seems little doubt that Dick at least never intended the case to go to court. There was good reason for that – he was, after all, a journalist himself and as the Lord Chief Justice, Lord Goddard, was eventually to say in the High Court, 'Dog does not eat dog.'[84] But Dick also had a less edifying motive for wanting to settle: the awkward fact was that, so far as Morgan Phillips was concerned, he knew that the *Spectator*'s imputation was perfectly

---

* Morgan Phillips (1902–63) was general secretary of the Labour Party 1944–61.

true. Indeed, a full two weeks before the *Spectator* article appeared, he had written in his own diary in reference to the general secretary of the Labour Party: 'He drank steadily . . . with the result he got tiddly by mid-day and soaked by dinner-time.'[85] The allegation against Dick – made even before his posthumous *Backbench Diaries* were published in 1981* – was, therefore, that he conspired to commit perjury. In those terms, the charge is certainly not true – although that Dick had an uneasy conscience about the action is demonstrated by the fact that he was by far the most reluctant partner in it. He made it clear from the beginning that all he wanted was an apology and nothing else.[86] In fact, the case would never have come to court if Ian Gilmour, the editor-proprietor of the *Spectator*, had been prepared to accept a form of words that Dick sent to him following a meeting over dinner at Roy Jenkins's home within a month of the original article being published.

Unfortunately, this incident later poisoned the atmosphere on both sides, since Dick – cavalierly disregarding the normal 'Without Prejudice' conventions – armed Arnold Goodman with all the details of the private negotiation and went on to make remorseless use of it when he appeared as a witness in the High Court in November. The final result, as Dick brazenly put it, was 'very satisfactory':[87] he, Bevan and Phillips were each awarded £2,500 damages after a highly tendentious summing up from Lord Goddard (the jury was absent for a mere thirty-eight minutes).[88] With typical candour, however, Dick commented in his diary on the same day as the verdict: 'I still think the risk we took was appalling.'[89] His critics (including Ian Gilmour), not unnaturally, tended to use the same adjective about his own conduct; but that seems a little harsh. Of the three plaintiffs Dick was the only one who showed any sensitivity to the moral dilemma involved in bringing the action at all (he blamed his lawyers for insisting on going to court). Yet in his own mind, as his diary bears out, the difficulty arose solely from the vulnerable position of Morgan Phillips. Finally, on the allegation specifically made by the *Spectator* it may be worth recording that Dick himself seldom drank whisky.

* In the *Spectator* (15 April 1978) Auberon Waugh claimed to have heard Dick boast that 'both he and Bevan had been pissed as newts' while attending what came to be jocularly known in the Labour Party as 'the Venetian blind'. His account of Dick's alleged words was subsequently vigorously challenged by Lord Goodman amongst others. Perhaps more significantly, the phrase 'pissed as newts' never formed a part of Dick's normal vocabulary – and indeed occurs not once in the nearly two million words of the published *Diaries*.

The *Spectator* libel action was not, however, the event that caused Dick most anxiety in 1957. That arose, more predictably, from something he had written himself. His *Mirror* column had not perhaps been quite the success that Cudlipp had hoped – indeed that autumn Cudlipp told him that he found it 'stuffy and pontifical'.[90] Coming when it did, that comment was a trifle unfair, for just two months earlier Dick had written what was probably the most controversial column of his entire *Mirror* career. The trouble was, though, that from the *Mirror*'s point of view it was controversial in quite the wrong way: it seemed, fatally, to reflect an attitude of academic snobbery. Dick appears to have been quite unaware of the offence his words were bound to cause. At the beginning of July, Sir Thomas Williamson – himself a former MP and that year's chairman of the TUC – had addressed the annual miners' conference on the need for the Labour movement to have more trade union MPs in Parliament.[91] Casting about for a theme for his *Mirror* column, Dick must have concluded that this was a safe enough one – here, after all, was a trade union leader saying something that was self-evidently true and needed to be rammed home. But the crucial difference was that, whereas Williamson had talked only about quantity, Dick proceeded to turn the discussion into one about quality. Even the heading the *Mirror* chose to put that Friday morning on his column – 'The Unions Must Send Better Men to Parliament'[92] – was, in retrospect, unwise: however unexceptionable the sentiment might appear elsewhere, it was hardly likely to be seen as anything but a reflection on their own talents by the ninety-seven trade-union sponsored MPs. Worse than that, in the body of his text Dick proceeded to deliver the Olympian judgment that of the entire membership of the trade union group 'only four suggest themselves for key jobs' – meaning as Cabinet Ministers in a future Labour Government. As a generic insult, that might have been, if not overlooked, then at least endured. Dick's act of monumental folly lay in naming the four individuals he had in mind – James Griffiths,* Aneurin Bevan, George Brown and Alfred Robens. As that meant ruling out the claims to Cabinet office of ninety-three of his parliamentary colleagues, only perhaps Dick could have been startled by the storm of wrath and fury that it provoked.

---

* James Griffiths (1890–1975), Labour MP for Llanelli 1936–66 had been elected Labour's deputy leader in succession to Herbert Morrison in 1956, defeating Nye Bevan by thirty votes. Minister for National Insurance and Secretary of State for the Colonies under Attlee, he served as Secretary of State for Wales in Harold Wilson's first Cabinet.

The awkward fact, of course, was that, even if what Dick wrote was true (and in essence it probably was), he was the last person who ought to have said it. The suspicion with which middle-class intellectuals were often regarded within the Labour movement was – then at least – never far below the surface. In his more sensitive moods Dick always knew that, talking quite openly of how people with his sort of background were merely 'tolerated' by the rest of the Labour Party.[93] Yet in the *Mirror*, of all places, Dick had not so much ignored such sensitivities as trampled all over them. He was to pay a heavy, and lasting, price for having done so.

Admittedly, the initial storm of fury blew itself out fairly quickly – partly, no doubt, because Gaitskell was determined that it should. Dick was summoned to meet the officers of the trade union group, and offered them a form of apology which he then followed up with a somewhat grudging recantation ('It was not my intention to compare the abilities of intellectuals and trade unionists at Westminster') in his *Mirror* column a week later.[94] That was not, as it turned out, enough to satisfy the *amour propre* of the Party's trade union MPs – who authorised their chairman and secretary to send a letter to the National Executive asking it 'to take note of Mr Crossman's conduct'.[95] By this stage, however, the leadership itself had become thoroughly alarmed. After the NEC meeting on 24 July, at which Dick was forced, this time abjectly, to apologise again, it was announced that 'continuation of the controversy could only result in harm to the Party – the incident is now closed'.[96]

So far as Dick's career prospects were concerned, that was a piece of wishful thinking. Although the *Sunday Times* exaggerated when it said of Dick, 'there are now serious doubts whether Mr Gaitskell could further affront the trade unionists by giving him preferment',[97] the damage to his standing and popularity within the Party was serious and enduring. It was first revealed in his vote for the National Executive at that year's October Conference at Brighton, which went dramatically down from 740,000 to 578,000. Although he succeeded in keeping his seat, it had been – as Dick himself admitted – 'a close shave'.[98] Fortunately for his peace of mind, however, he does not seem to have gone through his usual agony of apprehension, since he had more important matters to worry about. He had learnt the previous spring, to his astonishment and delight, that Anne was pregnant – and, because the baby was overdue and possible problems were suspected, he commuted for most of the week between Brighton and London. Anne was finally rushed to Westminster Hospital on the last full day of the Conference and their first child – a son, Patrick Danvers Crossman – was safely born on 5 October, the day after the proceedings finished.

The first night of the week, however, Dick did spend in Brighton. That was because he knew that the next day he faced the task of presenting Labour's policy document, 'National Superannuation', to the delegates. In fact, he frittered away the evening in the company of the *Daily Mirror* and only really started work on his speech the following morning. Despite his own foreboding 'that God would reward me for such gross negligence',[99] it turned out not to matter. At his own insistence winding up rather than opening the debate, Dick delivered one of those bravura displays of sheer expository power that no other figure in the Labour Party has ever been able to match.[100] He spoke with barely a note for nearly an hour and did not lose the rapt attention of his audience for a moment. No doubt, it represented the vindication of all those early years he had spent giving extra-mural university extension lectures up and down the land – something that Dick, with typical irreverence, acknowledged: 'Fortunately for me, I saw right in the middle [of the hall] Frank Cousins* who is the ideal WEA three-year tutorial class member – a long, not very intelligent face which nods when it's got it at last.'[101]

In the light of the commotion such views had caused only three months earlier, it was perhaps just as well that such a confession was made only in the privacy of his diary. At the time nothing detracted from the almost universal acknowledgment of what had been a spectacular conference performance. Even *The Times* was generous (and perceptive) in its praise:

> It was one of those delicious moments of personal triumph that come every now and again to a politician, and this time it came unexpectedly to Mr R. H. S. Crossman . . . He stood there looking quite shy and modest, as he swept back an unruly lock of grey hair from his brow, wondering what had so suddenly happened to him.[102]

For Dick, the triumph was probably all the more delicious in that it came at the end of the same morning as the constituency delegates had given him such a disappointing vote in the annual popularity poll to the NEC. It was almost a Morecambe 1952 in reverse, when electoral success had been swiftly followed by oratorical disaster

---

* Frank Cousins (1904–86), later briefly to be a colleague of Dick's in the Wilson Cabinet, was then the relatively newly elected general secretary of the Transport and General Workers' Union.

(see p. 168). Dick himself plainly preferred things the other way round – displaying some impatience with the 'curiously unimaginative' members of the Executive who remarked that if only he could have made the speech first, he would have topped the poll. ('Actually, I wouldn't have made nearly such a good speech from the top of the poll.')[103]

It says something for Dick's sense of realism that, even following so striking a platform success, he knew – in the wake of his débâcle with the trade union group – that he would be unwise to risk standing for the Shadow Cabinet. His immediate mood, in fact, appears to have been not just realistic but constructive as well: 'I am too old now to remain a young man with adventurous ideas and I had better therefore settle down to polishing myself for responsibility, even if this means my column becomes far too respectable for Hugh Cudlipp's taste.'[104] Alas, the latter prediction proved easier to promulgate than to fulfil. On the day after the new session opened, a glancing reference Dick had made to George Brown in his *Mirror* column led to Brown physically assaulting him in a House of Commons corridor.[105] Great efforts were made to hush up this incident – which ended with Dick knocking Brown to the floor and sitting on top of him – but it none the less surfaced within a week or two in the Cross-bencher column of the *Sunday Express*.[106] More seriously, Dick was soon in hot water again with his colleagues over criticisms he had made – this time at least generically – about the conduct of the Opposition in the Commons. A column he had published in the *Mirror* – headed 'Labour Must Stop These Milk-and-water Tactics in Parliament'[107] – caused particular offence. In the absence of Hugh Gaitskell on a visit to India, Dick found himself summoned by the deputy leader, James Griffiths, and the Chief Whip, Herbert Bowden,* to explain his criticisms. The determination to call him to book had originated in the Shadow Cabinet but, as its discussions had been extensively leaked, Dick was in quite a strong position to mount a counter-attack: the episode ended again (though this time it did not even reach the National Executive) with one of those bleak little Press announcements about 'no further action'.[108]

Probably it would never have gone as far as it did had Gaitskell not been away. For the most striking aspect of Dick's political

---

* Herbert Bowden was Opposition Chief Whip 1955–64. In Harold Wilson's first Government he was Leader of the House of Commons and subsequently (briefly) Secretary of State for Commonwealth Relations. Created a life peer as Lord Aylestone in 1967, he was that year appointed chairman of the Independent Broadcasting Authority, a post he held until 1975.

attitude at this period remains the closeness he felt to his Party leader. On the personal level that was manifested by his somewhat surprising decision – given his lack of religious beliefs – to ask Gaitskell to be godfather to his new-born son (Gaitskell accepted, though he did not attend the christening – held largely to please Dick's mother, then in her eightieth year).[109] On the more mundane political plane, a letter that Dick wrote to Gaitskell on the latter's return from India left very little doubt that he had come to see himself as his faithful liegeman:

> About politics I would rather talk to you than write. I presume that, before we meet, you will have heard a great deal of gossip, and some of it will be about me. Since most of this relates to an article I wrote in the *Mirror*, I am sending you a copy of it, so that you can judge for yourself whether I was guilty of any crime worse than writing for publication what people as respectable as Bob Mellish and Denis Howell* had been muttering round the lobby.
>
> Meanwhile there is only one thing I want to tell you in this letter. If anyone has whispered to you that I have been working against you in your absence, this is the sheerest invention. Ever since Attlee announced his resignation, I have regarded the acceptance of your leadership by everyone, including Nye, as the *sine qua non* of Party revival, and I am unlikely to have changed my views now that the Party has been reviving. . . .[110]

There could hardly have been a more explicit oath of fealty than that – and the next twenty-one months of Dick's political career were to turn him into something close to an Establishment figure within the Labour Party.

In part that was Gaitskell's doing as much as his own; for someone generally considered to be none too adept at political relationships Gaitskell handled Dick with extraordinary finesse. What he understood was that Dick felt fulfilled only when he was (in Lord Reith's phrase) 'fully stretched' – and he proceeded to make sure that this was generally the case. For the first time in his parliamentary life, Dick even found himself doing the dogged work on the Committee Stage of a Bill – the Government's National

---

* Robert Mellish, Labour MP for Bermondsey 1946–82, was to be Dick's own Under-Secretary at the Ministry of Housing and Local Government 1964–7, later becoming Government Chief Whip. He was created a life peer in 1985. Denis Howell, Labour MP for Birmingham, All Saints 1955–9 and for Birmingham, Small Heath since 1959, became Minister of Sport 1964–70 and 1974–9.

Insurance Bill produced as a direct rival to his own National Superannuation scheme. Although Dick was again disappointed in his
ambition to get elected to the Shadow Cabinet – standing for the
second time in November 1958 and collecting a respectable eighty-
seven votes (enough to put him fourth on the list of those not
elected) – that did not inhibit Gaitskell from deploying his talents on
the Front Bench. Dick made his maiden speech from the Dispatch
Box on 11 November 1958[111] winding up for the Opposition in a
debate on the Government's Pensions White Paper. After a wait of
thirteen years he might have expected it to be an ordeal but it
appears not to have been one – instead Dick reported in his diary 'a
sense of disappointment that one had got through yet another
experience without too much exaltation'.[112]

Gaitskell's real skill, however, lay in the way he harnessed Dick's
energies outside the House of Commons. Admittedly, here the
experiment started badly, with the leader recruiting Dick to an
informal, highly secret defence group charged with the task of providing the Party with a coherent policy on nuclear weapons. Here
Dick – with his idiosyncratic position of accepting the validity of the
deterrent theory but still objecting to the use of tactical nuclear
weapons – proved an awkward customer. But the group's discussions in March 1958 at least laid the foundations for the eventual
manifesto compromise whereby Labour, without renouncing the
American nuclear shield, proposed that Britain should take the lead
by founding a group of non-nuclear nations.* It was a policy essentially adopted in the interests of Party unity and it never satisfied
Gaitskell intellectually. Its endorsement by the Party, however, was
by no means Dick's sole responsibility: it owed far more to the
powerful advocacy of 'the non-nuclear club' by the *Manchester
Guardian*, whose support Gaitskell was very keen to have during
the election campaign.

But if Dick's first excursion into the realm of high policy-making
was not an unmitigated success, he fully redeemed himself by his
role in the sphere of policy presentation. Macmillan's announcement in mid-September 1958 that there would be no general election during the coming winter left the Labour Party's annual

---

* The policy was finally unveiled in June 1959 in a joint Labour Party–TUC
document entitled *Disarmament and Nuclear War: the Next Step* which made it
clear that Britain's renunciation of nuclear weapons would have to be conditional
on other nations being ready to do the same. Since it soon became evident that
there was little chance of their doing so, the proposal ran into the sand.

Conference at Scarborough in a state of limbo. It appears to have been Dick's idea that the way to keep up the momentum of the attack would be to produce a popular version of all the policy documents that the Party had published over the past year. He first prevailed upon Hugh Cudlipp to offer the full co-operation of the *Mirror* and then sold the notion of an 'overall policy pamphlet to end all pamphlets' to Hugh Gaitskell.[113] From Dick's point of view, compared with his triumph of 1957, the Conference may have been relatively flat – though his National Executive vote went satisfactorily back to 712,000 or roughly what it had been before his row with the trade union group. However, despite having spoken only on agriculture (successfully turning back a floor demand for land nationalisation),[114] he still left Scarborough in a mood of some excitement.

That was because he knew – and, no doubt, Gaitskell realised it, too – that the challenge he had set himself was one ideally suited to his talents. With the resources of the *Mirror* behind him, he was determined to demonstrate that a political Party's detailed policy proposals could be made palatable to the mass public. Dick threw himself into the enterprise with all the ardour of the propaganda expert he had once been. There was another echo from his wartime experience. Part of the strategy was that the new popular policy pamphlet should burst on the media world with the impact of a thunder-clap. This meant there must be no 'leaks' and as few people as possible should know about either its appearance or its contents. Here, again, by keeping the group of people working on it extremely small,* Dick succeeded. When the glossy and shining *The Future Labour Offers You* was launched – linked with a highly effective Party political broadcast – on 25 November 1958 even the newspapers conceded that something of a breakthrough had occurred in the art of political communication.[115]

Dick – whose own attitude to Gaitskell had gone through its ups and downs during the period of editing and preparation – was notably generous about his role once the pamphlet was safely published. The fact that the leader himself had shown 'a simple, passionate faith' in it had, he believed, made all the difference – 'If we had had Attlee leading and not believing in it, there would not

* Basically, they were Dick himself, Hugh Cudlipp and Sydney Jacobson, political editor of the *Daily Mirror*, with Gaitskell operating as chief sub-editor. Transport House supplied Peter Shore, then head of the Labour Party's Research Department, and later – as Labour MP for Stepney – to be a colleague of Dick's in the second Wilson Cabinet.

have been this strange belief spread about that something unique was occurring.'[116] Dick's jogging back to the days of Attlee reveals just how far he realised that not only the Party's – but his own – prospects had been transformed by Gaitskell's presence in the leadership. Even three years earlier, it would have been quite inconceivable that he would have been left in charge of a major propaganda project of this kind.

Miraculously, in the year that followed until Macmillan called the election for 8 October 1959, Dick managed to avoid blotting his copybook with the Party. It helped, no doubt, that he was away a good deal. With Patrick safely born, Dick embarked on a more regular pattern of foreign travel than at any other stage in his life (with the *Mirror* obligingly picking up the bill). He spent five weeks of the summer recess of 1958 in Russia and China,[117] two weeks in Algeria and Italy[118] during the Christmas recess, and two weeks in Israel (where he delivered three Weizmann Memorial Lectures) at Eastertime. If he did not go away again in the summer recess of 1959, it was not so much because of the imminence of the election as because Anne was expecting their second child – a daughter, Virginia, born on 20 August 1959.

It is possible that Dick regarded the period to the run up of the 1959 election as his most golden year to date. It had started auspiciously with his great success over *The Future Labour Offers You*, the same month (November) saw the publication to considerable acclaim of a book of his collected reviews, *The Charm of Politics*** and the end of the year was marked by his being singled out in a Conservative newspaper as 'the man who did most for his party'.[119] Of course, it could not all be smooth sailing. A letter Dick wrote to Hugh Gaitskell, following a disagreement between them over the relative merits of the Nenni and Saragat Socialists in Italy, reveals that even at the beginning of 1959 there could still be tensions in their relationship:

> I want to write you a very private and personal letter about the dinner on Wednesday. It was, I think, the first occasion on which I have quarrelled with you in the presence of others since you

---

* The book, published as usual by Hamish Hamilton, was tactfully, but none too truthfully, dedicated to 'K.M. and H.C., my two favourite editors' – meaning Kingsley Martin and Hugh Cudlipp. It received particularly glowing reviews from A. J. P. Taylor in the *Manchester Guardian*, Robert Blake in the *Sunday Times* and Harold Nicolson in the *Observer*.

became Leader, and the fact that I felt bound to do so worries me a great deal ... You may think it absurd to write to you about this. I am doing so because, although I am no doubt irresponsible about some things, I am not, and never shall be, irresponsible about my relations with you.[120]

Whatever the exact nature of the row – ignored by Dick in his diary – it does not seem to have upset the friendship between them. In fact, Gaitskell was soon replying, 'So far as our disagreement is concerned, please don't think about it any more'.[121] It is evident, indeed, that Dick continued to enjoy Gaitskell's confidence – although, as the election drew nearer, that was not entirely true the other way round. This was, no doubt, partly because throughout the spring and summer of 1959 Labour's prospects of victory seemed to recede, and Dick – to his frustration – was not even a member of the Party's campaign committee, selected by the NEC. Probably the greatest tribute to Gaitskell's faith in Dick's abilities lay in the speed and determination with which he moved, once the election became imminent, to change that. Originally told that he was to be 'available to steer the propaganda war',[122] Dick suddenly found himself informed by Gaitskell, while they were driving back from the TUC Congress at Blackpool, that he wanted him to take charge of Transport House during the period of the election campaign.[123] It was an unprecedented move – the Party, after all, already had a general secretary in Morgan Phillips – and only perhaps a leader enjoying all the authority of a potential Prime Minister could have got away with it. Gaitskell, however, secured the somewhat surly consent of the NEC and the deed was done.

Dick, of course, was in a relatively strong position because, under his guidance, the Party had just produced its follow up to *The Future Labour Offers You* in a fresh popular pamphlet entitled *The Tory Swindle 1951–9*. Although not glossy in format like its predecessor, it was another example of the techniques of popular journalism applied to politics – Dick once again had worked closely with the *Mirror* on it. Its success was assured once Lord Hailsham, as chairman of the Conservative Party, made the mistake of denouncing it as an example of 'a campaign of mud-slinging' (while Randolph Churchill vainly tried to get an injunction against it from the courts on the ground that it breached his copyright in his book, *The Rise and Fall of Sir Anthony Eden*). From Labour's point of view, this ensured that the campaign got off to a good start – and Dick himself was soon positively euphoric. His initial mood is perhaps best caught by a diary entry he made two weeks before polling day:

> In the last two days the Gaitskell boom has been rapidly swelling. How strange political leadership is! For months he was no bloody good because everyone said he was no bloody good. Now everyone says that Gaitskell is very good indeed and he becomes very good indeed, so that I can watch the godhead emerging from the man . . . But I am fully content to remain a man and even an acolyte.[124]

As the Party's base commander, Dick, of course, was more than that – indeed, four days later, he was writing, 'Hugh's chief of staff is an absolutely key position and I am having the time of my life.'[125] One reason for that was the undoubted success of the Labour Party's election broadcasts. Devised to follow the format of the then highly popular BBC *Tonight* programme – and produced under the guidance of its loaned editor, Alasdair Milne* – they broke new ground in the presentation of politics on television, leaving the Tories' rival efforts looking oddly old-fashioned and stale. At least until the end of September, the general impression was that, whatever might be the result, Labour was at least having the better of the campaign.

To be fair to Dick, however, his old psychological warrior's antennae did not let him down. He spotted instantly the moment things began to go wrong. On 28 September Gaitskell delivered a speech at Newcastle in which he promised 'no increase in the standard or other rates of income tax under the Labour Government so long as normal peacetime conditions continue'.[126] Since it was putting forward a costly programme, Labour's campaign was at once forced on to the defensive – with its position made even more vulnerable by the subsequent release in a Transport House background paper of a similar pledge about purchase tax. In Dick's own words, from then on 'we were struggling to maintain the image of the Party and to rebuild the image of integrity'.[127]

Even then Dick did not wholly succeed in banishing his original mood of optimism. When in the last week he finally got to his constituency – where his opponent was the future Conservative Cabinet Minister, John Biffen – the Coventry Labour Party struck him as having 'put up the best fight I have ever seen'; and even on

* Alasdair Milne subsequently went on to become Director-General of the BBC (1982–7).

polling day he admitted to having felt 'very enthusiastic'.[128] The eventual disappointment* was not, of course, as crushing for him as it was for Gaitskell – and Dick, even if deprived of his hopes of at long last becoming a Cabinet Minister, fully recognised that. In the post-election issue of the *New Statesman* he paid his patron a remarkable tribute – declaring that he had 'yet to meet a single Labour candidate who denies he was inspired by Gaitskell's leadership' and arguing that 'without it we might have lost not twenty-three but up to a hundred seats'.[129] If a generous postscript to the years 1955–9, it was soon to seem an ironic prologue to the years 1959–63.

* Although Dick's own majority went up marginally in Coventry East, the results in the other two Coventry constituencies were worse even than in 1955, with Maurice Edelman's majority going down by 2·1 per cent and Elaine Burton losing her seat on a 3·6 per cent swing. Across the country at large, the Conservative Government increased its majority from 60 to 102.

13 Rogue Elephant

Dick's estrangement from Hugh Gaitskell was neither precipitate nor premeditated. It took quite some time to develop – and, in Dick's view, was more Gaitskell's fault than his own. They met at Transport House on the day after the general election and together drafted the Party leader's statement – a dignified one, acknowledging the nation's verdict – for that afternoon's Press conference. Even more remarkably, Dick issued an invitation, which Gaitskell accepted, to come the following week to spend the night at Prescote. There was thus no initial sign of any threat to their close association of the previous four years.

By the time Gaitskell arrived at Prescote in the late afternoon of Tuesday 13 October, the clouds had already begun to gather. They were the result of personal factors as much as political ones. Dick had known since the end of August that his column in the *Mirror* would not continue after the election – the assumption being that, if Labour won, he would not be available while, if the Party were defeated, the paper would have to cut its losses and turn away (temporarily at least) from politics. The ending of his role as a twice-weekly columnist was a blow to Dick, although the *Mirror* did its best to soften it by offering him a most generous compensation settlement.* Inevitably, however, it still meant that he was at something of a loose end and all too anxious to involve himself in picking up the pieces after Labour's third consecutive defeat. It was, therefore, a serious error on Gaitskell's part to allow Dick to gather the impression that he was somehow being kept at arm's length and that

* To avoid tax on a lump sum, and on the advice of Arnold Goodman, the *Mirror* ended up by paying Dick a retainer of £1,000 p.a. as a 'political adviser' for a period of three years.

he was no longer considered an automatic part of the leader's inner circle. Unfortunately, that was the message that Dick chose to read into his discovery that on the Sunday immediately following the election a council of war had been held at Gaitskell's home in Hampstead from which he had been excluded.*

Hugh Gaitskell's visit to Prescote was, no doubt, intended to smooth ruffled feelings; but it ended up by having no such happy outcome. Here the fault was overwhelmingly Dick's – although Gaitskell, who had arrived from an apparently bibulous lunch at Nye Bevan's farm, could also be blamed for talking as freely as he did. What happened was that Gaitskell chose to unburden himself on the problems he faced, not just in terms of policies but of personalities, too. In particular, he made no secret of his desire to remove Harold Wilson from the Shadow Chancellorship – a piece of intelligence that Dick passed on within forty-eight hours to Wilson himself (whom he, not altogether surprisingly, reported in his diary to be 'furious and insecure').[1] It was a bad breach of trust and one that Gaitskell never found himself quite able to forgive.[2]

Dick himself does not seem ever to have realised the offence his indiscretion had caused. It may, though, simply have been a case of an old allegiance reasserting itself. His relationship with Wilson, after all, went back a long way – and he clearly resented the fact that Gaitskell had fallen into the hands of such exclusively right-wing advisers as Douglas Jay and Anthony Crosland. He was also apprehensive lest he himself should become too publicly identified with what was known in those days as 'the Hampstead set' – recoiling with horror when Roy Jenkins remarked to him casually, 'To judge from the Press, you are part of it now.'[3] To be fair to Dick, in doctrinal terms, he never was – and this was perhaps the underlying cause of his drift away from Gaitskell.

That process remained gradual. In fact, in November, within a month of the election, Dick found himself formally appointed the Party's official Front Bench spokesman on pensions – some consolation for his failure, yet again, to be elected to the Shadow Cabinet (although, with eighty-seven votes, he was only three votes behind the bottom elected candidate). His new Front Bench role soon posed him with a problem. In an effort to make up for his lost income from the *Mirror* he had agreed to become a regular panellist

---

* The occasion for the gathering was Gaitskell's wish to mark Hugh Dalton's retirement from the House of Commons – though, if Dick had realised that, it is a moot point (given their wartime association at Woburn) if it would have made him feel any better.

on a new Granada TV programme entitled *Who Goes Next?** The
programme was recorded in Manchester on Monday afternoons –
and, unfortunately for Dick, on the second Monday of the new
Parliament Pensions and National Insurance issues were due to
come up first at Question Time. With so embarrassing an absence in
prospect, Dick behaved honourably, immediately writing to the
Opposition Chief Whip and offering to resign from his new post
within a week of being appointed to it.[4] Luckily, it was a period in
which a fairly relaxed view was taken of Front Bench responsibilities, and Dick was not required to abdicate from his new Shadow
portfolio. It was not, however, the most auspicious of starts to what,
for other reasons, was to turn out to be an all too brief career as a
member of Gaitskell's Front Bench.

In the early days, the strains – if already apparent – did not
suggest any immediate breaking point in the relationship. Admittedly, Dick was worried by the 'revisionist' strategy Gaitskell
seemed determined to follow and, in particular, by his refusal to
repudiate the anti-public ownership positions taken up by a number
of his younger subordinates. His protective instinct towards the
Party leader was, however, demonstrated by a letter he wrote to
Gaitskell some ten days in advance of the special Conference at
Blackpool, which had been billed as 'the grand inquest' on the
Party's election defeat. If slightly nettled in tone, its purpose was
plainly intended to be constructive:

17 November 1959

Though I haven't had much luck with the suggestions I have made
to you since the election, I feel I must follow up our talk of the
other day.

The more I reflect on the arrangements for Blackpool, the
more unfortunate I find them. The natural time for the Leader to
speak would be on Sunday morning, when he gets the Monday
press and when he has had time to judge the mood of the Conference and, in part at least, to answer the debate. If, as is suggested, you start you are exposing yourself like St Sebastian to be
shot at by anybody and everybody, and the whole debate will take

---

* The programme was based on the strange device of putting three celebrities –
the original panellists were Dick, Malcolm Muggeridge and Peter Thorneycroft –
into separate sound-proofed boxes from which (without hearing one another's
answers) they responded from prepared texts to topical questions. Rather surprisingly, the programme survived for over a year, at one stage acquiring the future
Conservative Cabinet Minister, Michael Heseltine, as its studio chairman.

the form, whether it is intended or not, of letting off steam against the Leader. . . .

Is it too late to suggest a change of plan? The obvious way to make the Conference a success is to start it with a long report by Morgan Phillips, who is universally agreed by now to have been the architect of a brilliantly fought election campaign, who has never put a foot wrong* and who is a good working-class type untarnished by any association with intellectualism . . . Then you could start on Sunday morning and Nye close on Sunday afternoon . . . Any other arrangement must be disadvantageous to you personally.[5]

It was undeniably shrewd advice but Gaitskell, who wrote back cordially enough ('It was good of you to write and I much appreciated what you say'),[6] chose to disregard it. In the end, of course, he was saved by the magnanimity of Nye Bevan, who, after various dark rumours had swirled through Blackpool, chose to wind up the Conference on a note of unity. But that Gaitskell had taken a great risk – in particular by insisting that 'I speak for myself alone' – is acknowledged even by his official biographer.[7] He would certainly have lost nothing, and probably gained a good deal, if he had heeded Dick's advice.

The revealing fact, though, was that Dick thought it a warning worth delivering, which must banish any suspicion that he started out with the intention of undermining Gaitskell's position. As a natural violator of sacred cows, he was not even as shocked as many of his colleagues by Gaitskell's assault on Clause IV† at Blackpool, dismissing critics of the leader's speech as 'completely antediluvian'.[8] Yet the Party Conference of 1959 still marked the end of Dick's self-appointed role as adviser and candid friend to Gaitskell. Although they talked together a number of times between October and November, they did not have any further contact until well into the New Year. It was almost as if they both realised that they were set on a collision course – and that there was little or nothing to be done about it.

At Blackpool Dick had been elected the Labour Party's Vice-

---

* Some resentment, no doubt, lay behind this extravagant praise of Morgan Phillips. Dick was understandably put out that his own role in the campaign had never been officially acknowledged. See p. 226.

† Clause IV is the provision in Labour's constitution which pledges the Party to work to secure 'the common ownership of the means of production, distribution and exchange'. It remains extant to this day.

Chairman for the coming year. In normal times this would not have been a particularly momentous appointment – it came on the principle of Buggins's turn. Unlike Ian Mikardo, who was defeated in that year's NEC elections, he had retained his seat on the National Executive* and among the surviving MPs was next in order of seniority. (In strict terms of service, Dick was entitled to be elected Chairman but it had already been decided that, to avoid restlessness on the Party's industrial wing, that post should go to a trade unionist for the coming year.) On length of service, the Vice-Chairman's job could equally well have gone to Harold Wilson, but he saw nothing in it for him and encouraged Dick to take it on instead. What they, no doubt, both foresaw was that, in a likely period of confrontation between the leadership and the Party activists, it would be useful to have an essentially honorific office occupied by someone whose credentials rested solely in the confidence placed in him by the mass Party.

The contrast between Dick's success in regularly getting elected to the National Executive and his inability to command any similar support from his colleagues in the Commons meant inevitably that the role of the champion of the rank and file was attractive to him. In that sense, his elevation to the Party Vice-Chairmanship, with the almost automatic prospect of succeeding to the Chairmanship the following year, could hardly have come at a more awkward moment. From Gaitskell's point of view, it must have seemed as if a rogue elephant had been let loose to trample all over an always delicate, and now dangerous, territory: the constitutional relationship between the parliamentary Party and the Conference. Admittedly nothing happened instantly – partly because Dick was heavily engaged in turning the Weizmann lectures he had delivered in Israel the previous spring into a new book† and partly because the grim news that Nye Bevan was gravely ill with cancer imposed a temporary moratorium on the Clause IV debate.

That moratorium did not last long and it was Dick himself who broke it. On 29 January 1960 he addressed the annual dinner of the Coventry East Labour Party and used the occasion to call on the

---

* Dick was elected fourth with 652,000 votes – 200,000 votes fewer than Barbara Castle, who topped the poll. Ian Mikardo lost his seat to Tony Benn, who came on to the National Executive Committee for the first time.

† *A Nation Reborn* was published by Hamish Hamilton in London and by Atheneum in New York in autumn 1960. It lacked the first-hand vitality of *Palestine Mission* and, though it enjoyed a considerable success in the United States, was not one of Dick's more distinguished works.

leadership to 'drop the whole idea' of Clause IV revision and 'concentrate instead on reviewing the policies on which the Party had fought the last election'.[9] Although Dick seems to have taken care to brief friendly journalists and was rewarded with a particularly sympathetic article in the *Observer*,[10] his intervention does not appear to have been at all well received by his colleagues. Indeed, the following month's NEC meeting turned into something of a court martial with Gaitskell, who had already given a considered reply to Dick's speech to a regional conference at Nottingham,[11] making his own displeasure known. But it was mainly loyal trade unionists who made out the charge sheet against Dick, although they had to do so in his absence since he had left the meeting early in order to lunch with the film producer, Otto Preminger.[12] That this was a wrong choice of priorities is perhaps indicated by a letter that Dick circulated two days later to all the other twenty-seven members on the Executive:

26 February 1960

I had to leave the Executive last Wednesday punctually at 1 o'clock for an appointment I could not miss. I was therefore amazed to read the next morning of the proceedings after I left. In the course of them, I gather it was stated that 'a speech by the Vice-Chairman' was the last straw which provoked Mr Gaitskell's speech at Nottingham and further allegations of disloyalty were bandied about. Since what I had said on this occasion can have been read by few members of the Executive, I attach the press release I issued, for your information. But the purpose of this letter is to say to you in writing what I would have said if I had been at the Executive.

At present there is no decision by the Executive to consider a revision of Clause 4 of the Constitution. All we have is a powerful expression of opinion by the Leader of the Party, delivered at the Blackpool Conference, which he was fair enough to emphasise was a personal view, presented to Conference without authority and without even consultation with the Executive. In these circumstances I cannot understand how it is possible to question the right – or the propriety – of any of us, including the Vice-Chairman, expressing a different view.[13]

It was an oddly self-important letter for Dick to write but that its tone reflected his mood is confirmed by an even stranger covering note that Dick sent the same day personally to Gaitskell:

Personal *26 February 1960*

I am sending the attached to all members of the Executive today. Though I have only heard second-hand accounts, I must say that I was more than somewhat surprised to hear what happened at the Executive after I left. Apparently you took umbrage at my suggesting that the revision of Clause 4 should be quietly dropped and in no way protested when other members accused me of disloyalty to you. . . .

But it is not about this that I am writing to you: it is about your personal attitude. Having worked to heal the breach between the Gaitskellites and the Bevanites, I then worked pretty hard behind the scenes for you and the Party during the nine months before the election, and what I got in return for these labours was no thanks but dislike and suspicion. I am not complaining about that. What I want to say to you is this. When we last talked informally to each other a few days before Blackpool, I was trying to warn you against the advice Crosland and Jay were giving you and you remarked, 'Well, at least they have the courage to say unpopular things.' But, since I have begun saying unpopular things to you, you have not welcomed my courage but questioned my loyalty, and that is something I intensely resent. If only you could believe that I, and at least 10 other people whom I know and who share my view, are not disloyal when we try to deflect you from a course we think disastrous. We are doing the ultimate duty of a loyal friend, namely to tell the truth, even when the recipient reacts as you do.*[14]

It was an outburst to which Gaitskell, understandably, took some time to reply – and when he did some twelve days later it was in a distinctly frigid spirit ('On the personal side, I do not feel disposed to say much – I doubt if it would help.')[15] But by then Dick and he were engaged in a fresh controversy – and one which was to lead to the formal parting of the ways between them.

What, of course, shines through Dick's grand remonstrance to Gaitskell is a burning sense of grievance – summed up in that curiously injured phrase, 'What I got in return for my labours was no thanks but dislike and suspicion.' It was an uncharacteristic

---

* Although Dick obviously did not realise it, this was an unlikely argument to succeed with Gaitskell. According to Roy Jenkins, he once turned on him with the comment: 'Support me when I'm right? You're supposed to be a close friend of mine, you ought to support me when I'm wrong!'

posture for someone as robust as Dick to take up – and there seems little doubt that he had been badly hurt by Gaitskell's failure to express, formally or informally, any gratitude for all the work he had done both before and during the election.[16] It was certainly an odd omission on Gaitskell's part, not least because he enjoyed the reputation of having, in Jo Grimond's phrase, 'the best political manners of anyone'.[17] He could hardly have been expected to foresee the consequences that would flow from this one piece of negligence. For, not content with doing battle with his leader (and former patron) over Clause IV, Dick promptly proceeded to open up a second front over defence as well. Here he behaved with an unpredictability almost worthy of Aneurin Bevan. Having originally resolved that he would not take part in a scheduled left-wing rebellion in the annual two-day Defence White Paper debate due to open in the Commons at the end of February 1960,[18] he changed his mind at the last moment; he not only spoke highly critically of his own Front Bench from the back-benches[19] but joined forty-two other Labour MPs – what he himself rudely called 'all the odds and sods' – in abstaining on the official Opposition amendment.[20]

It is difficult to resist the conclusion that by now Dick had a political death wish – something he did not disguise when reflecting in his diary on what he had done:

> I must admit I walked home feeling much better to be back in my old *galère* as a free-thinker, as an awkward guy, as a Keep Leftist or whatever you like to call it, though by far the most accurate description would be that, after three years of uncomfortable lodging in the Labour Establishment, during which my talents have been ruthlessly exploited, I am now back in my natural habitat.[21]

Even that sense of liberation did not, however, prevent Dick from putting up something of a struggle to retain his Shadow pensions portfolio – or at least to make sure that Gaitskell incurred the obloquy for removing him from it forcibly. The negotiations between them dragged on for nearly ten days but, although Dick felt almost to the end that 'the whole thing had blown over',[22] the eventual outcome was probably pre-ordained. The tactical battle was fought more or less to a draw, with Gaitskell managing to avoid having to sack Dick but laying down stringent terms for the continuation of his spokesmanship role – terms which Dick promptly

19 The Anglo-American Commission arriving in Palestine in March 1946. Dick (*far right*) is standing next to Conservative MP, Reginald Manningham-Buller

20 Chaim Weizmann, first President of Israel

24 Hugh Gaitskell in his days as Chancellor of the Exchequer and his wife, Dora

25 Allies on the National Executive, Anthony Greenwood with Barbara Castle during the battle over Clause IV

19 The Anglo-American Commission arriving in Palestine in March 1946. Dick (*far right*) is standing next to Conservative MP, Reginald Manningham-Buller

20 Chaim Weizmann, first President of Israel

21 The *Sunday Pictorial* article which killed Dick's chances of ever holding office under Attlee

22 Dick and Harold Wilson in
the year of the Bevanite
triumph at Morecambe, 1952

23 Aneurin Bevan learning of
his defeat in the election for
the Treasurership of the
Labour Party in 1954

24 Hugh Gaitskell in his days as Chancellor of the Exchequer and his wife, Dora

25 Allies on the National Executive, Anthony Greenwood with Barbara Castle during the battle over Clause IV

characterised as making it 'quite impossible for me to remain on the Front Bench'.[23] The formal exchange of letters between them was prominently featured in all the newspapers on the morning of Tuesday 15 March and may well have contributed to Labour's loss of the first by-election of the new Parliament, held two days later at Brighouse and Spenborough.*

How irresponsibly had Dick behaved? In political terms, he certainly came near to winning the argument by skilfully asserting that, now that the Opposition Front Bench team numbered some forty-six MPs, it was monstrous to expect all of them to give up any right to criticism over every field of Party policy. It was a shrewd issue for Dick, an old opponent of 'oligarchies' and 'despotism', to take up – and he was rewarded with unexpected (though not unsolicited) support in a leader in the *Guardian*.[24] Nor in the short term had Dick made much of a sacrifice – as he himself cheerfully remarked, 'I'm only occasionally on the Front Bench, for 360 days of the year I'm only a back-bencher.'[25] But what perhaps he had done was to raise doubts about the seriousness of his dedication to politics and, indeed, his aptitude for being anything but a gadfly. *The Economist* undoubtedly reflected the voice of the Establishment when it pronounced that 'Mr Gaitskell's experiment of attempting to introduce this exceptionally talented man of ideas into the policy-making ranges of the parliamentary Party was a worthwhile one' – while going on to add sadly that it had all 'ended in grief'.[26] The same point was made even more ruefully from within the Gaitskell camp itself. 'I don't suppose', remarked Anthony Crosland at around this time, 'that Hugh has ever taken more trouble with any single individual than he did with Dick – and just look what happened there.'[27]

As proof of the sheer unpredictability of politics, Dick did not though suffer any lasting punishment in isolation or exile. An extraneous event came to his rescue – the announcement by the British Government[28] that it was abandoning its long-projected Blue Streak missile and that it was opening discussions with the US Administration on co-operating over a new nuclear delivery system. At once, the whole of Labour's own defence policy was thrown back into the melting pot – and Dick, since to some degree his anti-independent deterrent views had been vindicated, was invited by Gaitskell to

---

* As ill luck would have it, Brighouse was the most marginal seat held by Labour at the previous general election. The vacancy was caused by the death of the sitting Member, L. J. Edwards, who had won in October 1959 by just forty-seven votes.

become a member of a working party specially set up to draft a new defence document. That represented an astonishing turn in the wheel of political fortune, as the newspapers were not slow to rub in.[29] In truth, however, Gaitskell did not have much choice. Dick, after all, was still Vice-Chairman of the Party and in any successful formulation of a new defence policy the leader would need to carry the National Executive along with him. A body known as 'The Twelve Wise Men', drawn from the TUC, the NEC and the parliamentary Party, was set up, and by the end of June a fresh document – recommending leaving the development of thermo-nuclear weapons to the Americans and calling on NATO to reduce its dependence on the deterrent – had been satisfactorily agreed. A measure of the restored relations between Dick and his leader was an invitation to a party at Gaitskell's home at the beginning of September – where Dick and Anne, on the point of leaving, were startled to find themselves urged, 'Oh, do stay on, we haven't seen anything of you.'[30]

That apparent cordiality was all the more surprising as Dick had devoted a good part of his energies during the spring and summer to conducting a sustained critique of the 'revisionist' case for Labour Party reform. His opening shot came in the shape of an article in *Encounter* in April called 'The Spectre of Revisionism' – a not wholly convincing reply to a weightier piece by Anthony Crosland entitled 'The Future of the Left' in the previous month's issue. Written in knock-about, debating style, it amounted to little more than a spirited defence of Clause IV – provoking the *Spectator* (with little reason, admittedly, to feel friendly to Dick) to adjudicate loftily that it 'exposed Mr Crossman's limitations as a political thinker', as well as to wonder whether it had not been 'dashed off in some haste'.[31] (In fact, it had been – Dick had written it in the same week as he was sending his circular letter out to the members of the National Executive and composing his note of personal grievance to Gaitskell.)[32] He returned to the same theme, however, some two months later – and this time in the more substantial form of a Fabian pamphlet.

Labour in the Affluent Society[33] displayed all Dick's gifts at their most beguiling and perverse. Deploying his well-practised technique of broad screen projection, he immediately took the revisionists to task for 'their parochialism': in their obsession with the tastes of Western consumers, they had, he argued, entirely overlooked the fact that 'the Communists are overhauling us'. The main theme of his pamphlet was that there was 'a creeping crisis' for Western capitalism and that the only sensible course for the Labour Party to follow was to 'hold itself in reserve' waiting for the moment when all its own 'harsh predictions' came true. With a few flourishes added about the necessary distinction between 'a fighting Opposition and an Alternative Government', to say nothing of a sustained attack on 'the pendulum theory of politics', it was not surprising that Dick's thesis received a rapturous welcome on the Left. Less predictably, adjectives like 'brilliant' surfaced simultaneously in papers normally as far apart as the *Guardian* and the *Daily Express*.[34] More rigorous analysis tended to surface only in minority publications. In the *Spectator* Roy Jenkins mixed praise for its style with condemnation of its content describing it as 'a pamphlet in which every argument starts with its conclusion and then tries to batter the facts into supporting shape',[35] while in the undergraduate magazine, *Isis*, the young Peter Jay* was even more acerbic:

> Mr Crossman is in one sense a master of language, but he is also a slave of words. Over and over again he plays some slogan like a trump card without apparently the slightest attempt to understand what he is saying or to gain any insight into the problems with which he is dealing.[37]

In retrospect, it is easy to judge that such critics were right and that Dick had got his Cassandra-like warnings about the inevitable economic victory of Communism wholly wrong. In fairness, however, he was writing at a time when recent Soviet conquests of space had spread alarm and despondency throughout the West – and it was certainly a tribute to the verve and *brio* with which he made his case that it should have provoked as little disagreement as it did.† To the leadership of the Labour Party, however, the message to be drawn from his diagnosis remained fundamentally unhelpful: what he was, in effect, suggesting was that the Party should withdraw into its winter quarters until such time as an economic 'crash' floated it back into office. His old revisionist sparring partner, Anthony Crosland, was not the only socialist to find such an approach 'hideously immoral'.[38]

---

* Peter Jay was the son of Dick's Winchester and Oxford contemporary, Douglas Jay.

† Dick himself commented in a letter to his economist friend, Thomas Balogh, then in India, that the pamphlet had made 'an immense impact' – adding 'Roy, by the way, published the only effective reply to it in the *Spectator*'.[36] Letter dated 12 July 1960, RHSC's 'Autobiography' file.

In the short term there was no doubt, though, that Dick had succeeded in his objective. He had offered the Left a coherent body of doctrine, a kind of rival suit of ideological clothing to that worn by the revisionists. Did it represent any sort of bid for the leadership of the Left? Dick must have been aware that the long illness of Aneurin Bevan, who was to die on 6 July, had left a vacuum – but hard sense should have taught him that it was more likely to be filled by Harold Wilson than by himself. The year 1960 saw a gradual change in his attitude to Wilson. As late as March, and after his own Front Bench resignation, Dick told two ex-Bevanite colleagues that he would 'prefer to keep Gaitskell rather than work for Harold Wilson'.[39] All that, however, was to be overturned as a result of the drama leading up to the Party Conference held at Scarborough in October.

Overshadowed by the death of Bevan, who had salvaged the previous year's gathering at Blackpool with a rare generosity of spirit, the 1960 Labour Conference might have been expected to meet in sombre, if not chastened, mood. That it turned out instead to be an occasion dominated by rancour and antagonism had little to do with the argument over Clause IV – Gaitskell, at an NEC meeting in July, had reluctantly withdrawn his proposal to amend the Party's constitution and had settled in its place for 'a statement of aims' to be included in the NEC's annual report. In itself, that represented a significant climbdown by the Party's leader and Dick (with his consistent record of opposition to Gaitskell on this issue since his speech at Coventry in January) could certainly claim to have played a major part in bringing it about. The capitulation on the Party constitution did not, however, prove enough to guarantee peace and harmony at Scarborough. Ever since a succession of unilateralist votes at trade union conferences in the summer, it had been clear that the leadership was also in trouble over its defence policy – and this despite the fact that it was being presented as a joint TUC/Labour Party document. Dick, of course, had been one of its principal architects, having served as a member of the working party that drafted it. Yet behind the debate over the nuclear deterrent there was also an argument about the proper power balance within the Party – and it was this that Dick plunged into, initially with a signed article in the *New Statesman* almost two months before the Conference assembled.[40] The article was revealing in that it virtually assumed the inevitability of a defeat for the leadership on defence at the Party Conference and went on to discuss the consequences that would flow from that. It did so with some relish –

indeed, the suspicious-minded reader might well have gathered the impression that, far from dreading such an outcome, Dick was actively looking forward to it.

Was he, in fact, doing so? Here the evidence seems incontrovertible – since Dick himself told Harold Wilson at the end of August that he had 'come to the conclusion that, in the interests of the Party, it would be a good thing if we were defeated at Conference so heavily and ignominiously that Gaitskell had to resign'.[41] Although Dick was disappointed in that wish – the defence policy, after Gaitskell's 'fight and fight and fight again' speech, eventually went down at Scarborough by only just over a quarter of a million votes out of more than six million – it remains a confession that does something to explain his political behaviour over the succeeding months. From August onwards, if Dick was dedicated to one objective, it was to the overthrow of Gaitskell's leadership.

What made that particularly awkward, of course, was that – having successfully cleared the hurdle of the NEC elections once again* – Dick was now Chairman of the Party and so official spokesman of the rank and file membership. It was a role – partly because it was the nearest to a Party power base he had ever occupied – that Dick took very seriously. Sometimes he even contrived to imply that he regarded himself as a constitutional co-equal to Gaitskell. There was certainly more than a hint of that in the highly unorthodox party political radio broadcast that he delivered as Chairman of the Party within four days of the Scarborough conference ending:

> What I want to talk about this evening is the crisis in the Labour Party, and the listeners I mainly have in mind are the Party workers up and down the country. Many of you, I know, have been distressed and bewildered by the events at Scarborough because you feel there's now a contradiction between the Annual Conference which repudiated the official defence policy, and the Parliamentary Labour Party, most of whose members strongly supported it. Well, you're quite right to be alarmed, because if this is permitted to deepen into open conflict it could destroy the Labour Party as an effective force.[42]

It was Dick's belief that Gaitskell was determined to seek such an 'open conflict' that provided the continuing cause of the quarrel

---

* Dick was re-elected to the National Executive constituency section in fifth place with 677,000 votes.

between them. In fact, over the next six months they were to follow diametrically opposed strategies: Gaitskell resolved, whatever the risks, to try to reverse the Scarborough verdict and Dick intent at all costs to find a compromise formula that would spare the Party a constitutional collision.

There were respectable arguments on each side – but the defect behind Dick's case was that it was never quite as high minded as it seemed. His primary aim remained the removal of Gaitskell from the leadership – and that was not an objective that could easily or convincingly be combined with a campaign based on the importance of maintaining the unity of the Party. It was wholly typical of Dick, however, that he should neither have deceived himself about that, nor have sought to deceive his friends:

> As Chairman, my main job has been to block Hugh's attempts to use the new position in order to assert the authority of the Parliamentary leadership against the authority of the NEC. I have done so with some success and have made a series of week-end speeches which ostensibly are the most bromidic appeals for unity but which are universally and correctly diagnosed as attacks on the Gaitskell position – though his name, of course, is never mentioned.[43]

There were moments when even that self-denying ordinance could not be maintained – and Dick seriously undermined his position (even in the view of non-belligerents) when, in a statement issued on 29 October 1960, he came out firmly in support of Harold Wilson's bid for the leadership against Gaitskell.[44] In one sense he had no alternative, since he had been among those most actively encouraging Wilson to stand and in pressurising the unfortunate Anthony Greenwood to withdraw his own candidature (even though he had already effectively announced it by resigning from the Shadow Cabinet).* Some indication of how deeply Dick was involved in these preliminary tactical manœuvres is revealed by a letter he wrote to Greenwood on the day after Wilson had announced his decision to challenge Gaitskell:

---

* It was this resignation which allowed Dick to become, if only fleetingly, a co-opted member of the Shadow Cabinet. The experience, he claimed in a letter at the beginning of November to Thomas Balogh, 'taught me what a stuffy body it is and how disastrously without staff work or adequate preparation its proceedings are'. Whether for this or other reasons, Dick chose not to be a candidate for it in the November 1960 parliamentary Party elections.

21 October 1960

I want to write and thank you for what you have done during these last trying ten days – and also to say that you've earned the undying respect of one colleague at least, who in the past has been a bit narky about you . . . If ever the history of the Labour Party comes to be written and the story of how we began to pull out of the hopeless position into which we had sunk under the Gaitskell regime, what you did will be recorded as the turning-point. Because, if you hadn't done it, not only would Harold never have moved but a lot of other people, including myself, would have gone on saying that it was impossible to do anything . . . You set a spark alight that fired the whole show.[45]

Dick, of course, was never deluded enough to believe that 'the whole show' would culminate in the immediate deposition of Gaitskell. But any doubt of his ultimate objective is removed by a letter he wrote the same day to Harold Wilson:

21 October 1960

I think the most important lesson I draw (speaking as your old psychological warfare adviser) is that we have now thrown Hugh on the defensive on the key issue of unity. Thank God for the Tory press which on this occasion has dubbed you the Unity Candidate. I now feel that, with really hard work and consistent plugging of the Unity line, we can and shall achieve a better result than even you, in one of your optimistic moods, calculated. Indeed, if we can make this heave big enough, we may not need one more big heave but only one or two little heaves to finish the job.[46]

In that aspiration Dick was to be disappointed. The PLP ballot result, although by no means humiliating for Wilson, had the effect of shoring up Gaitskell's position. He won by 166 votes to 81 – or a margin of more than two to one. By the end, it was almost exactly the result Dick expected[47] – but that was only because he had already established that the Wilson leadership bid had failed to shift the allegiance of middle-of-the-road Labour MPs. Here Dick's own formal declaration of support had probably been counter-productive, as one aggrieved letter he received from a woman MP (and colleague on the NEC) should have taught him:

31 October 1960

Dear Dick,

I was about to send you a note to tell you with what pleasure I had been reading your Weizmann lectures. I have been but once to Israel and I found them most illuminating.

But now I must add a word of pained surprise. Why did you have to take sides publicly? You cannot speak other than as Chairman and it is bound to impair any chance you had of mediating on the NEC.

Yours,
EIRENE WHITE*[48]

Other critics, of course, were a good deal more forthright. Indeed, one of them – Hugh Gaitskell's most stalwart supporter, Sam Watson, the Durham miners' leader and chairman of the NEC's international sub-committee – actually drove Dick into attempting a reasoned defence of his decision:

2 November 1960

I am sorry that you should assume my impartiality as Chairman will have been in any way affected by the statement I made last week. I have never pretended to be neutral in this matter because neutrality is the spineless attitude of those who have no convictions. In my view, impartiality consists not in having no convictions but in being strictly fair, despite the fact that one has them. I happen to have strong views about the need for holding the Parliamentary Party and the Executive together and for achieving a new statement on foreign policy and defence. I have not concealed from you either my reasons for believing that Hugh's 'fight, fight, fight' had not assisted in this aim and might cause irreparable damage to the Party if it was continued.[49]

It was Dick's conviction on this last point that was to lead him astray throughout the following months. He became, in the *Sunday Times*'s phrase, 'the arch-priest of constitutionalism'[50] – and, as such, was constantly trying to patch together compromises that might succeed in re-uniting the views of the Conference with those of the parliamentary Party. From the start, it was probably a

---

* Eirene White, Labour MP for East Flint 1950–70, was a member of the National Executive 1947–53 and 1958–72. She served as a middle-ranking Minister in three Departments during Harold Wilson's 1964–70 Governments and was created a life peeress on her retirement from the Commons in 1970.

doomed enterprise (as well as being, on Dick's own admission, a disingenuous one). He was battling for a concept of the Labour Party that was already out of date:* the truth was that it had ceased to be, in any real sense, a mass movement and had become instead, like the Conservatives, a Party based on Parliament. Since Gaitskell still commanded the overwhelming loyalty of Labour MPs, there was no reason why he should be attracted by any effort to offer him a negotiated peace, least of all one sponsored by someone he had reluctantly come to identify as an opponent.[51] Nor, on the other side, were the nuclear disarmers much more sympathetic to any notion of a compromise settlement. Having carried the Labour Conference once on a unilateralist defence policy, they necessarily regarded any attempt to water that commitment down with intense suspicion.

Yet in personal terms, there was a further flaw in Dick's strategy – and one perhaps that he should have been able to foresee. It had never been part of Wilson's battle plan to go into exile once he had stood against Gaitskell, and Dick thus found himself without any convincing alternative to put in Gaitskell's place. There is some reason to believe that, in this respect, they may have been at cross-purposes from the beginning – certainly it was not long before Dick was complaining that Wilson had 'disappeared back into the Shadow Cabinet' and gloomily predicting that 'if he stood again next October, it would be difficult to get as many votes as we scraped together this year'.[52] That opened up for Dick, of course, an enticing prospect – although, as he made clear in a letter sent abroad to a friend, one that he seems to have treated only in a jocular spirit:

> You will be amused to hear that an organisation has been started in Cambridge for making Crossman run the Labour Party, and it already has a thousand members. So we can call it a mass movement. Anne is getting a little apprehensive, but I assure her that there's no danger to me as long as my parliamentary colleagues retain their implacable hostility and suspicion, which they show no signs of dropping.[53]

Sadly for any leadership hopes Dick may have concealed, that 'hostility and suspicion' was soon to spread beyond the parliamentary

---

* This was somewhat embarrassingly exposed by a prolonged debate in the correspondence columns of the *New Statesman*, which took place between Dick and the LSE political scientist, Robert McKenzie, during the summer of 1960. Dick had rather the worst of the exchanges initiated by McKenzie in a heavily ironical letter in the *New Statesman* (30 June 1960).

Party. At the last meeting in 1960 of the National Executive, the very body he had initially supposed he was championing, he was forbidden to brief the Press afterwards on the grounds that he could not be depended upon to be impartial.[54] The New Year found Dick driven back into one of his recurrent moods of disenchantment:

> The Labour Party has gone through many bad patches since '45 but I have never felt politics as gummed up and distressing as just now. If any opportunity for useful service outside were offered me, I am pretty sure I should take it since, despite incipient old age, I would reckon there are still at least eight years of useful work inside me. It's a strange thought that, in the whole period from 1945 till today, there were only three weeks during which I was given the chance of working all-out for the Party to which I have devoted my life. For what I did during those three weeks, which was quite first-rate, I shall never be forgiven by my colleagues, who at once saw the danger of having things run as effectively as all that. Is there any other occupation, or is there any Party in the history of politics, which feels such an instinctive hostility to creative ideas and bold decisions?[55]

It is only fair to add that this particular *cri de cœur* surfaced at a moment when Dick's spirits were low for other reasons. In January 1961 John Freeman had slid effortlessly into Kingsley Martin's editorial chair at the *New Statesman* ('There was no chance for any outsider to put his or anyone else's name forward'),[56] while the last month of the old year had seen the death, at the age of eighty-four, of Dick's mother, Lady Crossman. She had outlived her husband by almost twenty years – years in which her battles of the past with her son were forgotten – and, in Dick's own phrase, 'we managed to come together again'.[57] It was, therefore, a shock for Dick to discover that, alone among Helen Crossman's four surviving children, he had been excluded from her will. He actually wrote to her executor, the Public Trustee, to discover whether there was any deliberate intention behind this omission, and was much reassured to be told that it arose simply from his mother's feeling that he and his family were already adequately provided for (the estate anyway was a relatively modest one of some £7,659).[58] Probably what Dick minded most about was the seeming slight to his children,[59] Patrick and Virginia, who, he was almost certainly justified in claiming, had provided 'an unexpected, extra gift' to his mother in her old age.[60]

By 1961 the children directly affected his political life, when the family made its main home at Prescote instead of Vincent Square. The death of their maternal grandfather, Patrick McDougall, early in 1959 had something to do with this change, since it left Prescote uninhabited for most of the week; but a more crucial factor appears to have been the clear preference of their formidable nanny, a dedicated Plymouth Sister, for life in the country. Dick himself, perhaps as a result of his experience with Nye Bevan, was always particularly alert to the impact of geography on politics: and he was certainly not insensitive ('Where you live matters terribly')[61] to the likely influence of this change on his parliamentary life. Even so, it remains a matter for some surprise that in the whole of the 1960–1 parliamentary session he should have delivered just two Commons speeches.[62]

The substitution of Prescote Manor for 9 Vincent Square as the family's home was not the sole reason for that. Outside the Commons Dick may (as he put it) have been regarded as 'the patron saint of the constituency Parties'[63] but within the House he paid a price for that: he had come to be viewed as something of a pariah by the majority of his own Labour colleagues. Dick appears to have been genuinely taken aback by the indignation that his old-fashioned stand in favour of the sanctity of Conference decisions provoked – and on the first formal occasion (a meeting of the PLP on 14 December) when he was confronted with it clearly felt that he had given as good as he got. ('For the first time in my fifteen years in the Party Meeting I got across what I had to say.')[64] Even that form of self-confidence was not, however, to last for long. By the early months of 1961 – far from being seen as the champion of unity – he was forced to recognise that he was widely regarded as the prime wrecker of it. The immediate cause of this was a near success he enjoyed at the February meeting of the National Executive when an amendment he had cobbled together along with the shopworkers' president, Walter Padley,* to the Party's new statement of defence policy was defeated by only fifteen votes to thirteen. The narrow margin of victory was a shock to the leadership – and for a time it looked as if what came to be known as 'the Crossman–Padley compromise'† might succeed in rallying support at that

---

* Walter Padley (1916–84) was Labour MP for the Ogmore division of Glamorgan 1950–79. He served as Minister of State for Foreign Affairs 1964–7.

† While remaining solid on British membership of NATO, the Crossman–Padley proposals included a number of concessions to the unilateralists – including an implicit undertaking never 'to use the H-bomb or other nuclear weapons first' and an ambiguous promise 'to end the need for American nuclear bases in Europe, including Britain'.

autumn's Party Conference. That it failed to do so – and, indeed, was soon consigned to the lumber-room of Labour history – was at least partly Dick's own fault. By publicly denouncing Gaitskell's failure to embrace it as 'an absolute tragedy' – and solemnly warning that, as a result, 'there is a grave danger that the civil war in the Party will go on'[65] – Dick, not for the first time, overplayed his hand.

It was not so much a matter of the offence his remarks caused – though they led directly to a PLP meeting on 2 March which Dick characterised as 'the ugliest I have ever attended'.[66] Even more damagingly, he had gone on record with an analysis – and, indeed, risked a prediction – that events were to confound. The real secret of Dick's failure as a politician in the six months that followed the Scarborough Conference of 1960 lay in his placing a bet on the future that entirely failed to pay off. By the late spring of 1961 it was already clear that Gaitskell, far from facing a second defeat at that autumn's Party Conference, was on course for a massive victory.* Even 'the Crossman–Padley compromise' had ceased to be anything but an irrelevance – a fact that Dick had ruefully to recognise in conceding 'Gaitskell's defence triumph'.[67]

What saved Dick from being left high and dry was the Labour Party's periodic compulsion to produce a fresh, comprehensive, all-embracing home policy statement. At Scarborough in 1960, the Conference had been presented with a document called *Labour in the Sixties*. Its official status, however, had been merely that of a testament offered by the Party's general secretary, Morgan Phillips (who had been prevented from personally putting it before the delegates by a stroke he had suffered a fortnight before the Conference opened). In 1961 Gaitskell wanted a much more official update of Party policy – and for that purpose it had to be the joint work of the National Executive and the parliamentary Party. Having learnt enough about the disadvantages of more unwieldy bodies in preparing previous documents, Gaitskell resolved on this occasion to keep the drafting committee very small. For protocol reasons it would have been very difficult to exclude Dick, since he remained Chairman of the Party and was due to preside over that year's Party

---

* That the *bouleversement* was as sudden as any in modern British politics can be seen in two consecutive columns written by the *Observer*'s political correspondent, Hugh Massingham (30 April and 7 May 1961). The first included the prediction 'And the annual conference? Yes, Mr Gaitskell will almost certainly be defeated'; the second the pronouncement 'he can virtually count on victory at the annual conference in the autumn'.

Conference at Blackpool; but there was also the additional asset of Dick's skill and professionalism as a writer. In any event, Gaitskell swallowed whatever reservations he may have retained as a result of the defence controversy* and invited Dick to join George Brown (elected deputy leader in succession to Aneurin Bevan the previous November), Harold Wilson (who had succeeded Dick as Vice-Chairman of the Party) and himself on probably the most compact committee ever charged with the responsibility of putting together a Labour Party policy document.

Signposts for the Sixties was certainly produced in record time – scarcely more than a fortnight – and the fact that Dick was known to be its main author did a great deal to rehabilitate his reputation. It seems also to have been successful in restoring his relationship with Gaitskell – who, Dick noted, 'thanked me profoundly and sincerely, the first time in his whole life he has ever done such a thing, to me at least'.[68] Of course, with his defence battle safely won, Gaitskell may well have thought it prudent to get his formerly recalcitrant Party Chairman back on side before the Conference; and, if that was his objective, he attained it. At Blackpool in October Dick behaved with quite uncharacteristic responsibility, delivering a Chairman's address that in terms of loyalty and constructiveness could hardly be faulted[69] and following it up with a final speech which included the sentence, 'The leadership issue is once and for all out of the way.'[70] In fact, the only possible disappointment of the Conference lay in Dick's failure to lift his National Executive vote. Normally a year as Chairman of the Party was worth a minimum of 50,000 extra votes to a member of the constituency section – but 1961 was an exception to the rule. Although he went up from fifth to fourth in the order of candidates elected, Dick's vote was 2,000 fewer than it had been in 1960. No one could deny that he had spent an energetic year; but it was not perhaps surprising if the sheer kaleidoscopic nature of his performance had left the more conventional (not to say consistent) of the Party comrades a little bewildered.

If Dick had hoped for any reward for his reversion to responsibility, he was doomed to disappointment. He flirted with the idea of offering himself as the successor to Morgan Phillips, finally compelled to retire through ill health; Hugh Gaitskell's marked lack of enthusiasm for the notion soon persuaded him to abandon it. The

---

* He may have been helped to do so by Dick's (typically quixotic) remark, quoted in *The Times* (6 March 1961), that Gaitskell's presence in the leadership continued to be worth 'one million votes to Labour'.

same fate befell a further suggestion of his that he should take over the chairmanship of the Labour Party's publicity committee; this would have meant displacing a loyal Gaitskellite *apparatchik*. So it was probably just as well that, as soon as his chairmanship year was over, a new outlet should have opened up for Dick as a journalist. On Friday 20 October 1961 he began what was to be a two-year stint as a weekly back-page columnist of the *Guardian*.

It was, of course, a very different journalistic incarnation from his former one with the *Daily Mirror* – and not least financially (Dick was paid twenty guineas a week).* Yet in one sense Dick found himself in a uniquely privileged position since the editor of the *Guardian*, Alastair Hetherington, was also his lodger at 9 Vincent Square, occupying the top floor, which was no longer needed by the children, on his weekly trips from Manchester to London. They did not, however, see all that much of each other, as Hetherington – on the one or two nights a week he was actually there – normally came back late, after putting the paper's London edition to bed in Gray's Inn Road. The normal routine was that they would meet for breakfast, which Hetherington would cook and then summon Dick upstairs to eat.[71] It was plainly a convenient and congenial arrangement for both of them and it lasted for two and a half years, continuing even after Dick ceased writing the column in the autumn of 1963.

The column appeared on Fridays under the rubric 'Left of Centre' – though it tended to be less exclusively political in tone than its twice-weekly forerunner in the *Mirror*. At least, however, it provided Dick with an alternative interest to simply being a backbench Member of the House of Commons. (Against Gaitskell's advice,[72] he had stood for the Shadow Cabinet in November 1961, only to find himself snubbed once again by his colleagues.)† He did not, however, allow that to deter him from returning to the parliamentary fray. Between November and December 1961 he delivered three speeches in the House[73] – or one more than he had made in the entire 1960–1 session.

There was little question, though, that Dick had begun to regard himself as a political back number. Indeed, according to his own

---

* Dick used to like relating the story of how, on first negotiating the arrangement, he had raised the question of expenses with the *Guardian's* editor. 'Oh, we've thought of that,' replied Alastair Hetherington, 'ten guineas fee and ten guineas expenses.'

† With eighty-three votes Dick was not even the runner up. He came fourteenth, just behind one of the strongest Gaitskellite MPs, Christopher Mayhew.

testimony,[74] he had started to think seriously about reverting to academic life, casting occasional covetous glances both at Oxford and the London School of Economics. Since he had been away from professional academic life for a quarter of a century a post at either might well have proved more difficult to secure than he imagined – but in any event such aspirations depended on continued good health. And, at the beginning of 1962, just as he was entering his fifty-fifth year, it was that which came under question.

For the most part, Dick was lucky in seldom being bothered by illness – but, when he did get ill, he tended to get very ill indeed. That had been true of his phlebitis in 1943, his pleurisy in 1956 – and it was to prove to be once again the case with a burst duodenal ulcer in 1962. On 19 January he was visiting his constituency when he suddenly collapsed; he was rushed from Coventry to the Horton General Hospital in Banbury, where for two days he was on the danger list (he had suffered a massive internal haemorrhage and lost a great deal of blood). After seventeen days he was allowed home to convalesce – but with his doctors making it clear that, if his health would withstand it, they would still like to embark on major stomach surgery. The operation – a full gastrectomy – was duly performed on 3 March. Its seriousness was reflected by the fact that Dick did not return to the House of Commons for over ten weeks. When he finally reappeared, it was to a markedly cordial reception on both sides of the House[75] – a reminder perhaps that, whether he liked it or not, he was in danger of becoming something of a Westminster institution.

It was certainly not a role that Dick had ever aspired to – and he did little to cultivate it. In fact, no sooner was he back than he threw himself into the Labour Party's internal Common Market debate – in which the battle lines were similar to, though not identical with, the former struggle over 'revisionism'. If Dick nurtured any hopes of using the issue to revive the leadership question, they were squashed by the astonishingly tough anti-European line that Gaitskell took at the 1962 Brighton Conference. It was a Conference at which Dick, too, scored a significant personal success with yet another speech on pensions[76] and, although it brought no immediate preferment to the Front Bench, it apparently reconciled Gaitskell to the view that Dick would be the natural occupant of the Pensions and National Insurance Ministry in any future Labour Government that he led.[77]

It was not an intention that he ever communicated to Dick – and, even if he had done, it might not have made all that much difference. For what Dick hankered after was a role of central political influence; and that, given the wayward nature of his political behaviour from 1960 onwards, was not something ever likely to be on offer again while Gaitskell remained leader. He, therefore, threw himself back into the internal power politics of the Labour Party – now, from his point of view, provided with a new edge by the conflict over the Common Market. When Harold Wilson, partly on this issue, challenged George Brown for the deputy leadership in November 1962, Dick's was one of the guiding hands behind his campaign. Its failure – Wilson achieved only twenty-two more votes than he had won against Gaitskell and was comfortably defeated by a margin of thirty – convinced Dick that the Right was no longer prepared to give an inch. (His own defeat in the annual Shadow Cabinet elections – this time with nine fewer votes than he had got in 1961 – must have confirmed that impression.) By the end of 1962 he was once more in a mood of personal and political despondency – a mood that was to be banished only by one of those unpredictable upheavals that for Dick always remained part of 'the charm of politics'.

14   *The Gates of Paradise*

Hugh Gaitskell's death in the Middlesex Hospital on 18 January 1963 – from an obscure disease called *lupus erythematosus* – was not a total shock. The Labour leader had first gone into hospital on 15 December 1962 and, although he had been allowed home for Christmas, his return to hospital ten days afterwards did not look particularly reassuring. From early January onwards, a succession of ever gloomier medical bulletins not only alarmed the nation but alerted his colleagues to the need to make their dispositions. By the second week of the New Year, Dick was already backing the formation of a 'Regency', or a council of five to act in the leader's absence.[1] It was not a proposal that commended itself to many of his colleagues – indeed, on grounds of taste it was widely condemned. But Dick knew exactly what he was doing: if there was to be a temporary vacuum of authority at the top of the Labour Party, he was determined that the Right should not be allowed automatically to fill it. The clue to his support for the notion of a 'Regents' Council' lay in his realisation that, as the unofficial number three figure in the Party, Harold Wilson would have to be a member of it.

There was, as things turned out, no need for such contingency plans. Before Parliament reassembled on 21 January 1963, the fight for the succession had already started. No previous Leader of the Opposition had died in office in the twentieth century. The Labour Party thus found itself in an unprecedentedly vulnerable position – and its initial mood was one of considerable electoral apprehension. In public at least, Dick himself fully reflected it. Writing in the *Sunday Telegraph*, just two days after Gaitskell had died, he roundly declared that public opinion had begun 'to accept him unreservedly as a real national leader and potential Prime Minister' and even risked the judgment that his loss might prove 'irreparable'.[2] From the vantage point of a less than wholehearted loyalist, he went on to be even more generous, confessing that the achievements of Gaitskell's strong leadership had proved him 'wrong, wrong with many other sceptics. We can now see that what the Labour Party needed was to be dragged by the scruff of the neck and shoved into contact with the real problems of our age.'[3]

Did those, though, even at the time, represent Dick's genuine views? The question must be asked, since a decade later evidence emerged of his true, more brutal reaction to Gaitskell's death. In the Introduction to the first volume of his *Cabinet Diaries*, having dwelt on his own bleak prospects under the old regime, Dick could not resist adding: 'But as Harold Laski used to remind us, in British politics where there is death there is hope.'[4] Nor could he be accused of inventing such a reaction retrospectively. His own contemporary *Backbench Diaries* reveal all too clearly the sense of excitement, almost of elation, he felt as the realisation dawned upon him that Wilson stood the best chance of being elected as Gaitskell's successor. 'Of all the 249 members of the Parliamentary Labour Party,' he wrote at the time, 'Harold is the one person closest to me, the one I get on with best, the one whose relationships with me have been tested over twelve years by some fairly trying times.'[5]

Dick had, of course, known Hugh Gaitskell much longer – for more than forty years ever since they were first at school together. But that had tended, at least latterly, to be more of a personal complicating factor than any sort of political advantage. Now the slate had been wiped clean, and Dick could afford to start dreaming of a political future quite different in terms of influence from any that he could have contemplated under Gaitskell. To enjoy it, however, it was necessary first to get Wilson elected to the vacant leadership. It was an enterprise to which Dick brought not just invaluable confidence but a remarkable canniness as well.

If he was never the operating tactician of the leadership campaign – George Wigg was the principal source of intelligence for Wilson as to the voting intentions of his colleagues – Dick could claim from the outset to have been its chief strategist. It was his recommendation to Wilson that resulted in there being no overt campaigning at all. The practice of 'masterly inactivity' proved to be an inspired policy, not least because anything else would only have enhanced Wilson's existing reputation for machination and manœuvring. As it was, all the predictable allegations of undue pressure and arm-twisting tended to centre on Wilson's main opponent, George Brown, who reacted with especial vigour to James Callaghan's* decision to run as 'the third man' in the contest. Dick had rightly spotted from the start that a two-horse race was the one thing Wilson had to fear – as in those circumstances Brown could probably count on 'getting the Establishment vote as acting leader of the Party'.[6] Callaghan's intervention was, therefore, very helpful. It not only divided the Gaitskellites – with Roy Jenkins, for example, supporting Brown and Anthony Crosland backing Callaghan:[7] it also provided the hesitant with a respectable half-way house in which to take refuge before having to make their final decision – a decision which, in the nature of politics, was bound to be influenced by the two major contenders' rival showings on the first ballot. Unlike George Wigg, Dick never expected Wilson to win an outright victory,† and was more than content when he attained 115 votes to George Brown's 88 and Jim Callaghan's 41. That night, 7 February 1963, there was a very select supper party at 9 Vincent Square. The two main guests – perhaps in acknowledgment of Dick's role – were Harold Wilson and his wife, Mary.

Once the first ballot figures were known, the eventual result was inevitable and, when it was declared on 14 February, it showed a decisive victory for Harold Wilson with 144 votes to George Brown's 103. Dick had followed his own advice to Wilson and had contributed to his triumph by a display of astonishing self restraint. Although he continued writing his weekly column for the *Guardian*, he never once referred to the leadership contest until it was safely over. When he finally did so, it was in an understandable mood of gloating satisfaction. Recalling the *Observer*'s editorial forecast on 20 January that 'Gaitskell's death has not only robbed Labour of the chance of victory but probably means the end of the Party in its present form', Dick could not resist pointing to 'the response of the British voter to the *Observer*'s dirge': this revealed, he announced with relish, 'the biggest lead that has ever been registered by a British Party since George Gallup set up shop in this country'[8]

---

* James Callaghan was Labour MP for South Cardiff 1945–50, South-east Cardiff 1950–83 and Cardiff South and Penarth 1983–7. He was to be Dick's colleague as Chancellor of the Exchequer and Home Secretary in the Wilson Cabinets of 1964–70. He served as Foreign Secretary 1974–6 and after Dick's death became Wilson's successor as Prime Minister 1976–9. Leader of the Opposition 1979–80, he was created a life peer in 1987.

† George Wigg had a bet of £5 with the author that Wilson would do so. It may, of course, have been a wager made for purely psychological reasons. In any event, he paid up, though not with particularly good grace.

(Labour's lead in the Gallup Poll had increased from 9·5 per cent in the month before Gaitskell died to 18 per cent in the week that Wilson was elected). Since he also referred unkindly to 'the boneless wonders that go by the name of *Observer* editorials', this particular column, not unnaturally, attracted a tart reply from the paper's editor, David Astor, in the *Guardian*'s correspondence columns.[9]

Two days later, in the Labour Party's paper, the *Daily Herald*, Dick delivered an encomium on the new leader. Describing Harold Wilson as 'the cleverest man to have led a British political Party since Lloyd George' and calling him politically 'at least as professional as Mr Kennedy', he only fell into an élitist trap when he went on to dwell on the new leader's personal qualities: 'despite his intellectual brilliance he remains, like his wife, a sincere non-conformist who has escaped from the backstreets without acquiring either the sophistication or the tastes of high society – without any affectation he prefers the kind of unassuming, comfortable home life, which he shares with millions of ordinary families'.[10] Perhaps predictably, for the ranks of the sophisticated, this proved a bit much. Within a month, the *Spectator* was mischievously commenting on Dick's habit, with visitors to 9 Vincent Square, of pointing to a particular corner of his living-room and announcing reverentially, 'There is *his* chair.'[11]

Dick was vulnerable to such teasing because he was so clearly the outstanding beneficiary of the new regime. Less than a week after Wilson had been formally elected, he was translated from the backbenches to a Front Bench role – not the one he had expected (and half hoped for) of returning to pensions and social security but rather that of being the new leader's spokesman on science (and, in effect, the head of the Party's new policy brains trust that Wilson was determined to develop). With an eye perhaps on his own left-wing constituency Party, Dick put on a public show of lack of enthusiasm for his new status, telling his local evening paper: 'I was very reluctant to give up the freedom of speech which I had enjoyed and valued greatly for so many years. Mr Wilson was very insistent that I should take the job, however, and eventually I accepted.'[12]

That was a slightly graceless way of putting it, since Dick was understandably excited at being one of only two back-bench Labour MPs brought into the new leader's team. There was, however, one fly in the ointment: the Labour Front Bench already had a spokesman on science and, as ill luck would have it, he was the veteran

Labour MP, Gilbert Mitchison, QC,* the husband of Zita's great friend, Naomi, with whom Dick all those years ago had written his book on Socrates. Even before the final ballot was announced, Mitchison appears to have had some sort of intimation of the way things would go – saying to Dick in a conversation in the lobby of the House of Commons: 'No doubt you will be the Party spokesman on science. Be sure I bear you no ill-will if you take it over from me – at my age what can I expect from a young man like Harold?'[13] Alas, the brave front was not borne out by Mitchison's ultimate reaction to seeing himself displaced. The first sign that Dick had that all was not well came in the shape of a curiously stilted letter he received on the day his appointment was announced:[14] in it Mitchison pointedly offered no congratulations and simply announced that he was withdrawing the two questions he had set down for answer by the Parliamentary Secretary for Science (the Minister, Lord Hailsham, was in the House of Lords). For once, Dick reacted with consummate tact, if not perhaps with complete truthfulness – assuring Mitchison in his reply that 'there was nothing I wanted less than to deprive you of a task you were enjoying' and asserting that he had 'only accepted the job under protest because Harold insisted that he wanted to see me there as an act of loyalty to him'.[15] Mitchison, however, was not to be assuaged and, as an elected member of the Shadow Cabinet (which Dick was not), took himself off in some dudgeon to be the Party's spokesman on social security. At least initially, Dick remained unpersuaded that the change had been skilfully handled, confessing in his diary: 'It would have been much easier if Harold had let me do pensions and let poor Dick Mitchison – who will never forgive me for replacing him – carry on with science.'[16]

From the strictly House of Commons point of view, it was not much of a Shadow portfolio that Dick had been given. The Ministry for Science had only been created in 1959 by Harold Macmillan – apparently to find a berth for Lord Hailsham once he had removed him from the Tory Party chairmanship. The fact that the principal Government spokesman for the Department was in the House of Lords did not help his opposite number in the House of Commons – and a routine had more or less been established whereby scientific

* Gilbert ('Dick') Mitchison (1890–1970) was Labour MP for Kettering 1945–64. As a life peer, he subsequently served 1964–6 as Under-Secretary at the Ministry of Land and Natural Resources. He was one of only two members of the then Shadow Cabinet not to be given a Cabinet post when Wilson formed his first Government in October 1964.

issues received a formal airing once a year in a somewhat ritualised Commons debate. Before he even offered him the brief, however, Wilson had indicated to Dick that he wanted to change all that, explaining: 'The scientists, the technologists and their like felt excluded by the Gaitskell leadership, left out, not wanted. But if I get the job, I shall want to create an atmosphere where they all feel wanted in the Labour Party.'[17] He proved as good as his word – and Dick found himself encouraged to set up no fewer than four extra-parliamentary working parties that took to meeting in conditions of some secrecy at the Bonnington Hotel in Bloomsbury. Each had its individual chairman – not all of them scientists (Robert Maxwell was one, Noel Annan another) – and Dick was more the overall co-ordinator than anything else. But the enterprise at least made a propaganda point, which was demonstrated when headlines started surfacing in the Press like 'Labour Mobilises the Scientists'[18] or even 'The Tories in Danger of Losing the Battle of Brains'.[19] The objective was plainly to create the same atmosphere of intellectual excitement that had attended the launching of President Kennedy's New Frontier some three years earlier.

For such a role – as, in effect, Labour's ambassador to the academic community – Dick was probably as well cast as anyone could be. True, in the early days he tended to blunder into mistakes. The question of whether those taking part would need to be Party members became a particular bone of contention – with the NEC showing every sign of insisting on it and even the most sympathetic scientists fiercely resisting it. Characteristically, Dick found himself caught in the cross-fire – receiving stern demands from colleagues in the parliamentary Party that 'it surely goes without saying that only card-carrying Party members should be involved'[20] and at the same time being the subject of warnings from members of the scientific community that 'scientists have an over-riding loyalty to "science" (which is international and non-political)'.[21] The issue was eventually resolved in favour of the latter viewpoint – though not before Dick had caused some embarrassment to a young Labour Party colleague by appearing to railroad him into the secretaryship of the Socialist Scientists Association.[22]

Most of Dick's earliest efforts were devoted to activities outside Parliament, but he always recognised that the hour of reckoning would come when he would have to unveil his Party's plans for making science the new engine of socialism to the House of Commons. It was the one oratorical challenge of his career that genuinely intimidated him, and for an understandable reason. What

Dick had always prided himself upon in his Commons speeches was a complete mastery of his subject – something that may even have impeded the development of his political career since he tended to talk only on those topics where he felt he possessed some expertise. Yet here he was as every inch a classicist – after a six-month 'cram' course at the most – expected to outline not only his own but his Party's thinking in what was then the brand new area of relationships between Government departments, research councils and the industrial application of modern technology. He was further inhibited by knowing that what he said would be regarded as official Party policy; hence perhaps his anxiety to clear his speech with Wilson beforehand. In the week preceding the debate in July, he even went to the length of writing his leader a long letter outlining what he proposed to say and listing the commitments he wished to have permission to make.[23] Only one of them – a pledge to set up a Ministry of Science *and* Higher Education – appeared to bother Wilson when they eventually met. That, Dick was given to understand, might cause trouble with an NEC working party that had reported in the opposite sense on the same subject, so it might be prudent to soft-pedal it. By contrast, altogether more sweeping demands – such as doubling the numbers in higher education over a ten-year period or increasing Government grants to research institutes by £40 million annually – provoked no reservations from Wilson at all.[24]

On the day of the debate, 15 July, for the first time in his parliamentary life Dick had a bad case of stage fright. He arrived at the House too early and was reduced to wandering round the lobby and the Smoking Room with nothing really to do but fill in the time.[25] At 3.20 p.m., however, he took his seat on the Front Bench – the first time he had sat there for a debate since his quarrel over defence with Gaitskell more than three years earlier. At least, though, that memory gave him the chance of seeking to capture the sympathy of the House with his opening remarks – addressed, in accordance with parliamentary practice to the occupant of the Chair, the then deputy chairman of Ways and Means, Sir Robert Grimston: 'Having caught your eye, Sir Robert, with unusual facility, I am tempted to ask the indulgence of the Committee as a back-bencher who has spent nearly eighteen years on the back-benches and whose visit to the Front Bench a few years ago was extremely brief.'[26]

It was an engaging start and Dick's speech, even though delivered to a half-empty House on a Monday, proved a success. It earned the tribute of having a *Guardian* leader devoted to it[27] and even a Conservative newspaper described him as having spoken 'with tremendous fluency, force and vitality, dominating the Chamber with the flow of his thoughts rather in the manner of the late Aneurin Bevan'.[28] Probably, though, its most significant outcome emerged in a telephone conversation Dick had the next day with Wilson, who had rung him up to congratulate him on the reviews of his performance. According to his own contemporary account, Dick immediately urged his leader to make science and its relationship to the Labour Party the major theme of his own speech to that autumn's Party Conference, excitedly exclaiming: 'Look, Harold, this is the moment. We've got through this science barrier. Let's have a morning at Conference. You make your big speech on Labour in the Science Age and I will wind up the debate.'[29] At Scarborough in October that was exactly how things worked out, and Dick's claim to having been the godfather of Wilson's landmark speech identifying Labour with 'the white heat of the technological revolution' – though modestly never advanced in his lifetime – would seem to be incontrovertible.

There were always limits, however, to what Wilson could do in return for his most intellectually creative colleague. This was partly because on matters unconnected with his new Front Bench responsibilities Dick continued to follow his own wayward course. His attendance, for example, at the annual Anglo-German Königswinter conference in April 1963 provoked one of the early foreign policy squalls of the Wilson leadership. With his interest in Germany going back to the 1930s, Dick had long been a pillar of these gatherings, which are designed to promote Anglo-German understanding. On this occasion that was the opposite of what happened, since Dick allowed himself to be trapped into one of his frequent indiscretions. The trouble occurred not at the conference itself but at a dinner party British and American correspondents in Bonn gave in Dick's honour. There appears to have been a good deal of uninhibited discussion, with Dick (who was accompanied by an equally vocal Barbara Castle)* being particularly critical of the role played

---

* Barbara Castle, Labour MP for Blackburn 1945–79, was throughout her career a close political ally of Dick's. They sat together in Wilson's Cabinets of 1964–6 and 1966–70. Their friendship survived even her embracing, as First Secretary of State, the abortive trade union proposals of 1969, which Dick opposed. Leaving the House of Commons five years after Dick's death, she became the first leader of the democratically chosen British Labour Group in the European Parliament, following the direct elections of 1979. She was created a life peeress in 1990.

by the West German SPD in its new 'revisionist' phase. Within a day or two an account of the occasion had leaked and surfaced in the *New York Times*[30] – from which it was soon transferred in even more lurid versions to the British Press. From Dick's personal point of view, the most damaging account of all – though it did not touch on his view of the SPD – probably appeared in the *Spectator*:

> The most positive of all performances on the British side was, naturally, Mr R. H. S. Crossman's. Having confessed that, because he had at last backed a winner, he found an ox sitting on his tongue, he thereupon summoned up all his considerable powers of paradox and personality and told his audience that Britain had no place in Europe, that de Gaulle and his policies were nothing to be worried about, that we in Britain can generate a far greater stimulus outside Europe and that a socialist state can *only* be achieved in a small country . . . If these were the words that could get past the ox on the tongue of such a brilliant praetorian, what on earth were the thoughts that had been held back?[31]

As the meditations of a mere back-bench Member of Parliament on de Gaulle's rejection of Britain's first application to join the Common Market, Dick's views would probably not have attracted much attention – but he had plainly not yet got used to the inhibitions attached to being associated with a Front Bench team. He found himself summoned to answer for himself at a meeting of the Labour Party's foreign affairs group – and, though he refused to go, he thought it prudent to write a long and slightly exasperated letter of explanation ('I make no accusations as to who broke confidence, I do not know and I do not care')[32] to Patrick Gordon Walker, the Party's chief foreign affairs spokesman. He also suffered the indignity of seeing an official statement issued on behalf of the Labour Party, insisting: 'It is quite untrue that the British Labour Party and the German Social Democratic Party are opposed in their attitudes towards world problems.'[33]

This was by no means, though, the only incident in which Dick's conduct raised some hackles among his more conventional colleagues in the parliamentary Party. Just a month to the day after his appointment to the Front Bench, he joined with Barbara Castle and George Wigg in using the pre-Easter debate on the Consolidated Fund Bill to raise the speculation circulating around the model,

Christine Keeler (Keeler had just disappeared on the eve of a trial at
the Old Bailey at which she was due to be a witness). Dick's own
speech was extremely guarded – he simply referred to 'rumours
which have run round this House and the country'[34] – but that did
not save him from being subjected to what at the time seemed a
rather crushing intervention from his fellow Labour MP (and strong
George Brown supporter) Reginald Paget:*

> My Hon. Friend keeps on referring to rumours and rather deplor-
> ing what the Press is doing in regard to them . . . What do these
> rumours amount to? They amount to the fact that a Minister is
> said to be acquainted with a particularly pretty girl. I should have
> thought that was a matter for congratulation rather than inquiry.[35]

And, of course, in the short term it did look as if this concerted,
freebooting initiative had proved counter-productive. It – or rather
Barbara Castle's injudicious raising of the issue of a 'perversion of
justice' and coupling it with a reference to 'people in high places'[36] –
led directly to the War Minister, John Profumo's personal statement
the following day in which he categorically denied being 'connected
with or responsible for Keeler's absence from the trial at the Old
Bailey'. If he had not added the fatal phrase about there having
been 'no impropriety whatsoever in my acquaintanceship with Miss
Keeler',[37] that presumably would have been the end of the matter.
Far from launching what came to be known as 'the Profumo Affair',
Dick's late-night intervention – and those of his two colleagues –
would in all probability have effectively smothered it. Certainly, all
three had spoken without any real knowledge of the background,
apart from Fleet Street gossip (the osteopath, Stephen Ward's dos-
sier only reached Wigg five days after he had made his speech and
had not prompted it).[38] But, since in politics it is consequences that
count, Dick eventually emerged from this somewhat reckless
escapade looking vindicated.† He even risked drawing attention to
his part in instigating the hue and cry which brought the War Minister down in a speech he delivered in the Profumo debate on 17 June

---

* Reginald Paget (1908–90) was Labour MP for Northampton 1945–74, when he
was created a life peer. A former Opposition spokesman on Defence, he was
dropped by Wilson from his 1964 Government.

† His reputation with some critics did not, however, remain totally unscathed. A
savage onslaught on his role in the affair – written by H. G. Wells's son, Anthony
West – appeared in the *Spectator* (5 July 1963). The title of the piece, suggested by
the paper's proprietor, Ian Gilmour, was 'McCarthy in Westminster'.

1963.[39] Although Dick regarded it as 'a pretty good speech',[40] it was one of his less distinguished efforts, making barely a line of copy in any of the newspapers and having singularly little impact on the course of the debate (George Wigg's own contribution to the same debate was equally a non-event). In that there was some justice, for the security aspect to the affair was always pretty bogus* and, given the way in which they had both rushed in at the start with nothing to rely upon but Press innuendo, Dick and George Wigg had less claim than most to seek to exploit it.

So far as Dick was concerned, there was one curious and not very convenient legacy of the Profumo affair. When the Denning Report reviewing the history of the whole episode came out in September, it included in two of its paragraphs a rather muddled summary of what exactly had happened in the House of Commons on the night of 21–2 March 1963. The Report's author, despite his legal background, failed to draw any distinction between the precise point raised by Barbara Castle and the much more general, if mysterious, doubts expressed by Dick and George Wigg. All three speeches were lumped together as having represented 'remarks of much significance – they clearly imputed that Mr Profumo had been responsible for the disappearance of Christine Keeler'.[41] Not surprisingly, this particular passage was pounced on by the Conservative Party chairman, Iain Macleod, who, on the day the Report was published, called on all three of them to withdraw what they had said. Both Dick and George Wigg strenuously objected to Macleod's statement – and jointly wrote to him saying they had nothing to withdraw and demanding that he, in turn, apologise for suggesting that they had. Although Arnold Goodman was brought in to act as their adviser – and in the end a second legally threatening letter was sent[42] – it was an exercise that predictably ran into the ground. It was probably just as well that it did. Any libel jury might have concluded eventually that, in certain circumstances, just as important as the words that people use is the meaning they intend to have attached to them. And on that latter point Lord Denning may well have formed a legitimate judgment.

If his Profumo experience taught Dick one thing, it was perhaps the difficulty of trying to combine the roles of buccaneering back-

---

* Twenty-six years after the scandal, Sir Ian Gilmour revealed that even Wigg in a private document sent to Wilson had written: 'In my opinion, Profumo was never a security risk.' The document came into the *Spectator*'s possession when Wigg attempted to sue the paper for libel over the article mentioned above.

bencher and responsible Party spokesman. Certainly, in its aftermath, he tended to concentrate more and more on his Front Bench
sphere. But that was not the only sign that he was gradually adjust-
ing to the discipline involved in being a dedicated politician.
Another indication lay in the abrupt ending of his *Guardian* column
that autumn. True, the provocation was provided by the paper. In
the week of the Tory Conference in October 1963, Dick had written
his usual column for Friday on the Thursday morning in ignorance
that Harold Macmillan's impending resignation as Prime Minister
would be announced at Blackpool on the Thursday evening.
Although his lead item was devoted to the general theme of a future
contest for the Tory leadership, the news about the Prime Minister's
retirement necessarily made it seem – at least to the *Guardian's*
editor – somewhat stale. It was, therefore, 'spiked' – though
without Dick being afforded the courtesy of being informed. As is
usually the case in such contretemps, that was not so much anyone's
fault as the result of difficult and awkward circumstances: Dick had
been virtually incommunicado throughout the Thursday evening,
addressing a county National Union of Teachers dinner in Banbury.
That was not, though, something that he allowed to mitigate his
rage, which was not even mollified by a courteous letter that Alastair Hetherington (the *Guardian's* editor and still his lodger in 9
Vincent Square) sent him the next day:

11 October 1963

Dear Dick,
   I really am sorry about last night. I am not putting blame on
anyone else, and my decision may have been wrong. One must,
however, act quickly on such occasions, and it's useless to dither.
I had very little manœuvring room inside the paper. I also had a
number of other urgent things to attend to. Hence the decision.
   I feel fairly pleased with last night's work, though still very
sorry if I did wrongly over your column. I can well see how
irritating it must be to discover that it's out, and of course a
column ought to have continuity.

Yours,
ALASTAIR[43]

It says something about Dick's tendency always to act as a *prima
donna* in journalism that his immediate response to so friendly a
note should have been the comment in his diary, 'To think that this

little jackass* should have treated me in this way.'⁴⁴ No doubt, however, that spontaneous reaction merely reflected the genuine fury he felt – he even preserved the typescript of the thousand words he had sent in with a scrawl on the top: 'Last column written – was cut out by Editor.'⁴⁵ But behind Dick's anger another motive was at work. Typically, he did not seek to conceal it, even confessing in his diary about his column, 'The more I thought it over, the more I felt that this was my opportunity to drop it.'⁴⁶ Why, though, should Dick have had any such feeling? Again, his contemporary explanation could hardly have been more explicit. 'I had begun to realise that, with my present standing as one of the half-dozen top Opposition leaders, a column which had to be churned out each week was becoming an increasing embarrassment not only to myself but to my friends.'⁴⁷

The autumn of 1963, in that sense, probably marked a watershed in Dick's life. It was not that he gave way to self-importance – his domestic life at Prescote (where he faced the demanding challenge of being a 55-year-old father to two children of six and four) alone prevented that: it was rather that he had, however subtly, altered his priorities. He had always to some extent rung the changes between politics and journalism – and now politics was once again sounding the louder peal. In responding to it, Dick may, of course, have exaggerated his own career prospects. There is something poignant about that phrase 'one of the half-dozen top Opposition leaders' – especially when used by someone who a month later could not even get himself elected to the Shadow Cabinet. Of course, that merely demonstrated once again what an unforgiving body the parliamentary Party was – at the Party Conference at Scarborough Dick had enjoyed his second-best result ever for the National Executive, coming in fourth with 715,000 votes; but in the parliamentary elections, although for the first time he collected the votes of more than a hundred of his colleagues,† it was still not enough to make him anything better than runner up to the twelve elected candidates. The fact that Gilbert Mitchison – the man he had replaced as the Opposition spokesman on science – should have been the bottom elected candidate must have appeared only to add insult to injury.

In the end, though, this disappointment was hardly to matter.

---

* Alastair Hetherington, a fortnight later, had two relatively friendly conversations with Dick, in which the real reason for Dick's retaliatory decision to cease writing the column was finally revealed. Harold Wilson had advised him against continuing with it.

† Dick received 102 votes, twelve more than the next non-elected candidate.

Two external events underpinned and reinforced Dick's political position in the last months of 1963. The first was the publication of the Robbins Report on Higher Education[48] in October, putting the future of universities and polytechnics right at the top of the political agenda; the second – and more crucial from the parliamentary point of view – was the return of Quintin Hogg to the House of Commons after the failure of his attempt, as Lord Hailsham, to secure the succession to Harold Macmillan. In terms of his Front Bench responsibilities Dick was not the obvious beneficiary of either; Wilson, however, saw to it that he reaped the reward of both – and by the beginning of 1964 he was in all but name Quintin Hogg's opposite number on the Opposition Front Bench, conducting the argument with him not just on science but across the whole field of education.

The surprise elevation of Lord Home ('the 14th Earl' as Opposition spokesmen took care to call him) into the Prime Ministership was certainly not unhelpful to what had always been Wilson's aim of establishing complete personal authority over his own Party. At the start of the new Prime Minister's reign, the personal duel between them looked more and more like a contest between an attractive amateur and an accomplished professional. The fact that the Leader of the Opposition no longer needed to be too concerned about the sensitivities of his own Shadow Cabinet colleagues was demonstrated by the ease with which he now moved to offer Dick the opportunity to be the architect of Labour's entire approach to educational reform.* It was an exercise that required some finesse – if only because the parliamentary Party already had its official education spokesman in an ex-school teacher elected member of the Shadow Cabinet, Frederick Willey.† From the time of the Queen's Speech debate in November – when Wilson himself laid out the Opposition's response to the Robbins Report[49] – Willey's role, however, became ever more shadowy and Dick's more and more substantial. Fresh from the success of his speech winding up

---

* Dick always maintained that he had had to press Harold Wilson to give him this starring role, but that does not alter the fact that it was Wilson who took the risk of bestowing it upon him.

† Frederick Willey (1910–87) was Labour MP for Sunderland 1945–50 and Sunderland North 1950–83. He was the first, and only, Minister of Land and Natural Resources in the Wilson Government of 1964 when he again ran into collision with Dick as Minister of Housing and Local Government. His ministerial career ended in 1967 but he eventually became chairman of the Parliamentary Labour Party 1979–81.

the science debate at the Labour Party Conference,[50] Dick had launched his own pre-emptive strike in a long letter to *The Times*[51] even before the Robbins Report was published. The paper conveniently headed it 'Planning for Research: What Labour has in Mind' and, although the views it put forward did not ultimately carry the day (Dick came out in favour of a new autonomous Ministry to be responsible for the universities and research), it certainly put down his own personal marker in a debate that was to rumble on till February 1964 when the Government announced its considered response to the Robbins recommendations.

When that announcement finally came, it was given significantly by the Prime Minister in reply to a Front Bench parliamentary question from Dick[52] – and it could hardly have been of more assistance to his own position. Sir Alec Douglas-Home (as he had become following his translation from the Lords to the Commons) revealed that the Government had decided against the Robbins proposal for two separate Ministries of Education – one for universities and research and the other for schools. Instead, there would be one super-Department, to be known as 'the Ministry of Education and Science'. Even in terms of the argument, this did not represent a rebuff for Dick, since as early as the previous November he had reversed his previous support for a Ministry of Higher Education and Research and had come out, if a little reluctantly, in favour of a single unified Department as 'the lesser of two evils'.[53] More to the point, however, were the personnel dispositions that the Prime Minister also announced. The first Minister of Education and Science, he told the House of Commons, would be the then Minister for Science and Lord President of the Council, Quintin Hogg, with Sir Edward Boyle, who for the previous eighteen months had headed the Education Ministry, serving under him as a Minister of State (though retaining his seat in the Cabinet). Although an awkward administrative solution from the Government's point of view, it was the ideal political answer so far as Dick was concerned. It meant that he inherited, as of right, the task of shadowing Hogg – now the undisputed number one figure in the new combined Ministry – while the unfortunate official education spokesman, Fred Willey, was relegated to the status of being the opposite number to a mere Minister of State. Wilson's dilemma about promoting Dick over the head of an already established Front Bench education spokesman had obligingly been solved for him by the action of the Government.

For the remaining six months of the 1959–64 Parliament, Dick took remorseless advantage of the political opportunity offered to him. It was not just a question of his being matched against Hogg in all major Commons exchanges – though, since they were both rival debating stars, these tended to attract a good deal of Press attention. The issue that Dick made his own was that of 'the brain drain' – the emigration of British scientists, particularly to the United States, in search not just of higher salaries but of better laboratory facilities as well. This became very much the theme of their first full-dress encounter against each other – a Commons debate held in the same month that Hogg's appointment was announced. There were documented figures of 160 scientists having left Britain for work abroad in the previous year[54] and in the debate Dick made great play not just with the statistics but with an insensitive letter of rebuke that Hogg had written to a young scientific research student who had asked his advice on whether he should emigrate or not.[55] For his part, Hogg replied with some fairly effective mockery of the various changes of mind Dick had gone through over the type and number of research and education Ministries needed in Whitehall[56] and, indeed, not for the first time in his life, Dick had hardly been consistent.

These purely oratorical displays were never, however, likely to get Dick into trouble with the Parliamentary Labour Party. He was a formidable Front Bench performer, and even his critics on the benches behind him had to recognise his debating abilities. Tensions, though, were still running not far below the surface and these were publicly exposed when Dick, perhaps rashly, moved to extend his empire into that of policy-making over primary education. Wearing his National Executive hat, he had for some months chaired a study group on the supply of teachers – and, when its report came out in May 1964, it was found to include, as one of its ten recommendations, a proposal for half-day schooling for children between five and six. That was not the kind of policy initiative likely to commend itself to the National Union of Teachers, to whom it seemed a short-cut device for reducing the employment prospects of its members. Within two days of presenting the document to a Press conference at Transport House, Dick found himself humiliatingly repudiated – with even the *Daily Mirror* reporting: 'A Labour plan for half-day schooling for children under six has been killed stone dead by Harold Wilson and his Shadow Cabinet. The Shadow Cabinet's decision is a sharp setback for Mr Richard Crossman.'[57]

'Sharp setback' or not, it certainly looked as if Dick had been the victim of a 'mugging' by his enemies – and an editorial note in the weekly periodical *Education* may well have let the cat out of the bag. Headed 'Who Does What?' it argued that the incident

> is bound to raise the whole question of what exactly Mr Cross-man's role now is in the Parliamentary Labour Party. He is supposed to be the Labour Party's spokesman for science; Mr Willey is handling education. Yet somehow the impression has been created that Mr Crossman is entitled to the mantle of Mr Hogg; he certainly acts as though this were the case. Mr Willey is said to resent this keenly and it seems that resentment is spreading within the Parliamentary Labour Party. Mr Crossman's latest brilliant indiscretion may bring matters to a head.[58]

Harold Wilson, of course, had no intention of allowing that to happen – though his acquiescence in the snub to Dick may well have been the price he had to pay for forestalling any outright revolt against his protégé's admittedly somewhat anomalous position. What Dick perhaps ought to have been able to foresee was that in setting himself up as an expert in the area of primary education he was bound to look vulnerable. How much could the product of a prep school, Winchester and New College, Oxford be expected to know about the sort of infant education experienced by 95 per cent of the population? In fact, though, Dick may well have known rather more than his critics thought. His son, Patrick, went to the local primary school in Cropredy, the near-by village to Prescote, and Dick himself was one of its 'managers'. Over the previous year he had engaged in correspondence with the chairman of the Oxford-shire County Education Committee about its plans for rebuilding the school. Even the most antagonistic member of the NUT might have been softened by the discovery that one of the first points he put in his opening letter was: 'Apparently there is to be a "staff room" without windows. I do ask you to reconsider whether it is wise to spend money on creating a Black Hole of Calcutta and calling it a "staff room".'[59]

Given the susceptibilities, not to say the jealousies, of his colleagues in the Parliamentary Labour Party it was perhaps just as well that another exercise Dick embarked upon just before the October 1964 general election never became public knowledge. Partly at the instigation of George Brown – who, improbably, was a governor of Repton School which lay in his constituency of Belper – he agreed to meet a group of five public school headmasters in order to seek to establish what chance, if any, there would be under a Labour Government of fee-paying schools having a relationship with the State system. A dinner took place at the United Universities Club in London on 15 July with five headmasters present, in addition to Dick and George Brown. The proceedings were sufficiently formal for a minute of the discussions to be drawn up, which one of the headmasters (Frank Fisher, the Warden of St Edward's, Oxford) subsequently sent to Dick for his approval.[60] It reveals nothing very compromising. Dick is shown as having stood out throughout for a minimum participation of 50 per cent of pupils from the State sector if the public schools wished to be involved in any way in Labour's educational plans. But the mere notion of conducting any negotiations with the representatives of such entrenched citadels of privilege would certainly have alarmed the more fundamentalist members of the PLP. It was just as well for Dick's standing and reputation with his colleagues that not a word of these conversations – or, indeed, of an earlier meeting that he had attended, under the auspices of the Fabian Society, with the headmasters of Malvern and Winchester[61] – ever surfaced.

The main significance of both these confidential encounters lies in the light they shed on Dick's state of mind in the immediate run up to the 1964 general election. The fact that, in the interests of a long-term educational strategy, he was ready to take risks of this kind suggests that he had very little doubt that he was destined to be Minister of Education and Science in any Labour Government that was formed after the election. In a way, this confidence of his was curious. A favourite journalistic game in the months leading up to the pre-ordained ending of the 1959–64 Parliament lay in working out the various permutations of a future Labour Cabinet. One such article, a full year earlier, had accurately forecast Dick's future – predicting that, rather than being placed at education, he was 'far more likely to be found some new world to conquer such as Housing and Local Government'.[62] Probably, though, it suited Dick to keep his own mind rigorously on the task in hand, if only to prevent himself from day-dreaming. In the earliest days of Wilson's leadership, he had fallen victim to imagining that he was being kept in reserve for something much bigger – and that something much bigger in his mind was always his original ambition of the Foreign Office.[63]

As the months, however, went by he had been forced to recognise that this was an increasingly unrealistic prospect. It would have required, for one thing, a much closer working partnership with

Wilson than he enjoyed. Against all his own expectations, Dick had a rather more distant personal relationship with the new leader than he had established with Gaitskell, at least in their pre-1959 honeymoon period. They were, of course, very different figures – Gaitskell social and gregarious, Wilson wary and almost, by instinct, a lone wolf. That was brought home to Dick after the first six months of the new regime. On the eve of the summer recess in 1963 he had inquired casually what Wilson would be doing in the first week of August and wondered whether there would be any chance of their seeing each other. 'Oh well,' came the reply, 'let's make an appointment. The diary is getting full.'[64] It was, as Dick immediately detected, a sure sign that the days of political intimacy were over and that their relationship from now on would proceed on a much more formal basis.

15   *Cabinet Minister*

To his surprise and mortification, Dick played a much less active part in the election campaign of 1964 than he had in that of 1959. Unlike Gaitskell, Harold Wilson appointed no *ad hoc* campaign committee and was content to use the chairmen of the various NEC sub-committees – of which Dick had never been one – as his standing advisory body on election strategy. Their responsibilities were hardly onerous; in planning and preparing for the election Wilson took virtually all the threads into his own hands. That was true also of the campaign. The Party leader controlled its running and direction just as completely as his face dominated the hoardings and the hustings. Even within Transport House, there was no room for Dick to play the kind of role as chief of staff and base commander that he had filled five years earlier. As his own seat was in no conceivable danger, he remained in London until the last week of the campaign. But because Wilson did the same (always, until the last five days, taking the Press conference at Transport House in the morning before journeying out to deliver a major speech each evening) there was remarkably little for Dick to do. He was reduced to justifying his existence by fulfilling speaking engagements, largely in London and the Home Counties.

Since Labour won the election – overturning a Tory majority of 100 to snatch victory by four seats – the impression was subsequently created that its campaign had been a story of copybook success. That was not the way it looked to Dick at the time. The election date – 15 October – had, of course been widely predicted,[1] and it was his lack of active involvement in the preparations for it that provoked Dick's initial mood of disquiet. In contrast to 1959, he was not concerned with the final drafting of the manifesto* – although at least he was shown it before most members of the National Executive and the Shadow Cabinet, who only saw it when it was on the point of going to the printers.[2] He was surreptitiously slipped a copy by Wilson, who cannot have been gratified by his reaction. Dick found it 'not at all good, absolutely flat' – and blamed that on the fact that it had been almost exclusively written by those already entrenched in the woodwork.[3] Increasingly, that became the main burden of his criticism – 'Harold's such a natural conservative that he does everything in an Establishment way, through the proper channels, all that sort of thing.'[4] In blurting that out, Dick was betraying a premonition of what was later to be one of his principal reservations about Wilson as Prime Minister.

Once established in No. 10 Wilson at least had high-class staff work, and Dick was not alone in feeling that one of the deficiencies of Labour's 1964 campaign was the calibre of the people the leader chose to rely upon. Even George Brown (never a close friend) felt that it had been a 'a mistake to ease Dick out' and loudly complained against 'a completely bureaucratic regime'.[5] But Wilson may not have had much choice. He had, after all, assumed for himself the starring part that Morgan Phillips, the Party's then general secretary, had played at the Press conferences in 1959 – and that meant that he had to find at least some behind-the-scenes role for Phillips's successor, Len Williams.† In private he was certainly under no illusion as to the capacity of the Party's new general secretary: 'It would have taken more even than Dick's teaching talents to get Len up to the Morgan Phillips level. The way I'm doing it is the only way to run it.'[6]

That, though, was scant consolation for Dick at finding himself excluded from even a back-room role in the campaign. He was not, as he had been in 1959, given oversight of the election broadcasts; these, reflecting Wilson's belief in an ordered chain of command, came under the control of the Party's broadcasting officer. No doubt all the resentments at being held at arm's length over the previous months contributed to his mood, but by the time the campaign proper began this had shifted from political admiration almost to personal resentment:

* Dick had, however, done some preliminary work on it during a fortnight's holiday he spent at Scarborough with his family in August.

† Len Williams (1904–72) had been the Labour Party's national agent before becoming general secretary in succession to Morgan Phillips in 1962. Knighted in 1968 when he was appointed Govenor-General of Mauritius, he died there before his term was completed.

Of course, we've all been downgraded because Harold's so
absolutely determined to be the sole man. I honestly think that I
had more influence on Hugh than I have on him. When I take him
to Coventry tomorrow, those two-and-a-quarter hours in the train
will be the longest time I've spent with him since he became
leader.[7]

As the campaign gathered pace Dick began to cheer up. He liked
elections and 1964 was the sixth he had fought in Coventry. This
time there was a clear challenge facing the City Labour Party – to
regain the Coventry South division (Elaine Burton's old seat, which
had been lost to the Conservatives in 1959). It had always been
Dick's habit to keep out of the way until he was needed – and the
presence of a 27-year-old fellow-Wykehamist as his Conservative
opponent* in Coventry East did not seem to his constituency Party
to demand his presence until the closing days of the campaign. This
led to a predictable charge from the youthful Tory candidate about
Dick taking the constituency for granted, but his local Party officers
were old hands at seeing off that kind of protest.[8]

In his own constituency Dick had a highly satisfactory personal
result – raising his 1959 majority of 7,762 to 13,038 and coming
within a whisker of matching the 60 per cent of the total poll that he
had achieved at his first contest in Coventry in 1945. Even more
gratifying for the Coventry Party, Labour won back the third seat in
the city from the Tories – ensuring that there was a mood of left-
wing jubilation at Coventry City Hall, where all three results were
simultaneously declared on the night of Thursday 15 October.[9]
Things looked rather more encouraging for Labour that night than
they turned out to be the next day. The returns from the county
constituencies tilted the balance back in the Conservatives' favour;
Wilson did not know whether he would be in a position to form a
Government until the mid-afternoon of Friday 16 October. Once,
however, the result from Brecon and Radnor gave him his overall
majority he moved very quickly. He was at the Palace by four
o'clock and by 4.30 pm was installed in Downing Street. That evening he announced the first six apppointments to his Cabinet.

Dick's name was not among them. He may have given way to a
secret hope that it would be, for one of the few Labour casualties at

* Ian Gow, Conservative MP for Eastbourne 1974–90. He became Parliamentary Private Secretary to Margaret Thatcher and a Minister of State at the Department of the Environment and briefly at the Treasury before resigning in 1985 over
the Anglo-Irish Agreement. Murdered by the IRA in July 1990.

the election had been Patrick Gordon Walker, who lost his seat at Smethwick largely on the immigration issue. But in a typical piece of early Wilsonian defiance, the new Prime Minister nominated him to the Foreign Office regardless. Whatever aspirations Dick may have harboured of getting the Foreign Secretaryship vanished in a matter of hours. But he was still in for a surprise when he was eventually summoned to Downing Street on the Saturday morning. He was offered not the Department of Education and Science which he had confidently anticipated but the Ministry of Housing and Local Government. What prompted this last-minute switch remains a mystery, although at least one advance hint of it had appeared in the Press over a year earlier (see p. 260). It seems likely, therefore, that it had been in Wilson's mind for some time – and perhaps for no better reason than an anxiety on his part lest his Cabinet should simply look like a replica of his Shadow Cabinet. This was a fear that Dick shared, though only, understandably, in an abstract form. For once, his and Wilson's versions of his reaction to the offer tally. In Dick's own words he was 'disconcerted',[10] while Wilson himself years afterwards recalled him as having 'somewhat unhappily accepted'.[11]

It is possible, though, that there was a more personal motive for the new Prime Minister's decision. Before Wilson even became Labour's leader Dick had described him as 'probably the only member of the Parliamentary Labour Party who is not afraid of my brutal brain power'.[12] If that was no longer true, he had only himself to thank. In March 1963 he had published a highly praised long Introduction to a new paperback edition of Bagehot's classic work, *The English Constitution*.[13] It was a remarkably forceful essay, revealing strong convictions about the way in which, since Bagehot's own day, Cabinet Government had been allowed to fossilise into merely a 'dignified' part of the constitution. Dick was, in effect, sounding a warning against the dangers of 'Prime Ministerial Government'. If there was one reader to whom its central message was not only unwelcome but alarming it must have been Labour's aspirant Prime Minister. He could hardly be blamed for concluding that the best thing to do with Dick was to confront him with an intellectual challenge that would exhaust his energies, leaving no time for contemplation of such matters as the proper nature of Cabinet Government.

Yet if that was the Prime Minister's strategy – and there is some evidence of it in his later complaint, 'Dick never understood Cabinet Government, his mind was made up long before he was sworn of the Privy Council as a member of the Cabinet'[14] – it was always inevitable that there would be a price attached to it. This was paid in the first instance by the Civil Servants at the Ministry of Housing and Local Government, and in particular by the Department's redoubtable Permanent Secretary, Dame Evelyn Sharp. The first woman to rise to the top rank in Whitehall, she enjoyed a formidable reputation as a particularly tough-minded official long before Dick's arrival. One of Wilson's stranger notions of the time was concerned with the advantages of 'creative tension'* – and he probably saw that as one benefit of putting two such strong characters alongside each other.

However, he miscalculated their personal chemistry. Whatever Dick himself may have felt – and his views varied between respect for her experience and exasperation with her judgment – there is no doubt that Evelyn Sharp came to look back on her last eighteen months in the Ministry of Housing as the most frustrating of her entire Whitehall career. Although, like most Civil Servants, she tended to be discreet in public, she broke with the habits of a lifetime to give one totally uninhibited background interview to a journalist† just before the publication of Dick's first volume of *Cabinet Diaries*. In it she spared Dick nothing:

> He arrived in, as he admits himself, incredibly raw. He knew virtually nothing about our side of things. The first words he ever said to me were, 'I don't know what I've been put here for' – and this was rather how he felt about it. The whole thing was an uninterested feeling at that stage. And he never – it wasn't in his temperament – sat down and said, 'I'm going to find out what the Ministry deals with and the way it's accustomed to dealing with things' in order that he should know what he wanted to change, if he did want to change. But he shot straight in with a complete lack of confidence in civil servants but, more than that, with a conviction that their purpose in life was to obstruct Ministers. Now, all this meant that he was very slow to gather what it was all about anyway.
>
> I would say that administration really irked him. This made it very difficult for him, perhaps particularly in a Ministry like Housing which does really deal with a mass of petty decisions as well as

---

* Wilson first used the phrase in order to justify his creation of a Department of Economic Affairs as a rival to the Treasury.

† Simon Jenkins, editor of *The Times*, most generously made the tape of this interview available to me.

some quite important ones. He found this, I think, a real burden –
though he became fascinated, particularly by travelling round the
country, which he did every Friday. But he never got into the skin
of being a Minister, he never really could bear the burden of
being a Minister – and it is a burden.

He would *not* listen. He distrusted us from the start and made
that clear. He was a bully. Meetings with him were simply a
turmoil. He was a bull in a china shop and he felt like a bull in a
china shop. I think he *wanted* to be a bull in a china shop, he
wanted to hear the china smashing.[15]

That reads very much like the reaction of a well-ordered mandarin
mind, provoked perhaps beyond endurance by Dick's posthumous
breach of confidence in recalling private conversations in his *Diaries
of a Cabinet Minister*. (On another occasion Evelyn Sharp was to
refer to his conduct in this respect as simply 'terribly bad
manners'.)[16] But her charges nevertheless deserve to be examined.
They represent, naturally, a wholly departmental assessment, taking no account of Dick's political role outside his own Ministry. Yet,
in Dick's own eyes, a departmental Minister was what he essentially
was during his first period in the Cabinet: he was quite ready to
accept it as 'a fair criticism' when he was teased for taking the view
that 'the really important business of this Government gyrates
round the Ministry of Housing and Local Government'.[17] He had
not been in office twelve weeks before the realisation struck him,
while at Labour's victory Conference at Brighton, 'how isolated we
have all become in our Ministries'[18] – adding a year and a half later
the perceptive comment that, from the Prime Minister's vantage
point, 'it's much easier to have departmentally minded Ministers
who stay departmental'.[19]

He would hardly, therefore, have quarrelled at having his performance judged – at least in the first of the three Cabinet offices he
held – by what he did in his own Department. The view of his own
Permanent Secretary was, bluntly, that 'he was not a good Minister'[20] – but it is not a verdict that, for obvious reasons, need automatically be accepted. It was certainly at variance with most
journalistic judgments reached at the time. Before he had been in
office a year, the *Spectator* had no hesitation in citing him as 'one of
the strongest and most decisive Ministers in the Government' –
adding perhaps significantly: 'In a Department that has traditionally
been subject both to pressure groups from without and to powerful civil servants from within, he has emerged as the undisputed

master.'[21] The *Observer* specifically referred to his initial apprehensions of being 'buried in a bureaucratic cocoon' having come to nothing and even wrote of 'the crushing task of decision-making at Housing' being for him 'the spice of life'.[22] What outsiders instinctively recognised – even if those on the inside had more difficulty in coming to terms with it – was that Dick had established his claim to be a dominant Minister who really ran his own Department.

From the more jealous bureaucratic viewpoint, therein lay his offence. It is a naive mistake to believe that Civil Servants welcome weak Ministers: they do nothing of the sort – they want, after all, a politician with sufficient stature and weight to win the Department's battles, if necessary at Cabinet level. But, equally, they have always felt entitled to have certain courtesies observed – of which probably the most cherished is that they and the political head of the Ministry are engaged in a joint endeavour. It was Dick's cavalier disregard of this *esprit de corps* that led him into a good deal of unnecessary difficulty. From the moment – during his first month in office – that he chose to consult Arnold Goodman, rather than take advice from his Department, over the drafting of his earliest piece of legislation (an anti-Eviction Bill designed to protect sitting tenants), he had lost the good will of his own top officials. Their feeling appears to have been that, far from regarding them as natural allies, the new Minister was determined to see them as his chosen enemies.

In detecting that kind of hostility on Dick's part, the permanent officials at the Ministry of Housing and Local Government may have exaggerated a little – but not much. Indeed, Dick himself was quite explicit over his reservations about *them*. In a conversation with Alastair Hetherington towards the end of 1964, he was even more forthright than he was later to be in his *Diaries of a Cabinet Minister*:

> Dick said he'd been struck by how 'terribly second rate' most of the civil servants were. Among the top few with whom he was dealing he had expected to find a number who were an intellectual match for him. There wasn't one, with the possible exception of 'the Dame'. Most of them had no originality, conformed to a set pattern, were negatively concerned with what you couldn't do, and – worst – didn't know the way people lived in the outside world. They were isolated and knew nothing of what happened outside Whitehall.
>
> He said he didn't get on well with Dame Evelyn. Both of them liked to throw out outrageous ideas, and both needed a brake to act upon them. Therefore they weren't a good pair to work

together. He couldn't trust Dame Evelyn's ideas, and she didn't much like him. She preferred a young man like Keith Joseph,* whom she could steer and direct.

He said rather bitterly that among the civil servants there was nobody you could trust. Nor could he bring his own people in, as was possible under the American system. The civil servants didn't bring things forward until they were ready to do so. They didn't tell you what was happening. They delayed your letters if they didn't approve of them. (One had actually not been posted for ten whole days after he'd written and signed it because they didn't like it.) They made minor amendments to your letters, but didn't point these out, when bringing your letters forward for signing. They exchanged memoranda behind your back. He couldn't prohibit people in his Ministry from sending out policy documents that he hadn't seen. It would be physically impossible. But the civil servants treated you as a Minister who was only there for two years or so, while they were there for ever. They got on with what they wanted to do.[23]

It was a revealing indictment, and does much to explain why Dick's great weakness as a Minister lay in his failure to operate the Whitehall machine at all effectively.[24] He certainly conceded the efficiency of that machine, at least in terms of its internal communication – protesting to an interviewer that 'although his office was only 200 yards from the Cabinet Room, by the time he got back from a Cabinet meeting, the Dame and others at the top always knew what he'd said, how he'd done and what had been decided'.[25] To balance this kind of 'mandarin power', he deliberately set about building some self-protective ramparts around his own Private Office. There were teething troubles at first with the two Private Secretaries he inherited from his Conservative predecessor – and graver difficulties later on when the senior of them was promoted and was replaced by a nominee of the Dame's. This unfortunate figure failed to survive for more than a fortnight,[26] but Dick's own selection of his successor, John Delafons, proved a great success. Delafons not only was able to stand up to his Minister but actually contrived to

* Sir Keith Joseph, Conservative MP for Leeds North-East 1956–87, and later a life peer, had been Dick's immediate predecessor at the Ministry of Housing and Local Government. He was subsequently to succeed him in 1970 at the Department of Health and Social Security. By then at least Dick had come to develop a considerable regard for Sir Keith, who went on to be Secretary of State for Industry and for Education.

command his admiration while doing so;* he also found considerable favour with Dick by displaying a remarkable facility for writing speeches in his own idiosyncratic style. Under him, the Private Office became, in his political chief's revealing phrase, 'the political machine I needed for controlling the Department'.[27]

The Private Office in a large Ministry is a pretty substantial institution. On Dick's own estimate, by the time he left the Department of Housing and Local Government, 'there were some sixty people there to help the Minister and his four political colleagues'.[28] It was in this light that he always saw its function – and he certainly ended up by making it work on his own behalf. He won one early battle by getting his own private secretary, Jennie Hall, installed in it, and she soon won golden opinions (even prompting the Dame to pay her a lavish tribute when she eventually left to have a baby).[29] The efforts to infiltrate his two successive Parliamentary Private Secretaries – Tam Dalyell and Geoffrey Rhodes† – into its working did not go so smoothly, partly because of the characteristic reluctance of the Civil Service to allow confidential material to fall into unauthorised hands. But Dick enjoyed extremely good relations with the Department's long-standing chief information officer, Peter Brown, who had started off by serving under Harold Macmillan when he was Minister of Housing in the Churchill Government of 1951: he became, in effect, an integral part of the Private Office operation, with a particular skill in guiding Dick through his various Press conferences whether held in London or out in the regions.

There is always a sense in which any Minister has to be his own public relations officer – and in this role, at least when he had a large Ministry behind him, Dick possessed all the qualifications to be successful. He knew about the art of propaganda, he understood journalists and he relished the task of exposition. Mishaps which occurred tended to have their origins in accidents far away from the complex world of housing policy. There was the occasion, for example, when – returning from a debate at London University

---

* This feeling was not apparently reciprocated. After his retirement in 1989, Delafons was quoted in a newspaper interview as saying: 'I didn't like the man actually.' He did, however, pay tribute to Dick as 'one of the biggest personalities I've ever encountered'.

† Tam Dalyell, Labour MP for West Lothian 1962–83 and for Linlithgow from 1983, served as Dick's PPS 1964–5 and 1966–70. Geoffrey Rhodes (1928–74), Labour MP for Newcastle East 1964–74, filled in none too happily for the intervening eighteen months. Dalyell was also the tenant of the upstairs flat at Vincent Square 1965–74. He subsequently drew on his experiences to write a book, *Dick Crossman: a Portrait* (Weidenfeld & Nicolson, 1989).

against Iain Macleod – he chose to treat himself to a solo supper at Prunier, a very grand seafood restaurant in St James's. Not wishing to be seen sitting in solitary splendour studying Cabinet papers, he tucked them beneath his seat and instead read *Hansard*. The result was all too predictable. On departing from the restaurant to go home, Dick forgot about the sheaf of Cabinet papers and left them under his seat, where they were found by a fellow diner who, though a retired Army officer, made off with them. Before handing them over to the police, he showed them to the *Daily Express*. The result two days later was a front-page headline in the paper (complete with the Prunier restaurant symbol) declaring 'Cabinet Papers Left by Crossman Handed to the Police'.[30] 'Nothing', Dick candidly confessed in his diary, 'could have been more unpleasant.'[31] However, the storm blew itself out quickly, largely because Wilson showed considerable nerve by insisting on making an official statement to the House of Commons the following week in which he successfully deflected criticism away from Dick and on to the conduct of the man responsible for the leak (sarcastically referred to by the Prime Minister as 'an officer and a gentleman').[32]

A second Press episode, which followed hard on its heels, was a good deal more wounding. On the estate at Prescote were a number of cottages – mainly inhabited by those who worked on the farm. One of them, however, was lived in by a man and his mother who had been there ever since Anne's father had bought the cottage to add to the farm estate in the 1930s. They paid a peppercorn rent and had resolutely refused all offers to have their home modernised in return for an increase in rent. The cottage was part of a pair – and the other half, until recently lived in by the Prescote cowman, had been thoroughly renovated. At a time when the rights of tenants were very much part of the new Government's legislative agenda, the contrast between the condition of the two properties – both owned by the Minister of Housing – proved an irresistible target for the right-wing newspapers. A particularly brutal story, complete with photographs, appeared in the *News of the World*, which was followed up by the *Daily Telegraph*.[33] It was a far more upsetting experience for Dick than his contretemps with the Cabinet papers, if only because it impinged on what he had always until then regarded as the haven of his home life at Prescote. To make matters worse, Anne inevitably bore the brunt of all the gossip – and village recriminations – it left in its wake.[34]

The importance to Dick of the sense of contentment and independence that Prescote gave him is hard to exaggerate. His

third marriage was his only completely successful one and it provided him with emotional as well as financial security. He may have
seen his children only at weekends, but the unexpected prize of a
happy family life was something that had come to him relatively late
and so he valued it all the more highly. It meant, in his own eyes at
least, that he had ceased to be simply a career politician – and he
freely admitted to the feeling of reassurance he got from knowing
that 'the moment anyone says that my life at the Ministry has got to
end there is an alternative life ready'.[35] He saw, of course, the
professional part of that life as lying in writing, and was marginally
disappointed when a book he published within six months of becoming a Cabinet Minister failed to generate much excitement. Entitled
Planning for Freedom,* it was – like its predecessor, *The Charm of
Politics* – merely a collection of essays that had already appeared in
print; but on this occasion, perhaps because the essays were concerned with ideas rather than with people, it received far less sympathetic treatment. In Dick's own words, it turned out to be 'a
pleasant, harmless flop' – with the reviewers tending to suggest that
'I am not a serious thinker but a political journalist who takes
himself a bit too seriously.'[36] Was Dick hurt by the general unenthusiastic reception? There is one piece of evidence that suggests he
may have been. When told by his American publisher that his book
would be coming out in the United States in November 1965, he
rested content with making the single comment in his diary: 'I
couldn't care less.'[37]

But by then, of course, Dick was firmly into his stride as a Cabinet
Minister. He had not found the adaptation to his new role at all
daunting – indeed, his Civil Servants might have been even more
critical than they were had they known that his immediate reaction
on taking charge of the Department was that 'it's far easier work
than the arduous strain of writing for popular papers'.[38] A few
months later, though, he did betray some awareness of the demands
of his job – telling a visitor that 'he knew very little of what was
going on outside his own Department: he had never been blinder or
more ignorant about the country or the world in general'.[39] In the
Whitehall context, Dick certainly counted as a Minister who insisted
on absorbing himself in the work of every aspect of his Department;
and, for that reason alone, it is probably worth attempting an assessment of the record of the Ministry during his 22-month reign there.

---

* *Planning for Freedom*, a volume of collected pieces written between 1938 and
1964, was published by Hamish Hamilton in March 1965.

In legislative terms, it was highly active. The first measure Dick brought before the Commons was an anti-Eviction Bill, over whose drafting he had caused such offence by consulting Arnold Goodman in his first days at the Department. Once that administrative hiccough was out of the way, the Bill's parliamentary passage was remarkably swift: it went through both Houses of Parliament by the first week of December and was on the Statute Book by Christmas. Since it was designed as no more than a holding operation until a major Rent Bill could be introduced, speed was the essence of the exercise, and the ease with which Dick negotiated it through the Commons did his reputation, and the morale of the Department, nothing but good. The far more formidable challenge of the Rent Bill itself followed in the spring of 1965 and, although it took until October to become law, it ended up as another feather in Dick's cap. (Its contribution to the solution of the national housing problem was more questionable, since its general effect was to dry up the supply of rented properties.) No sooner, however, had Dick put these two legislative achievements behind him than he embarked upon a pair of fresh measures – a Rates Rebate Bill, for which he worked up a good deal of enthusiasm, and a Leasehold Enfranchisement Bill (a product of the 1964 Labour manifesto) on which he was much less keen. The latter eventually went through after the 1966 election and, as well as remedying some outstanding injustices in South Wales, mightily gratified middle-class professional leaseholders in London who found themselves able to translate their leasehold properties into freeholds at a very modest cost. (In that sense, since the original promise was repeated in the 1966 manifesto, it probably did no harm to Labour's election prospects.) A Housing Subsidies Bill also came on stream after the 1966 election, although by the time it was presented to the Commons Dick had already left the Department.

It was an impressive showing for a new Minister who had virtually vaulted from the back-benches straight into the Cabinet and who had never previously piloted a Bill through the Commons. Here, though, Dick was right to recognise that he owed a debt to the Department and even to the Dame; despite the squalls over his taking of outside advice (repeated in the case of the Leasehold Enfranchisement Bill, on which he recruited two Labour MPs to prepare a departmental brief on which legislation could be based)[40] they were as anxious as he was to ensure that their Ministry got its fair share of the new Government's legislative programme.[41] Pride in the Department dictated no less – and there were obvious advantages, when it came to asserting priorities within Whitehall, in having a Permanent Secretary who had been in office for more than ten years and who had served no fewer than five former Housing Ministers.

The problems arose in the area where the Ministry basically lacked any expertise. When Dick arrived at the Department, he was appalled to discover that 'there was no housing programme, there was no information and no plan, there were just a lot of meaningless figures'.[42] Remarkably, although its very title suggested that it should be concerned with the building of houses, the Ministry of Housing had seldom viewed that as its primary concern: it was a matter left largely to local authorities. The one exception was while Harold Macmillan was Minister, when a pledge given in Opposition at the Conservative Conference of 1950 that 300,000 houses would be built a year dictated the Department's strategy. Dick came to office with no such mandate – and the best he was initially able to extract from the Prime Minister was a private commitment to the building of 150,000 houses in the public sector (and 250,000 by private building) for the year 1965.[43] This, when revealed to the Cabinet, caused ceaseless anxiety to the Chancellor, James Callaghan, and Dick was soon reduced to a humiliating process of haggling with the Treasury: in the end the target was not reached, and Dick was left to reflect bitterly on the fact that the Chancellor, rather than the Minister of Housing, controlled house building.

However, he never sought to disguise that he had made his own mistakes. The one he is most often reproached with – the promotion of systems building, leading to the replacement of sound council houses with high-rise blocks – is a little unfair. This had been the Ministry's policy, supported by subsidy, long before he arrived and, if at first he did little to challenge it (even recruiting an outsider from Costain's to co-ordinate such projects), his own instincts in favour of conservation as against wholesale redevelopment gradually came out on top. It was an area where his views came to clash with those of the Department, and it was by no means the only one. He had, he confessed, come far too late to the realisation that what counted was getting the co-operation of the great conurbations and allowing them far more than their proportional share of the national housing-start allocation.[44] The Department firmly opposed such an approach but Dick finally got it through: the change featured in the same White Paper which rashly forecast the building of a total of 500,000 houses a year, in the public and private sectors, by 1970.[45] This

26 Anne and Dick's wedding, 3 June 1954. George Wigg (*left*) was best man. George Hodgkinson (*right*) was Dick's first agent in Coventry

27–8 Patrick and Virginia with their parents (*left*) and with Nanny (*right*)

29 The politician as populist. Dick in a miners' canteen

30 The 1964 Labour Cabinet in the garden at No. 10, with Cabinet Secretary, Sir Burke Trend standing far right

latter commitment was even more recklessly characterised by Wilson during the 1966 campaign as 'not a lightly given pledge – it is a promise'.[46]

Dick himself rightly regarded the 31 March 1966 general election as the high-water mark of the 1964–70 Labour Government. He did not have the slightest doubt that Labour would win – indeed, by predicting 'a gain of 70 or 80 seats'[47] he rather overestimated Labour's actual performance of gaining 48 seats. But he never concealed, at least in the privacy of his own diary, his sense that it was a triumph dictated more by the luck of timing than anything else.[48] His own majority at Coventry East went up gratifyingly to 18,696 – won against the future Conservative Chief Whip and Cabinet Minister, John Wakeham – and he finally attained the 60 per cent of the total poll that had eluded him since 1945. By now he had, of course, become part of the political fabric of the city; three months before the election his local party had made him a presentation commemorating his twenty years as their MP. The occasion prompted Dick to ruminate on what his association with the constituency had meant. He did so in typically forthright fashion:

The luck of my being chosen [as prospective candidate] in 1937 has kept me in Parliament with a huge cast-iron majority and with a particular kind of party behind me which has deeply influenced my thinking, keeping me much more on the Left than I would by nature have been. And this has meant that I have not had any of the pressures that are exerted on MPs in marginal constituencies: I have never in my political life had to bother about appeasing industrialists, or right-wing groups, churches or chapels.

Coventry East would simply not have allowed me to be a right-winger, to be an anti-Bevanite, for example. On the other hand, they have given me their loyalty and their permission to be a very egocentric politician with ideas of my own; and though they have often disagreed with me they have given me pretty solid support.[49]

As Dick himself foresaw, that support was soon to come under strain. His position in the Labour Government complicated his relationship with his constituency, not least because he was beginning to think more as a Minister than as a left-wing politican. That was shown in his reaction to the 1966 election. Although this time he did have an informal backroom role – breakfasting every morning with the Prime Minister at No. 10 and then going over to Transport House to communicate Wilson's thoughts to James Callaghan, who took the Press conferences – his mind remained predominantly on his Department. He continued to spend most of the day there until the last week when he made his usual pilgrimage to Coventry; only a matter of days before going there, he exposed his priorities by grumbling that the campaign had meant 'that the work of the Department is being slowed down – the officials don't want any issues brought up to the Minister'.[50] There could, however, have been another reason. In March 1966, Dame Evelyn Sharp, already two years beyond the normal Civil Service retirement age of sixty, finally left the Ministry in which she had spent the past fifteen years; after much bargaining with the Prime Minister, the Department acquired a new Permanent Secretary, Sir Matthew Stevenson, from the Ministry of Power. Dick's relationship with him during his remaining five months at the Ministry was to be a good deal less stormy than that with the Dame – though, given his own mercurial temperament, perhaps also a trifle enervating. ('He looks', Dick bleakly recorded on first meeting him, 'like an insurance representative from the Prudential.')[51]

Once the election was over, yielding Labour a comfortable overall majority, there was the usual anticipation of a widespread Cabinet reshuffle, and Dick appears briefly to have thought that he might be moved to take George Brown's place at the Department of Economic Affairs. Wilson had hinted as much to him during one of their breakfast meetings during the campaign. Dick found the prospect 'disconcerting – it would mean giving up all the projects I have been working on for the past eighteen months'[52] – and was probably relieved when it did not take place (George Brown had prudently resisted the offer of being Deputy Prime Minister without a Department). But Dick had enough self-knowledge to realise that there was a case for a move, if not necessarily to the DEA. The election victory, indeed, provoked a mood of contrition on his part in which he set down what he thought was not only the Department's but the Whitehall grapevine's assessment of his performance: 'Their view is that I don't handle civil servants well; I am far too rough with them, scare them stiff, make hasty judgments and very often scrawl rude things on paper which upsets them, especially when I haven't read the file carefully enough before scrawling.'[53] It was a striking indication of the maturity that eighteen months' experience as a Minister had brought to his outlook; his final months at the Ministry were in marked contrast to the turbulent days that had followed his arrival –

days that years later still stuck in Baroness Sharp's* memory.

This was partly because, as Dick himself somewhat ruefully recognised, the Department itself had now moved into a quieter phase – 'We've done all the new exciting things, now everything depends on administrative drive and follow-through.'[54] But it was also the result of Dick feeling on top of his job and, therefore, starting to play a more influential role in the life of the Government as a whole. Back in the autumn of 1965 he had been given the job of chairing the Liaison Committee, which was supposed to keep Transport House and particularly its publicity department in touch with the Government and No. 10. It had not proved an easy task, partly because George Wigg, who had held the post previously, keenly resented being displaced. Another factor may well have been the suspicion with which Dick tended to be regarded by the senior staff of the Party organisation. Paradoxically, that mattered less at a time when even the most recalcitrant Party officer had to acknowledge that the Government was engaged in a day-to-day fight for survival. Now, however, that Labour enjoyed a majority of ninety-seven in the Commons there was bound to be a much greater degree of vigilance – and Dick was among the first to recognise the importance of seeing to it that the Party, both in its headquarters organisation and its membership, did not become increasingly alienated from the Government.

For all his premonitions about the hollow nature of the triumph the Government had won at the polls, Dick can hardly have foreseen how quickly things would begin to go wrong. Trouble started with the seamen's strike, which began two months after the election. The strike, paralysing the docks, lasted seven weeks and, although it ended with a victory for the Government, it had a devastating effect on the balance-of-payments position. Dick was repelled by the tactics Wilson employed in order to defeat the seamen's pay claim – the Prime Minister had first spoken in the Commons of 'a tightly knit group of politically motivated men'[55] and then eight days later gave the House the details of the names and movements of the individual members of the Communist Party he had in mind[56] – but he reluctantly conceded the success of the coup Wilson had pulled off. It represented, he wrote in his diary,

---

* Exceptionally for the permanent head of a Home Department, outside the Treasury and the Cabinet Office, Dame Evelyn Sharp (1903–85) was created a life peeress on her retirement. Dick, who retained occasional social contacts with her after she left the Civil Service, would certainly have had to be consulted over this nomination.

'the apex of his luck'[57] – and this despite the fact that earlier on Dick had made a far gloomier forecast about the strike: 'We are drifting on to the rocks and another July crisis is almost certain.'[58] In fact, both statements proved to be true. Wilson's laurels won against the Communist Party and the Seamen's Union withered very soon. By the time the Prime Minister left for a visit to Moscow in mid-July not only was the pound once more under severe pressure; the Cabinet itself was seething with division.

The legend of 'the July plot' against Wilson was to become a key part of Labour's mythology – but, as its supposed target made clear some years later: 'There was no plot, no conspiracy, no cabal, no organisation.'[59] Dick himself usually tended to be a little more circumspect, on one occasion going so far as to say: 'Insofar as there was one, it was Roy Jenkins, Tony Crosland and Tony Wedgwood Benn* and me who were implicated in it, along with George Brown.'[60] The significance of these names is that they belonged to the members of the Cabinet who were also the most prominent advocates of devaluation, or at least of the pound finding its own level at a floating rate. And if there was a rebellion (though hardly 'a plot') against Wilson in July 1966, it centred on this issue. It was one on which Dick could claim a consistent record. He had recognised the case for devaluation almost from the moment Labour came to office;[61] and although he may have exaggerated a little in describing himself in July 1966 as 'a counter force inside the Cabinet round which people were grouped'[62] he probably was, at least on political grounds, Wilson's most formidable opponent. Mainly, no doubt, this was because he had always before been regarded as a natural ally of the Prime Minister; but it must also have owed something to the temerity displayed by a senior and relatively successful departmental Minister in challenging the central economic strategy of the Government.

Dick's own first, instinctive reaction was that by challenging and losing the battle – the package of deflationary cuts duly went through the Cabinet without any concessions being made over the defence of sterling – he had risked bringing his own ministerial career to a close. He certainly took the threat sufficiently seriously to discuss the prospect of an enforced early retirement from the Cabinet with Anne – who, he wryly reported, 'wants that with her

* Tony Benn, as he later took to calling himself, had just entered the Cabinet as Minister of Technology. He came gradually to exasperate Dick, who once described him as 'an intellectually negligible whizz-kid'. Benn went on to be Secretary of State for Industry and then for Energy in the 1974–9 Labour Government.

whole heart'.[63] But, although Dick was probably right to feel that he had alienated himself from the Prime Minister without commending himself even to George Brown (whose dramatically threatened resignation he felt ought to have been accepted), he also showed a surprising innocence of Wilson's character. It was always the Prime Minister's inclination, as long as that remained feasible, to buy off his opponents rather than to cut them down. Sure enough, within a fortnight, both Brown and Dick found themselves in new and super-ficially more impressive roles within the Cabinet.

There had been a hint of what was in store for Dick when, a week before Parliament broke up for the summer recess, he had been warned by the Chief Whip, John Silkin,* not to rush off to join Anne and the children, who were already on holiday in Cornwall, without first clearing his departure with him. Dick correctly surmised that this must mean a reshuffle was being planned – but he remained in the dark until, a week later, Silkin let the cat out of the bag by saying that, though he was sworn to secrecy, what was being proposed 'gives me enormous pleasure because it means you and I will be working together'.[64] It was hardly a very cryptic remark: only one other Minister – apart from the Prime Minister – works intimately with the Government Chief Whip, and he is always the Leader of the House of Commons. When Dick was summoned the next day to see Wilson at No. 10, he was, therefore, forewarned, if not necessarily forearmed: since being invited to become Lord President of the Council and Leader of the House of Commons involved (as he himself put it) being 'catapulted into the strato-sphere',[65] it was an offer he could hardly refuse. It was none the less one that almost instantly he regretted having accepted.

What Dick had done, as he very soon came to realise, was to exchange power for status. Whatever gratification he may have felt about the way his promotion was treated in the Press† – where it was

---

* John Silkin (1923–87) was Labour MP for Deptford 1963–87. A close ally and associate of Dick's during his period as Leader of the House, he later became Minister of Public Building and Works 1969–70 and Minister of Agriculture 1974–79.

† There were, however, two sour notes. On 11 August both the *Daily Express* and the *Daily Sketch* explained Dick's move in terms of his failure to get sufficient houses built. So far as the motives operating in the Prime Minister's mind went, this was the reverse of the truth. His appointment of the former Minister of Overseas Development, Anthony Greenwood (1911–82) as the new Minister of Housing suggested that he wanted as Dick's successor someone who would not kick up too much fuss if the Department's budget continued to be cut. Dick himself was 'shocked' by the appointment.

regarded as almost as significant as George Brown's move to the Foreign Office – was quickly dissipated. Its real meaning, at least to Whitehall professionals, was brought home to him in the most humiliating manner possible. One of his last acts at the Ministry of Housing and Local Government had been to persuade the Ministry's chief information officer, Peter Brown, with whom he had got on remarkably well, to join him in his new unofficial role, supposedly co-ordinating all Government information. Brown's appointment was duly announced in the newspapers ('Crossman gets own PRO'),[66] only to be embarrassingly cancelled within a fortnight ('No Press Officer for Mr Crossman').[67] What had happened was that, after proposing this new sphere of responsibility for Dick, the Prime Minister had failed to deliver on his promise. Opposition from within No. 10, where Wilson already had his own two Civil Service press officers as well as a political one in the person of the young Gerald Kaufman,* had put an end to any idea of Dick acting as the effective supremo of the Government's public relations. As a veteran of Whitehall's internal wars, Peter Brown spotted the impossibility of the job even before Dick, and lost no time in pleading to be allowed to go back to his old post at the Ministry of Housing. ('He had seen the red light and realised there was no future for him in my office because Downing Street was determined to down me.')[68]

It was hardly an auspicious start, and it had a depressing effect on Dick's spirits. By mid-September he was already confiding to the editor of the *Guardian* that he was 'discontented with his move and that being Lord President and Leader of the House wasn't a real job'.[69] It was certainly not a job for which he was ideally cut out. The flummery of the Lord President's office – with its regular contact with the monarch through meetings of the Privy Council – had little or no appeal for him; and, although Dick was to come to have a sneaking respect for the Queen herself, the repeated ritual trips – frequently not even to Buckingham Palace but to Balmoral and Sandringham – were to prove a perpetual irritant.

Nor perhaps was he much better suited to his role in the House of Commons. The most successful Leaders of the House tend to be those with a natural talent for disarming criticism and turning away wrath. Men like Herbert Morrison and R. A. Butler were adept at lowering the temperature in the Commons rather than raising it.

* Gerald Kaufman, Labour MP for Manchester Ardwick 1970–83 and for Manchester Gorton since 1983, had worked as Dick's researcher during his days as a *Daily Mirror* columnist. There was always a certain acerbity in their relationship.

With all his zest and gusto, it was not an emollient facility that Dick was ever likely to develop – indeed, his own rumbustious approach made him a highly improbable pourer of oil on to troubled waters. Why, then, did Wilson appoint him and why, even more, did Dick agree to take the job on?

The answer is that both men recognised one of the stronger political currents running at the time – the feeling, particularly prevalent among the new MPs on Labour's back-benches, in favour of parliamentary reform. But whereas Dick believed passionately in the cause, the Prime Minister – as conservative in his attitude to the Commons as in much else – was never really prepared to pay it much more than lip service. A lot of Dick's difficulties over the next twenty months were to flow from this difference in commitment between them. For Wilson, the important thing was to make sure that the new boys among the Government's supporters – and there were sixty-six of them in the new Parliament – were kept happy; for Dick, what mattered was making sufficient changes in the way the Commons was organised to ensure that they had a worthwhile and fulfilling role to play. This contrast in their respective attitudes was to create much trouble for Dick.

The first signs came over the question of televising – if only on a closed-circuit experimental basis at first – the proceedings of the House of Commons. The product of a recommendation from the House's own Select Committee on Broadcasting, the idea greatly excited Dick; he even put a paper before the Cabinet on 10 November 1968 enthusiastically backing the proposal. He found, however, that the Prime Minister was implacably opposed to the idea and around the Cabinet table he could muster the support of only five colleagues. This was, as he put it, 'a terrible blow'[70] – and it inevitably meant that when he spoke in the Commons a fortnight later (both opening and widening up the debate)[71] he had to be careful to put forward only a personal viewpoint without in any way committing the Government. It may be that, as a result, he leaned over too far in order to given an entirely fair presentation of both sides of the case.* But the defeat of the television proposal – it went down on a free vote by 131 votes to 130 (a much narrower margin than in most subsequent debates over the next twenty years)† – undoubtedly left

---

* This was Dick's own view in later life. In recalling the occasion, he would ruefully explain: 'By trying to be dispassionate, I blew the whole thing.'

† Television cameras were eventually installed in the House of Commons in November 1989, nearly five years after they had been admitted by the House of Lords.

Dick not only with a sense of frustration but of bitterness, too. Apart from the Chief Whip, no one supported him on the Treasury Bench and in the division lobby he found himself the sole Cabinet Minister voting for the proposal. That night he wrote in his diary of 'feeling absolutely sick of life and furiously angry with my colleagues for letting me down'.[72]

Of course, Dick can hardly have thought that the televising of debates would by itself blow all the cobwebs from the Commons away – though, under the initial disappointment of having his own support for the scheme turned down by the Cabinet, he did resentfully record the judgment: 'I was left with all my programme for parliamentary reform in ruins.'[73] Where, however, he may well have been right was in sensing that the presence of the cameras in the Chamber would have created a new climate in which everything else he wanted to do would become much easier. (Like Nye Bevan before him,* Dick had always felt that one of the hidden dangers to democracy in Britain lay in the gulf which existed between the people and their elected representatives.) As it was, however, he had no alternative but to press ahead with his programme of reform without the transformation in atmosphere that he had hoped television would bring about. Although he enjoyed a considerable personal success with his December speech arguing the case of modernising the House's procedure,[74] getting Parliament to accept the two main changes he had in mind proved much more difficult. The first, the introduction of morning sittings twice a week, was thoroughly unpopular with MPs and within a year Dick had to recognise that the experiment had failed and announce that it would not be continued in the new parliamentary session.[75] Over the second, the establishment of Specialist Committees vaguely on the American congressional pattern, the obstacles lay not so much with ordinary Members of Parliament as with Ministers: none of his Cabinet colleagues, Dick soon discovered, saw much reason why the work of their Departments should be scrutinised by a bipartisan Select Committee of backbench MPs. The result was that only two such bodies were established during Dick's time in office – one a departmental committee on agriculture and the other what was cautiously known as 'a subject committee' on science and technology. Although their number was to grow later, Dick's claim to being the godfather of the Commons Specialist Committee system is

* Aneurin Bevan's last major speech in the House of Commons, delivered on 3 November 1960, included a plea – not cleared with the Labour Party leader, Hugh Gaitskell – for the televising of the proceedings of Parliament.

a little tenuous. The most he had done was to assert the principle: he had been effectively blocked from putting it into effect.

That was also to be his experience with a third, and more directly constitutional, reform on which he also embarked while Leader of the House. Arguably, if Dick had not felt under-employed, the 1966–70 Labour Government would never have got involved in the legislative fiasco of its attempt to reform the House of Lords. The long-forgotten Parliament (No.2) Bill – with its provision for separate categories of 'speaking' and 'voting' members in the Upper House – may have been launched on its ill-fated passage through the Commons well after Dick had gone back to being a departmental Minister; but no one doubted that it was substantially his brainchild, the product of his determination to leave his mark not merely as a parliamentary but as a constitutional reformer. It certainly took up a disproportionate amount of his time during his latter months as Leader of the House, and at first the prospects of getting an agreed, bipartisan approach to Lords reform did not look wholly unfavourable. Dick certainly worked very hard at it – establishing particularly close links with the Conservative Leader in the Lords, Lord Carrington, and his deputy, Lord Jellicoe, both of whom favoured rationalising the composition of the House, although they were always less enthusiastic about measures limiting its powers. The difficulty, however, was that all such contacts had to be confidential and there could be no real test of the acceptability of what had ceased, in effect, to be cross-Party proposals* until they were published in a White Paper[76] and presented to Parliament. But by the autumn of 1968, Dick himself – though he continued to take a fatherly interest in the scheme – had moved to other responsibilities. It remains an arguable point whether, if he had been left to deploy all his debating skill on trying to navigate the resulting Bill through the Commons, it would have hit the rocks as disastrously as it did.[77]

What Dick discovered was that the way of the parliamentary reformer, like that of any transgressor against tradition, will always be hard. He had acknowledged from the beginning that 'no one can reform the House of Commons if the House of Commons doesn't want to reform itself'[78] – and that, he reluctantly appears to have accepted, was the case. He did his best to console himself by reflecting

---

* The rejection by the House of Lords in June 1968 of an Order imposing sanctions against Rhodesia, in line with a United Nations resolution, led to the Government breaking off its talks with the Opposition. Although the Lords later rescinded its action, confidence between the two sides was never fully restored.

that, so far as Wilson was concerned, this particular side of his job had never been what mattered: 'Why he wants me close to him is for the battle for power inside the Cabinet and the reorganisation of the Parliamentary Party.'[79] 'Reorganisation of the Parliamentary Party' was probably too strong a term: what Dick had been brought in to do was to temper the rather regimental discipline that had characterised the role of his predecessor, Herbert Bowden. The PLP's standing orders were not formally suspended during his twenty-month reign but they were interpreted more liberally. This soon set Dick and the Chief Whip, John Silkin, on a collision course with the chairman of the PLP, Emanuel Shinwell, who in turn was backed by a similar martinet, the Paymaster-General, George Wigg. Their conflict ran on for months and was finally resolved when Shinwell resigned in April 1967, followed by the departure of George Wigg from the Government some six months later. By then, however, Wilson had made his own 'dog licence' speech* to the parliamentary Party and Dick had his work cut out to persuade those on the Government back-benches that anything had changed from the bad old days of the Attlee Government.

If eventually he succeeded in doing so, the achievement was, to some degree, the result of his own remarkably uninhibited personality. Provided they were prepared to take him on, he happily engaged in dialectical combat with the most junior members of the Parliamentary Labour Party – arguing with them for hours on end in the Commons tea-room[80] and never being tempted to pull rank or seniority. In his sixtieth year, he had become something of a legend in and around Westminster – which presumably explains why *Panorama*, the BBC's flagship current affairs programme, decided in the summer of 1967 to devote half of one of its regular Monday editions to a profile of him. The work of the programme's then presenter, Robin Day, it was a serious piece of television journalism over which time and trouble had clearly been taken. For the benefit of the BBC cameras, Dick had even been inveigled into a discussion session with the students at the newly founded Warwick University – a discussion which produced the best quote of the whole programme (and a text perhaps for Dick's entire career): 'My main central belief is that the Establishment when tested will be found

---

* On 2 March 1967 the Prime Minister, in a speech to the Parliamentary Labour Party, had included the warning that, although every dog is entitled to one bite, if he makes a habit of it, his owner may have doubts about renewing his licence. This infelicitous reference was not cleared in advance with Dick and caused him great fury.

wanting – that on any issue where the Establishment says "I know", I instinctively wonder if they do, and nearly always I'm right.'[81]

Dick was somewhat apprehensive about the effect this star treatment – the programme's cast list included Michael Foot, Quintin Hogg, Emanuel Shinwell, Kingsley Martin and A. J. Ayer – would have on his colleagues at Westminster. But he need not have worried. The Commons tends to take a pride in its own – and Dick was soon happily commenting: 'Many of my colleagues seemed somehow gratified that I had been described as one of the most brilliant and incalculable politicians alive and that so much time had been devoted to me on television. Yes, it had gone over pretty well.'[82]

Whatever his disappointments as a parliamentary reformer, Dick's first year as Leader of the House established him as a politician of considerable stature. He had become, in effect, public orator to the Labour Party – and, although not all his excursions on to weekend platforms pleased the Prime Minister,[83] they almost always commanded Press attention. So it was curious that at his moment of greatest national renown Dick took the one step that effectively ruled him out from ever going much higher in Labour politics. After fifteen years of being regularly elected to it, he announced in August that he was not accepting nomination for that year's National Executive elections.[84] It was not a wholly voluntary choice; an indication of the restiveness the Government's record was provoking among the rank and file came from his own constituency Party executive, which the month before had supported a resolution calling on him to stand down on the grounds that the NEC already contained far too many Ministers.[85] This unforeseen development seems to have been a bad blow to Dick's pride – and he later came to believe that he had reacted to it over-hastily. Of course, after he joined the Government, the NEC carried much less significance in his life. He no longer had the time or the inclination to worry about his showing in the annual popularity contest – although that had been perfectly respectable, with his vote remaining steady and his position out of the seven elected candidates alternating between fourth and fifth place. There was no realistic threat of his being defeated, even though as Leader of the House he necessarily played a less prominent part in policy debates at Conference than he had done as Minister of Housing. Why, then, did Dick react to his constituency Party's action as impulsively as he did?

The explanation is that his critics within his local Party were, in a sense, pushing at an open door. Dick, with his romantic allegiance to Labour as an essentially grassroots Party, always believed that there was something improper about the National Executive being stacked high with Ministers – all of whom were bound to support, rather than criticise, the policy of the Government. He had come close to resigning a year earlier – and only the threat posed by Frank Cousins's resignation from the Government* had persuaded him that it was his duty to stay put.[86] The fact remains, however, that in June 1967 – only a month before his constituency Party intervened – he had made a firm personal decision not to stand down: 'Frankly, there is not nearly as strong a reason this year as last for my trying to set an example by showing that one Minister at least is prepared to resign and give way to younger people outside Parliament.'[87] The Coventry East resolution was thus far more than the catalyst for his gesture of renunciation: it was its cause. Untypically, Dick initially tried to deny that even to himself: 'It does seem to me it's a genuine advantage to get out this year';[88] but he could not keep up that level of self-deception and it was not long before he was writing with perhaps some evident bitterness:

> I feel more strongly than ever that this is a resignation with no return. I've never walked out on anything in quite this fading-out style. I shall never go back to the NEC and they'll never want me back. And it's also an acceptance of the failure of Harold's idea that I should combine the Leadership of the House with Party liaison, as well as an acceptance of a new idea of myself – not as a failing politician but as a politician who's reached his zenith and must now stay on this level or gently move towards retirement.[89]

No doubt, these comments owed something to Dick's concealed resentment at the treatment he had received at the hands of his own local Party; but as an appraisal of what the decision implied for his own political future it was hard to fault. His withdrawal from the NEC meant that he had sacrificed the one position he had won for himself and had been relegated to the status of being, as he ruefully put it, 'Harold's henchman'.[90]

None the less it was a role that had always half-attracted him – and the misfortune for Dick was that it had come too late. During his last six months as Leader of the House he was probably as close

---

* The publication of the Government's Prices and Incomes Bill in July 1966 – effectively freezing all price and wage increases for six months – caused Frank Cousins to resign from the Government. From his powerful post as General Secretary of the Transport and General Workers' Union, it was feared that he would lead a revolt against the Government's whole handling of the economy.

to the Prime Minister as any member of the Government. The departure in November 1967 of George Wigg to the Horserace Betting Levy Board left a vacuum that he was able to fill. But by the beginning of his fourth year at No. 10 Wilson, inevitably, was already set in his ways – and Dick soon found himself engaged in a tug of war with the Civil Service Establishment (and, in particular, with the Secretary of the Cabinet, Sir Burke Trend) in which his will by no means always prevailed. His moment of greatest influence came when the entire economic strategy of the Government collapsed with the forced devaluation of November 1967.* It was a vindication of the sceptical line Dick had consistently taken and, although he fully recognised it as a serious defeat for the Government, he also saw in the decision the chance of starting afresh. Wilson was later to hold him responsible for offering unwise advice on this point – and, indeed, in his memoirs specifically blamed him for the upbeat tone of the Prime Ministerial broadcast he delivered on the Sunday after devaluation was announced.[91] This, however, is in direct conflict with Dick's own contemporary testimony: in his diary, he records the difficulty he faced getting the Prime Minister to acknowledge that a defeat had taken place at all. There may conceivably be truth in both versions, although Dick's quotation of a remark made by Wilson ('Ah, Dick, you like admitting defeats . . . but I never do that sort of thing')[92] unquestionably carries a ring of authenticity.

It was in the gloomy aftermath of the devaluation announcement that Dick came into his own. He certainly justified his claim to being a foul-weather friend of the Prime Minister – and, for a time at least, Wilson depended on him quite heavily. It helped, no doubt, that he was not seen within No. 10 as a plausible successor – although Dick himself, on at least one occasion, could not resist a flight of fancy ('In certain ways I am the Macmillan who could take over from Harold') while going on instantly to recognise its improbability ('but the chances of my doing so, thank God, are utterly remote').[93] He displayed a record of notable loyalty in the traumatic Cabinet debates that followed devaluation – supporting Wilson over continuing the ban on sales of arms to South Africa, firmly backing the new Chancellor, Roy Jenkins, on the fresh round of public expenditure cuts and becoming one of the most stalwart proponents of the need for a British military withdrawal east of Suez. It was all

* The reduction of the parity rate of the pound to the dollar from $2.80 to $2.40 was announced in a statement from the Treasury on the evening of Saturday, 18 November 1967. It followed a week in which there had been a horrendous run on sterling.

the more impressive a performance, since in private at least Dick was under no illusion as to the significance of all that had occurred: 'This Government has failed more abysmally than any Government since 1931.'[94]

Of course, there were personal consolations: it had taken economic catastrophe to bring it about, but Dick had come very near to playing the role of Prime Minister's confidant to which he had always aspired. Wilson even took to dangling new jobs in front of him – what about taking on the Home Secretaryship and combining it with being Leader of the House (as Rab Butler had done in the early days of the Macmillan Government)?[95] That proposal fell through once Jim Callaghan decided, after all, to stay in the Government after leaving the Treasury. Within a fortnight, however, the Prime Minister, by now irate at Denis Healey's part in a Cabinet revolt designed to restore arms sales to South Africa, had another idea. Why should Dick not take his place at the Ministry of Defence and really tackle the job of cutting down on Britain's overseas military commitments?[96] To his credit, Dick jumped at neither offer – realising perhaps more shrewdly than Wilson that the last thing the Government needed, after the blow it had suffered, was the shock of further ministerial changes.

Yet when a major change was forced on the Prime Minister some three months later by George Brown's protest resignation from the Foreign Office,* Dick was without doubt keenly disappointed. For all his political life he had wanted to be Foreign Secretary and, if only on grounds of political good behaviour, plainly felt that this time he had some hope of getting the post.[97] However, once Michael Stewart's† appointment had been announced, he bravely faced up to the uncomfortable fact that 'Harold never even conceived the possibility of making me Foreign Secretary' – venting his

---

* On 15 March 1968 the gold markets of the world were closed pending a conference of central bankers in Washington to fix an official price for gold. This took place on the weekend of 16 and 17 March. George Brown was not consulted about the decision and took great umbrage – sending a formal letter of resignation to Wilson which included a specific complaint about 'the way this Government is run'.

† Michael Stewart (1906–90) was Labour MP for Fulham East 1945–55 and for Fulham 1955–79, before being created a life peer on leaving the Commons. He had become Secretary of State for Education and Science in place of Dick in October 1964. Three months later he moved to the Foreign Office for the first time when Patrick Gordon Walker lost the Leyton by-election. Having succeeded George Brown at the DEA in August 1966, he now succeeded him again as Foreign Secretary.

frustration merely by referring to the man who had got the job for the second time round as 'a dull, dumpy, substitute'.[98] The main legacy of the whole episode was to leave him restive and resentful – a mood that Wilson quickly detected. Within two days Dick found himself in No. 10 having an entirely different future mapped out for him.

On this occasion, in contrast to 1966, it was not a future that he had in any way foreseen. The Prime Minister's proposal was that he should assume the title of 'First Secretary of State', relinquished by Michael Stewart on moving to the Foreign Office, and become the ministerial head of a mammoth new department to be welded together out of the then separate Ministries of Health on the one hand and National Insurance on the other. It was not, in truth, much of an offer to a politician who had already had the prospect of the Home Office or the Ministry of Defence held out to him – and, at first, Dick seems to have been inclined to refuse it. Wilson, however, displayed some skill in suggesting that he had it in him to be the natural successor to William Beveridge, the original architect of the Attlee Government's post-war scheme of universal social security; he displayed perhaps some cunning also in making it clear that, if the answer was still 'No', he would immediately offer the same post to Barbara Castle.[99] If Dick's resistance had not totally crumbled by the time he left No. 10, it certainly had by lunch time; he took his wife, Anne, to the Farmers' Club in Whitehall Court, where she told him, 'It's an ideal job for you – it would be silly not to take it.'[100]

For Dick, however, there was one drawback and a touchingly human one. The more formal duties of being Lord President may never have held much attraction for him but one reward of the job he had always prized was the extremely grand room in the Privy Council offices that went with it. He had gone to considerable trouble to obtain pictures for it from both the National Gallery and the National Portrait Gallery and his pride and joy was an enormous Teniers painting that almost covered an entire wall. If he now moved to be First Secretary of State, it would inevitably mean parting from a magnificent room that he had come to love – and that he was very unwilling to do. Fortunately, the Prime Minister had broached the matter with him early enough for alternative arrangements to be made* and Barbara Castle found herself the surprised

---

* The Cabinet changes were not announced until 6 April – or a full three weeks after Dick's first conversations with the Prime Minister. Since Wilson had the reputation of always playing his cards very close to his chest, that in itself was a striking mark of the confidence that had grown up between them.

recipient of an offer from Dick: he suggested that she should take the title of First Secretary rather than himself. Facing a move herself to an enlarged department but still then bearing the somewhat drab title 'Ministry of Labour', she was understandably delighted – and, with the Prime Minister's authorisation, the deal was done. It was not perhaps quite 'the very generous'[101] action, given Dick's main motive, that it immediately appeared to a mystified Wilson; but it was still an oddly quixotic gesture for a professional politician. It was not long before Dick himself had second thoughts about it – plaintively wondering, even ahead of the reshuffle, 'whether I haven't given my future away'.[102]

In fact, however, Dick had done that by assenting to the substance rather than the original packaging of the Prime Minister's offer. By accepting an essentially overlord role supervising the work of two existing Government departments, he had sentenced himself to a period in limbo, at least until such time as the two departments were formally merged (and the Prime Minister had always planned, without perhaps making it entirely clear to Dick, that this would not be until the autumn when the Commonwealth Relations Office was also due to be merged with the Foreign Office).[103] The result was that Dick was left as something of a loose cannon in Whitehall – applying himself neither to the work of structural bureaucratic reorganisation (which plainly bored him) nor to the drafting of a new post-Beveridge social security system (for which, fatally, he seems to have believed there would be plenty of time once the new joint Ministry was established). Since the Government was already approaching its half-way mark – the 1966 general election had taken place over two years earlier – the lack of urgency that Dick brought to the task of ensuring that a new earnings related pensions scheme got on to the Statute Book remains the most puzzling aspect of his tenure at the DHSS. He did not get his White Paper on National Superannuation published until March 1969 and the resulting Bill did not start its passage through the Commons until January 1970, inevitably falling when Wilson called an election for the following June. By the time of the Queen's Speech in October 1969, Dick had already become apprehensive ('I am a bit concerned to get the Superannuation Bill published and put on the Statute Book in time')[104] but by then things had slipped dangerously far. He should have insisted that the Bill was included in the 1968–9 legislative session rather than the 1969–70 one. And in his earlier, more zestful incarnation at the Ministry of Housing and Local Government he would certainly have done so.

The trouble was that his period as Leader of the House had altered Dick's perspective. He was now preoccupied with the troubles of the Government as a whole rather than with the challenge of administering a single department. (Once the merged Ministry was established, his Permanent Secretary remembers him as having 'left the department to get on very much on its own'.)[105] It was a fault of which he was aware, while remaining quite unrepentant about it:

> If only I could be a decent departmental Minister and keep my nose to the grind-stone of the job I would be entirely happy. But it can't, and mustn't, be done. I have to do what I can to save this Government, a backbreaking, dispiriting, unsuccessful business.[106]

That comment, admittedly, was made against the background of the main political drama of 1969 – the Labour Government's abortive effort to introduce its trade union reform legislation based on Barbara Castle's White Paper, *In Place of Strife*.[107] Here Dick played a somewhat convoluted role. Excluded from the very small group of Ministers who were let into the secret of the Prime Minister's and the First Secretary's intentions, he nevertheless started off trying to salvage what he was sure had been a thoroughly reckless initiative in terms of correct Cabinet procedure. In itself that was not surprising: Barbara Castle was a friend of long standing and, although Dick was not as close to the Prime Minister as he had been during his period as Leader of the House, he retained some loyalty – though no longer much respect – for him.

If Dick's attitude changed later – and he eventually became one of the most forthright opponents of legislation against the trade unions – this was probably the result of psychological as much as political factors. Not the least of these was his sense of grievance that his own pet projects had become the casualties of the Government's new-found obsession with trade union reform. Not only was his own White Paper on National Superannuation (he got the *Daily Mirror* to produce a popular version again) totally overshadowed by *In Place of Strife*, which was published a matter of days ahead of it; worse, the threat of a major parliamentary row on the Industrial Relations Bill led to the Government deciding to sacrifice the Parliament (No. 2) Bill, the product of all Dick's work on Lords Reform.[108] There was one other motive at work, too. Dick, as the years of his conflict with Gaitskell showed, consistently took a slightly sentimental view of the significance of the Labour Party as a mass movement. When it became clear that the idea of introducing penal sanctions against trade unions was deeply unpopular with Party activists – in Coventry his agent reported in April that he could not even raise twenty-five members to attend the local Party's annual dinner[109] – the fact that public opinion generally welcomed it counted for nothing with Dick. There was, he instinctively recognised, only one side of the argument for him to be on – even if it meant severing ties with old allies like Wilson and Castle. With the latter, a form of friendship was maintained. One of the more bizarre episodes of the whole crisis was the holiday the Crossmans and the Castles took together, cruising in the Mediterranean on Charles Forte's yacht a fortnight before the Cabinet forced the Prime Minister and the First Secretary to withdraw the Industrial Relations Bill in return for 'a solemn and binding undertaking' from the TUC.

After the crucial Cabinet meeting on 17 June – and a second one which ratified the agreement with the TUC the next day – Dick did something he had never done before. He sat down and wrote a long, highly personal letter to the Prime Minister. Since it provides the most concise summary of his own position on *In Place of Strife* – as well as throwing an astonishing light on his relationship with Wilson* – it is reproduced here almost in full:

PRIME MINISTER

Though I did not shout for joy like some of our colleagues, I was feeling an enormous sense of relief when you were able to come back and tell us what you had achieved in yesterday's negotiations with the TUC. When the time comes to write history, I feel pretty sure that the change in the responsibility and powers of the TUC which you and Barbara set in motion will be seen as one of the most important events which occurred under this Government . . .

Nevertheless all this has not been achieved without damage. One part of that damage are the wounds we inflicted on each other in last Tuesday's Cabinet discussions. I certainly know how much some of the things said to you must have hurt, and I presume you know how much some of the things hurt which you said to us . . .

---

* The feeling of Dick's wife, Anne, was that the letter should not be sent: 'It sounds like a headmaster addressing a pupil.' To that, Dick cheerfully replied: 'Not exactly, it's like a senior housemaster addressing an unsuccessful headmaster.' The letter went anyway.

Let me start from the charges you made against us. You expressed an outraged resentful bitterness at being let down by colleagues whose nerve had failed them in the hour of crisis. You said that your colleagues were not only soft and cowardly but dishonourable in 'ratting' on Cabinet decisions. I want you to understand what it is that makes honourable, decent colleagues behave in what you feel is such an unworthy way. The prime cause of the ever-growing split between you and the Cabinet on the Industrial Relations Bill was the way you and Barbara put it over us last January. To put it bluntly, we felt you deliberately bounced us into accepting the White Paper and the appalling risks it implied . . .

I am not arguing that Prime Ministers are *never* entitled to take only a few colleagues into their confidence on making a big decision and then swing the Cabinet behind. But you can only afford to do so on rare occasions. I think you ought to realise the damage done to your personal relations with some of us when we realised we had been committed to what we felt a reckless and possibly disastrous policy without any consultation.

What made things worse was the thought that so many of the other strategic decisions which determined the fate of the Government since 1964 had been taken in small conclaves without prior Cabinet consultation. This applied particularly to the so-called '100 days' in 1964 and to the weeks leading up to devaluation . . .

Of course I admit that there is a positive strength in this kind of leadership. Your unique and most exhilarating quality is your combination of resilience in adversity with total absorption in day-to-day combat. But this quality has its defect. It has meant that your leadership in the past five years has consisted of a series of sudden adventures and new initiatives, in launching each of which you have associated with you a different group of colleagues. Someone less energetic and bouncy would have kept a better continuous control of the Government's whole strategy and had more time to observe the morale of the Cabinet and indeed of the Government . . . The whole point of this minute is to urge you to consider the desirability of becoming less personally identified with particular aspects of Cabinet policy, more detached and giving yourself more time for central oversight of Government policy and more time for consultation with Cabinet colleagues. These may seem minor matters of behaviour but I am convinced that it is in our behaviour to each other that we fall

down as a Cabinet and that, unless we can improve, demands for
leakproof loyalty to Cabinet decision will be in vain.

June 1969[110]

Not many Ministers can ever have presumed to address a Prime
Minister in that fashion* – and it may be that Dick already sensed
that his Cabinet career was drawing to a close.[111] Although initially
his reputation had ridden rather high during the protracted struggle
over *In Place of Strife* – he had again begun to tinker with the notion
that he might yet be Wilson's successor[112] – a classic political gaffe
committed in the Commons at the beginning of May drastically
affected his standing with his colleagues. Three days before local
elections were due in England and Wales, he had, as Secretary of
State for the Social Services, announced an increase in the charges
for both false teeth and spectacles under the National Health
Service regulations.[113] Although a routine announcement, and one
that had already been foreshadowed in the Budget, it was the kind
of blunder in terms of timing that was guaranteed to rouse the wrath
of the Labour Party both in Parliament and the country. By revealing that he had forgotten all about the local elections, Dick hardly
made matters any better, and he was probably right to regard it as
'the worst clanger in my political career since my *Mirror* article on
the trade unions'.[114]

The incident was all the more unfortunate as it followed very
swiftly upon what threatened at first to be a major departmental
scandal. Here, though, Dick had emerged with his reputation
enhanced. When he took over at the DHSS he had inherited an
83,000-word Report, commissioned by the previous Minister of
Health, into criminal malpractices at the Ely Mental Hospital, Cardiff. Unknown to Dick, officials at the Department had been conducting a six-month wrangle with the author of the Report, the
young Conservative barrister Geoffrey Howe,† over how little of his
indictment they could get away with publishing. When the matter
came to him for decision, he saw instantly that by disclosing the
contents of the Report in full, the Department could do something

---

* Wilson sent no written answer to the minute, though he did, a few days later,
at one of their late evening meetings together, 'read aloud, very fast' to Dick from
a long detailed reply which he claimed to be preserving for his own memoirs.

† Sir Geoffrey Howe, elected to Parliament in 1964 had lost his seat at Bebing-
ton in the 1966 election. Returned to the House of Commons in 1970 for Reigate,
he was subsequently to have a highly distinguished ministerial career becoming
Chancellor of the Exchequer in 1979, Foreign Secretary in 1983 and Deputy Prime
Minister and Leader of the House of Commons in 1989.

to awaken the conscience of the nation to the conditions prevailing in far too many mental hospitals. Although it involved overruling nearly all his Civil Servants, Dick successfully insisted on publication of the whole Report, combined with a simultaneous announcement of an entire new system of inspectors, reporting direct to the Secretary of State, for all sub-normal, geriatric or psychiatric hospitals. It was, perhaps, the outstanding example of Dick's zeal for open government being carried forward to practical, reforming effect. He certainly transformed a potential administrative disaster for the Department into the occasion for putting the spotlight on what until then had been a shamefully neglected area of the Health Service.

The episode proved that when he applied his mind – and, even more important, had his interest aroused – Dick was still capable of being as creative and imaginative a Minister as anyone in the Government. But at the purely departmental level this gradually became more the exception than the rule. Again, the reasons were partly psychological. In October 1968, when the Departments of Health and National Insurance were finally merged – and Dick formally became Secretary of State for the Social Services – he had to sacrifice not only his title as Lord President of the Council but also the room in the Privy Council Offices that went with it. Settings and surroundings were always very important to Dick and, although, at the suggestion of the Cabinet Secretary, Sir Burke Trend, he acquired the use of the Lord Privy Seal's room in the Cabinet Office, the main part of his ministerial life was inevitably spent in the headquarters of the new joint Ministry at the Elephant and Castle. Known as Alexander Fleming House (named after the pioneer of penicillin) it is a large modern office block of no distinction and sited inconveniently both for Westminster and Whitehall; Dick had wanted to establish himself in the old Ministry of National Insurance building in John Adam Street off the Strand, but this was found to be impractical on grounds of space – there were four other Ministers at the new merged department and they and their top officials all obviously needed to be in the same place. Dick never really took to ministerial life at the Elephant and Castle – describing it from the beginning as being 'out there in exile'.[115] His worry, of course, was that he might become remote from Government's power centre, and it may be that he over-compensated. Certainly, he was much more involved in the broad sweep of Government policy than he had been at Housing; but at the same time he never achieved the total absorption in the affairs of his new department that had marked his period as Minister of Housing and Local Government at the start of the Labour Government.

There were, no doubt, other contributory causes as well. Dick himself ruefully noted at the end of 1968 that, in the past year, 'I seem to have grown a good deal older . . . I am definitely losing political zest, looking and feeling more detached with less zoom, watching, not believing in things, not as enthusiastic or inspired.'[116] But the real trouble perhaps was that he was simply bored. On the social security side he had lived too long with the world of pension policy-making to get much intellectual excitement out of it. His Permanent Secretary, Sir Clifford Jarrett, was astonished to discover that 'he hardly ever interfered and on matters relating to the State Earnings Related Pension Scheme was pretty receptive to advice'.[117] Health interested him more, but here again the presence in the Ministry of an old New College contemporary, Sir George Godber, as Chief Medical Officer, appears to have had the effect of inducing an uncharacteristic humility in Dick. It was largely during his latter days in the Cabinet, on matters beyond the purview of his own department, that he tended to throw his weight around. In September 1969, for example, he addressed a long minute to the Prime Minister about the Common Market, arising out of reading a Foreign Office telegram which reported a fairly insignificant conversation between a British diplomat and a Federal German official.[118]

Such trespassing on the territory of other Cabinet members is never particularly popular and it was probably just as well for his colleagues' peace of mind that an event supervened to temper even Dick's enthusiasm for such excursions. There were already signs that he had not completely cut the painter from the world of journalism and writing. He devoted an inordinate amount of his attention, during the first six months of his new supervisory role, to preparing a Granada lecture on broadcasting which he delivered in October 1968 at the Guildhall.[119] The lecture – a wide-ranging critique of the way politics was presented on television – attracted a considerable amount of newspaper attention[120] and led in the same week to an hour-long BBC TV discussion programme, in which Dick was the central figure.[121] At the time the experience must have seemed to offer little more than a welcome break from ministerial routine – a routine with which Dick had lived now for more than four years. A sharper reminder of the world he had left behind came with the death of his old editor, Kingsley Martin, some four months later:* Martin no longer, of course, occupied the editorial chair at the *New Statesman* so there was nothing professionally unsettling about the news of his death. Understandably, though, it tempted Dick back to remembering their journalistic time together – a joint past he evoked with great brilliance at the memorial meeting the *New Statesman* held in honour of its former editor in March 1969.[122]

The man who presided at that meeting was the chairman of the *New Statesman's* board of directors, Lord Campbell of Eskan, a socialist businessman who for fourteen years had run the large public company of Booker McConnell. He already knew Dick as something more than a social acquaintance but the bravura performance that evening plainly made its mark. Six months later, when he faced the task of finding a new editor for the paper,† Campbell had no doubt about whom he should turn to first. Over lunch at Prescote in October 1969, he put the proposition to Dick; to his gratification, the response was positive – on condition that he would not be expected to take up the post until the end of the then Parliament and that complete secrecy could be maintained.[123] Within ten days a memorandum recording the agreement between them had been formally drawn up.[124]

Dick thus knew from the autumn of 1969 that his ministerial career was on its last lap. Remarkably, it was a piece of knowledge he kept entirely to himself; none of his Cabinet colleagues appears to have guessed anything. If, from time to time, they noticed a less interventionist, assertive or aggressive attitude, they no doubt put it down to the softening effects of age or even the battle-weariness of someone who had been a Cabinet Minister continuously since 1964. Only perhaps on one occasion did Dick allow the mask of 'business as usual' to slip – and that was when in April 1970 he went to the United States to give the Godkin Lectures at Harvard. Delivered on three successive evenings to a combined audience of faculty and students, these turned out to have a distinctly valedictory ring.[125] This did not, however, matter. As Dick himself subsequently wrote: 'If you do not provide any "advance", it is very much easier now

* Kingsley Martin died in Egypt on 16 February 1969. There had been some *rapprochement* between them in his later years. Dick had been touched by his participation in the BBC's *Panorama* profile and in July 1967 happily attended his seventieth birthday party.

† Paul Johnson, who had succeeded John Freeman as editor of the *New Statesman* at the beginning of 1965, wished to give up. He had intimated his willingness, however, to stay on until an appropriate successor could be found.

than in the days when any competent reporter knew shorthand to address a public meeting without being reported.'[126] He might have added that any British politician was bound to be of less interest speaking in Cambridge, Massachusetts than Cambridge, England. But in any event his secret was kept. He went into the election – called by an over-confident Wilson for 18 June 1970 – as the one member of the Labour Cabinet who knew for certain that, whatever happened at the polls, he would not be returning to Parliament as a Minister.

16   *Old Statesman*

Dick was not in England on the day, 18 May 1970, when the Prime Minister formally announced the date of the general election. He had gone abroad on a pre-planned family holiday in Malta,* and did not return until 26 May (leaving Anne and the children behind). If Harold Wilson thought his absence odd, he did not have to wait long for the explanation. In a telephone call made within three days of his return Dick finally let the Prime Minister in on his secret. Typically, Wilson gave nothing away – leaving Dick to comment, slightly irritably: 'He managed to completely conceal his reaction.'[1]

Probably that was just as well, for the news can hardly have come as an unmitigated blow to Wilson. Dick, after all, was already sixty-two and any Prime Minister welcomes the chance to make Cabinet changes painlessly: a prospective vacancy at the DHSS offered him the opportunity to do just that. It was a realisation that Dick may even have shared. His main pitch in their telephone conversation together consisted of a plea to Wilson to give his job after the election to Barbara Castle[2] – a proposal that hardly suggests he had much doubt about the eventual result. Dick's mood of confidence persisted right through until polling day, when his observation of the sluggish pattern of voting, particularly in the safe Labour wards of Coventry East, first aroused his alarm. In the event, his own majority tumbled from 18,696 to 12,265 and the swing against him – no doubt, in part, punishment for having been a Cabinet Minister in a Government that had disappointed the trade unions – was double that in either of the other two Coventry seats. At 5·5 per cent it was, however, only just above that in the country at large, where an

* Dick had been invited by Dom Mintoff, then the island's Leader of the Opposition. The Crossman family stayed in his seaside villa.

average 4·7 per cent swing allowed the Conservatives to sweep to victory with a majority of forty-three over Labour. On the afternoon of Friday 19 June Edward Heath succeeded Harold Wilson as Prime Minister.

If the result was a shock to Dick, it was plainly not the same sort of disappointment to his career that it was to most of his ministerial colleagues. He had embarked on the election in an understandably detached spirit – even condemning the Labour Party's initial poster campaign (featuring photographs of Tory ex-Ministers under the slogan 'Yesterday's Men')* as 'a thoroughly ill-judged publicity stunt'.[3] Only at his own count at Coventry City Hall, when it was already clear that Labour was going down to defeat, did any real sense of frustration break through. He got involved in some kind of quarrel with a BBC camera crew – causing Anne to write afterwards to Dick's agent, Winnie Lakin, thanking her for 'the angelic way you coped with his irritations – I do hope his outburst about the BBC at the count didn't upset you'.[4]

In that same letter, Anne expressed her own sense of thankfulness that Dick was now 'out of it'[5] – but he was still, of course, a Member of Parliament. His determination to continue as an MP provoked the first complication in his relationship with his new employer, the *New Statesman*. No evidence of any formal commitment survives, but clearly the paper's Board expected that Dick would resign from Parliament on taking up the editorship.[6] That hope – and this appears to have been all it was – argued a certain naivety on their part: Dick may never have loved the House of Commons but he had got used to being there – and to expect him to cut himself off from the friends and colleagues he had come to know over a quarter of a century was asking a lot. (So, for that matter, was expecting him to sacrifice £3,750 a year when the paper itself was to pay him a salary of only £7,000 with, unlike the House of Commons, no pension rights attached.)[7] Since he intended to be a writing editor, Dick was also entitled to claim that he needed to keep all his lines of communication open – if only to provide material for the weekly 'London Diary', which he had already decided he would sign as 'Crux'. The amount of purely parliamentary copy he included, not only there but in the paper generally, was later to become one of the principal grounds of disagreement between Dick

---

* The phrase was later to haunt the Labour Party. It was the title of a controversial BBC documentary looking at Labour ex-Ministers a year after they had lost power. The programme incensed Dick, who devoted a whole leading article in the *New Statesman* to attacking it.

and the Board. But, initially, no one seems to have been willing to force a *démarche* on the issue of his continuing in Parliament; and it was very much as a politician, if now a back-bench one, that Dick arrived in Great Turnstile, at last as editor, on Monday 29 June.

At the outset his strongest feeling seems to have been one of vindication. The eighteen years he had spent serving Kingsley Martin – like his nineteen years on the back-benches before becoming a Minister – had finally found their fulfilment. That sense was not confined to him alone. After his death, one member of the *New Statesman* Board explained that, in appointing him to the editorship, they felt that they were 'performing a belated act of justice'.[8] Compensating for the errors of the past is seldom the best motive for appointing anyone to a job, although, at first, it was only Anne who privately wondered whether Dick's return to the *Statesman* was not altogether too tied up with ancient history for any good to come of it.[9] In public, however, even she maintained a brave front – writing to a close friend: 'I think he is going to have enormous fun with the *Statesman*.'[10]

In the first few months Dick undoubtedly did. The announcement of his appointment had been of incalculable news value to the paper – and the fact that industrial troubles at the printers prevented his first issue from coming out served only to whet the Press's appetite for news about him. At the end of his first abortive week both the *Sunday Times* and the *Observer* carried accounts of the impact his arrival had made on the *New Statesman*'s predominantly young staff[11] – and, though the stories infuriated Dick, there was no question that such coverage provided wonderful free publicity for the paper. The early issues produced under his editorship brought a marked improvement in sales, with circulation by the end of September touching 80,000 copies a week. It was a notable achievement as the July–September quarter is notoriously the most difficult one for periodicals as well as newspapers.

Unfortunately, however, in appointing Dick the *New Statesman* Board had overlooked a very important factor. The one area in which he had virtually no experience or expertise – after 1948 Kingsley Martin had not allowed him to take charge of the paper even when he himself was away – was as a strictly editorial journalist. He never mastered the arts of sub-editing copy. In seeking to improve a manuscript he invariably made a terrible mess on it, and – perhaps worst of all – he could rarely work up much enthusiasm for (or even interest in) articles that he had not written, or re-written, himself. These may not have been limitations that mattered when he

had been a reviewer or columnist; but as an editor they were bound
to be serious defects. To be fair to Dick, he showed some awareness
of this himself – complaining within two months of taking over the
editorial chair that he felt the paper was 'doughy and dumpy' but
not apparently being able to link this feeling to his own sense week
by week that 'the whole thing is really over by Wednesday lunchtime'.[12] For a committed editor, like Kingsley Martin, it never, of
course, had been: he ate, drank and slept the paper seven days a
week. But somehow all the years spent as a journalistic *prima donna*
inhibited Dick from doing that. No one could have put the point
more openly than he did: 'There is a big pressure on me on Mondays
and Tuesdays but it is finished by Tuesday evening for that is when I
have to finish the actual writing and once the anxiety of writing is
over, one settles down.'[13] Dick certainly enjoyed the rest of the
week – indeed, he soon collected a Cabinet-in-exile around the
boardroom table in Great Turnstile. At least at the start of his reign
three former members of the Labour Cabinet* came regularly to his
Thursday morning conferences – conferences that he initially tried
to keep quite separate from the more routine gatherings of most of
the actual editorial staff. Fortunately, it was not long before he was
persuaded out of maintaining so invidious a distinction[14] – though it
still remained far from clear what such predominantly political
animals had to contribute to the journalistic business of producing a
weekly periodical.

That was never a concern that bothered Dick. He saw his new
post, first and foremost, as providing him with a platform from
which he could continue to influence the policy of the Labour Party
and, on appropriate issues, even dictate the strategy of the leadership. The first such issue he took up was the Common Market, on
which he was convinced the Party should reverse the position it had
adopted in Government and come out in opposition to British entry.
The leading article in the fifth number of the *New Statesman* he
edited was headlined 'The People v. the Market: Who Has the Last
Word?'[15] It amounted, in effect, to a challenge to the Labour Party
to demand a fresh general election on the question of principle

* The three were Barbara Castle, Harold Lever and Tony Benn – though Benn
soon fell by the wayside, affronted at finding himself surrounded by 'right-wing
Gaitskellites who are really columnists for the Establishment'. A subsequent
regular attender was the former Minister for Disarmament, Lord Chalfont, later to
be an overt supporter of Mrs Thatcher but at that stage still a member of the
Labour Party. At Dick's invitation, he briefly became the *New Statesman*'s foreign
editor.

before any negotiation was completed. It was not very welcome advice to the Labour leadership; but, worse, it was probably never an issue likely to commend itself to the *New Statesman*'s essentially cosmopolitan, middle-class readership. When the *Daily Mirror*, a long-standing supporter of British entry, struck back with an editorial headed 'Dirty Work at the Crossroads'[16] (which was reproduced in a full-page advertisement in the *New Statesman*),[17] it evoked a response among the paper's own readers; whatever their own views, they were able to recall that it was the Wilson Government which, only a few months earlier, had decided to re-apply for membership. Dick, however, was not to be deterred. That winter a series of eleven articles started, all appearing under the rubric 'The Price of Europe'. As one relentlessly succeeded another, they inevitably led to a falling circulation graph.

Dick himself, while not apologising for what he had done about Europe ('We first made our real impact with our sustained anti-Common Market campaign',)[18] later came to concede that initially he had not got the paper's journalistic formula wholly right: 'In the first six months I was far too conscious of and preoccupied with goings on at Westminster – as a result the paper was a bit stodgy and many opportunities were lost.'[19] It was a characteristically honest admission – but he still failed to draw the obvious inference from it. He was 'preoccupied with goings on at Westminster' because he was going there every day. The PLP, since it comprised the one part of the *New Statesman*'s readership to which he had regular and immediate access, necessarily became his target audience (and, perhaps more dangerous than that, the catchment area from which he drew his potential contributors). The charge, though only whispered at first, gradually became louder and more insistent: the *New Statesman* was in danger of becoming the parish magazine of the Parliamentary Labour Party.

In retrospect, it is hard to resist the conclusion that the initial instinct of the *New Statesman*'s Board was correct. It would have been difficult enough to graft an ex-Cabinet Minister in his sixties on to the life of a weekly periodical in any circumstances: Dick's insistence on continuing with his parliamentary career made it virtually impossible.* After his writing days on Monday and Tuesday he was seldom seen in the afternoons in the *New Statesman*'s offices –

---

* In March 1971 Dick reluctantly announced – the decision was not wholly voluntary – that he would not be standing in Coventry at the next election. That still, however, implied another three or even four years in Parliament.

he was always, as the staff's wry phrase of the time had it, 'down at the House'. (He even took, on parliamentary high days, to holding editorial conferences there in his shared MP's room.) Nor, once an early and not very reliable version of a fax machine had been installed at the *New Statesman*'s new printers at Southend connecting it with Great Turnstile, did he make much pretence of seeing the paper through the press. That was a matter of relief rather than resentment to his colleagues. Dick's own total lack of editorial skills (extending to an inability to master the normal reader's marks on a proof) tended on press days to create havoc and confusion. Deliverance, however, was by no means complete once he ceased going. Even after the paper had moved its printing arrangements to Southend in August 1971 – the previous printers at High Wycombe had the dubious advantage of being on Dick's direct route home to Prescote – he would continue to bark peremptory and often not very practical 'subbing' instructions down the phone. If the press time was still met, it was largely due to the professionalism and expertise of the *New Statesman*'s deputy editor, Tom Baistow.

However, what Dick did bring to Great Turnstile was an air of exhilaration and excitement. All through the twenty-two months of his editorship, he remained a figure very much in the public eye – revelling in the controversies he provoked (the most notorious of which was probably an attack on what a *New Statesman* front page called 'The Royal Tax Avoiders'),[20] appearing regularly on television and radio and, as often as not, journeying out on Friday evenings to deliver speeches just as if he were still a leading member of a Government. All this energy and activity naturally taxed the back-up resources of a small weekly paper – and Dick was fortunate in being able to bring in his wake to the *New Statesman* his former personal secretary in the Civil Service, Janet Newman. He was quite blunt about what had prompted him to ask her to join him:

> The truth, of course, is that with me here – with me as an MP as well as an Editor – the whole dimension of the job has changed for the *New Statesman* secretarial staff. It changed in the Private Office when I arrived at the Elephant and Castle. I create more work to be done, and having Janet is an enormous relief.[21]

It was a relief, too, to his editorial colleagues – for Dick had not emerged unscathed from his previous six years of being cosseted by a personal staff in Whitehall. To claim that he had forgotten how to cope with the routine problems of everyday existence – and needed

a personal nanny – may sound unduly offensive; but unquestionably
he did not find the adjustment to everyday life altogether easy.
Mervyn Jones, a regular contributor to the *New Statesman*, puts the
point vividly in his autobiography:

> My own view is that he would have made a good editor had he
> secured the job ten years earlier. The trouble wasn't so much his
> age (he was sixty-two) as the fact that he had spent most of the
> intervening period in the rarefied atmosphere of the corridors of
> power. It was phenomenal to see how insulated he had been from
> life in the real world; he seemed to peer about, vainly seeking to
> pick up the threads, like Dr Manette after his release from the
> Bastille. There were many anecdotes about his ignorance of what
> anything cost – a round of drinks, the train fare to Brighton, the
> stamp on a letter. More fatally, he was no longer able to tell the
> difference between a good article for a weekly paper and a
> satisfactory departmental memorandum.[22]

In truth, Dick's problems as a journalist, which were created by his
Whitehall experience, went beyond that. He no longer *wrote* anything. Instead, he would pace up and down dictating – while Janet
Newman or the other editorial secretary, Sheila Draper, would take
his words down on a pad. They would then be typed and Dick would
correct the typescript – usually scrawling illegibly all over it. The
process – complete with dictation – would then be repeated, with
even a 200-word London Diary paragraph sometimes going through
four or five drafts before a final version was found acceptable. As a
means of composition, it was not only wasteful of time and effort; it
also led to a writing style without much flow or rhythm. Anyone
puzzled by the contrast between the easy prose that Dick wrote, for
example, in *The Charm of Politics* and the much more *staccato* style
that characterised his articles as an editor of the *New Statesman*
need not look further for an explanation.

Worse, though, he liked to try to impose his own building-block
approach on other writers. The poet James Fenton, at the time on
the *New Statesman*'s staff, once comically described his own deal-
ings with him:

> I would bring in a first draft. Now, he would say, this is very good
> but there are one or two ways in which it can be improved. Then
> he would take a pen and excise, infallibly, everything of which
> one had been most proud. Now, he would say, the thing is – the
> sentences are in the wrong order – watch. And so he would insert

the most extraordinary lines and loops turning the page into a wild game of snakes and ladders . . .

He *did* indeed teach me a lot, but what he taught me was cunning and guile. To say what you wanted, you had to express it in some manner that simply defied censorship. It had to be protected also. A useful ruse was to plant a few decoy sentences which would draw his fire while the rest escaped to the printers.[23]

It was a trick others came to learn. Dick was particularly savage on first paragraphs – so his wilier contributors grew accustomed to clearing their throats for half a page and then starting the article they wanted to write with the first sentence of paragraph two. 'There you are,' Dick would exclaim triumphantly, 'as I've told you before, first paragraphs never say anything' – and the article would be sent on its way to the printers with its first paragraph slashed out. Honour would have been satisfied all round, if by a circuitous route.

One of the eventual allegations made against Dick by his enemies on the Board centred on 'his inability to handle his staff and contributors with tact and respect'.[24] That charge over-simplified matters: with many of his contributors and some of the staff he established an immediate rapport, though there were certainly others for whom their experiences, in what Alan Watkins later described as 'Crossman's dialectical gymnasium',[25] produced bruises and strains which were not easily forgotten. But this was not peculiar to life at the *New Statesman*. Even on social occasions Dick could behave just as roughly. 'Well,' he would often say, briskly rising after reducing some supper party to an argumentative shambles, 'I enjoyed that – it was a jolly good set-to'; it never occurred to him that what he had left behind was a kind of emotional field dressing-station. His conduct as editor was in this respect part and parcel of his whole personality – and, if criticisms were to be made, they perhaps applied more properly to those who had offered him the job in the first place.

A more serious weakness lay in the failure of the *New Statesman* to absorb all Dick's attention, or even to satisfy his ambitions. It was not just a question of his attitude to politics – though there was perhaps something ominous in his confession made within four months of becoming editor: 'I miss the big swim. Yes, we are a little swim, a side eddy here now. A place from which we see the big swim and they come to see us but we're suffering from a feeling we are out of it. We are in this delicious, pleasant, exhilarating place but how long shall I keep my bounce, my energy as Editor?'[26] Even

31 The Cabinet Minister as candidate. Dick with Anne after handing in his nomination papers in Coventry, 1970

32 In the editorial chair. Dick on his first day as editor of the *New Statesman*

33 Dick on the farm at Prescote

more alarmingly, Dick's thoughts had already started to reach to a future beyond the *New Statesman*. The catalyst here was a proposal from the publisher, George Weidenfeld, that he should write the official life of his old Zionist hero, Chaim Weizmann. This inevitably provoked some complications, as he was already under contract to produce two books for Hamish Hamilton over the next five years – one on the English constitution and the other to be what was still referred to as his 'Memoirs' rather than his 'Diaries'. Weidenfeld's offer – an advance of £30,000 – seemed, however, too good to sacrifice;* and by the end of October Dick had already signed up to produce not two but three books over the next five years. It was not long before he was writing: 'It looks as though I shan't be wanting to be Editor of the *New Statesman* much after three years from now.'[27] As a prediction delivered within six months of taking up the editorship, it hardly reflected a mood of total dedication to making a success of the paper.

The truth was that, once the novelty had worn off, Dick rapidly became depressed. He was hurt by the fact that circulation had failed to grow – indeed, was now falling rather more abruptly than before he came on the scene. He attributed this to lack of publicity, ruefully noting: 'No other paper mentions what we say or do. We are absolutely out of the news as a paper. We just were a stunt, an amusing story for a few months in July, August and September. Now the *Statesman* is just another place, another weekly with no facilities and no special advertisement.'[28] But the trouble, of course, was really the product. Under Dick's guidance, the paper was still insisting on talking in internal Labour Party terms to a left-wing audience that, after the Wilson years, was largely disillusioned with orthodox parliamentary politics.

If that was obvious to outsiders – including the new readers who had taken the paper only to drop it again – it was a lesson that took some time to sink in with the paper's Board. When the directors did take action, the result was disastrous. Their first move was to call for a re-jig of the paper's format – involving a pictorial cover, photographs scattered inside and the sectionalisation of subject matter. This was known in Great Turnstile as 'the New Look' and Dick, essentially a words man, was never happy about it. By acquiescing,

---

* Dick had little need to worry about money. In 1970–1 the farm at Prescote, which now extended to 500 acres, made the biggest profit it had ever made, more than £20,000. Dick's freelance earnings in his first year at the *New Statesman* also came to well over £2000 – a pleasant surprise for someone who had not been allowed to accept any fees as a Minister.

however, he assented to a decisive shift in power from the editorial to the management floor. Indeed, during the autumn of 1971, when the changes were being prepared, he was to be found sitting morosely at his desk staring uncomprehendingly at a *mélange* of proposed cover styles. Any attempted criticism immediately produced the despairing cry: 'I know they're no bloody good, but it's what *they* say has got to be done.' The bewildered, defeated impression he created presented a poignant contrast to the picture of the self-confident editor he had given only a year earlier.

The format changes had barely been put in place* before Dick once again became seriously ill. He all but collapsed in the office in January 1972 and, although he bravely returned to work, after two days spent undergoing tests in hospital, he was back there again for a major operation a week later. He had always regarded the ten years following his gastrectomy in January 1962 as offering an unlooked-for bonus to his life, and he approached his new operation – this time for cancer of the intestine† – in a remarkably courageous spirit. He found great encouragement in the fact that he was not only in the same hospital (Horton General at Banbury) but in the same bed that he had occupied exactly a decade earlier, viewing it as a lucky omen.[29] The operation was a success‡ – and Dick was back on the phone to the *New Statesman*'s offices three times in one morning within a week of its taking place.[30] Its seriousness was, however, underlined by the fact that he did not return to work for almost two months.

When he did so on Monday 13 March, it was to confront a thoroughly disagreeable shock. Lord Campbell, the *New Statesman*'s chairman, had been insistent that, before going into the office, Dick should breakfast with him at his flat in Eaton Square.

---

* These were first visible in the *New Statesman*'s issue of 10 December 1971, which carried a half-pictorial and half-photographic representation of the Queen and the Duke of Edinburgh as vagrants on the cover. This montage referred, though none too convincingly, to a leading article (now relegated to p.2) attacking the provisions of the latest Civil List.

† There had been a previous cancer scare over a shadow on Dick's lung in 1960. It came to nothing, though it persuaded Dick to give up smoking cigarettes for ten years. He resumed the habit again, if slightly surreptitiously, once he became editor of the *New Statesman*.

‡ The surgeon could give no assurance that the cancer would not come back elsewhere in his body. This was certainly said to Anne, who never, however, raised the matter with Dick as the surgeon had assured her that he had said the same thing to him. Dick later strenuously denied having been given any such warning. It may be, of course, that he simply chose to blot it out from his mind.

Dick subsequently confessed to having been 'puzzled'[31] by this request, but he complied with it all the same. It was only then that he discovered that, in his absence, the Board had held an informal meeting and decided that it would be in the paper's best interests if he were immediately to resign on grounds of ill health. That anyway was Dick's version, as given to the readers of the *New Statesman* ten days later.[32] It was not, however, an account accepted by Lord Campbell, as he made clear in a private letter written to Dick the following month:

> At that dreadful breakfast I did *not* tell you that the Board decided you must be immediately removed. What I told you, as spokesman for the Board, was that they thought it only fair to tell you at once that they had decided they did not want you to carry on after the end of the year; that because both sides were subject to six months' notice that would mean informing you of this in June; and that they felt that you might prefer to resign on health grounds straight away.[33]

The differences between the two versions are perhaps matters of nuance rather than substance – though, in fairness to Lord Campbell, he had been Dick's last champion on the Board* and had no appetite at all for the task he had been given. In his reluctance to humiliate Dick he had extracted a concession from his colleagues that soon proved an expensive blunder. When most editors are fired, they are specifically required to clear out of their offices in a matter of hours. It is a brutal procedure but at least it minimises the embarrassment of their staffs and limits the potential damage to the paper. The *New Statesman* behaved in a much more gentlemanly fashion with Dick – actually requesting him 'to carry on until a successor was found and appointed'.[34] It was a mistake that only the journalistically naive would have made: certainly from then on, at least so far as the Board was concerned, the propaganda war was lost.

For three days Dick kept his own counsel – though he looked so shattered and dispirited on the day he returned to work that one member of his staff suspected that he 'must have been given his cards'.[35] On the morning of Thursday 16 March, the day after a

---

* Dick himself in a letter written to a friend on 18 March acknowledged that Lord Campbell's had been 'the only vote against the decision to get rid of me forthwith'.

Board Meeting had discussed terms for his departure, Dick finally broke the news to his editorial colleagues. No doubt he hoped that they would stand solid behind him – perhaps even threaten a strike on his behalf. He was disappointed; there was no majority for any action beyond deploring the circumstances of his dismissal and serving notice on the Board that they would expect to be fully consulted – as the staff had not been when Dick was appointed – over the choice of his successor. For this somewhat unchivalrous attitude on the part of the staff he had only himself to blame. When he was convalescing at Prescote, he had summoned his principal colleagues down to see him. Six or seven people had journeyed from Paddington on the train to Banbury, armed with two bottles of Krug champagne and determined to do their best to cheer him up. All they got for their pains was a lecture on how inadequate the paper had been in his absence, combined with a paean of praise for the *New York Review of Books*. It may be, of course, that Dick was still in considerable pain – but, if so, he should have postponed calling the meeting. Certainly, for some (though not all) of those there, the boorishness of his behaviour that day proved the last straw.

The outside world, however, knew nothing of that background. To the Labour Party, in particular, it seemed as if a great socialist had been felled by a largely capitalist Board.* And, because the axe had fallen on him the moment he had returned from illness, Dick could count on wider sympathy than that. He played it for all it was worth – using all his own psychological warfare skills to make sure that it was his version of the truth that got across. Even before he provided the *New Statesman*'s readers with his own 'blow by blow' account of his Eaton Square breakfast with Lord Campbell,[36] the initiative was already clearly his. The first and most devastating salvo he fired probably landed in the columns of the *Evening Standard*, via an interview with Mary Kenny:

> Richard Crossman, the newly sacked editor of the *New Statesman* was today a very angry, hurt, peeved and cross man indeed because of his Board's decision to dispose of him just as he had returned from his sickbed.
>
> 'I feel very angry,' he said emphatically, 'They just shouldn't

* The *New Statesman* at the start of the 1970s was still trading profitably. A private company, it had been paying dividends of as much as 22·5 per cent to its largely hereditary shareholders, as well as substantial annual bonuses to its staff.

behave in this way. They knew what I was like when they got me, and now they're sacking me because of what I'm like.'[37]

It was a fair point, and there was never a convincing answer to it. Lord Campbell nevertheless did his best to provide a response in an interview he gave to Chris Dunkley (then of *The Times*) three days later:

I thought he would stand outside Labour politics. We appointed him not because he was a Labour leader, but because he was Dick Crossman. I certainly had not realised how the Labour statesman would be so apparent.

We were trying an experiment of appointing as editor a sixty-year-old former Cabinet Minister – despite the fact that he was sixty, and despite the fact that he was a former Cabinet Minister. But there were a number of other cross-currents: his age, his health, his manner, which some of the staff found hectoring, as well as the concentration on Westminster politics.[38]

Not unnaturally the flavour of those remarks infuriated Dick – and effectively guaranteed that he would use his control of the paper's editorial content during the weeks that remained to belabour the Board mercilessly.* On 24 March 1972, he devoted his entire London Diary – changing its name for the occasion to 'Great Turnstile Diary' – to giving his own account of the events that had led to his dismissal and virtually inviting the paper's readers to rise up in rebellion against it. Many of them, including a number of old political colleagues, eagerly accepted the invitation – and for five successive issues the *New Statesman*'s correspondence columns rang with protests against the Board's action. It was an unprecedented spectacle in any part of the Press – but Dick himself undoubtedly derived some comfort from it. 'I think', he wrote with evident satisfaction to a friend abroad when all was over, 'that the Board of the *New Statesman* got the worst end of the stick.'[39]

That did not alter the fact, however, that he had been deeply hurt – something that all his various references to having been 'a cuckoo in a nest of sparrows' or 'a pike in a pond of minnows'[40] could not wholly disguise. Dick had seldom known professional failure – and, whatever the clumsiness of the Board's behaviour in the way they got rid of him, it was hard to claim that his tenure of the editorship

---

* He was, however, notably generous about his successor, calling him 'the right man' and commending him to the paper's readers in his final London Diary (28 April 1972).

had been a success. He particularly resented the charge that he had failed to get on with the editorial staff – and was touchingly pleased when they insisted on giving a dinner for him at which he was presented with three volumes of a new edition of *The Diaries of Samuel Pepys*.

If there were compensations for being sacked, they lay in two areas. The first was that no longer being tied to the *New Statesman* meant that he could see far more of his family – indeed, according to Lord Campbell, his parting remark on leaving their notorious breakfast together had been: 'I can tell you one thing, Anne will be delighted'.[41] He returned to that theme in many of the letters he wrote to those who had sent him private notes of sympathy. In at least one of them, he almost admitted to a feeling of guilt:

> You will be glad to hear that my wife and children were delighted at the news. I had promised them that when I ceased to be a Minister I would have more days at home and see more of them. Actually, being editor of the *New Statesman* absorbs nearly as much energy as being a Minister and has kept me in London five days a week.[42]

The other aspect of his life over which Dick clearly felt some sense of relief was purely professional. It arose from the commitments he had taken on as an author who had already received advances from both Hamish Hamilton and Weidenfeld & Nicolson. Again, at least in his private correspondence, he was quite explicit about it:

> I came back from convalescence fit as a fiddle to find that the Board of the *New Statesman* in my absence had decided to get rid of me. From my point of view, it is no great disaster since I can now get down to writing the books which I am contracted to write and which I couldn't write while I was in the editorial chair.[43]

Against that, however, there was one regret that Dick ventilated publicly – telling a reporter on the *Daily Telegraph* that he now felt he had decided to leave Parliament too soon and that he would have made a different decision had he been able to anticipate what would happen at the *New Statesman*.[44] (Since his decision not to stand again had, in effect, been forced on him by his local Party, this was perhaps a case of special pleading.) In any event, Dick had started to wind down his parliamentary career once he ceased to be a Minister, using the House of Commons more as a social club than a political forum and intervening only occasionally in debates.*

Dick's release from the chores of editorship meant, however, that he enjoyed something of an Indian summer at least as a journalist and commentator. An invitation from William Rees-Mogg led to his writing a regular Wednesday column in *The Times*, starting in June 1972 and continuing until three weeks before his death. Liberated now from virtually all forms of constraint, it was a much better column than the one he had previously written for the *Guardian* – and, with the ornament of a wonderful Marc† sketch of Dick in heavy glasses, it became one of the weekly high spots of the paper. The column tended to be much more personal in tone (it was called 'Personal View') than anything he had written before, at least outside his Crux Diary in the *New Statesman*. He would usually divide it into two parts – and if the opening item was serious and political, the tailpiece would often be designed to be of simply human interest. Sometimes, though, that would be the case with the whole column. An example was one he wrote in April 1973 on the staple liberal dinner-party topic of State v. fee-paying education:

> My wife and I continue to thank our lucky stars that we live in North Oxfordshire and therefore have been denied freedom of educational choice. To be exact, we were left with the choice of accepting the single school provided by the county or choosing a school to our taste in the fee-paying system . . .
>
> When our children left the village school there was no choice – we were compelled to let them go on to what, I fancy, is at the moment one of the best schools in England. I say 'at the moment' because the headmaster who created Banbury Comprehensive is leaving after twelve years . . .
>
> I can understand why middle-class parents buy private education where the state system is still unsatisfactory. But why do they do so in North Oxfordshire? When I ask about it, I am told as often as not: 'Of course, you have to because of your politics, but we just couldn't. After all, it's the child's future that is at stake.

---

* He did, however, make one notable speech in the Commons on 28 March at the height of the *New Statesman* row in which he warmly welcomed the imposition of Direct Rule in Northern Ireland and called for the withdrawal of British troops within a year. This demand echoed a call already made in a *New Statesman* editorial: 'One Year, Then Out' (13 August 1971).

† Mark Boxer, who died in 1988, had been one of Dick's own imports to the *New Statesman*. Boxer considered him 'one of the few editors who see the point of drawings rather than suffering them'. Dick also introduced the cartoonist Nicholas Garland into the columns of the *New Statesman*.

> So we have to pay the fees, though we can't really afford it.' Some
> of the mothers who talk this way are frankly envious but still
> cannot get over the guilt they would feel if they opted out of the
> private sector . . . [45]

In fact, Dick was being a shade less than candid – there had been at
least two moments when he himself had almost decided to opt out of
the public sector. His son, Patrick, had originally been put down for
the Dragon School, Oxford (where an uncle by marriage taught)
and matters had gone far enough for four years' fees to be paid in
advance.[46] He had also at one stage wanted Patrick to go to Winchester – even taking Anne there on a Sunday evening to look at
College Meads – 'the most beautiful place in the world'.[47] In the
case of Patrick and Virginia it was not really Dick's views that
mattered; what counted was their mother's determination that they
should not be sent away to boarding school.

For the last two years of his life Anne's was a decision that
brought Dick nothing but delight. If he had been something of an
absentee father before, he was now very much a full-time parent, to
two teenage children who went daily to Banbury Comprehensive
and came home each evening. At last Prescote had become the kind
of complete family home that Dick had always intended. He worried a bit about Patrick's lack of educational progress compared
with his own at the same age – but consoled himself with the reflection that 'he seems to be growing up more naturally with his own
tastes, his own relationships, and this is what has been given to him
by the State system'.[48] Wisely, Dick resisted the temptation 'to push
and shove him'[49] – though the pressures of their father's fame can
never have been easy either for Patrick or Virginia.*

That fame did not diminish once Dick had left the *New Statesman*.
Indeed, if anything, thanks to television, he became an even greater
celebrity. At the beginning of 1973 he launched a series of late
evening interview programmes on BBC1 called *Crosstalk*, which
proved a great success with the more discriminating viewer. The
format at the start was a little stilted, as the BBC fought shy of
letting Dick loose alone and insisted on the presence of a studio
chairman. (Derek Hart, the former *Tonight* interviewer, was cast
for this role, but he soon found he had remarkably little to do and
had disappeared by the time the BBC brought the series back fifteen

---

* Virginia became Head Girl of Banbury Comprehensive and later took up a
career as a researcher. Patrick killed himself at the age of seventeen in February
1975, nearly a year after his father's death.

months later.) At their best, the programmes were genuine personal conversations – and, as Dick's guests ranged from Enoch Powell to Harold Wilson or (outside Parliament) from his old *Mirror* boss, Cecil King, to his former Civil Service adversary, Baroness Sharp, they were seldom less than stimulating. The *Guardian* was later to judge that they had 'produced some of the best political reminiscences and insights of the decade'.[50]

But that was not the limit of Dick's new incarnation as a TV star. During the February 1974 election he was offered the opportunity – along with the Conservative MP, Sir John Foster, who was also due to retire – of starring for three consecutive weeks in one of ITV's prime current affairs programmes. Granada TV's *World in Action* devoted itself for the period of the campaign to describing a political journey both the ex-MPs made across the length and breadth of Britain. For Dick, in particular, it was a gallant venture, since he already knew by then that he was a dying man. As a device for current affairs coverage of a campaign, it was not wholly successful – there was something sedentary about two elderly politicians sitting on the touchlines and merely watching what was going on – but it at least had the virtue of novelty. It also offered the poignant spectacle of Dick, by now ravaged by cancer, delivering what was to be virtually his last political tutorial.

His final illness stole up very quickly. Until September 1973, when it was discovered that he had cancer of the liver and was told that he probably had no more than six months to live, he led a relatively active life. His main preoccupation was getting on with his books – and he initially concentrated almost exclusively on his life of Weizmann, visiting Israel twice to pursue his research at the Weizmann Institute at Rehovot. That in itself was evidence that he had either not taken in, or had chosen to disregard, his surgeon's earlier warning about the possibility of the cancer returning – for, if he had realised that he might be facing a race against time, he would certainly have given priority to his *Diaries*. Once he went back to reading them in transcript form, he immediately resolved to abandon the project of using them as the basis first for a book on the British constitution and then for one of memoirs – and instead decided to let them speak for themselves. Because, however, the centenary of Weizmann's birth was due to fall in 1974 – and the publishers wished his official biography to be published in that year – he felt he had no choice but to try to get that commission out of the way first. It was not until he learned that he had so little time left that he reversed those priorities. Even then he waited until the beginning of 1974 formally to break the news to Meyer Weisgal, the chairman of the Weizmann Institute in Israel:

> *29 January 1974*
>
> My dear Meyer,
>   I am writing to tell you that since my rapidly declining health excludes any chance of my completing the Weizmann Biography, I have decided that the fairest thing is for me to abandon the project and let you at once proceed to choose my successor. As I know you will realise, I have come to this conclusion with the greatest reluctance. It is a terrible thing to give up when one has spent nearly two years learning how to do a tremendous task and when I thought I have got the picture right at least up to 1917. But I now feel that in your interests as well as my own there is really no alternative . . . [51]

During the last few months of his life Dick had to write a number of letters of that kind – including one to the literary editor of the *New Statesman*, to which he had only recently agreed to return as a reviewer:*

> *27 February 1974*
>
> During the fortnight when I have been touring England for Granada TV, I have also been thinking about my literary future. As you may know, I have not been well since last autumn. The doctors leave me free to do entirely what I like in living, eating and drinking (which I have ceased to like) but my physical strength is, month by month, becoming severely limited. Very reluctantly I have decided that until I have completed the text of my diaries for publication, I must give up everything and only retain my weekly *Times* article to keep the wolf from the door. [52]

In fact, Dick was able to retain even that only for another two weeks – although one week after writing that letter he did bravely embark on his second series of *Crosstalk* in which he interviewed Lord Butler, Jack Jones and Jeremy Thorpe before his painfully obvious failing strength forced the curtailment of the series at the half-way mark. There remained, however, two things that gave Dick real satisfaction. The first was that, by a supreme effort of will, he

---

* Since leaving the *New Statesman* in April 1972, Dick had been a regular contributor to the book pages of the *Listener*. His allegiance, however, had been very much a personal one to its editor, Karl Miller, who resigned in 1973.

managed to complete preparing the first volume of his *Diaries* for publication, even writing the Introduction and actually seeing a sample page and the proposed dust jacket for it (which the publishers had rushed through) some six weeks before he died. The second cause of comfort to Dick was something he had hardly dared to expect but was all the more gratifying for that.

Throughout the February 1974 general election he had taken a gloomy view of the Labour Party's prospects of victory. On the eve of the election he had written in his column in *The Times*: 'Unfortunately, I see few signs of a Labour Government emerging tomorrow night. In order to halt the Tory juggernaut, something like an old-fashioned Labour revival was required. It has not taken place.'[53] And he was equally pessimistic in private, writing to an old *New Statesman* colleague on the same day: 'I have been enjoying myself during the election campaign with John Foster, since Granada looked after us very well. I don't, however, look forward to the result with much pleasure.'[54] The result, therefore, when it came – leaving Labour with the largest number of seats, enabling it to form a minority Government without an overall majority – not only surprised but delighted Dick. It meant that he had lived to see the return of Harold Wilson to No. 10, and, not for the first time, he found himself rejoicing in the sheer unpredictability of politics.

Dick's last public outing was a lunch at Downing Street with the new Prime Minister. It took place on Monday 23 March, and no one else was present. Wilson, however, later gave his own account of the occasion, revealing that in the course of it he had offered Dick a life peerage, and that he had accepted[55] (the formal announcement was to wait until a full batch of new life peers had been assembled). Probably they both knew that it was an offer he was unlikely ever to be able to take up – though neither can have known that, within three days of their meeting, Dick would collapse and sink into a coma from which he never regained consciousness.

On the last Sunday of her husband's life, Anne spoke movingly to a newspaper reporter of what it had meant to live under the shadow of an incurable illness: 'You value the time together. None is wasted. And afterwards you don't get the feeling of "Oh, if only I'd done more" because you have done more, and that is a marvellous feeling.'[56]

By then, of course, Anne had been forced to recognise the imminence of Dick's death, even defying the still prevailing reluctance to mention cancer by carefully explaining that was what her husband had. She was forthright about this because she and Dick had agreed there should be no pretence or disguise. Nor was there – with Anne going on to say, 'He has refused to give up but now I think he has to.'[57]

Dick died at home at Prescote, as he had wished, on Friday 5 April 1974. He was only sixty-six – a fact that may have surprised those for whom he had seemed for so long an enduring, colourful presence in British politics. But then, as he himself put it, 'I have certainly led an interesting and varied life.'[58] It was a proposition on which, for once, he could probably count on commanding almost universal assent.

Notes and References

I THE CLAIM TO FAME

1 RHSC, *The Diaries of a Cabinet Minister* (Hamish Hamilton/Jonathan Cape, 1975), vol. I, p. 505. Entry for 21 April 1966.
2 Interview, Graham C. Greene, 11 December 1989.
3 C. H. Rolph, *Further Particulars* (Oxford University Press, 1987), p. 217.
4 Hugo Young, *The Crossman Affair* (Hamish Hamilton/Jonathan Cape, 1976).
5 The dates for these discussions, according to RHSC, *The Diaries of a Cabinet Minister*, vol. II (Hamish Hamilton/Jonathan Cape, 1976) were 26 January 1967 and 21 September 1967. The entry for the former occasion even includes a verbatim extract from the Cabinet Minutes, twenty-one years ahead of its official release under the thirty-year rule.
6 *Observer* (22 January 1967). The paragraph appeared in the paper's Pendennis gossip column.
7 Letter from the Cabinet Secretary to the editor of the *Sunday Times*, 28 January 1975. The text is given in full in Young, *The Crossman Affair*.
8 *Hansard* (11 April 1975), vol. 889, written answers, col. 483.
9 *Listener* (25 September 1980). Foot's review of Barbara Castle, *The Castle Diaries 1974–76* (Weidenfeld & Nicolson, 1980) fully reflects his own distaste for the whole genre. It was headed: 'To set diary against diary is to spread endless misapprehension.'
10 An article entitled 'The Jigsaw of Truth' – including the verbal recollections of a number of Labour ex-Cabinet Ministers – had appeared in the *Sunday Times* (22 June 1975).
11 Cmnd 6386 (22 January 1976).
12 RHSC preserved these handwritten notes in his 'Autobiography' file. They are dated 11 August 1945.

2   AN EDWARDIAN CHILDHOOD

1   Interview, Lord Wilberforce, 13 January 1988.
2   Interview, Geoffrey Crossman, RHSC's elder brother, 7 February 1988.
3   RHSC, 'My Father', *Sunday Telegraph* (16 December 1962).
4   Interview, Mary Woodhouse, RHSC's youngest sister, 21 December 1987.
5   RHSC, 'My Father'.
6   See Leo Abse, *Private Member* (Macdonald, 1973), pp. 139–41.
7   RHSC, 'My Father'.
8   Interview, Geoffrey Crossman.
9   Letter from RHSC to Zita Baker undated but from internal evidence written in August 1937, four months before their marriage. In it he speaks of the Old Rectory, Ashmore, as 'fearfully comfortable' and describes it as 'a marvellously appointed house with endless bathrooms'.
10 Interview, Geoffrey Crossman.
11 Interview, Mrs Geoffrey Crossman, 7 February 1988.
12 Interview, Mary Woodhouse.

3   THE WYKEHAMIST

1   See James Sabben-Clare, *Winchester College* (Paul Cave, Southampton, 1981).
2   *New Statesman* (18 September 1954). The review is reproduced in RHSC *The Charm of Politics* (Hamish Hamilton, 1958).
3   Interview, Michael Hope, 5 January 1988.
4   RHSC, *The Diaries of a Cabinet Minister* (Hamish Hamilton/ Jonathan Cape, 1977), vol. III, p. 862.
5   BBC 2, *Reputations* (5 April 1979), interview, Sir William Hayter.
6   Chamber Annals – Short Half 1920 – Cloister Term 1921 by DGS.
7   Ibid.
8   Chamber Annals – Cloister Term 1924 by DHMC. The 'analyst' belatedly dated his report 23 November 1925.
9   RHSC, *The Charm of Politics*, p. 115.
10 *The Wykehamist*, no. 634 (3 November 1923).
11 Ibid., no. 647 (23 May 1924). The performance of *Dr Faustus* took place on 31 March 1924.
12 *The Wykehamist*, no. 653 (21 November 1924).
13 RHSC, 'My Father', *Sunday Telegraph* (16 December 1962).
14 Interview, Stephen Spender, 15 February 1988.
15 Prefect of Hall Ledger 1920–9, held at Winchester College. Entry signed R. H. S. Crossman.
16 Ibid.

17   Notes supplied by Ernest Sabben-Clare.

18   It was included in John Betjeman's first collection, *Mount Zion* (The James Press, 1931). It was dedicated to Randolph Churchill – leading to some confusion among the ignorant as to whether or not he was the model for it (Churchill, in fact, went to Eton). Subsequently Betjeman expanded the dedication to read: 'To Randolph Churchill, but not about him': Bevis Hillier, *Young Betjeman* (John Murray, 1988), pp. 356–7.

4   UNDERGRADUATE AND DON

1   BBC Radio, *Youth Looks Ahead* (4 February 1935) and BBC 1, *A Chance to Meet* (21 February 1971).

2   Taken from RHSC's own account of his speech in his unpublished *New Statesman* diaries. Entry 23 October 1970.

3   Interview, Sir Stephen Spender, 15 February 1988.

4   RHSC's 1928–9 diary. Entry 23 May 1929. The holiday, in April, was at Porthcothan near Padstow.

5   Ibid. Entry 25 December 1928. The cousin's name was Rosemary Howard.

6   Ibid. Entry headed simply 'Sunday' – but, from internal evidence, the first Sunday of Hilary Term 1929.

7   Undated letter from RHSC to his mother, presumably written in February 1928.

8   Undated letter from RHSC to his mother, presumably written in March 1928.

9   'This is a gorgeous place: better than I thought possible' – letter, 21 March 1928, sent from Caen by RHSC to his mother.

10   RHSC's 1928–9 diary. Entry, 25 December 1928. The cousin's name was Amie Walters. She never married.

11   Interview, Ruth Harris, daughter of Ellen Murray, 25 January 1988. According to Mrs Harris, 'Dick wasn't the beginning of a flirt. He wasn't stylish or elegant or any of those things. It was basically that he was so terribly clever and that he had this fantastic vitality.'

12   Undated letter from RHSC to his mother presumably written in March 1928.

13   Interview, Michael Hope, 5 January 1988. Michael Hope inherited the part of Socrates. The 'personal favourite' added to the cast – in Hope's former role of Chorus – was an undergraduate named Francis King.

14   Interview, Sir Stephen Spender, 15 February 1988. At a dinner at the Garrick Club in 1970 Auden apparently responded to a question from RHSC, 'Don't you remember my writing poetry?' with the answer, 'I remember nothing at all about it – you were only interested in politics.'

15   *Crosstalk* (28 January 1973).
16   RHSC's letter to Tom Braddock, 7 February 1973. Crossman Papers, Modern Records Centre, University of Warwick Library, MSS. 154/3/BR.
17   Interview, Gabriel Carritt, 14 March 1988.
18   Interview, Lord Jay, 20 January 1988. Jay was apparently prepared to go on to Southampton but Dick, uncharacteristically, drew the line at that.
19   RHSC's 1928–9 diary. Entry 23 May 1928.
20   Interview, Sir Isaiah Berlin, 3 January 1988.
21   Letter from New College dated merely 'Sunday' but plainly written after one first mentioning the topic, 2 February 1930.
22   Ibid. Dick's mother's reply is scribbled in pencil on the back of his letter.
23   Letter from New College, 15 February 1930.
24   Ibid.
25   Letter from New College, 22 February 1929, plainly an error for 22 February 1930.
26   Ibid.
27   Ibid.
28   RHSC, interview 3 July 1971 with C. H. Rolph then writing the biography of Kingsley Martin. The original tape of the interview is held at Surrey University.
29   Ibid.
30   Letter from RHSC to his mother, 'Thursday 30 x 30, Frankfurt'.
31   Letter from RHSC to his mother, 31 January 1931.
32   Letter from RHSC to his mother, 'Monday', written from Greece.
33   Ibid.
34   Letter from RHSC to his mother, 14 May 1931.
35   Interview, Professor H. L. A. Hart, 3 May 1988.
36   Letter from RHSC to his mother, 19 June 1931.
37   RHSC, interview with C. H. Rolph.
38   Remark of RHSC's quoted in Anthony Howard (ed.), *Selections from the Crossman Diaries* (Hamish Hamilton/Jonathan Cape 1979), Introduction, p. 14.
39   Crossman Papers, Modern Records Centre, University of Warwick Library, MSS. 154/3/DHS.
40   RHSC, interview with C. H. Rolph.
41   Ibid.
42   Interview, Lord Jay.
43   W. H. Auden, *The Orators* (Faber, 1932), p. 67.
44   Interview, Mary Woodhouse, 21 December 1987: 'My poor mother completely fell for her.'
45   Letter to Zita Baker, 24 February 1935.
46   Letter to Zita Baker, 11 August 1934.
47   Interview, Mary Woodhouse: 'Dick was entranced by her. He had

never had a woman before and she demonstrated to him that he wasn't just a one-sided scholar.'

48 Interview, Sir Isaiah Berlin.

49 Interview, Professor H. L. A. Hart. The best efforts of the then Dean of Divinity of New College, the Rev. J. P. Sheehy, have failed to establish any record of the ceremony – no doubt for the reason given.

50 Interview, Sir Isaiah Berlin.

51 Ibid.

52 Interview, Anne Crossman, 9 January 1989.

5   BROADCASTER AND CELEBRITY

1 Notes supplied by Ernest Sabben-Clare.

2 RHSC, interview with C. H. Rolph, 3 July 1971. There Dick dated these sentiments to 1932.

3 Interview, Maurice Latey, 25 August 1988.

4 *Sunday Times* profile (25 May 1969). Dick himself is quoted there as saying, 'although there are very few things in life one can say one knows, I know I was a good teacher'.

5 BBC Written Archives Centre (WAC), Caversham. Talks, Crossman, Richard H.S. 1934–6 File 1. Letter from Charles Siepmann, 20 April 1934.

6 Ibid., letter from RHSC dated simply 'Saturday'.

7 Ibid., letter from J. R. Ackerley, 26 April 1934.

8 Ibid., letter dated simply 'Friday'.

9 Crossman Papers, Modern Records Centre, University of Warwick Library, MSS. 154/4/BR.

10 BBC WAC, Caversham. Talks, Crossman, Richard H. S. 1934–6 File 1. Letter from Ackerley to RHSC, 30 April 1934.

11 Ibid., Internal memo.

12 Crossman Papers, Modern Records Centre, University of Warwick Library, MSS. 154/4/BR.

13 RHSC's letter to Zita Baker dated merely 'Wednesday' but from internal evidence written on 4 July.

14 Ibid.

15 Ibid.

16 Crossman Papers, Modern Records Centre, University of Warwick Library, MSS. 154/4/BR.

17 PRO. FO 395/453; P 418/39/150.

18 Londoner's Diary, *Evening Standard* (25 July 1935).

19 Letter to Zita Baker datelined Meyersheim.

20 BBC WAC, Caversham. Talks, Crossman, Richard H. S. 1934–6 File 1.

21 Ibid., letter, 26 July 1935.

22 Ibid., letter dated simply 'Saturday' but received at the BBC on 23 April 1934.

23   RHSC, interview with C. H. Rolph.

24   The broadcasts went out, respectively, on 4 September and 8 October 1934. The first was reprinted in the *Listener* and the script of the second is held at Caversham.

25   BBC WAC, Caversham. Talks, Crossman, Richard H. S. 1934–6 File 1. Letter, 2 October 1934.

26   Ibid., letter, 28 December 1934.

27   Ibid., memo, 4 January 1935.

28   Ibid., letter from Siepmann to RHSC, 15 January 1935.

29   Ibid., PS to letter from RHSC to Major Gladstone Murray, 16 January 1935.

30   Ibid., letter from Gladstone Murray to RHSC, 25 January 1935.

31   Ibid., memo from Gladstone Murray to Director of Talks, 19 January 1935.

32   *Daily Herald* (12 February 1935). The broadcast was also reprinted in the *Listener* (6 February 1935).

33   Handwritten letter from RHSC to his parents, undated but presumably written some time in the latter half of December 1934.

34   BBC WAC, Caversham. Talks, Crossman, Richard H. S. 1934–6 File 1. Undated letter.

35   Ibid., letter, 4 June 1934.

36   Ibid., undated postcard.

6   AN OXFORD SCANDAL

1   Letter from RHSC to Zita Baker, undated but retained in envelope postmarked 16 December 1934.

2   Letter from RHSC to Zita Baker, 1 January 1935. A second letter on the same day offered an apology – though only on strictly limited grounds.

3   Letter from Zita Baker to RHSC, 'New Year's Day'.

4   Letter from RHSC to Zita Baker, 'Thursday a.m.', apparently written from Germany in early August 1934.

5   Letter from RHSC to Zita Baker written from Marberg, 16 June 1934.

6   Poem entitled 'Hohens Taufer', 14 July 1934 and, therefore, written in Germany. It is dedicated 'For Zita from Dick'.

7   Letter from Zita Baker to RHSC from 94 Woodstock Road and dated 'Monday' – but from internal evidence written in the first week of January 1935.

8   Ibid.

9   Letter from Zita Baker to RHSC dated merely 'Friday' but plainly written in the first half of January 1935.

10   Letter from RHSC to Zita Baker dated 'Saturday evening' and written from 'Winsford's Farm, Holford, Bridgwater'.

11   Letter from RHSC to Zita Baker, 25 February 1935.

12 Letter from RHSC to Zita Baker, 5 March 1935.

13 Letter from Zita Baker to RHSC from New York, 9 February 1935.

14 Letter from RHSC to Zita Baker, 5 March 1935.

15 Interview, Naomi Mitchison, 6 January 1988.

16 Letter from RHSC to Zita Baker, 10 March 1935.

17 Ibid.

18 Letter from Zita Baker to RHSC from Cairo Hotel, Washington DC, 22 March 1935.

19 Ibid.

20 BBC WAC, Caversham. Talks, Crossman, Richard H. S. 1934–6 File 1. Letter, 11 September 1935.

21 Ibid.

22 Ibid., letter, 27 January 1936.

23 Letter from Zita headed 'Harrison's Hotel, Brighton' and dated simply 'Friday' – presumably 17 January 1936.

24 BBC WAC, Caversham. Talks, Crossman, Richard H. S. 1934–6 File 1. Letter from Roger Wilson to RHSC, 17 January 1936. Nearly a month later Wilson was still complaining about Dick's 'hammer blows of emphasis'. Letter, 13 February 1936.

25 Ibid., 'Internal Circulating Memo', 13 February 1936.

26 Ibid., memo written by Roger Wilson.

27 Letter from Zita headed 'Harrison's Hotel, Brighton' and dated 'Friday'.

28 BBC WAC, Caversham. Talks, Crossman, Richard H. S. 1934–6 File 1.

29 Interview, Mary Nicholson, 19 September 1988.

30 BBC WAC, Caversham. Debates and Discussions File 1A 1926–36.

31 *Oxford Mail* (16 February 1937), Report of John Baker's evidence at divorce hearing held at Devon Assizes at Exeter.

32 Private information but confirmed by two independent sources.

33 Letter from RHSC to Zita dated simply 'Monday' and reporting on 'a terrific blow-up' with Naomi Mitchison. The letter appears to have been written in January 1937.

34 Interview, Mary Nicholson.

35 Letter from RHSC to Zita dated simply 'Tuesday afternoon' but probably written late in 1936.

36 Letter from RHSC to Zita written in pencil from Manchester Station in March 1937.

37 Letter from RHSC to Zita undated but plainly written in the latter half of February 1937.

38 Letter from RHSC to Zita undated but apparently written on 4 March 1937.

39 Letter from RHSC to Zita dated 'Tuesday', but evidently written in the first quarter of 1937.

40 Letter from RHSC to Zita reporting on a conversation with his agent,

J. T. Baxter. It is dated 'Friday p.m.' but was plainly written early in the campaign.

41 Letter from RHSC to Zita from the Central Committee Room, Hockley Hill, Birmingham, sent on 11 April 1937.

42 Letter from RHSC to Zita from the Central Committee Room, Hockley Hill, Birmingham, dated 'Monday'.

43 Letter from RHSC to Zita from the Central Committee Room, Hockley Hill, Birmingham, dated 'Friday'.

44 Letter from RHSC to Zita from the Central Committee Room, Hockley Hill, Birmingham, undated.

45 *Daily Herald* (21 April 1937).

46 Letter from RHSC to Zita from the Central Committee Room, Hockley Hill, Birmingham, undated, apparently written on 19 April 1937.

47 Interview, Sir Isaiah Berlin, 3 January 1988.

48 Letter from RHSC to Zita undated but clearly written some time after her decree nisi had been granted.

49 Letter from RHSC to Zita written on 4 March 1937.

50 Letter from RHSC to Zita in Bolton postmarked 12 October 1937.

51 Ibid.

52 Letter from Buckhurst Hill House, 11 December 1937.

53 Interview, Carrie Hodgkinson, widow of George Hodgkinson, secretary of Coventry City Labour Party, 12 April 1988.

7   PRODIGY POLITICIAN

1 Letter from RHSC to Zita, 29 October 1937.

2 Letter from RHSC to Zita, 11 November 1937.

3 Undated letter from RHSC to Zita giving details of his programme in advance of their marriage.

4 Letter from RHSC to Zita headed 'Burton, Tuesday morning'. Both RHSC's brothers were still unmarried and his mother had been for the past four years 'Lady Crossman'.

5 Letter from RHSC to Zita, dated 'Friday'.

6 Interview, Venice Barry, Zita's and John Baker's daughter, 10 April 1988.

7 RHSC's reports appeared in the *Daily Herald* on 19, 23, 24 and 27 May 1938. The last was an interview with the Foreign Minister, Dr Kamil Krofta.

8 Letter from Hotel Ambassador, Prague to Zita, dated 'Tuesday'.

9 Undated letter from RHSC to Zita.

10 *New Statesman and Nation* (8 August 1936).

11 *New Statesman and Nation* (22 May 1937).

12 RHSC, interview with C. H. Rolph, 3 July 1971, where the point was made that Martin acted out of fear of losing him to the *Spectator*.

13 *Oxford Mail* (18 May 1935).

14 RHSC, interview with C. H. Rolph.

15 Letter to Zita, dated 'Friday afternoon'.

16 Letter to Zita, dated 'Tuesday' but evidently written after a meeting of the Headington Party which, alone of the Oxford City Party branches, came out against supporting Sir Stafford Cripps. Dick also opposed endorsement of the Manifesto at the meeting of the Party's General Committee held in February 1937.

17 Crossman Papers, Modern Records Centre, University of Warwick Library, MSS. 153/3/RES. Letter to Peter Drake, 14 November 1973.

18 Letter to Zita, dated 'Friday evening' but probably written early in 1937.

19 *Oxford Mail* (19 October 1937). The other three speakers were Lady Violet Bonham Carter, Dr Nathaniel Micklem and Roy Harrod.

20 *New Statesman and Nation* (12 November 1938).

21 A. S. Knight, 'The Oxford City By-Election and Appeasement'. Written in 1964 as the Trevelyan thesis, a typed copy is held at the *Oxford Mail*.

22 C. H. Rolph, *Kingsley* (Gollancz, 1973), p. 249.

23 RHSC, interview with C. H. Rolph.

24 Ibid.

25 Ibid.

26 *New Statesman and Nation* (3 July 1937). The reviewer was Roger Manvell.

27 Introduction to Anthony Howard (ed.), *Selections from the Diaries of a Cabinet Minister* (Hamish Hamilton/ Jonathan Cape 1979), p. 9.

28 Interview, Sir Isaiah Berlin, 3 January 1988.

29 Ibid.

30 RHSC, interview with C. H. Rolph.

31 Rolph, *Kingsley*, p. 242.

32 *New Statesman and Nation* (3 June 1939).

33 Ben Pimlott (ed.), *The Political Diary of Hugh Dalton 1918–40, 1945–60* (Jonathan Cape, 1986), p. 267.

34 RHSC, interview with C. H. Rolph.

35 Letter to Zita, undated but clearly written in August 1939 before the Nazi-Socialist Pact.

36 Letter to Zita, dated 'Monday' but plainly written in September 1939, probably on 4 September.

37 Letter to Zita, undated but evidently written in the very early days of 'the phoney war'.

38 Letter to Zita, dated 'Monday', probably written on 11 September 1939.

39 Letter to Zita, undated but presumably written in October or November 1939.

40 *Daily Express* (7 December 1939).

41 *New Statesman and Nation* (20 January 1940). The editorial was headed 'Speculation and Reality'.

42   Ibid.
43   Ibid. (17 February 1940).
44   Ibid.
45   *New Statesman and Nation* (15 June 1940). The article was actually a book review and was, somewhat ironically, headed 'War Aims'.

8   PSYCHOLOGICAL WARRIOR

 1   BBC WAC, Caversham. Talks, Crossman, Richard H. S. 1937–42 File 2.
 2   Ibid. Ogilvie's MS note is dated 1 May.
 3   Ben Pimlott (ed.), *The Second World War Diary of Hugh Dalton* (Jonathan Cape, 1986), p. 171.
 4   Ibid., pp. 65–6.
 5   Ibid., p. 284.
 6   Hugh Dalton, *The Fateful Years: Memoirs 1931–45* (Muller, 1957), p. 380.
 7   Lecture to Royal United Services Institution 20 June 1952, published in *RUSI Journal* (August 1952), pp. 319–32.
 8   Ellic Howe, *The Black Game: British Subversive Operations against the Germans in the Second World War* (Michael Joseph, 1982), p. 85. I am indebted to Mr Howe's admirable book for a good deal of material on the early days at Woburn.
 9   PRO, FO 898/9.
10   Howe, *The Black Game*, p. 85.
11   PRO, FO 898/8. The request is recorded in the minutes of the meeting for 17 March 1941.
12   PRO, FO 898/8. The date of this minute is 15 July 1940.
13   Sefton Delmer, *Black Boomerang* (Secker & Warburg, 1962), p. 46.
14   PRO, FO 898/4.
15   PRO, FO 898/181. The minute is dated 14 April 1941.
16   Ibid. Voigt's memorandum is dated 'March 1941'. It was not seen at Woburn till 12 April 1941.
17   PRO, FO 898/183. The minute is dated 3 November 1941.
18   Ibid.
19   *Second World War Diary of Hugh Dalton*, p. 351.
20   PRO, FO 898/60. The letter was drafted by Reginald Leeper.
21   Ibid.
22   Ibid.
23   Sefton Delmer, 'H.M.G.'s Secret Pornographer', *Times Literary Supplement* (21 January 1972).
24   Kenneth Young (ed.), *The Diaries of Sir Robert Bruce Lockhart*, vol. II, *1939–65* (Macmillan, 1980), pp. 153–4.
25   R. H. Bruce Lockhart, *Comes the Reckoning* (Putnam, 1947), p. 171.
26   PRO, FO 898/317.

27 Ibid. Both this and the previous quotation appear in the 'as broadcast' script.

28 Ibid.

29 House of Lords, *Hansard* (4 August 1942), vol. 124, cols 181–4.

30 Ibid. The peers were the Marquess of Crewe, Lord Ailwyn and the Earl of Mansfield.

31 *News Chronicle* (31 July 1942).

32 Lockhart, *Comes the Reckoning*, p. 173. In this account of the incident, published in 1947, Sir Robert Bruce Lockhart does not reveal Dick's identity, calling him simply 'my expert'.

33 PRO, FO 898/317.

34 Ibid.

35 Ibid., FO 898/183.

36 Ibid.

37 Interview, Leonard Miall, 26 October 1988. Miall was then serving with the British Political Warfare Mission.

38 *Kurzwellensender Atlantik* was sired by Naval Intelligence, with whom Delmer had established close contacts. It first broadcast on 22 March 1943.

39 It was entertained, however, by at least one of his 'white' broadcasting contemporaries. Interview, Marius Goring, 30 November 1988.

40 *Diaries of Sir Robert Bruce Lockhart*, vol. II, p. 156.

41 PRO, FO 898/183.

42 Harold Macmillan, *War Diaries: Politics and War in the Mediterranean, January 1943–May 1945* (Macmillan, 1984), p. 125.

43 RHSC, 'The Making of Macmillan', *Sunday Telegraph* (9 February 1964).

44 Alistair Horne, *Macmillan 1894–1956* (Macmillan, 1988), p. 215.

45 Macmillan, *War Diaries*, pp. 168, 192. The entries are for 29 July and 25 August 1943.

46 RHSC, 'The Making of Macmillan'.

47 Ibid.

48 RHSC's essay in Daniel Lerner, *Sykewar: Psychological Warfare against Germany, D-Day to VE-Day* (George W. Stewart, New York, 1949), p. 345.

49 Susan Barnes, *Behind the Image* (Jonathan Cape, 1974), p. 48.

50 *Diaries of Sir Robert Bruce Lockhart*, vol. II, p. 274.

51 RHSC's essay, *Sykewar*, p. 346.

52 Ibid.

53 Delmer, *Black Boomerang*, p. 201.

54 RHSC, 'Black Prima Donna', *New Statesman* (9 November 1962). The article – a review of Sefton Delmer's book, *Black Boomerang* – is a paean of praise to Hugh Greene of the BBC.

55 RHSC's essay in Lerner, *Sykewar*, pp. 331–2. In a later lecture delivered at the RUSI in February 1952, RHSC estimated that the policy of unconditional surrender had 'postponed the end of the war

by a year' – giving on that occasion as the ground for his belief that 'it prevented the military conspiracy of 20 July being a success'. *RUSI Journal* (August 1952), p. 330.

56   Solly Zuckerman, *From Apes to Warlords* (Hamish Hamilton, 1978), p. 331.
57   Interview, Naomi Mitchison, 6 January 1988.
58   *Observer* (26 June 1945). The article by RHSC is headed 'AMG Policy in Germany is Failing'.
59   PRO, FO 371/C3220.

9   ZIONIST CONVERT

1   RHSC, letter to Tom Harrisson, 20 June 1973.
2   Kenneth Young (ed.), *The Diaries of Sir Robert Bruce Lockhart*, vol. II, *1939–65* (Macmillan, 1980), pp. 435–6.
3   Ibid.
4   RHSC's Introduction to George Hodgkinson, *Sent to Coventry* (Robert Maxwell, 1971), p. xxi.
5   Jack Jones, *Union Man* (Collins, 1986), p. 122.
6   Letter from Zita to RHSC dated 'V Day 1945'.
7   RHSC, 'A Midland Election', *New Statesman and Nation* (30 June 1945).
8   Ibid.
9   Diary note by RHSC, 11 August 1945.
10   Interview, Sir William Hayter, 21 December 1987.
11   *Diaries of Sir Robert Bruce Lockhart*, p. 477. This diary entry, recording a meeting with RHSC, is dated 1 August 1945.
12   Notes in pencil made by RHSC in a hardback notebook with a cover bearing the legend 'Minutes'.
13   RHSC, *Palestine Mission* (Hamish Hamilton, 1947), p. 11.
14   *Hansard*, vol. 415, cols 1927–34.
15   RHSC, *Palestine Mission*, p. 12.
16   Ibid.
17   Crossman Papers, Middle East Centre, St Antony's College, Oxford, DS 126.4. Letter from *Queen Mary* dated 'New Year's Day'.
18   Ibid.
19   Ibid.
20   Ibid. DS 126.4. Letter from *Queen Mary*, 'Sunday 30th' [December 1945].
21   RHSC, *Palestine Mission*, p. 43.
22   Ibid., p. 46.
23   Ibid., p. 57: 'Crossing the Atlantic we had our first experience of British Foreign Office organisation. No one had told the Cunard line who we were and some were given fourth priority.'

24 Ibid., p. 66.
25 Crossman Papers, St Antony's College, DS 126.4. Nine typed pages headed 'Diary'.
26 Susan Barnes, *Behind the Image* (Jonathan Cape, 1974), p. 47.
27 RHSC, *Palestine Mission*, p. 66.
28 'Report of the Anglo-American Committee of Enquiry Regarding the Problems of European Jewry and Palestine'; Cmd 6808, Preface.
29 RHSC, *Palestine Mission*, p. 110.
30 Crossman Papers, St Antony's College, DS 126.4. RHSC's diary entry for 6 March 1946.
31 Ibid.
32 Ibid., letter, '23rd' (March).
33 Ibid., letter, 'Tuesday 12th' (March).
34 Ibid., diary entry, '15th March'.
35 Ibid., undated letter probably written on 8 March 1946.
36 Ibid., letter, 'Friday'.
37 Ibid., undated letter evidently written after 10 March 1946, when RHSC visited Dr Weizmann at Rehovot.
38 By his friend, Meyer Weisgal, in *The Times* (24 April 1974). The article was headed, 'A Frank and Loyal Friend of Israel'.
39 Ibid.
40 *Sunday Times*, colour magazine (29 November 1970). The article is reproduced in Barnes, *Behind the Image*, pp. 40–59.
41 Crossman Papers, St Antony's College, DS 126.4. Copy of Memorandum sent to Hector McNeil.
42 Ibid.
43 'Report of the Anglo-American Committee', p. 2.
44 RHSC, letter to Zita dated 5 April 1946.
45 Crossman Papers, St Antony's College, DS 126.4
46 Ibid., letter, 16 March 1946.
47 RHSC, letter to Zita undated but on internal evidence written 8 April 1946.
48 RHSC, *Palestine Mission*, p. 199.
49 Crossman Papers, St Antony's College, DS 126.4.
50 Ibid.
51 *Hansard* (1 July 1946), vol. 424, cols 194–9. RHSC spoke again on the same subject on 31 July, *Hansard*, vol. 426, cols 1007–18.
52 The lecture was delivered on 13 June 1946. Its title was simply 'The Palestine Report'. Lord Astor's introduction was not helpful – his concluding chairman's remark being that 'Britain alone could not bear the burden.'
53 Crossman Papers, St Antony's College, DS 126.4. The letters were from Judge J. C. Hutcheson Jr (the American chairman) and Ambassador William Phillips. They are dated respectively 16 August 1946 and 26 August 1946.
54 Ibid. The letter from Rehovot is dated 22 May 1946.

55 Ibid., letter from the School of Mathematics at Princeton, 3 June 1946.
56 When Dick's friend, the economic journalist, Nicholas Davenport sent him a draft of his memoirs in February 1974 the one passage to which Dick took exception was that arising from the accusation that he had never been consistent on anything. He replied rather sharply: 'I appreciated always that my battle with Bevin and my support of Israel was rather a bore to you. But even so you might have been willing to admit in print that, in taking the line I did, I forfeited any chance of a job with the Attlee Government and made myself extremely unpopular with the Establishment.' Crossman Papers, Modern Records Centre, University of Warwick Library, MSS. 154/3.

10   BACKBENCH REBEL

1 *Daily Herald* (27 October 1945).
2 *Labour Party Conference Report* (1946), pp. 160–1.
3 Ibid., pp. 164–5.
4 *Hansard* (17 November 1954), vol. 533, col. 486. The accusation, surprisingly, came from the moderate-minded Conservative MP for Kelvingrove, Walter Elliot.
5 *Tribune* (12 April 1974). The description of the debate occurs in Michael Foot's posthumous tribute to RHSC entitled 'The Left Will Not Forget'.
6 *New Statesman and Nation* (14 September 1946).
7 *Jewish Standard* (12 July 1946).
8 *Hansard* (31 July 1946), vol. 426, cols 1017–18.
9 Interview, Lord Cudlipp, 16 March 1988. Generously, Hugh Cudlipp insisted that the credit for RHSC's original recruitment belonged to Cecil King.
10 Diary entry for 25 October 1946.
11 *Washington Daily News* (19 November 1946). The phrase was the heading to a column about RHSC written by Richard Hollander.
12 Diary entry for 29 October 1946.
13 *Sunday Pictorial* (10 November 1946).
14 Kenneth Harris, *Attlee* (Weidenfeld & Nicolson, 1982), pp. 300–1.
15 Typed letter on House of Commons notepaper from RHSC to Zita, then in New Haven, Connecticut.
16 Ibid.
17 Ibid.
18 *Hansard* (18 November 1946), vol. 430, col. 527.
19 Ibid., col. 577.
20 Ibid., col. 590. The two ILP MPs were John McGovern and Campbell Stephen.

21 *The Times* put the figure for deliberate abstentions at 122; *Tribune*, remarkably, as low as 82.
22 Letter from RHSC to C. D. Jackson dated 20 February 1947.
23 Ibid.
24 *Hansard* (1 April 1947), vol. 435, col. 1869.
25 No announcement was made to the Commons. The Government simply put down its amendment on the Order Paper the day the House rose for the Easter recess.
26 e.g. the *Manchester Guardian* (5 April 1947) and the *Daily Telegraph* (10 April 1947).
27 The pamphlet was published on 1 May 1947 by the *New Statesman* at one shilling. 'Our Red Paper' is the authors' own description of it in their foreword, 'How This Book Came About'.
28 Ian Mikardo, *Back-bencher* (Weidenfeld & Nicolson, 1988), p. 110.
29 Michael Straight, *After Long Silence* (Collins, 1983), p. 102.
30 Undated memo written by Kingsley Martin, presumably some time in the 1950s, arguing the case against RHSC ever being allowed to become editor of the *New Statesman*.
31 *Time and Tide* (19 April 1947).
32 *Saturday Evening Post* (3 January 1948). The article, in which RHSC's side of the story appears, is entitled 'Britain's Jeering Section' and bears the byline of Ernest O. Hauser.
33 RHSC's letter to C. D. Jackson, 22 April 1947.
34 *Labour Party Conference Report* (1947), p. 106.
35 Ibid., p. 141.
36 Ibid., p. 164.
37 Ibid., p. 179.
38 *New Statesman and Nation* (7 June 1947).
39 *Birmingham Post* (28 May 1947).
40 Alan Bullock, *Ernest Bevin: Foreign Secretary 1945–1951* (Heinemann, 1983), p. 78.
41 RHSC, *A Nation Reborn* (Hamish Hamilton, 1960), p. 70.
42 Conversation with the author 1970. Bullock, *Ernest Bevin*, dates a version of this story to the 1946 Party Conference but, given Bevin's speech, that can hardly be correct.
43 RHSC, letter to C. D. Jackson, 24 May 1947.
44 *New Statesman and Nation* (25 October 1947).
45 But see *Hansard* (11 December 1947), vol. 445, cols 1239–40. In an adjournment debate opened by the Colonial Secretary, Arthur Creech Jones, the temptation to count the cost of imposing 'a non-policy' in Palestine proved too strong to resist. RHSC put it at £200 million.
46 *Hansard* (23 January 1948), vol. 466, col. 566.
47 RHSC, interview with C. H. Rolph, 3 July 1971.
48 *Manchester Guardian* (19 March 1948).
49 RHSC, interview with C. H. Rolph.
50 RHSC (ed.) *The God that Failed* (Hamish Hamilton, 1950), p. 7.

51 Ibid.
52 Letter to RHSC from Councillor A. J. Waugh, Secretary of the Coventry East constituency, 29 May 1948, preserved in RHSC's 'Autobiography' file.
53 *Coventry Tribune* (24 January 1948).
54 RHSC, interview with C. H. Rolph.
55 *Coventry Standard* (11 September 1948). Article entitled 'Manifold Duties of an MP's Wife'.
56 RHSC, interview with C. H. Rolph. Kingsley Martin is quoted in the transcript as having said: 'I've left Dick in charge *once* and he's proved he is just a politician trying to use the paper for his purposes.'
57 Crossman's Column, *Sunday Pictorial* (9 February 1949).
58 Ibid. (16 February 1949). The article appeared as the newspaper's 'splash' story.
59 Ibid.
60 'Notes of the Week', *The Economist* (29 January 1949).
61 *Sunday Pictorial* (23 January 1949).
62 *Hansard* (26 January 1949), vol. 460, col. 991.
63 'The Week in Parliament', *News of the World* (30 January 1949).
64 *Sheffield Telegraph* (31 January 1949).
65 *Tribune* (4 February 1949). The comment was included in a column written by RHSC's fellow Labour MP, J. P. W. Mallalieu.
66 *Daily Telegraph* (27 January 1949). News story headed 'Position of Mr Bevin Shaken'.
67 *Coventry Evening Telegraph* (21 January 1949).
68 Ibid. (31 January 1949). News story headed 'Mr Crossman Explains His Trips Abroad'.
69 Crossman's Column, *Sunday Pictorial* (3 April 1949).
70 Ibid.
71 *Hansard* (6 April 1949), vol. 463, cols 2059–111.
72 RHSC, 'Thoughts before Blackpool', *New Statesman and Nation* (28 May 1949).
73 Crossman's Column, 'How to Defeat the Coming Crisis', *Sunday Pictorial* (26 June 1949).
74 Crossman's Column, *Sunday Pictorial* (29 April 1949).
75 Crossman's Column, *Sunday Pictorial* (31 July 1949).
76 *Sunday Dispatch* (15 January 1950) and *Sunday Chronicle* (15 January 1950).
77 London Letter, *Manchester Guardian* (16 January 1950).
78 The pamphlet was again published by the *New Statesman*. It was launched on 12 January 1950 at 6d.
79 *Daily Worker* (12 January 1950).
80 Crossman's Column, *Sunday Pictorial* (26 February 1950).
81 Ibid.
82 Typed copy of original letter preserved in RHSC's 'Autobiography' file.

83 Typed copy of original letter dated 27 March 1950 preserved in RHSC's 'Autobiography' file.

84 Ibid.

85 c.f. Anthony Crosland, *Can Labour Win?* (Fabian Society, 1960), p. 14. 'What is damaging is the appalling uncertainty as to what the Party really wants to nationalise, and the constant vague threat that it is thought to offer to the whole of private industry.'

86 Typed copy of letter, 27 March 1950, preserved in RHSC's 'Autobiography' file.

87 Iain Hamilton, *Koestler* (Secker & Warburg, 1982), pp. 291–2.

88 *Hansard* (24 June 1950), vol. 476, col. 2045.

89 *The Times* (31 July 1950). RHSC replied on 2 August 1950.

90 *Hansard* (27 July 1950), vol. 478, col. 723.

91 Ibid. (14 September 1950), vol. 478, col. 1263.

92 Crossman's Column, *Sunday Pictorial* (29 April 1951).

93 Philip M. Williams (ed.), *The Diary of Hugh Gaitskell 1945–56* (Jonathan Cape, 1983), p. 332.

11   INDEPENDENT BEVANITE

1 Crossman's Column, *Sunday Pictorial* (29 April 1951).

2 *Truth* (29 June 1951). RHSC's remark is quoted in an article by J.R. Bevins headed 'A Socialist Awakes'.

3 These included RHSC. 'Mr Churchill has achieved office without effective power': Crossman's Column, *Sunday Pictorial* (28 October 1951).

4 *Manchester Guardian* (29 October 1951).

5 RHSC, *The Backbench Diaries of Richard Crossman*, ed. Janet Morgan (Hamish Hamilton/Jonathan Cape, 1981), p. 31. Diary entry for 6 November 1951.

6 *New Fabian Essays*, Introduction by Margaret Cole and R. H. S. Crossman (Turnstile Press, 1952).

7 Ibid., Introduction to the third impression by RHSC (Dent, 1970).

8 *Hansard* (5 March 1952), vol. 497, col. 482.

9 *Backbench Diaries*, p. 85. Entry for 5 March 1952.

10 Ibid., p. 410. Entry for 24 March 1955.

11 Ibid., p. 328. Entry for 11 March 1954.

12 *Birmingham Post* (20 June 1951). The numbers had already gone up to twenty-nine by the time of the October 1951 general election.

13 *Coventry Evening Telegraph* (29 March 1952). The story appeared under the headline 'Bevanite Answers by Mr Crossman'.

14 *Backbench Diaries*, pp. 90–1. Entry for 10 March 1952.

15 *Observer* (9 March 1952).

16 *Daily Express* (8 March 1952).

17 Ibid. (13 May 1951). The front-page story was headed 'Bevan 13 form the Bevan Party'.

18 BBC WAC, Caversham. Talks, Crossman, Richard H. S., 1949–52, File 4. The author of the memo was Archie Gordon, who later became the Marquess of Aberdeen.

19 Crossman Papers, Modern Records Centre, University of Warwick Library, MSS. 154/3/LPO.

20 *Sunday Mercury*, Birmingham (28 October 1951).

21 See p. 57 above.

22 *Backbench Diaries*, p. 120. Entry for 23 July 1952.

23 Interview, Bishop George Reindorp, 12 February 1989. George Reindorp was at the time vicar of St Stephen's, Rochester Row.

24 Ibid.

25 *Backbench Diaries*, p. 126. Entry for 23 July 1952.

26 Butler Papers, Trinity College, Cambridge, G24.

27 *Backbench Diaries*, p. 126. Entry for 8 August 1952.

28 Interview, Carrie Hodgkinson, 12 April 1988.

29 *Backbench Diaries*, p. 136. Entry for 8 August 1952. 'Her reaction was that in that case I wouldn't be Foreign Secretary and that anyway there would be too much entertaining for her.'

30 RHSC's 'Autobiography' file.

31 *Backbench Diaries*, p. 151. Entry for 1 October 1952.

32 *Labour Party Conference Report* (1952), p. 107.

33 *Evening Standard* (1 October 1952).

34 Crossman's Column, *Sunday Pictorial* (5 October 1952).

35 *Backbench Diaries*, p. 152. Entry for 1 October 1952.

36 *Labour Party Conference Report* (1957), pp. 119–24.

37 *Daily Herald* (14 October 1952). Gaitskell's article carried the headline 'Bevanism – a Dangerous Game'.

38 Ibid.

39 RHSC's 'Autobiography' file. Letter dated 20 October 1952.

40 Ibid. Letter from Hugh Gaitskell dated 23 October 1952.

41 *Sunday Pictorial* (11 January 1953). For once his report appeared not as 'Crossman's Column' but as a news story headed 'Neguib Says "Hurry up Mr Eden".'

42 RHSC's articles appeared on 17 and 24 January 1953, the first called 'Egypt's Nine Just Men', the second 'Why We Must Evacuate Suez'.

43 RHSC's 'Autobiography' file. The letter from Sadat is dated 19 February 1953 and that from Nasser 16 April 1953.

44 *Backbench Diaries*, p. 195. Entry for 20 January 1953.

45 *Backbench Diaries*, pp. 248, 259. Entries for 24 June 1953 and 9 November 1953.

46 Ibid., pp. 218–20. Entry for 22 April 1952.

47 *Backbench Diaries*, p. 219.

48 Interview, James Greene, 26 September 1988.

49 Ibid.

50 Ibid. The delights of 'fresh blue trout' are also mentioned by RHSC in a 'Salzburg Diary' he contributed from holiday to the *New Statesman and Nation* (29 August 1953).

51 *Backbench Diaries,* p. 260. Entry for 9 September 1953.

52 'A Newspaper Tells Its Secrets – Nothing that Shocked Has Been Left Out', *Sunday Pictorial* (6 September 1953).

53 *Hansard* (17 December 1953), vol. 522, cols. 659–73.

54 *Backbench Diaries*, p. 282. Entry for 18 December 1953.

55 Ibid., p. 283.

56 'Report on Mau Mau' (23 January 1954) and 'What Went Wrong in Uganda?' (6 February 1954).

57 *Daily Express* (9 January 1954).

58 *Time and Tide* (2 January 1954). The piece was headed 'Crossman for Quitting' and appeared under the byline of the well-known right-wing journalist, John Connell.

59 *Backbench Diaries*, p. 326. Entry for 6 May 1954. RHSC at least had the grace to record that 'Anne was a bit upset'.

60 *Hansard* (13 April 1954), vol. 526, col. 971. Denis Healey, in a column he wrote at the time for the *New Republic*, described Bevan as having intervened 'red as a turkey-cock and in a voice shrill with emotion'.

61 In addition to RHSC's own *Backbench Diaries*, detailed accounts of this episode are given in Philip M. Williams, *Hugh Gaitskell* (Jonathan Cape, 1979) and Michael Foot, *Aneurin Bevan 1945–1960* (Davis-Poynter, 1973).

62 *Backbench Diaries*, p. 313. Entry for 21 April 1954.

63 Ibid. 'He was obviously extremely, if coldly, angry.'

64 *New Statesman and Nation* (24 April 1954). RHSC's admission to having written this leader appears in his *Backbench Diaries*, p. 317. Entry for 28 April 1954.

65 Crossman's Column, *Sunday Pictorial* (18 April 1954).

66 Both phrases appear in Hugh Dalton, *High Tide and After: Memoirs 1945–60* (Muller, 1962), pp. 409, 369.

67 RHSC's 'Autobiography' file. The letter to Harold Wilson is dated 22 April 1952. A full version of it appears in *Backbench Diaries*, pp. 315–17.

68 Williams, *Hugh Gaitskell*, p. 327.

69 Crossman's Column, *Sunday Pictorial* (2 May 1954).

70 *Backbench Diaries*, pp. 340–1. Entry for 13 August 1954.

71 'Crossman Cross-examined', *Sunday Pictorial* (26 September 1954).

72 RHSC wrote two articles in the *New Statesman and Nation* on the Oppenheimer Case – the first appearing on 23 October and the second on 30 October 1954.

73 *Backbench Diaries*, p. 350. Entry for 1 October 1954. The claim is made there that Nye Bevan shared the same view.

74 *Labour Party Conference Report* (1954), p. 113. The delegate who put RHSC right was Mrs L. Tweed from Cambridge.

75 *Backbench Diaries*, p. 352. Entry for 1 October 1954.

12   TEMPORARY GAITSKELLITE

1 *Observer* (5 December 1954). The item appeared in the paper's 'Pendennis' gossip column.

2 RHSC, *The Backbench Diaries of Richard Crossman*, ed. Janet Morgan (Hamish Hamilton/Jonathan Cape, 1981), p. 375. Entry for 9 December 1954.

3 *New Statesman* (22 October 1960). The leading article that week – headed 'The *Observer* in Trouble' – recalled 'a libellous paragraph' that the *Observer* had printed six years earlier.

4 *Observer* (12 December 1954). The original paragraph had mischievously characterised John Freeman as 'the sort of man who would add tone to any good regimental mess'.

5 *New Statesman and Nation* (26 February 1955). The supplement was called 'The Dilemma of the H-bomb'. RHSC took the same line in Crossman's Column, *Sunday Pictorial* (20 February 1955).

6 *New Statesman and Nation* (26 February 1955).

7 *Backbench Diaries*, p. 386. Entry for 22 February 1955. This was, of course, the view to which Bevan reverted with his 'naked into the Conference chamber' speech at Brighton in 1957.

8 Ibid., p. 387.

9 'American Bases in Britain', *Tribune* (26 February 1955). Aneurin Bevan cited the H-bomb as the reason why Britain was 'no longer defensible with or without the presence of American bases'.

10 *Hansard* (2 March 1955), vol. 537, col. 2122. The speech, however, was mainly notable to the next morning's newspapers for bringing Churchill to his feet to acknowledge that he had had a stroke in 1953.

11 Ibid., col. 2176.

12 The remark was not recorded in *Hansard*. It is, however, quoted by his official biographer: Michael Foot, *Aneurin Bevan 1945–60* (Davis-Poynter, 1973), p. 464.

13 *Backbench Diaries*, p. 393. Entry for 3 March 1955.

14 Ibid., p. 395.

15 *Tribune* (4 March 1955). The piece under the rubric 'Speaking for Myself' was headed 'Dick Crossman's Bombshell' and was signed by the editor, Robert J. Edwards, later to become editor of the *Daily Express*.

16 *Daily Express* (5 March 1955). The story, 'There *may* be two Labour Parties', was written by Derek Marks, who ten years later also became the paper's editor.

17 *Coventry Evening Telegraph* (5 March 1955). The story was 'clarified' in the same paper two days later: 'Statement on position of Mr Crossman', *Coventry Evening Telegraph* (7 March 1955).

18   *Backbench Diaries*, pp. 399–400. Entry for 15 March 1955. The two
     colleagues who accompanied him were Barbara Castle and Anthony
     Greenwood.
19   Crossman's Column, *Sunday Pictorial* (6 March 1955), headed
     'Bevan – His Own Worst Enemy'.
20   *Backbench Diaries*, p. 389. Entry for 23 February 1955.
21   Ibid., pp. 409–11. Entry for 24 March 1955.
22   *Daily Express* (19 March 1955). The election actually took place on
     26 May 1955.
23   RHSC's 'Autobiography' file. There is no record of any response
     from Bevan.
24   *Backbench Diaries*, p. 419. Entry for 19 April 1955.
25   Ibid. Entry for 3 May 1955.
26   Ibid., p. 420.
27   RHSC's letter to Gilbert Baker, 2 June 1955, 'Autobiography' file.
28   RHSC's letter to David Butler, 7 June 1955, 'Autobiography' file.
29   RHSC's letter to H. R. Underhill, then the Labour Party regional
     organiser in Birmingham, 2 June 1955, and marked 'Private and
     Confidential', 'Autobiography' file.
30   RHSC's letter to Gilbert Baker, 2 June 1955, 'Autobiography' file.
31   Ibid.
32   *Backbench Diaries*, p. 433. Entry for 30 June 1955.
33   Ibid., p. 434. Entry for 15 July 1955.
34   Interview, Paul Johnson, 25 February 1989.
35   *Backbench Diaries*, p. 435. Entry for 15 July 1955.
36   Ibid., p. 436.
37   Undated memo written by Kingsley Martin. It was discovered among
     Martin's papers by his biographer, C. H. Rolph.
38   RHSC's 'Autobiography' file. The letter was signed 'Yours ever,
     John'.
39   Ibid. The letter, significantly or not, was signed 'Yours, Kingsley
     Martin'.
40   Ibid. John Roberts himself left the paper some eighteen months
     later.
41   Ibid. The arrangement had been that RHSC should stay until John
     Freeman's holiday was over.
42   *Backbench Diaries*, p. 439. There is no date for this entry and the
     original MS of this section of the *Diaries* appears to be lost.
43   RHSC's 'Autobiography' file. The letter was written from the old
     Mirror headquarters, Geraldine House, Fetter Lane, EC4.
44   *Daily Mirror* (20 September 1955).
45   *Backbench Diaries*, p. 44. Entry for 23 September 1955.
46   'Tory Fruits of Victory Begin to Go Sour', *Daily Mirror* (10 October
     1955).
47   *Manchester Guardian* (14 October 1955). The story was written by its
     political correspondent, Francis Boyd.

48　*Truth* (14 October 1955). The report was still, however, accurately entitled 'Attlee's Last Conference'.

49　*Tribune* (16 December 1955).

50　'Now Bevan Backs Herbert Morrison', *Daily Mirror* (10 December 1955).

51　*Tribune* (16 December 1955). Foot's best phrase lay in his reference to Dick and the *Mirror* as 'the loudest bagpipe on the squeaking train'.

52　Ibid. (30 December 1955). RHSC's own letter – basically a refutation of the charge that he had ever been part of a concerted *Mirror* campaign to get rid of Attlee – appeared on the previous page.

53　Philip M. Williams, *Hugh Gaitskell* (Jonathan Cape, 1979), p. 369.

54　Ibid.

55　*Backbench Diaries*, p. 466. Entry for 19 January 1956.

56　*Hansard* (24 January 1956), vol. 548, col. 103. The row rumbled on, particularly in Scottish newspapers, for some weeks.

57　*Backbench Diaries*, p. 467. Entry for 19 January 1956.

58　'The New Despotism' and 'The Party Oligarchies', *New Statesman and Nation* (14 and 21 August 1954).

59　*The Economist* (11 February 1956).

60　*Banbury Guardian* (21 May 1956).

61　*Backbench Diaries*, p. 408. Entry for 21 March 1956.

62　*Hansard* (13 May 1956), vol. 552, cols 1776–82. The *Daily Telegraph* called it 'by far the best speech of the evening' and the *Sunday Times* 'the most brilliant contribution to the debate'.

63　Ibid. (8 June 1956), vol. 553, cols 1499–1513. The *Manchester Guardian* devoted a leading article to the themes arising out of this speech – 'Controlling Ministers' (9 June 1956).

64　*Observer* (26 June 1960). The remark appeared in an 'Observer Profile'.

65　*Hansard* (12 September 1956), vol. 558, cols 84–97.

66　*The Times* (21 September 1956).

67　*Coventry Evening Telegraph* (22 September 1956).

68　Ibid.

69　*Backbench Diaries*, p. 517. Entry for 28 September 1956.

70　Ibid., p. 524. Entry for 26 October 1956.

71　Ibid.

72　Ibid., p. 521.

73　*Daily Telegraph* (23 October 1956).

74　*Hansard* (13 November 1956), vol. 560, cols 858–62.

75　e.g. 'Eden's Gamble on Quick Success Can Lead Only to Disaster', *Daily Mirror* (3 November 1956). RHSC's column always appeared with its central message distilled in bold type above the body of the text.

76　*Backbench Diaries*, p. 554.

77　Ibid., p. 556. Entry for 18 December 1956.

78 Ibid., p. 566. Entry for 15 January 1957.

79 Ibid., p. 585. Entry for 3 May 1957.

80 Interview, Lord Jay, 20 January 1988.

81 *Hansard* (17 April 1957), vol. 568, cols 1975–87.

82 *Spectator* (1 March 1953).

83 Crossman Papers, Modern Records Centre, University of Warwick Library, MSS.154/3/SPL. Letter dated 5 March 1957 and from initials at the top dictated by Arnold Goodman.

84 *Backbench Diaries*, p. 631. Entry for 22 November 1957.

85 Ibid., p. 574. Entry for 14 February 1957.

86 Crossman Papers, Modern Records Centre, University of Warwick Library, MSS.154/3/SPL. As late as July RHSC wrote to Arnold Goodman: 'Personally I would be perfectly content with an apology as I stated from the first.'

87 *Backbench Diaries*, p. 633. Entry for 22 November 1957.

88 *The Times* (23 November 1957).

89 *Backbench Diaries*, p. 632. Entry for 22 November 1957. Alan Watkins argues persuasively in *A Slight Case of Libel* (Duckworth, 1990) that this remark was intended to refer only to 'the risk' the plaintiffs had taken in turning down the settlement offer the defendants had made to them on the opening day of the trial.

90 *Backbench Diaries*, p. 603. Entry for 13 September 1957.

91 *Manchester Guardian* (4 July 1957). The story by its Labour Correspondent, John Cole, was headed 'TUC Warns Labour'.

92 *Daily Mirror* (5 July 1957).

93 RHSC's address to Westminster School Political and Literary Society, 12 December 1949. The author was present.

94 *Daily Mirror* (12 July 1957).

95 *Manchester Guardian* (17 July 1957).

96 *Manchester Guardian* (25 July 1957). The report claimed that RHSC 'admitted that his article was unwise'.

97 *Sunday Times* (21 July 1957). The comment appeared in a column under the by-line 'A Student of Politics' – in fact the paper's political correspondent, James Margach.

98 *Backbench Diaries*, p. 616. Entry for 4 October 1957.

99 Ibid.

100 *Labour Party Conference Report* (1957), pp. 119–24.

101 *Backbench Diaries*, p. 616. Entry for 4 October 1957.

102 *The Times* (2 October 1957). The story was written by its political correspondent, David Wood.

103 *Backbench Diaries*, p. 616. Entry for 4 October 1957.

104 Ibid., p. 622. Entry for 24 October 1957.

105 Ibid., pp. 637–8n. All RHSC had done in his *Mirror* column of 6 November 1957 was to suggest that Antony Head would prove a more formidable opponent for his successor as Defence Minister, Duncan Sandys, than his Labour 'Shadow' George Brown.

106 *Sunday Express* (17 November 1957).
107 *Daily Mirror* (3 December 1957).
108 *Daily Mirror* (13 December 1957).
109 Interview, Anne Crossman, 9 February 1989.
110 *Backbench Diaries*, pp. 646–7. Entry for 20 December 1957.
111 *Hansard*, vol. 595, cols 298–310.
112 *Backbench Diaries*, p. 722. Entry for 14 November 1958.
113 Ibid., p. 714. Entry for 8 October 1958.
114 *Labour Party Conference Report* (1958), pp. 133–6.
115 e.g. *News Chronicle* (26 October 1958).
116 *Backbench Diaries*, p. 724. Entry for 27 November 1958.
117 This trip produced eight columns in the *Daily Mirror* published
     between 22 August and 19 September 1958. RHSC subsequently
     published a more considered piece in the *New Statesman* (27 Septem-
     ber 1958) which some months later drew a magisterial rebuke from
     the noted Cambridge Sinologist, Joseph Needham (*New Statesman*,
     31 January 1959).
118 Five columns in the *Mirror* appeared between 7 and 20 January 1959.
119 *Evening Standard* (30 December 1958). The piece, 'Wonders of
     Westminster', was written by the paper's political correspondent,
     George Hutchinson.
120 Crossman Papers, Modern Records Centre, University of Warwick
     Library, MSS.154/BD/8. The letter is dated 20 February 1959.
121 Ibid. Gaitskell's letter is dated 23 February 1959.
122 *Backbench Diaries*, p. 771. Entry for 26 August 1959.
123 Ibid., p. 772. Entry for 15 September 1959.
124 Ibid., p. 780. Entry for 24 September 1959.
125 Ibid., p. 781. Entry for 28 September 1959.
126 *The Times* (29 September 1959).
127 *Backbench Diaries*, p. 785. Entry for 5 October 1959.
128 Ibid., p. 786. Entry for 9 October 1959.
129 *New Statesman* (17 October 1959). The article was headed 'The
     Stimulus of Defeat' and went on to develop a case for the Party
     leader being allowed to nominate his own Shadow Cabinet.

13   ROGUE ELEPHANT

1 RHSC, *The Backbench Diaries of Richard Crossman*, ed. Janet
   Morgan (Hamish Hamilton/Jonathan Cape, 1981), p. 791. Entry for
   19 October 1959.
2 Interview, Lord Jay, 20 January 1988. The story of the failed
   manœuvre also surfaced in the *Sunday Times* (25 October 1959 – 'Who
   Are the Jay-walkers?' by A Student of Politics).
3 *Backbench Diaries*, p. 797. Entry for 27 October 1959.

4   Letter from RHSC to Herbert Bowden, 17 November 1959, 'Autobiography' file.
5   RHSC's 'Autobiography' file.
6   Ibid. Gaitskell's reply was dated 18 November 1959.
7   Philip M. Williams, *Hugh Gaitskell* (Jonathan Cape, 1979), p. 352.
8   *Backbench Diaries*, p. 803. Entry for 9 December 1959.
9   *Coventry Evening Telegraph* (30 January 1960). The somewhat misleading heading to the story was 'Postpone Debate on State Control – Mr Crossman'.
10 *Observer* (31 January 1960). Its political column, written as usual by Hugh Massingham disguised under the byline 'Our Political Correspondent', carried the headline 'A Breather for Clause Four'. A much harsher view, plainly inspired by the Gaitskell camp, appeared in that same day's *Reynolds News* in a column written by its political correspondent, Ivan Yates.
11 *Guardian* (15 February 1960).
12 *Backbench Diaries*, p. 813. Entry for 26 February 1960.
13 RHSC's 'Autobiography' file.
14 Ibid.
15 Ibid. This letter – also marked 'Personal' – is dated 9 March 1960.
16 *Topic* (6 October 1961). The cover story in this early version of a British news magazine expressly alludes to RHSC's resentment of 'Gaitskell's strangely cavalier treatment of him'.
17 *Hansard* (22 January 1963), vol. 670, col. 48. Grimond made the remark in his Commons tribute to Gaitskell after the Labour leader's death.
18 *Backbench Diaries*, p. 815. Entry for 26 February 1960.
19 *Hansard* (1 March 1960), vol. 618, cols 1058–67.
20 *Backbench Diaries*, p. 818. Entry for 2 March 1960.
21 Ibid.
22 Ibid., p. 825. Entry for 18 March 1960.
23 *The Times* (15 March 1960).
24 *Guardian* (15 March 1960).
25 *Daily Express* (15 March 1960).
26 Editorial note, 'Exit Mr Crossman', *The Economist* (19 March 1960).
27 *Time and Tide* (11 June 1960). The remark is quoted in a profile of RHSC entitled 'Political Problem Child'.
28 *Hansard* (13 April 1960), vol. 621, cols 1265–6. The announcement was made in a Commons statement by the Defence Minister, Harold Watkinson.
29 One provincial newspaper, the *Western Daily Press* (26 May 1960) actually carried the headline 'Crossman Back in Labour Defence Fold' – which, though an exaggeration, was perhaps a pardonable one. There were also cartoons by Illingworth and Vicky (*Daily Mail* and *Evening Standard*, 27 May 1960) both drawn at Gaitskell's expense.

30 *Backbench Diaries*, p. 870. Entry for 1 September 1960.
31 *Spectator* (18 March 1960).
32 *Backbench Diaries*, p. 813. Entry for 26 February 1960. RHSC had obviously been shown a proof of Crosland's article in advance.
33 Fabian Tract 325 (June 1960).
34 The pamphlet was reviewed in both papers on 7 June 1960. Less surprisingly, the adjective 'brilliant' was also used by Bernard Crick in a signed review in the *New Statesman* (18 June 1960).
35 *Spectator* (17 June 1960). Jenkins's lengthy review was headed 'The Fallacies of Mr Crossman'. The pamphlet had also been attacked by Bernard Levin in his political column the previous week.
36 Letter, 12 July 1960, RHSC's 'Autobiography' file.
37 *Isis* (15 June 1960).
38 Anthony Crosland, *Can Labour Win?*, Fabian Tract 324 (May 1960).
39 *Backbench Diaries*, p. 829. Entry for 22 March 1960.
40 *New Statesman* (6 August 1960).
41 *Backbench Diaries*, p. 866. Entry for 30 August 1960.
42 Transcription of party political broadcast delivered on the BBC's Light Programme, 11 October 1960.
43 RHSC's letter to Thomas Balogh in India, 13 December 1960, 'Autobiography' file.
44 *Observer* (30 October 1960).
45 RHSC's 'Autobiography' file.
46 Ibid.
47 *Backbench Diaries*, p. 897. Entry for 3 November 1960. RHSC's private forecast of the result was astonishingly accurate – 'Harold will get 80 votes and Hugh 160'.
48 RHSC's 'Autobiography' file. RHSC replied on 2 November 1960, somewhat defiantly declaring: 'I think I disapprove of Hugh's behaviour more than that of anyone else's behaviour except Ernest Bevin's in Palestine.'
49 Ibid., RHSC's letter to Sam Watson.
50 *Sunday Times* (18 December 1960). The phrase appeared in the regular weekly column by 'A Student of Politics'.
51 *Backbench Diaries*, p. 884. Entry for 18 October 1960. RHSC there quotes Gaitskell as saying: 'I see you are against me, not on my side.'
52 RHSC's letter to Thomas Balogh, 13 December 1960, 'Autobiography' file.
53 RHSC's letter to Thomas Balogh, 3 November 1960, ibid.
54 *Daily Mirror* (22 December 1960). The story was headed 'Ban on Crossman'.
55 RHSC's letter to Frank Longford (previously Pakenham), 6 January 1961.
56 RHSC's letter to Thomas Balogh, 13 December 1960.
57 RHSC's letter to Frank Longford, 6 January 1961.

58 RHSC's original letter to the Public Trustee does not survive but the latter's response (3 January 1961) records its receipt. To the Public Trustee's own letter RHSC replied: 'It puts everything in an entirely different light.' Crossman Papers, Modern Records Centre, University of Warwick Library, MSS.154/3/PER. Letter, 6 January 1961.

59 The fact that they, too, were excluded from their grandmother's will was duly noted by the Press when the will was published – e.g. *Evening News* (13 March 1961).

60 RHSC's letter to Frank Longford, 6 January 1961. The occasion for the letter was a note of sympathy from Longford on hearing of Lady Crossman's death.

61 *Backbench Diaries*, p. 900. Entry for 23 November 1960.

62 These were on the Army and Air Force Bill on 2 February 1961 (*Hansard*, vol. 633, cols 1245–61) and in the 1961 Defence White Paper Debate on 28 February 1961 (*Hansard*, vol. 635, cols 1431–8).

63 *Backbench Diaries*, p. 900. Entry for 23 November 1960.

64 Ibid., p. 910. Entry for 14 December 1960.

65 The quotations are taken from RHSC's handout of his speech delivered at Transport Hall, Cardiff on 25 February 1961.

66 *Backbench Diaries*, p. 938. Entry for 3 March 1961.

67 Ibid., p. 950. Entry for 14 June 1961.

68 Ibid., p. 952. Entry for 28 June 1961.

69 *Labour Party Conference Report* (1961), pp. 82–4.

70 Ibid., p. 252.

71 Letter to the author from Alastair Hetherington, 12 August 1989.

72 *Backbench Diaries*, p. 960. Entry for 28 November 1961.

73 Two were on the Army Reserve Bill and one on the Christmas adjournment. They are to be found, respectively, in *Hansard* (27 November 1961), vol. 650, cols 95–105; (19 December 1961), vol. 651, cols 1238–43; (20 December 1961), vol. 651, cols 1382–91.

74 RHSC's Introduction to *The Diaries of a Cabinet Minister*, vol. I, ed. Janet Morgan (Hamish Hamilton/Jonathan Cape, 1975).

75 *Coventry Evening Telegraph* (16 May 1962). The story was headed 'MPs Cheer Mr Crossman'.

76 *Labour Party Conference Report* (1962), pp. 101–6. RHSC's speech was heavily praised in the daily briefing issued at the conference by the *New Left Review*.

77 Baroness Gaitskell, interview with the author, 13 June 1979.

14 THE GATES OF PARADISE

1 RHSC's 'Left of Centre' column, *Guardian* (11 January 1963).

2 *Sunday Telegraph* (20 January 1963). The article on the paper's leader page was headed 'Inner Strength of Hugh Gaitskell'.

3   Ibid.

4   RHSC, *The Diaries of a Cabinet Minister*, ed. Janet Morgan (Hamish Hamilton/Jonathan Cape, 1975), vol. 1, p. 11.

5   RHSC, *The Backbench Diaries of Richard Crossman*, ed. Janet Morgan (Hamish Hamilton/Jonathan Cape, 1981), p. 972. Entry for 8 February 1963.

6   Ibid., p. 969.

7   Anthony Howard and Richard West, *The Making of the Prime Minister* (Jonathan Cape, 1965), p. 17.

8   RHSC's 'Left of Centre' column, *Guardian* (15 February 1963).

9   *Guardian* (16 February 1963).

10 *Daily Herald* (17 February 1963).

11 Notebook, *Spectator* (22 March 1963).

12 *Coventry Evening Telegraph* (22 February 1963). The news item was headed, 'Mr Crossman's New Role "After Persuasion" '.

13 *Backbench Diaries*, p. 975. Entry for 12 February 1963.

14 RHSC's 'Autobiography' file. Mitchison's handwritten letter is dated 21 February 1963.

15 Ibid. RHSC's typewritten letter is dated 25 February 1963.

16 *Backbench Diaries*, p. 987. Entry for 5 March 1963.

17 Ibid., p. 972. Entry for 8 February 1963.

18 *The Times* (4 June 1963).

19 *Sunday Times* (21 July 1963).

20 RHSC's 'Autobiography' file. Note to Dick Crossman from Judith Hart, 27 July 1963.

21 Ibid. Letter from Stephen Taylor, a medical member of the House of Lords, 21 July 1963.

22 Ibid. Letter from RHSC to Tam Dalyell, 23 July 1963, explaining that he had never had any intention of 'press-ganging you into anything'.

23 Ibid. Copy of letter from RHSC to Harold Wilson, 10 July 1963.

24 *Backbench Diaries*, p. 1013. Entry for 17 July 1963.

25 Ibid., p. 1019.

26 *Hansard* (15 July 1963), vol. 681, col. 35.

27 *Guardian* (16 July 1963). The leader was entitled 'The Exodus of Scientists'.

28 *Yorkshire Post* (16 July 1963). The tribute appeared in its diary column.

29 *Backbench Diaries*, p. 1020. Entry for 17 July 1963.

30 *New York Times* (8 April 1963).

31 Notebook, *Spectator* (12 April 1963).

32 RHSC's 'Autobiography' file. Typed copy of letter from RHSC to Patrick Gordon Walker, 24 April 1963.

33 *The Times* (10 April 1963). The statement was issued in Berlin by Edward Short, the Deputy Opposition Chief Whip, who himself had attended the Königswinter conference.

34 *Hansard* (21 March 1963), vol. 674, cols 726–31. The occasion for the

debate was the case of the two journalists, Reginald Foster and Brendan Mulholland, imprisoned as a result of the Vassal Tribunal.

35 Ibid., col. 727.

36 Ibid., cols 737–42.

37 *Hansard* (22 March 1963), vol. 674, col. 810.

38 Lord Wigg, *George Wigg* (Michael Joseph, 1972), p. 269.

39 *Hansard* (17 June 1963), vol. 679, cols 119–28.

40 *Backbench Diaries*, p. 1001. Entry for 22 June 1963.

41 Cmnd 2152, para 170.

42 RHSC's 'Autobiography' file. Both RHSC's original draft and Lord Goodman's amended version of it survive along with Macleod's initial robust reply sent on 7 October 1963.

43 Ibid. Hetherington's letter was a handwritten note.

44 *Backbench Diaries*, p. 1029. Entry for 15 October 1963.

45 RHSC's 'Autobiography' file. The typescript, presumably a duplicate for the one submitted, even has manuscript corrections on it.

46 *Backbench Diaries*, p. 1029. Entry for 15 October 1963.

47 Ibid., p. 1040. Entry for 2 December 1963.

48 Cmnd 2154. The Report was published on 23 October 1962.

49 *Hansard* (19 November 1963), vol. 684, cols 810–30.

50 *Labour Party Conference Report* (1963), pp. 150–3.

51 *The Times* (8 October 1963).

52 *Hansard* (6 February 1964), vol. 688, cols 1339–45.

53 RHSC's letter in the *Teacher* (18 November 1963). He ratified his conversion with a speech at Edinburgh reported in the *Observer* (15 January 1964).

54 *Daily Telegraph* (14 February 1964).

55 *Hansard* (24 February 1964), vol. 690, cols 39–54.

56 Ibid., cols 68–9.

57 *Daily Mirror* (14 May 1964). The story appeared on the paper's front page.

58 *Education* (15 May 1964).

59 RHSC's 'Autobiography' file. Letter to Mrs P.M. McDougall dated 25 March 1963. Mrs McDougall replied, rather curtly, on 12 April 1963, whereat RHSC wrote again on 18 April 1963.

60 Crossman Papers, Modern Records Centre, University of Warwick Library, MSS.154/3/Ed. Fisher's letter enclosing the draft minutes is dated 27 July 1964. RHSC replied to it suggesting some minor emendations on 5 August 1964.

61 Ibid. This meeting, which apparently took place on 7 July 1964, is referred to in a letter from Shirley Williams, then the general secretary of the Fabian Society, to RHSC, dated 22 July 1964.

62 *Sunday Times* (28 July 1963). The article was headed 'Wilson's Men' and carried the byline of the author.

63 *Backbench Diaries*, p. 982. Entry for 19 February 1963.

64 Ibid., p. 1023. Entry for 26 July 1963.

15   CABINET MINISTER

1   e.g. by the *Observer* (17 May 1964). The Prime Minister had ruled out a spring or summer election on 19 April 1964.
2   *Sunday Times* (6 September 1964). Leader page article headed 'A Gamble on One Man'.
3   RHSC, interview with the author, 3 September 1964.
4   Ibid.
5   Interview, George Brown, 3 September 1964.
6   Interview, Harold Wilson, 1 September 1964.
7   Interview, RHSC, 3 September 1964.
8   *Birmingham Evening Mail* (12 October 1964). RHSC's election agent, Winnie Lakin, is quoted there as having said: 'Seven days will be quite enough to deal with Mr Gow.'
9   *Coventry Evening Telegraph* (16 October 1964).
10 RHSC, interview with Alastair Hetherington, 18 October 1964. *Guardian* Archives Series C5/132/1, Manchester University Library.
11 Harold Wilson, 'A Desire to Educate', *Listener* (5 January 1978). A transcript of Wilson's review of the third volume of RHSC's *Diaries* broadcast on Radio 3.
12 RHSC, *The Backbench Diaries of Richard Crossman*, ed. Janet Morgan (Hamish Hamilton/Jonathan Cape, 1981), p. 972. Entry for 8 February 1963.
13 Published by Collins/Fontana (1963). The paperback ran into ten impressions by the time of RHSC's death and is still a standard work for students.
14 *Listener* (5 January 1978).
15 Interview with Evelyn Sharp by Simon Jenkins, 2 October 1975. A slightly abbreviated version of the opening of a not always very audible tape.
16 'The Chronicler of the Cabinet' transmitted on BBC2, 5 April 1979.
17 RHSC, *The Diaries of a Cabinet Minister*, ed. Janet Morgan (Hamish Hamilton/Jonathan Cape, 1975), vol. 1, p. 433. Entry for 23 February 1966.
18 Ibid., p. 97. Entry for 13 December 1964.
19 Ibid., p. 534. Entry for 13 June 1966.
20 Interview with Evelyn Sharp by Simon Jenkins.
21 Alan Watkins, 'The Academic in Office', *Spectator* (9 October 1965).
22 *Observer* (28 March 1965). The comments appeared in a Profile entitled 'A Maverick in Harness'.
23 RHSC, interview with Alastair Hetherington, 15 December 1964. *Guardian* Archives Series C/5/198/5, Manchester University Library.
24 See Roy Jenkins, 'His Own Worst Enemy', *Observer* (1 October 1989). Lord Jenkins was reviewing Tam Dalyell's book *Dick Crossman: a Portrait* (Weidenfeld & Nicolson, 1989).

25 RHSC, interview with Alastair Hetherington.

26 *Diaries of a Cabinet Minister*, vol. I, pp. 183–4. Entry for 21 March 1965.

27 Ibid., p. 613. Entry for 24 August 1966.

28 Ibid.

29 Ibid., p. 443. Entry for 31 January 1966. RHSC quotes Evelyn Sharp as having said of Jennie Hall that 'she loved her dearly'.

30 *Daily Express* (13 May 1965). The story was written by Chapman Pincher.

31 *Diaries of a Cabinet Minister*, vol. I, p. 217. Entry for 7 June 1965.

32 *Hansard* (18 May 1965), vol. 712, cols 1208–10.

33 *New of the World* (23 May 1965) and *Daily Telegraph* (24 May 1965).

34 *Diaries of a Cabinet Minister*, vol. I, p. 244. Entry for 7 June 1965.

35 Ibid., p. 112. Entry for 3 January 1965.

36 Ibid., p. 183. Entry for 23 January 1965.

37 Ibid., p. 359. Entry for 22 October 1965.

38 Ibid., p. 67. Entry for 22 November 1964.

39 RHSC, interview with Alastair Hetherington, 27 April 1965. *Guardian* Archives Series C/5/280/1, Manchester University Library.

40 Leo Abse, *Margaret, Daughter of Beatrice* (Jonathan Cape, 1988), p. 122. The two MPs were Abse himself and Sam Silkin, later, as Attorney-General, to bring the action designed to prevent the publication of RHSC's *Cabinet Diaries*.

41 *Diaries of a Cabinet Minister*, vol. I, p. 619. Entry for 24 August 1966.

42 RHSC, interview with Alastair Hetherington, 15 December 1964.

43 *Diaries of a Cabinet Minister*, vol. I, p. 108. Entry for 18 December 1964.

44 Ibid., pp. 625–6. Entry for 24 September 1966.

45 Cmnd 3163.

46 Wilson's statement was made at Bradford on 27 March 1966. It is recorded on p. 194 of Paul Foot, *The Politics of Harold Wilson* (Penguin, 1968).

47 *Diaries of a Cabinet Minister*, vol. I, p. 482. Entry for 19 March 1966.

48 Ibid., p. 89. Entry for 1 April 1966.

49 Ibid., p. 416. Entry for 18 December 1965.

50 Ibid., p. 480. Entry for 17 March 1966.

51 Ibid., p. 470. Entry for 3 March 1966.

52 Ibid., pp. 484–5. Entry for 27 March 1966. The diary entry recalls a meeting that took place on 23 March 1966.

53 Ibid., p. 490. Entry for 3 April 1966.

54 Ibid.

55 *Hansard* (20 June 1966), vol. 730, col. 42.

56 Ibid. (28 June 1966), vol. 730, cols 1603–27.

57 *Diaries of a Cabinet Minister*, vol. I, p. 581. Entry for 24 July 1966.

58 Ibid., p. 542. Entry for 19 June 1966.

59 Harold Wilson, *The Labour Government 1964–70* (Weidenfeld & Nicolson, 1971), p. 256.
60 RHSC, *The Diaries of a Cabinet Minister*, ed. Janet Morgan (Hamish Hamilton/Jonathan Cape, 1976), vol. II, p. 70. Entry for 12 October 1966. RHSC in a report of a conversation with James Callaghan.
61 *Diaries of a Cabinet Minister*, vol. I, p. 70. Entry for 24 November 1964.
62 Ibid., p. 583. Entry for 24 July 1966.
63 Ibid.
64 Ibid., p. 606. Entry for 10 August 1966.
65 Ibid., p. 612. Entry for 24 August 1966.
66 *Sunday Telegraph* (4 September 1966).
67 *The Times* (15 September 1966).
68 *Diaries of a Cabinet Minister*, vol. II, p. 35. Entry for 13 September 1966.
69 RHSC, interview with Alastair Hetherington, 14 September 1966. *Guardian* Archives Series C/5/292/1, Manchester University Library.
70 *Diaries of a Cabinet Minister*, vol. II, p. 118. Entry for 10 November 1966.
71 *Hansard* (25 November 1966), vol. 736, cols 1606–21, 1723–30.
72 *Diaries of a Cabinet Minister*, vol. II, p. 136. Entry for 24 November 1966).
73 Ibid., p. 118. Entry for 10 November 1966.
74 *Hansard* (14 December 1966), vol. 738, cols 471–94.
75 Ibid. (14 November 1967), vol. 754, col. 244.
76 Cmnd 3799. The White Paper was published on 1 November 1968.
77 The Parliament (No. 2) Bill was withdrawn by the Government on 17 April 1969 after it had consumed eleven days of parliamentary time.
78 *Diaries of a Cabinet Minister*, vol. II, p. 137. Entry for 25 November 1966.
79 Ibid.
80 See Wilson, *The Labour Government*, where on p. 257 RHSC is described as 'giving instruction to the young in the Commons tea-room'.
81 Transcript of *Panorama* broadcast, 17 July 1967.
82 *Diaries of a Cabinet Minister*, vol. II, p. 430. Entry for 17 July 1967.
83 Wilson, *The Labour Government*, includes a veiled criticism on p. 378 of 'a speech by Dick Crossman at Morden, Surrey, glorying in his liberal policies'.
84 *Coventry Evening Telegraph* (14 August 1967).
85 *Diaries of a Cabinet Minister*, vol. II, p. 449–50. Entry for 29 July 1967.
86 *Diaries of a Cabinet Minister*, vol. I, p. 558–9. Entry for 3 July 1966.
87 *Diaries of a Cabinet Minister*, vol. II, p. 396. Entry for 24 June 1967.
88 Ibid., p. 450. Entry for 29 July 1967.
89 Ibid., p. 452. Entry for 31 July 1967.

90 Ibid., p. 453. RHSC was to use the same phrase about himself for the second time five weeks later: p. 467. Entry for 7 September 1967.

91 Wilson, *The Labour Government*, p. 463.

92 *Diaries of a Cabinet Minister*, vol. II, p. 578. Entry for 17 November 1967.

93 Ibid., p. 592. Entry for 26 November 1967.

94 Ibid., p. 626. Entry for 31 December 1967.

95 Ibid., p. 596. Entry for 28 November 1967.

96 Ibid., p. 598. Entry for 12 December 1967.

97 RHSC, interview with Alastair Hetherington, 21 March 1968. *Guardian* Archives Series C/5/334/5, Manchester University Library.

98 *Diaries of a Cabinet Minister*, vol. II, pp. 716–17. Entry for 17 March 1968.

99 Ibid., pp. 721–2. Entry for 19 March 1968.

100 Ibid., p. 723.

101 Ibid., p. 763. Entry for 4 April 1968.

102 Ibid.

103 Wilson, *The Labour Government*, p. 521. But see RHSC, *The Diaries of a Cabinet Minister*, ed. Janet Morgan (Hamish Hamilton/Jonathan Cape, 1977), vol. III. Entry for 26 May 1968, where RHSC records his hope of getting the merger by July.

104 *Diaries of a Cabinet Minister*, vol. III, p. 683. Entry for 14 October 1969.

105 *Contemporary Record* (Summer 1987), vol. I, no. 2. Sir Clifford Jarrett's recollections are included in a symposium, 'The Crossman Diaries Reconsidered'.

106 *Diaries of a Cabinet Minister*, vol. III, p. 469. Entry for 18 April 1969.

107 Cmnd 3888, *In Place of Strife*, was published on 17 January 1969, eleven days before the White Paper on National Superannuation, Cmnd 3883.

108 After a prolonged cross-bench filibuster, the Prime Minister announced the withdrawal of the Bill on 17 April 1969. *Hansard*, vol. 781, cols 1338–44.

109 *Diaries of a Cabinet Minister*, vol. III, p. 448. Entry for 21 April 1969.

110 RHSC's 'Autobiography' file. The minute preserved is a carbon copy of the original. The exact date was presumably added later – though from internal evidence, the minute was plainly written on 19 June 1969.

111 *Diaries of a Cabinet Minister*, vol. III, p. 531. Entry for 20 June 1969. RHSC records his dominant feeling as having been, 'What have I got to lose or gain?'

112 Ibid., p. 448. Entry for 20 April 1969.

113 *Hansard* (5 May 1969), vol. 733, cols 42–50.

114 *Diaries of a Cabinet Minister*, vol. III, p. 476. Entry for 5 May 1969.

115 Ibid., p. 249. Entry for 2 November 1968.
116 Ibid., p. 297. Entry for 24–7 December 1968.
117 *Contemporary Record* (Summer 1987), vol. I, no. 2.
118 RHSC's 'Autobiography' file. The minute is dated 15 September 1969 and refers to a conversation held in London on 10 September 1969 between Sir Con O'Neill and the chargé d'affaires at the West German Embassy.
119 The lecture, entitled 'The Politics of Viewing' was given as part of the Granada Lecture series on 21 October 1968. It is reproduced in full in the *New Statesman* (25 October 1968).
120 *The Times* (22 October 1968) devoted a whole page to it.
121 *Diaries of a Cabinet Minister*, vol. III, pp. 237–8. Entry for 24 October 1968.
122 The meeting was held at Friends' Meeting House, Euston Road on 20 March 1969. RHSC's address appears in Mervyn Jones (ed.), *Kingsley Martin: Portrait and Self-Portrait* (Barrie & Jenkins, 1969).
123 Interview, Lord Campbell of Eskan, 4 December 1989.
124 The memorandum no longer survives but it is referred to in a letter to RHSC from the Company Secretary dated 26 June 1970.
125 The lectures were published in 1972 under the title *The Myths of Cabinet Government* by the Harvard University Press in the United States and later with the title *Inside View* by Jonathan Cape in Britain.
126 Introduction to *The Myths of Cabinet Government*, p. xii.

16   OLD STATESMAN

1 RHSC, *The Diaries of a Cabinet Minister*, ed. Janet Morgan (Hamish Hamilton/Jonathan Cape, 1977), vol. III, p. 930. Entry for 29 May 1970.
2 Ibid., p. 931.
3 Letter to the Very Rev. H. C. N. Williams, Provost of Coventry, 14 May 1970. Crossman Papers, Modern Records Centre, University of Warwick Library MSS.194/DHS/3.
4 Letter from Anne Crossman, 24 June 1970 to Winnie Lakin, who supplied the author with a copy.
5 Ibid.
6 Interview, Lord Campbell of Eskan, 4 December 1989.
7 Letter from J. A. Morgan, Company Secretary, to RHSC, 26 June 1970. This letter represented his only contract with the paper and offered no security of tenure beyond a provision for six months' notice on either side.
8 Paul Johnson, 'Crossman and the *New Statesman*', *Encounter* (August 1974).
9 Interview, Anne Crossman, 9 February 1989.

10 Letter from Anne Crossman to Winnie Lakin, 24 June 1970.
11 The stories appeared in the Atticus column of the *Sunday Times* and the Pendennis column of the *Observer* (5 July 1970).
12 RHSC's unpublished *New Statesman* diary. Entry for 31 August 1970.
13 Ibid. Entry for 24 July 1970.
14 See Alan Watkins, 'Fine Reviewer, Fair Journalist, Poor Editor', *Spectator* (18 November 1989).
15 *New Statesman* (7 August 1970).
16 *Daily Mirror* (10 August 1970). The article was the work of RHSC's old mentor, Hugh Cudlipp.
17 *New Statesman* (21 August 1970).
18 Crux, Great Turnstile Diary, *New Statesman* (24 September 1972).
19 Ibid.
20 *New Statesman* (28 May 1971). The leading article was, in fact, written by Paul Johnson. A follow-up article, 'Supplementary Benefits' (10 December 1981) was, however, the work of RHSC.
21 *New Statesman* diary. Entry for 7 July 1970.
22 Mervyn Jones, *Chances: an Autobiography* (Verso, 1987), p. 230.
23 James Fenton, 'Mr Crossman's Dogsbody', *New Review* (November 1976).
24 Paul Johnson, 'Crossman and the *New Statesman*', *Encounter* (August 1974).
25 Alan Watkins, *Brief Lives* (Hamish Hamilton, 1982), p. 42.
26 *New Statesman* diary. Entry for 18 October 1970.
27 Ibid. Entry for 10 December 1970.
28 Ibid. Entry for 19 November 1970.
29 Letter from RHSC to Sir Alan Marre, former Second Permanent Secretary at the DHSS, dated 9 February 1972.
30 Crucifer, London Diary, *New Statesman* (4 February 1972).
31 Crux, Great Turnstile Diary, *New Statesman* (24 March 1972).
32 Ibid.
33 Letter from Lord Campbell of Eskan to RHSC, 12 April 1972.
34 Ibid. Lord Campbell drew attention to this phrase in an effort to rebut RHSC's suspicion that there had been an intention of keeping him out of the office.
35 James Fenton, 'Mr Crossman's Dogsbody', *New Review* (November 1976). The member of the staff, according to Fenton, was the author.
36 Crux, Great Turnstile Diary, *New Statesman* (24 March 1972).
37 *Evening Standard* (17 March 1972).
38 *The Times* (20 March 1972).
39 Letter from RHSC to Frau Lilo Milchsack, 4 May 1972. Crossman Papers, Modern Records Centre, University of Warwick Library, MSS.154/3/MIS.
40 These were phrases that regularly recur in RHSC's replies to the huge volume of private correspondence he received.
41 Interview, Lord Campbell of Eskan, 4 December 1989.

42 RHSC's letter to Eliahu Elath in Israel, dated 21 April 1972.
43 RHSC's letter to Hans Rosenhaupdt in Princeton, New Jersey, dated 28 March 1972.
44 *Daily Telegraph* (20 March 1972), Story headed 'Crossman Admits "I Quit Parliament too Soon" '.
45 *The Times* (25 April 1973).
46 RHSC, *The Diaries of a Cabinet Minister* ed. Janet Morgan (Hamish Hamilton/Jonathan Cape, 1975), vol. I, p. 278. Entry for 18 July 1965.
47 *New Statesman* diary. Entry for 23 October 1970.
48 Ibid.
49 Ibid. Entry for 20 December 1970.
50 *Guardian* (6 April 1974). The tribute was included in its obituary of RHSC.
51 RHSC's letter was reproduced by Meyer Weisgal in a posthumous tribute that appeared in *The Times* (24 April 1974).
52 RHSC's letter to Claire Tomalin, then literary editor of the *New Statesman*. Crossman Papers, Modern Records Centre, University of Warwick Library, MSS.154/3/MIS.
53 RHSC, 'Personal View', *The Times* (27 February 1974).
54 RHSC's letter to Corinna Adam, 27 February 1974. Crossman Papers, Modern Records Centre, University of Warwick Library, MSS.154/3/MIS.
55 Harold Wilson's address at the Memorial Meeting for RHSC held at Church House, Westminster on 15 May 1974.
56 *Daily Express* (1 April 1974).
57 Ibid.
58 RHSC's letter to J. R. L. Anderson dated 27 February 1974. Crossman Papers, Modern Records Centre, University of Warwick Library, MSS.154/3/MIS.

Bibliography

PRIMARY SOURCES

The principal Crossman archive is kept at the Modern Records Centre of the University of Warwick. The collection of papers maintained there is formidable in scope, but is primarily concerned with its subject's years of official celebrity and fame. It provided an invaluable source for me in writing this book, but without the complementary personal papers, loaned to me by Mrs Anne Crossman, the task would have been impossible. Happily, the two sets of papers are now to be united at Warwick. It was always Crossman's intention that there should be one centre where biographical material upon him could be found; and that purpose will now be achieved.

The only other significant first-hand documentation on Crossman's career is at the Middle East Centre, St Antony's College, Oxford. For reasons which remain obscure, the letters he wrote to his second wife, Zita, while serving on the Anglo-American Palestine Commission, were deposited there long ago, together with portions of a contemporary diary he kept, which later formed the basis for his book, *Palestine Mission*. This material also includes a number of letters that Crossman himself received during the same period – including notes from Clement Attlee and Ernest Bevin. From an even earlier phase of Crossman's career, the Library at New College retains a number of letters and postcards that he wrote to his tutor, Christopher Cox, both while an undergraduate and later during the year he spent abroad before joining the Senior Common Room.

The BBC, a model guardian of its own history, also holds a number of early letters that Crossman wrote – though rather more of its own characteristic internal memos written about him. The research facilities afforded by its Written Archives Centre at Caversham were of enormous assistance to me in writing Chapters 5 and 6. So were the *Guardian* Archives, held at Manchester University (to the existence of which I was first alerted by the *Guardian*'s former editor, Alastair Hetherington, and through whose relevant material I was expertly guided by the paper's Northern Librarian) for research on Chapter 15.

The Public Record Office at Kew proved its usual, muddled, infuriating self. Since I did not wish to wait to bring out this book until the year 2001, there was never any possibility of official records providing corroboration or otherwise of Crossman's own account of the Labour Government of 1964–70. That Government's own action in reducing the former fifty-year rule to a thirty-year one meant, however, that at least I could look at the Whitehall documentation on Crossman's performance as a temporary Foreign Office servant during the Second World War.

I cannot complain at some of the insights which turned up; but I can, and do, protest at the casual arrogance with which one is informed, nowadays normally by a computer, that a particular document, half a century after the event, is 'not available'. Subsequent inquiry would usually reveal that no one quite knew why. Indeed, the best explanation I was offered was: 'Maybe someone at the FO itself is interested in it. It's not, after all, as if it is officially "closed".' It was at such moments that Crossman's whole campaign against official secrecy seemed to acquire an extra justification.

BOOKS BY AND ABOUT CROSSMAN

During his life Crossman was author, co-author or editor of ten books, all of which are mentioned in the text. None was specifically autobiographical – although *Palestine Mission* (Hamish Hamilton, 1947), *The Charm of Politics* (Hamish Hamilton, 1958) and *Inside View* (Jonathan Cape, 1972) all possess autobiographical elements. The preponderance of his autobiographical writing was, however, published only after his death – in the three volumes of his *Diaries of a Cabinet Minister*, ed. Janet Morgan (Hamish Hamilton/Jonathan Cape, 1975, 1976 and 1977) and in his *Backbench Diaries*, ed. Janet Morgan (Hamish Hamilton/Jonathan Cape, 1981). There is little question in my mind, though, that he had originally intended to publish his own memoirs. He maintained for over forty years an 'Autobiography' file – with contents going back to 1928 – and his original contract with both Hamish Hamilton and the *Sunday Times* envisaged just such a volume. His excuse for abandoning it was the belief that his *Diaries* would speak more effectively for themselves – although it remains legitimate to wonder whether the real reason was not more to do with his having taken a commission from another publisher to write the life of Chaim Weizmann. As it was, the nearest approach to a memoir that Crossman ever wrote was a 3,000-word essay entitled 'My Father' that appeared in the *Sunday Telegraph* on 16 December 1962. It is a splendidly evocative piece that makes it all the sadder that he never tried his hand at autobiography over a more sustained length.

There has been only one previous biographical study – Tam Dalyell, *Dick Crossman: a Portrait* (Weidenfeld & Nicolson, 1989). A work plainly conceived in affection by an author who was Crossman's Parliamentary Private Secretary, it successfully captures several aspects of its subject's character. It is, however, far from reliable on fact – with a marked shakiness over dates – and suffers to some extent from its author's inability to decide whether he or his hero should be centre stage.

An altogether more professional work is Hugo Young's *The Crossman Affair* (Hamish Hamilton/Jonathan Cape, 1976). Its focus is narrow, since it tells the story simply of the Wilson Government's efforts to ban the publication of the first volume of the *Diaries of a Cabinet Minister*. What it sets out to do, it does, however, extremely well – and by no means its least touching aspect is its brief picture of Crossman, as a dying man, determined at all costs to see that his *Diaries* should come out.

In many ways, the most entertaining verbal snapshot of Crossman is contained in Susan Barnes's profile of him originally published in the *Sunday Times* Magazine (29 November 1970). It is reproduced in her book, *Behind the Image* (Jonathan Cape, 1974), and has a real feel of Crossman's personality about it. Again, however, it is not wholly dependable. If the camera cannot lie, the sitter can always pull a face – and in this case seems deliberately to have done so more than once. Some of its anecdotes need to be treated with reserve.

The two outstanding obituaries published after Crossman's death appeared in the *Guardian* and *The Times* (6 April 1974), while a later symposium in *Encounter* (August 1974), with contributions from Paul Johnson, Hugh Cudlipp and Maurice Edelman, is also worthy of note. A booklet produced by Dick's friends consisting of the addresses given at his memorial meeting held at Church House, Westminster on 15 May 1974 offers little in the way of special illumination. It does, however, obligingly preserve for posterity the warm terms – recalling his 'inspiration of the Labour movement' – in which Harold Wilson, as Prime Minister, praised his old friend before the storm broke. A distinctly cooler tone – 'Dick Crossman never understood politics, only journalism' – surfaces in his eventual review of the *Diaries* in the *Listener* (5 January 1978).

GENERAL

Abse, Leo, *Private Member* (Macdonald, 1973).
——, *Margaret, Daughter of Beatrice* (Jonathan Cape, 1989).
Addison, Paul, *The Road to 1945* (Jonathan Cape, 1975).
Attlee, C. R., *As It Happened* (Heinemann, 1954).
Balfour, Michael, *Propaganda in War 1939–45* (Routledge & Kegan Paul, 1979).
Barman, Thomas, *Diplomatic Correspondent* (Hamish Hamilton, 1968).
Benn, Tony, *Out of the Wilderness: Diaries 1963–7* (Hutchinson, 1987).
——, *Office Without Power: Diaries 1968–72* (Hutchinson, 1988).
Berlin, Isaiah, *Personal Impressions* (Hogarth Press, 1981).

Bethell, Nicholas, *The Palestine Triangle: the Struggle for the Holy Land 1935–48* (Putnam, New York, 1979).

Brown, George, *In My Way* (Gollancz, 1971).

Bruce Lockhart, Robert, *Comes the Reckoning* (Putnam, 1947).

Bullock, Alan, *Ernest Bevin, Minister of Labour* (Heinemann, 1967).

——, *Ernest Bevin, Foreign Secretary 1945–51* (Heinemann, 1983).

Burridge, Trevor, *Clement Attlee, a Political Biography* (Jonathan Cape, 1985).

Butler, D. E., *The British General Election of 1951* (Macmillan, 1952).

——, *The British General Election of 1955* (Macmillan, 1955).

Butler, D. E., and Rose, Richard, *The British General Election of 1959* (Macmillan, 1960).

Butler, D. E., and King, Anthony, *The British General Election of 1964* (Macmillan, 1965).

——, *The British General Election of 1966* (Macmillan, 1966).

Butler, D. E., and Pinto-Duschinsky, Michael, *The British General Election of 1970* (Macmillan, 1971).

Butler, Lord, *The Art of the Possible: the Memoirs of Lord Butler* (Hamish Hamilton, 1971).

Callaghan, James, *Time and Chance* (Collins, 1987).

Campbell, John, *Roy Jenkins: a Biography* (Weidenfeld & Nicolson, 1983).

——, *Nye Bevan and the Mirage of British Socialism* (Weidenfeld & Nicolson, 1987).

Castle, Barbara, *The Castle Diaries 1964–70* (Weidenfeld & Nicolson, 1984).

Churchill, Randolph, *The Rise and Fall of Sir Anthony Eden* (MacGibbon & Kee, 1959).

Cosgrave, Patrick, *The Lives of Enoch Powell* (Bodley Head, 1989).

Crum, Bartley C., *Behind the Silken Curtain* (Simon & Schuster, New York, 1947).

Cudlipp, Hugh, *At Your Peril* (Weidenfeld & Nicolson, 1962).

——, *Walking on the Water* (Bodley Head, 1976).

Dalton, Hugh, *The Fateful Years, Memoirs 1931–45* (Muller, 1957).

——, *High Tide and After. Memoirs 1945–60* (Muller, 1962).

Davenport, Nicholas, *Memoirs of a City Radical* (Weidenfeld & Nicolson, 1974).

Delmer, Sefton, *Black Boomerang* (Secker & Warburg, 1962).

Dilks, David (ed.), *The Diary of Sir Alexander Cadogan 1938–43* (Cassell, 1971).

Donoughue, Bernard, and Jones, G. W., *Herbert Morrison, Portrait of a Politician* (Weidenfeld & Nicolson, 1973).

Driberg, Tom, *Ruling Passions* (Jonathan Cape, 1977).

Eden, Anthony, *Full Circle* (Cassell, 1960).

Edwards, Ruth Dudley, *Victor Gollancz, a Biography* (Gollancz, 1987).

Fisher, Nigel, *Iain Macleod* (André Deutsch, 1973).

Foot, Michael, *Aneurin Bevan: a Biography* vol. I, *1897–1945* (MacGibbon & Kee, 1962).

——, *Aneurin Bevan: a Biography*, vol. II, *1945–1960* (Davis-Poynter, 1973).

Foot, Paul, *The Politics of Harold Wilson* (Penguin, 1968).

Glasser, Ralph, *Gorbals Boy at Oxford* (Chatto & Windus, 1988).

Goodman, Geoffrey, *The Awkward Warrior, Frank Cousins: His Life and Times* (Davis-Poynter, 1979).

Halcrow, Morrison, *Keith Joseph, a Single Mind* (Macmillan, 1989).

Hamilton, Iain, *Koestler* (Secker & Warburg, 1982).

Harris, Kenneth, *Attlee* (Weidenfeld & Nicolson, 1982).

Healey, Denis, *The Time of My Life* (Michael Joseph, 1989).

Hennessy, Peter, *Whitehall* (Secker & Warburg, 1989).

Hillier, Bevis, *The Young Betjeman* (Murray, 1988).

Hodgkinson, George, *Sent to Coventry* (Robert Maxwell, 1971).

Horne, Alistair, *Macmillan 1894–1956* (Macmillan, 1988).

——, *Macmillan 1957–1986* (Macmillan, 1989).

Howard, Anthony, and West, Richard, *The Making of the Prime Minister* (Jonathan Cape, 1965).

Howe, Ellic, *The Black Game: British Subversive Operations against the Germans in the Second World War* (Michael Joseph, 1982).

Hyams, Edward, *The New Statesman: the History of the First Fifty Years 1913–63* (Longman, 1963).

Inglis, Brian, *Downstart* (Chatto & Windus, 1990).

James, Robert Rhodes, *Anthony Eden* (Weidenfeld & Nicolson, 1986).

Jay, Douglas, *Change and Fortune: a Political Record* (Hutchinson, 1980).

Jay, Peggy, *Loves & Labours* (Weidenfeld & Nicolson, 1990).

Jones, Jack, *Union Man: the Autobiography of Jack Jones* (Collins, 1986).

Jones, Mervyn, *Chances: an Autobiography* (Verso, 1987).

King, Cecil, *The Cecil King Diary 1965–70* (Jonathan Cape, 1972).

——, *The Cecil King Diary 1970–4* (Jonathan Cape, 1975).

Leigh, David, *The Wilson Plot* (Heinemann, 1988).

Lerner, Daniel, *Sykewar: Psychological Warfare against Germany, D-Day to VE-Day* (George W. Stewart, New York, 1949).

Lloyd, Selwyn, *Suez 1956* (Jonathan Cape, 1978).

Longford, Elizabeth, *The Pebbled Shore* (Weidenfeld & Nicolson, 1986).

McCallum, R.B., and Readman, Alison, *The British General Election of 1945* (Oxford University Press, 1947).

MacDonogh, Giles, *A Good German: Adam von Trott zu Solz* (Quartet, 1990).

Macmillan, Harold, *War Diaries: Politics and War in the Mediterranean, January 1943–May 1945* (Macmillan, 1984).

——, *Memoirs II, The Blast of War* (Macmillan, 1967).

——, *Memoirs III, Tides of Fortune* (Macmillan, 1969).

——, *Memoirs IV, Riding the Storm* (Macmillan, 1971).

——, *Memoirs V, Pointing the Way* (Macmillan, 1972).

Macmillan, Harold, *Memoirs VI, At the End of the Day* (Macmillan, 1973).

Marsh, Richard, *Off the Rails* (Weidenfeld & Nicolson, 1978).

Martin, Kingsley, *Editor* (Hutchinson, 1968).

Maudling, Reginald, *Memoirs* (Sidgwick & Jackson, 1978).

Mayhew, Christopher, *Time to Explain* (Hutchinson, 1987).

Mikardo, Ian, *Back-bencher* (Weidenfeld & Nicolson, 1988).

Morgan, Janet, *The House of Lords and the Labour Government 1964–70* (Oxford University Press, 1975).

Morgan, Kenneth O., *Labour in Power 1945–51* (Oxford University Press, 1984).

——, *Labour People* (Oxford University Press, 1987).

Newman, Michael, *John Strachey* (Manchester University Press, 1989).

Nicholas, H.G., *The British General Election of 1950* (Macmillan, 1950).

Nicolson, Nigel, *People and Parliament* (Weidenfeld & Nicolson, 1958).

Pakenham, Frank, *Born to Believe* (Jonathan Cape, 1953).

Pimlott, Ben, *Hugh Dalton* (Jonathan Cape, 1985).

——, (ed.), *The Political Diary of Hugh Dalton, 1918–40, 1945–60* (Jonathan Cape, 1986).

——, *The Second World War Diary of Hugh Dalton, 1940–5* (Jonathan Cape, 1986).

Ponting, Clive, *Breach of Promise: Labour in Power 1964–70* (Hamish Hamilton, 1989).

Punnett, R.M., *Front-Bench Opposition* (Heinemann, 1973).

Reith, J.C.W., *Into the Wind* (Hodder & Stoughton, 1949).

Rolph, C.H., *Kingsley: the Life, Letters and Diaries of Kingsley Martin* (Gollancz, 1973).

——, *Further Particulars* (Oxford University Press, 1987).

Sabben-Clare, James, *Winchester College* (Paul Cave, Southampton, 1981).

Seldon, Anthony, *Churchill's Indian Summer* (Hodder & Stoughton, 1981).

Short, Edward, *Whip to Wilson* (Macdonald, 1989).

Stewart, Michael, *Life and Labour: an Autobiography* (Sidgwick & Jackson, 1980).

Straight, Michael, *After Long Silence* (Collins, 1983).

Sykes, Christopher, *Troubled Loyalty: a Biography of Adam von Trott zu Solz* (Collins, 1968).

Thomas, Hugh, *John Strachey* (Eyre Methuen, 1973).

Thorn, John, *The Road to Winchester* (Weidenfeld & Nicolson, 1989).

Tracey, Michael, *A Variety of Lives: a Biography of Sir Hugh Greene* (Bodley Head, 1983).

Vansittart, Lord, *The Mist Procession* (Hutchinson, 1958).

Watkins, Alan, *Brief Lives* (Hamish Hamilton, 1982).

——, *A Slight Case of Libel* (Duckworth, 1990).

Weisgal, Meyer W., and Carmichael, Joel (eds), *Chaim Weizmann: a Biography by Several Hands* (Weidenfeld & Nicolson, 1972).

Wheen, Francis, *Tom Driberg: His Life and Indiscretions* (Chatto & Windus, 1990).

Wigg, Lord, *George Wigg* (Michael Joseph, 1972).

Williams, Marcia, *Inside Number Ten* (Weidenfeld & Nicolson, 1972).

Williams, Philip M., *Hugh Gaitskell: a Political Biography* (Jonathan Cape, 1979).

——, (ed.), *The Diary of Hugh Gaitskell 1945–56* (Jonathan Cape, 1983).

Wilson, Harold, *The Labour Government 1964–70* (Weidenfeld & Nicolson, 1971).

Wyatt, Woodrow, *Into the Dangerous World* (Weidenfeld & Nicolson, 1952).

——, *Confessions of an Optimist* (Collins, 1985).

Young, Kenneth, *Sir Alec Douglas-Home* (Dent, 1970).

——, (ed.), *The Diaries of Sir Robert Bruce Lockhart*, vol. II, *1939–65* (Macmillan, 1980).

Zuckerman, Solly, *From Apes to Warlords* (Hamish Hamilton, 1978).

Index